The Word of a Prince

Elizabeth I: the 'Ermine' Portrait. Attributed to William Segar (The Marquess of Salisbury, Hatfield House)

MARIA PERRY

THE WORD OF
A PRINCE

A Life of Elizabeth I from Contemporary Documents

THE BOYDELL PRESS

First published 1990 by The Boydell Press, Woodbridge

Reprinted in paperback 1996, 1999

ISBN 0 85115 261 9 hardback
ISBN 0 85115 633 9 paperback

The Boydell Press is an imprint of Boydell & Brewer Ltd
PO Box 9, Woodbridge, Suffolk IP12 3DF, UK
and of Boydell & Brewer Inc.
PO Box 41026, Rochester, NY 14604–4126, USA

A catalogue record for this book is available
from the British Library

Library of Congress Catalog Card Number: 90–39847

This publication is printed on acid-free paper
Printed in Great Britain by
St Edmundsbury Press Ltd, Bury St Edmunds, Suffolk

For G.R.E.

Henry VIII and his family; showing (from left to right) Jane, the Fool; Princess Mary; Edward; Henry VIII enthroned: Jane Seymour: Elizabeth: and Will Somers, Henry's jester. The picture was not painted from life as Jane Seymour died in child birth.

CONTENTS

ACKNOWLEDGEMENTS

My thanks are due first and foremost to Sir Geoffrey Elton without whose help and guidance this book could not have been written. We conceived the idea of letting Elizabeth 'tell her own story' over lunch at Clare College, Cambridge on the Ides of March 1984. Dr Stephen Medcalf of Sussex University added his sponsorship to Sir Geoffrey's and the British Academy kindly funded much of the research. It took four years longer than I originally anticipated, but as I worked almost exclusively from manuscript sources a bibliography would mean little to the general reader. Early in the study, Professor Conrad Russell influenced me more than he may realise by repeating Elton's exhortation to 'read the documents'. I thought two such luminaries could not possibly be wrong. I must thank Professor Russell and Dr David Starkey for allowing me to attend their Tudor and Stuart Seminars at the Institute of Historical Research, where I learned a great deal about methods of searching for unpublished material, and where I made friends with Professor Geoffrey Parker, Dr Peter Lake, Dr Mia Rodriguez-Salgado, Dr Maria Dowling, and Miss Frances Devereux, Honorary Archivist to the Royal Fusiliers, the City of London Regiment, who all supplied information for this book – mostly over tea, which at the Institute is served by Kathy McKeown.

The staff of the British Library have been wonderful. In particular I want to thank Mr Julian Conway, Superintendent of the Manuscript Students' Room, Mr John Barr of the North Library, Mrs Nina Evans of Book Delivery Services, and her predecessor, Mr Edwards, also Miss Williams of the British Museum's Prints and Drawings Department. At the Bodleian Library, Oxford I have been helped by Dr Bruce Barker-Benfield of the Western Manuscripts Department; at the Public Record Office by the knowledgeable Mr Evans; at Hatfield by the Marquess of Salisbury's Librarian, Mr Robin Harcourt-Williams; at Longleat by Miss Kate Harris and in the Muniments Room of Westminster Abbey by Mrs Nixon and Miss Christine Reynolds. Mr Toon and the staff of the Reference Services of the Kensington Library have been most helpful in producing their copies of the State Papers on days when I could not get to the British Library. As I wrote some of this book while I was ill, I must also thank Dr Morgan of Charing Cross Hospital and Dr McGreevey for encouraging me to continue.

The translations of Elizabeth's Latin are by Dr Elisabeth Leedham-Green, Assistant Keeper of the University Archives, Cambridge, by Mr Sedley Andrus, Beaumont Herald Extraordinary, and by my son, Ralph Perry Robinson. Professor Lino Pertile of Edinburgh University advised on the Italian translation. Further material was supplied by Dr Katherine Duncan-Jones of Somerville College, Oxford, Dr T. E.

Acknowledgements

Hartley of Leicester University, Miss Katharine Pantzer of the Houghton Library at Harvard and Mr Theo Mathew, Windsor Herald. By appearing in Alan Ereira's BBC2 documentary *Armada* I also gained a firsthand knowledge of the conditions at Tilbury.

Lord Weymouth's flashlight snapshot of the Longleat portrait of Lettice Knollys was the beginning of the picture research. His rendering of Lettice's pearls is both artistic and unforgettable. Thanks are due to Miss Bridget Ayers of The Queen's Gallery, Buckingham Palace, Mrs Jane Alway of Sotheby's, Mr Henry Bedingfeld, Rouge Croix Pursuivant of the College of Arms, Mr Lars Sjoberg, the Curator of the Royal Castles' Collections in Stockholm, Mr Jonathan Franklin of the National Portrait Gallery's Archive Division at Lewisham, and Mr James Taylor of the National Maritime Museum, also to Dr Robert Oresko and Mary Anne Stevens for allowing me to attend the Swedish Colloquium at the Royal Academy at short notice. I also wish to thank my two industrious picture researchers, Sophie Thornton and Carolyn Smith. For their moral support during this long study I should like to thank Patrick Cafferkey, Christopher Andreae, my mother and Julian Perry Robinson who gave unstinting help and encouragement. Mr George Sadler was a tower of strength. He also gave me a ream of typing paper, when the rest of the world bullied me to own a word processor – a man who recognises a technologically unsophisticated woman when he sees one.

EDITORIAL NOTE

Queen Elizabeth dated her letters according to the Julian Calendar. The dates used throughout this book are therefore the Old Style used in the English State Papers. New Style dating came into use in Europe in 1582. Some dates will therefore differ by ten days from those used by modern authorities which rely on European State Papers. For example the OS dates for the Battle of Gravelines and Elizabeth's speech at Tilbury in Chapter XI are ten days earlier than the NS dates used by Colin Martin and Geoffrey Parker in their book *The Spanish Armada*, which adopts the Gregorian Calendar.

Spelling and punctuation in quoted material have been partially modernised to facilitate reading. In the holograph material we have retained Elizabeth's capitalisation.

INTRODUCTION

Orator, wit, stylist and Queen, Elizabeth Tudor was one of the most prolific writers of the golden age which bears her name. Few people realise that her first book was published when she was fourteen and a half – by John Bale, a controversial heretic whose works had been banned in England by Elizabeth's father, King Henry VIII. After this unorthodox literary début, she wrote, studied or translated something most days of her life, exceptions being made for 'holydays and hunting'.

Her writing is often brisk, vivid and entertaining. Many of her letters are as lively now as the day they were penned. She wrote, and spoke, French and Italian almost as fluently as English. Throughout her youth she poured out letters to family and friends; later to courtiers, diplomats and her brother sovereigns, the Kings and Queens of Europe. She also wrote poems, prayers and graffiti. Deprived of writing materials while under house arrest at Woodstock, when she was unjustly suspected of treason in her sister Mary's reign, Elizabeth defiantly inscribed a couplet on a window pane with a diamond. She could speak extempore Latin that would put a university chancellor to shame and, to the delight of her assembled courtiers, she spontaneously denounced an ambassador in that language when she was over sixty. Roger Ascham, her most celebrated tutor, continued to read the classics with her long after she had left the schoolroom. He said the Queen tackled more Greek in the library at Windsor Castle than most churchmen managed in a lifetime.

Formidably educated, she could, when she chose, hide plain meaning in great swathes of circumlocution, although she detested the language of lawyers and often ridiculed their long-windedness. Her own speeches became more elaborate as she grew older. The Renaissance prose of her later years would not be everyone's idea of bedtime reading, and for the purposes of this book it has been necessary to make a selection of her words rather than a collection. Some documents, such as the eight-page letter to Catherine de' Medici expressing Elizabeth's unvarnished opinions of Mary Queen of Scots, who had just connived at murdering her, have also been abridged. But the source material is marvellous, and studied in sequence her writings have ghosted themselves into a posthumous autobiography, which I hope will be of interest to both historians and lovers of the English language.

Surprisingly, no one has yet attempted to print Elizabeth's 'Collected Works'. There are selections of her letters, and an excellent book on her poems. Dr T. E. Hartley is also assembling and annotating her parliamentary speeches, of which there are so many differing texts. My task has been lighter, for although I have dealt with a broader spectrum of her writings, I have tried to catch the authentic voice of Elizabeth, deliberately excluding documents jointly composed by the Queen and her Council. This has meant searching out manuscripts in which she 'tells her own story', and I have concentrated where possible on documents written in Elizabeth's own hand, or contemporary copies, usually endorsed with William Cecil's unmistakable superscription in the top left corner, 'Copy of Her Majesty's letter to . . .' (for the filing system of the Queen's great Secretary of State was impeccable).

Prominence has been given to the early holograph material, which has proved especially fascinating, since it provides new insights into Elizabeth's character and spiritual development. It also throws certain aspects of her life into fresh perspective, in particular her feelings towards her father (whom she adored unequivocally); her relationship with Robert Dudley, Earl of Leicester; her attitude to her work of government, and her firm belief in later life that she had been destined to rule the English people by the will of an omniscient God. After the defeat of the Spanish Armada in 1588 this conviction grew. Philip II sent other fleets against England, and when his ships could not leave their ports in 1593 because of bad weather, Elizabeth, convinced that the very elements were on her side, became obsessively interested in the idea of predestination. That autumn, shortly after her sixtieth birthday, she sat down in the library at Windsor Castle to translate Boethius' *Consolation of Philosophy* from Latin into English, to riddle out for herself the various theories of divine foreknowledge.

Born a girl when Henry VIII urgently desired an heir to secure his kingdom's future, declared a bastard, excluded from the succession by her brother Edward VI, accused of misconduct with her stepmother's husband, and imprisoned by her own sister, Elizabeth survived a youth fraught with difficulties and dangers. Yet when she is studied through the medium of her own words, a picture emerges which is more cohesive and less psychologically baffling than many offered by her biographers. Several historians suggest that her mother's execution before she was three years old was Elizabeth's most traumatic experience. *She* states quite clearly that imprisonment in the Tower during her sister Mary's reign was the episode which went deepest into her conscious memory. 'I stood in danger of my life,' she told Parliament, 'my sister was so incensed against me.' That she got out of the Tower alive seemed to her a miracle comparable with any escape story in the Old Testament. She referred to her deliverance many times, thanking God for it to the end of her days. On a practical level she owed her life to her brother-in-law, King Philip, who saw that it would have been politically inexpedient to execute the heiress to the throne, since Queen Mary was apparently unable to bear him children. But Elizabeth had prayed to Almighty God to save her, and He had done so. Her release from the grim fortress, where both her mother, Anne Boleyn, and her cousin, Lady Jane Grey, had been executed, confirmed everything she had been taught in the schoolroom about faith, and proved, in her view, the validity of prayer. When she was setting out from the Tower on the day of her Coronation procession, Elizabeth thanked God publicly for snatching her like Daniel from the 'mouths of the greedy and raging lions', who sought to devour her. Her imagery was simple, her sense of theatre superb, and

Henry VIII at the time of Elizabeth's infancy c. 1536

ANNA BOLINA VXOR— HENRI· OCTA

Anne Boleyn at the time of Elizabeth's infancy c. 1536

captive lions in the Tower menagerie, which was one of London's principal tourist attractions, served to back up the suitability of the parable. Her people roared their approval, as she rode in triumph through the City, but the Tower remained a private nightmare. Twenty years later in a prayer for her personal use she still praised God for 'pulling me from the prison to the palace'.

There is not much evidence that the execution of Anne Boleyn had any immediate impact on her two-and-a-half-year-old daughter. When she was three months old, Elizabeth had been put in the care of Lady Bryan, who had brought up the King's other children, Princess Mary and the illegitimate Henry Fitzroy, Duke of Richmond. There was a brief period in the summer of 1536 when it was said openly that Elizabeth was not the King's child. After the sensational charges against Anne, who was accused of adultery with six men, one of them her own brother, the Court was a hotbed of gossip. Messire Eustace Chapuys, the Imperial ambassador, sent by Charles V to protect the interests of Henry's first wife, Katharine of Aragon, hated Anne Boleyn so much that he referred to her in despatches as 'the Concubine'. He told the Emperor that even Elizabeth's godfather Archbishop Cranmer had declared she was 'a bastard by Mr Norris and not the King's daughter'.

There must have been many at Court who knew the charges against Anne were trumped up, and Professor Ives has recently demonstrated that, of the twenty offences alleged, the majority would have been impossible, because the Queen and the 'co-respondents' were not even in the same palaces when the love-making was supposed to have taken place. Nevertheless rumour was rife, and an order went through to Sir John Shelton, Master of Elizabeth's household at Hunsdon, that it was 'the King's pleasure that my Lady Elizabeth shall keep her chamber'. The order was probably a reply to the famously distraught letter from Lady Bryan, written to Cromwell shortly after the Queen's execution.

Anne had dressed her daughter beautifully. Her mercers' bills record purchases of orange velvet, russet velvet, yellow satin and white damask for Elizabeth's kirtles. Her caps were of white satin, richly embroidered with gold, and of crimson satin costing a total of £7 13s 4d in one month alone. A purple satin cap required boat journeys from Greenwich to London and back for a fitting and a further trip when the cap needed mending. Lady Bryan's letter has mostly been quoted to show that the baby princess had grown out of her clothes.

'She has neither gown nor kirtle nor petticoat, nor linen for smocks, nor kerchiefs, sleeves, rails, body stychets, handkerchiefs, mufflers, nor begens [sic],' she told Cromwell.

The first part of the letter makes it clear that no official directive about Elizabeth's future had yet arrived at Hunsdon:

'Now as my lady Elizabeth is put from that degree she was in and what degree she is at now, *I know not but by hearsay*. I know not how to order her, or myself or her women or grooms,' protested the poor woman, who was a stickler for etiquette, since part of her job was to see that all Henry's children were brought up with beautiful manners.

Lady Bryan's memories of the upset there had been at Elizabeth's birth, when Mary, stubbornly loyal to her divorced mother, had refused to acknowledge Anne as Queen or her father as Supreme Head of the English Church, were painfully recent. Mary had the sympathy of the Pope, the Emperor and all Catholic Europe, but Henry, outraged both as a King and as a pater-familias, punished her by reducing her to the status of one of Elizabeth's ladies-in-waiting. When he visited any of the manors where his new daughter was staying, Mary had to keep to her chamber. Henry refused to speak to her for two years, though on one occasion at Hatfield Mary appeared on the battlements of the tower as Henry was leaving. He doffed his hat to her and rode away.

Lady Bryan, who had brought Mary up until she was six, had been accustomed to treat her as the heiress to the throne for seventeen years. She must have been profoundly embarrassed when the girl was sent to share Elizabeth's household with orders to ride behind the baby's litter on progress, and to cede the seat of honour even when the infant was still in the care of a wet-nurse. Mary's servants were stripped of their livery and she was placed under the surveillance of Lady Shelton, Anne Boleyn's aunt. Persuaded by Cromwell to submit to her father, she had been forgiven, but was still living with Elizabeth and Lady Bryan at Hunsdon in the tense months after Anne's execution. Nobody knew what course Henry's wrath would take this time, and there must have been anxious conferences about Elizabeth's future. Mary wrote to the King on 21 July:

'My sister Elizabeth is well, and such a child toward as I doubt not but your Highness shall have cause to rejoice of in time.'

Lady Bryan used the same adjective:

'She is as toward a child, and as gentle of condition as ever I knew in my life. Jesu preserve her Grace,' she assured Cromwell.

In addition to all this, Elizabeth was cutting her teeth; Lady Bryan's second husband, David Soche, had just died, and Sir John Shelton was insisting that, as no orders had been given to the contrary, Elizabeth should dine in public in the great hall at the board of estate. This saved the bother of serving two dinners, one in the hall and one in the nursery. It also made Lady Bryan, who was a baroness in her own right and with the status of a very superior royal nanny, see red. She could not stop Elizabeth from grabbing the grown-up food, 'divers meats, fruit and wine', which she considered unsuitable for her young charge. 'She is too young to correct greatly,' she pointed out to Cromwell. 'I beg she may have a good mess of meat to her own lodging with a good dish or two meet for her to eat of, and the reversion of the mess shall satisfy her women, a gentleman usher and a groom, which been eleven persons on her side. This will also be more economical.' Sir John was outmanoeuvred. Elizabeth continued to be brought up calmly in the way Lady Bryan approved, while the general fuss died down.

Although her mother had been publicly branded a whore, the child remained heiress to the throne through May and June. At this point the Duke of Richmond was still alive, and to many he seemed eligible for the succession, despite his illegitimacy. Cromwell and Henry's new wife, Jane Seymour, were suing for Mary to be allowed back at Court. Henry, meanwhile, had been told that Anne had plotted before her death to poison both Mary and Richmond to assure Elizabeth's future. It was a preposterous suggestion, but according to Chapuys the King believed it:

'When the Duke of Richmond went to say goodnight to his father and ask for his blessing after the English custom, the King began to weep', saying Richmond and Mary 'were greatly bound to God for their deliverance'.

It seems probable that there was a brief period when Henry felt he could not bear to set eyes on Elizabeth. She was formally bastardised by the savagely worded Act of Succession of July 1536 and deprived of the title of Princess. The Act said Anne Boleyn had confessed to impediments in her marriage to 'the most reverend father in God, Thomas Archbishop of Canterbury'. It barred Elizabeth from the succession, making it treason to refer to either Mary or Elizabeth as legitimate. Nevertheless Elizabeth was at Court again with the royal family by October, and an observer writing to Cardinal du Bellay at the time of the Pilgrimage of Grace recorded that Henry loved her very much.* Earlier that year on the night Katharine of Aragon died, the King, dressed all in yellow, had danced about the Court with Elizabeth in his arms, showing her off to all the courtiers, radiant with joy because, on that January evening in 1536, he still believed that the child of which Anne miscarried a month later would be a boy.

Elizabeth was two years old and this whirling jig must have been one of her earliest memories of her father. We do not know, and are never likely to know, at what age she learned the shattering details of the charges against her mother; but despite the harsh wording of the 1536 act, nobody can seriously have supposed that the little girl with the pale skin and red-gold hair was not Henry's child. She spent the Christmas of 1536 at Court and throughout her childhood she was present on State occasions. Several incidents suggest she often stole the show. In Edward's christening procession she carried the chrisom even though she was so small that she had to be carried herself by Viscount Beauchamp. Like many royal four-year-olds she grew restive during the ceremony, and afterwards she stepped forward with Mary and Lady Herbert of Troy to help carry the baby Prince's train in the long procession back to Jane Seymour's apartments.

* Fearing treachery from the Londoners, Henry withdrew to Windsor Castle with Jane Seymour, Mary and Elizabeth. Du Bellay's correspondent suggests he used the two princesses to influence public opinion: 'To soften the temper of the people he caused his two daughters Mesdames Marie and Isabeau to come thither.' The writer implies that at Windsor Elizabeth ate in the nursery as Lady Bryan had prescribed, but she was around the Court and he noticed that Henry was very affectionate to her.

Prince Edward as a baby: Holbein's New Year gift to Henry in 1540

Elizabeth's illegitimate status was to trouble lawyers and diplomats charged with arranging foreign marriage alliances for the next decade. In the spring of 1537 Sir Thomas Wriothesley wrote a memorandum to himself:

'The King has two daughters and as Princes commonly conclude amity and things of importance by alliance it is thought necessary that these two daughters shall be made of some estimation.'

Nothing was ever done towards legitimising Mary or Elizabeth, but legal bastard-isation made little difference to the way Elizabeth was treated at home. She was the King's daughter, the Lady Elizabeth's Grace, a princess in all but name. After Anne Boleyn's fall, Mary took precedence as the older sister with a quota of forty-two household servants to Elizabeth's thirty-two, but in the Act of Succession of 1543, declaring that any issue from the King's sixth marriage to Katherine Parr should have a claim to the throne, Elizabeth was restored to the succession in a very specific way. In the event of Edward's death and if Henry and Katherine had no children, the Crown was to go to Mary. If she died without issue it went to Elizabeth. Section 2, which deals with Elizabeth's claim, made it clear that Mary's rights were conditional upon her agreeing to certain letters patent, which the King was then preparing. It provided for a safeguarding of the new Church settlement by stating that if Mary did not keep the special conditions, Elizabeth should inherit, '*as though the said Lady Mary were then dead*' (my italics).

The conditions were not outlined in the act, but they clearly included the proviso that neither Mary nor Elizabeth was free to marry without the consent of the Council. It goes without saying that the King required his daughters to live in unblemished chastity before marriage. Assuming Elizabeth learned the reasons for Anne's fall in adolescence, this may explain why she set a defensively high value on her own reputation. Elizabeth Jenkins, in her biography *Elizabeth the Great*, explains the tenacious clinging to virginity as stemming from a deeply-rooted fear of sex, which she connected with her mother's execution and with that of Henry's fifth wife, Elizabeth's cousin, Katherine Howard. Since Katherine's dizzying indiscretions are supposed to have started when she was twelve years old, Elizabeth, as Anne's daughter, was encouraged from puberty to read grave and godly texts, which placed a high emphasis on purity. That she later came to value virginity for its own sake was in some part the result of her education. Even her pious great-grandmother, Lady Margaret Beaufort, the benefactress of St John's College, Cambridge, had approved of French romances, but there is no record that the adolescent Elizabeth ever read anything but the scriptures and the classics.

Not long after Anne's death there was another scandal in the royal family. Lady Margaret Douglas, the King's niece and ward, fell in love with Lord Thomas Howard, a younger brother of the Duke of Norfolk. The extent of their indiscretion was an exchange of gifts. He gave her a cramp ring, and she gave him her miniature. Lord Thomas was executed, and Lady Margaret was technically under sentence of death, a clause being added to the 1536 Act of Succession underlining that it was a capital offence to 'espouse, marry or deflower being unmarried' any of the King's female relations. Commenting on the severity of the sentence Chapuys said Margaret Douglas deserved pardon since in her case 'copulation had not taken place', and even if it had, he added tartly, she could scarcely be blamed 'seeing the number of domestic examples she has seen and sees daily'.

Henry was furious. His niece had been brought up at the English Court from earliest childhood, when the Pope had scandalised Henry by granting a divorce between her mother, Margaret of Scotland, and her second husband, the Earl of Angus. The Defender of the Faith had taken his elder sister,s child morally and spiritually under his wing. As a royal ward she had no business to go about disposing of her heart as she pleased. He thundered that she had 'behaved herself so lightly as was greatly to our dishonour'. Margaret of Scotland threatened to disown her daughter, but after a short spell in the Tower and some contrite letters to Cromwell, Lady Margaret returned to Court, apparently quite undeflowered. Her experience served as a stern object lesson against romantic dalliance both to her cousins and to Henry's other ward, the giddy Mary Howard, widow of the Duke of Richmond.* The 'Princess of Scotland' remained in her uncle's household until her marriage to the Earl of Lennox in 1544. Although Elizabeth was too small to understand its implications at the time, the episode must have remained in the memories of her ladies, and her own experience in 1548, when she was accused of misconduct with Thomas Seymour, was a frightening parallel, since she must have felt, despite her innocence of the charges, that it was on account of her own blood royal that he died.

No Tudor monarch employed a speech-writer. Prince Edward, sent to welcome a foreign ambassador at eight years old, agonised in a letter to Katherine Parr that he would have to make a Latin speech of welcome. Trained by Roger Ascham, who had been Public Orator at Cambridge, Elizabeth was so well grounded in Cicero by the time she ascended the throne that speech-making came naturally to her. She quickly developed this talent with such style and flamboyance that contemporary annalists treasured even her most casual sayings. Thanks to their zeal most of her parliamentary speeches are preserved, though when she spoke extempore the short-hand writers had to make rapid guesses.

Henry himself set the precedent and indeed the pattern for Elizabeth's great parliamentary orations when he addressed the House of Commons on Christmas Eve 1545. They had somewhat reluctantly voted him the income from the Chantries, Colleges and Hospitals to cover the cost of his wars with France and Scotland. When

---

* When Cromwell examined Margaret Douglas's servants it emerged that Mary Howard, who was considered too young to be a proper chaperone, had been present when the lovers met. Henry and Norfolk had corresponded about daughters and the trials of fatherhood. The King chose Mary as a wife for the Duke of Richmond. After Richmond's death Norfolk sued for his daughter's jointure, which was not immediately forthcoming; he worried that she would marry someone unsuitable. Henry regarded his widowed daughter-in-law as a useful acquisition, including her in schemes for matrimonial alliances as a fourth choice after the Ladies Mary, Elizabeth and Margaret Douglas.

the King went to dismiss Parliament, the Speaker offered thanks and praise. Traditionally the Lord Chancellor replied on the sovereign's behalf, but suddenly Henry himself rose to thank the Commons heartily for the subsidy, promising the poor and sick would not suffer as a result of the changes. Then he spoke of religion, taking St Paul's Epistle to the Corinthians as his text. He berated the members soundly for their lack of charity towards each other. As Supreme Head of the Church, he wanted uniformity; he did not wish his flock to call each other 'heretic', 'anabaptist' and 'papist'. He blamed the preachers. Some were too stiff in their old 'Mumpsimus', some too busy with their new 'Sumpsimus'. Few, he said, truly preached the word of God. The scriptures had become a topic for common debate. He was sorry to hear 'how unreverently that most precious jewel the word of God is disrupted, rhymed, sung and jangled in every alehouse and tavern contrary to the true meaning of the same'. A correspondent of Lord Paget, probably Sir William Petre, was present and reported that several of the Commons burst into tears.

The spontaneity of Henry's gesture took everyone by surprise. There is no suggestion he had prepared what he was going to say, but Petre's letter to Paget implies that in Court circles people were accustomed to Henry breaking into long harangues. The novelty this time lay in his addressing not the courtiers but the Commons.

Elizabeth could not have been present, for she was staying that Christmas at Hertford Castle. There is no record that she ever heard her father give a formal address, but the startling resemblance of the Mumpsimus Sumpsimus outburst to her own speeches on uniformity of religion suggests she knew its contents by heart. At times her language echoes Henry's so closely that we may be certain that she had, like Paget and Petre, heard her father in full flow many times. For her the address at the end of the session became an established tradition, a way of accounting for her actions and policies to her subjects, or like her father correcting them when she believed they erred. In Parliament Elizabeth spoke from the heart, drawing on her unique reserves of personal experience, as well as on her great store of learning. In her youth, when it was rumoured she was pregnant by Thomas Seymour, she had defended herself to Protector Somerset against the 'shameful slanders' to her 'honour and honesty'. She valued both throughout her life and she set a high value on telling the truth. For her country she could be magnificently devious, complex and prevaricating, but she saw herself as straightforward, plain-dealing and bound by an invisible power, higher than hers, never to go back on her word – 'the word of a Prince'.

CHAPTER I

The Italian Letter

Elizabeth's earliest surviving letter was written from St James's Palace, when she was ten years old. It is in Italian and addressed to her fourth stepmother, Queen Katherine Parr. The Queen had been made Regent while Henry VIII was in France supervising the siege of Boulogne. Dismissed usually as a 'schoolroom exercise', the letter reveals a good deal about Elizabeth's childhood feelings, and her growing trust in her new stepmother, but it has rarely been studied in context.

Elizabeth had met Katherine Parr, then Lady Latimer, in June 1543 at Greenwich and was present when Henry married her at Hampton Court a month later. The wedding was a private affair in a small oratory, 'the Queen's Privy closet'. Only close friends and Henry's immediate family attended. Bishop Gardiner officiated, and as the King repeated the marriage vows for the sixth time in his life, a broad grin spread across his face. Afterwards the royal couple went to Oatlands on honeymoon progress. Princess Mary remained with them, but Elizabeth was sent back to continue her studies in the household she was then sharing with her brother Prince Edward.

The following year, in the midst of hectic preparations for the French campaign, Henry's niece and ward Lady Margaret Douglas was betrothed to the Earl of Lennox. The marriage took place a few days before the King set out for Boulogne. On 26 June Elizabeth, Mary and Edward dined in state with their father as part of the marriage celebrations. For Elizabeth and Edward this must have been a colourful and memorable occasion with the twin excitements of Henry's impending departure and the feasting and jousting for Lady Margaret's wedding. London was full of soldiery, a fine sight for children of six and ten. The day ended with an al fresco supper in Hyde Park. The Queen was not present at the banquet, although she attended the nuptial Mass on 29 June. Elizabeth was apparently not at the church ceremony, so the child and her stepmother missed each other by three days in the whirlwind of royal engagements.

Despite the pressures of State business which Katherine shouldered as Regent, she remained steadily concerned with the welfare of the King's younger children, who had seen two stepmothers, the unsuitable Anne of Cleves and the indiscreet Katherine Howard, come and go since the death of Edward's mother, Jane Seymour. During that busy July Elizabeth was separated from Edward. Up to the age of six he had been educated, as he was later to remark in his journal, 'among the wemmen'. As heir to the throne he was now set up in his own household with Dr Richard Cox, a former headmaster of Eton, to teach him Latin and Sir John Cheke, Regius Professor of Greek at Cambridge, appointed 'as a supplement to Mr Cox for the better instruction of the Prince and the diligent teaching of such children as be appointed to attend upon him'. While Edward travelled to Hampton Court with the Queen, Elizabeth remained at St James's. Although once a leper hospital, it had been recently modernised, and by the summer of 1544 was a pleasant royal house, the ceilings painted by Holbein, and with a suite of rooms which the Queen kept for her own use. The bosses in the vaulting of the gatehouse still bore the carved initials of Elizabeth's parents, H and A, lovingly intertwined.

Messengers were sent continually between the royal households. While Henry was in France, Katherine wrote five times during July and August mentioning the children's health. She was particularly careful of the delicate Edward. Each time his household removed, scouts were sent ahead to check there was no sickness in the district. Elizabeth and Edward clearly adored the Queen, an engaging and motherly figure with a collection of little lapdogs, who signed herself K.P. and found time not only to enquire about their progress in Latin, but to take lessons to improve her own. To alleviate the discomforts of siege warfare she sent Henry a boatload of venison from the home park at Hampton Court. She was also busy at this stressful period collecting *Prayers and Meditations*, a small volume which she published with the King's approval the following year. It included a Prayer for the King's Safety, and a pious prayer for the use of armies before entering battle, which requests the Almighty to grant the English victory 'with small effusion of blood and to the little hurt and domage of innocents'.

Cut off from the rest of her family Elizabeth was struggling with Italian subjunctives and learning courtly forms of address. We do not know exactly how long she remained at St James's but by September, when the plague had broken out in London, the Queen had removed, first to Oking and later to Eltham, the moated palace south of the river. Elizabeth was at Eltham, apparently ahead of the Queen's luggage, though we do not know if she accompanied Katherine to Otford, where the Queen awaited Henry's return in the first week of October.* The Italian letter, despite the grand phrases suggested by a tutor or transcribed from a copy book, immediately establishes by its confiding tone how much Elizabeth trusted Katherine. It also reveals the mingled awe and pride which overcame her whenever she thought of her magnificent father. She comments on the ill luck and everlasting round of

---

* The Queen's household expenses indicate that Elizabeth was removed quickly from St James's to one of the country manors. By September 1544 she was at Oking with the Queen, who had spent August hunting. Katherine was a keen sportswoman and ordered a dozen new strings for her bow; the accounts are full of presents of buck, which the Queen shot and sent to friends. When the plague broke out in London and Westminster Katherine issued a proclamation that no one who had been in the capital should come near Oking, for fear of infecting the King's children. Later the rule had to be relaxed, when the Queen sent to London for 'starch, pins and other necessaries'.

events (*volutrice de cose humane*)* which have prevented her from seeing the Queen for a whole year. She has not dared to write to Henry herself, but thanks her stepmother for doing so. She describes her present position away from the rest of the family as '*exilio*'. Much has been made of this word: Mumby in *The Girlhood of Queen Elizabeth* assumes that she had offended the King, and been sent away from the Court. Elizabeth Jenkins repeats the assumption, but there is no foundation for the story, and if it were true it would almost certainly have reached the ears of Chapuys, who lost no opportunity to report any evil about the child of 'la Ana'.† Elizabeth shrewdly points out to Katherine that she has entreated the Lord God to send Henry '*successo bonissimo*', the very best success against his enemies. Finally, remembering the splendours of the State banquet a month earlier, she hints broadly that she hopes to be at Court again very soon, so that she and Katherine can rejoice together at the victor's return.

❦ Unkind fortune, envious of all good and the continuous whirl of human affairs, has deprived me for a whole year of your most Illustrious presence. And not content with this, has again robbed me of the same pleasure. This would be unbearable for me, if I did not expect to enjoy it again soon. And in this my exile, I know well that in your kindness, your highness has had as much care and solicitude over my health as the King's Majesty. So that I am bound to serve you and to revere you with a daughter's love, since I understand that your most Illustrious Highness has not forgotten me every time you have written to the King's Majesty, which it was my duty to have requested from you, since I have not dared to write to him myself. I now humbly beseech your most Excellent Highness that when you write to his majesty you will recommend me to him, praying always for his sweet blessing and similarly entreating our Lord God to send him best success and the obtaining of victory over his enemies in order that your highness and I may as soon as possible rejoice with him on his happy return.

I pray God that he will preserve your most illustrious highness to whose grace, kissing your hands, I offer and recommend myself.

From St James's this 31st July

Your most obedient daughter and most faithful servant,

Elizabeth

* '*Volutrice*' does not exist in Italian, but Elizabeth literally meant 'that which turns human affairs', from the Latin '*volutare*'.

† Chapuys to the Emperor, 13 August 1543 – a typical reference: 'the daughter of Ana Bolans, the King has sent to be with the Prince his son'. In earlier letters he called her 'the Bastard', or to distinguish her from Richmond, 'the little Bastard'.

Nothing done as it should be

Scattered references in the State Papers suggest the royal children usually kept Christmas together. In 1539, when Edward was two, Mary and Elizabeth had him with them at Hertford Castle. In December 1544, after Henry had returned victorious from Boulogne, the two younger children were together at Ashridge, the house near Berkhampstead noted for its healthy air. Dr Cox wrote from Ashridge on 10 December to report to Sir William Paget that the Prince could decline his Latin nouns and conjugate his verbs. He was tackling the parts of speech with the same gusto the King had shown when attacking Boulogne, and he was ready to start Aesop's *Fables*.

Elizabeth wrote from Ashridge on 31 December. During the peace negotiations Cardinal du Bellay had made a suggestion that she should marry a French prince and return Boulogne to France as part of her dowry. It followed that particular attention was being paid to her French. She had made a New Year's present for the Queen, a translation of Marguerite of Navarre's poem *The Mirror of the Sinful Soul*. Marguerite was Francis I's sister and she and the King's mistress, Madame d'Estampes, headed an 'English party' at the Valois Court, so the choice was a graceful one. The poem's title echoed another literary feat, for Elizabeth's famous great-grandmother, Lady Margaret Beaufort, had 'Englysshed' an earlier poem, *The Myrour of Golde for the Synfull Soule*, in 1506. Lady Margaret was a patroness of both William Caxton and Wynken de Worde, and de Worde had printed *The Myrour* from Fleet Street in 1522 and again in 1526.

Sir John Neale has called Marguerite's work 'an excessively dreary French poem'. More recently Anne Lake Prescott, in *The Pearl of the Valois and Elizabeth I*, marvelled at its unsuitability 'as a means of displaying Elizabeth's talents', since the poem presents God 'as a great king and judge who is kind to daughters and does not execute adulterous wives'. In fact the metre is light and lilting and the poem lends itself easily to literal translation despite its high seriousness. Jean Belmain, the French tutor laconically mentioned in Edward's journal, had recently joined the household. He probably helped with the translation, so Elizabeth cannot have found the language too difficult. The labour lay in writing it out.

The script she uses for *The Mirror* is not quite as careful as that of the Italian letter, written five months earlier. The first twenty-seven pages suggest the writer was having a terrible battle to get the tails of her 'g's aligned and that she was undecided about how to form the letter 'k'. The pages of the 'book' are much smaller than the large single sheet she used to write her letter to Katherine during the summer. The book must have been finished in a hurry, since the dedication is dated on the last day of the old year. Elizabeth had obviously transcribed her first draft from 'rough' to 'best'. On f. 34 she wrote, 'for my mind was in other places'. Clearly it was; she copied the phrase out twice, firmly scoring through the repetition. She had grasped the poem's main theme, the complete dependence of the soul upon God, which she set out in the introduction, but chiefly she was concerned to get the thing down in English, and at eleven she was painfully aware of her own grammatical shortcomings.

Traditionally she is supposed to have embroidered the cover herself. The needle-work must have been more fun than the translation. The book is bound in blue cloth, festively embroidered with forget-me-nots on the spine, and with heartsease worked in violet, yellow and green silk at the corners. Elizabeth stitched the Queen's initials, 'K.P.', on the front cover in silver, framing them in a rectangular design. One side of the rectangle is longer than the other so the effect is slightly lopsided. At first sight the silver stitching is minute, but closer examination suggests that Elizabeth actually used the silver braid manufactured for the royal liveries, sticking or stitching it to the blue cloth.* The heartsease symbolised the domestic harmony Katherine had brought to the royal household, but, alas, Elizabeth got the colours upside down, making the upper petals yellow and the lower ones purple, a condition not usual in pansies.

Professor Prescott has studied Elizabeth's mistakes carefully, citing her occasional omissions and gender confusions as the signs of subconscious anger against her father, but I believe that these, like other small faults of grammar and calligraphy, are the natural errors of a child who was battling heroically against time to complete a task that stretched her powers of comprehension and concentration to the limit. The poem is prefaced by a touchingly funny letter of dedication showing only too clearly how Elizabeth's mind worked on this occasion. She begins with a flourish of fine phrases and imposing metaphors, including the precept that idle minds are best kept busy, but she dwindles half-way down the second page to an anxious plea that the Queen will not show the gift around too much until she has corrected the mistakes. 'Nothing', winces the royal pupil in a burst of panic-stricken parentheses, 'is done as it should be', and a few lines further on she repeats the phrase. A tutor may have helped with the translation but both the panic and the parentheses suggest the letter was Elizabeth's own composition.

CҔ To Our most Noble and Virtuous Queen Katherine, Elizabeth her humble
daughter wisheth perpetual felicity and everlasting joy.

Not only knowing the affectuous will and fervent zeal, the which your Highness hath towards all godly learning, as also my duty towards you (most Gracious and Sovereign Princess) but knowing also, that pusillanimity and idleness are most repugnant unto a reasonable creature, and that (as the philosopher sayeth) even as an instrument of iron or other metal waxeth soon

---

* The thread is tarnished and discoloured. I had the good fortune to be holding the manuscript when, oblivious to the laws of conservation, a ray of sunshine struck through the windows of Duke Humphrey's Library and fell directly on to the embroidery, lighting up the colours. It is impossible to tell whether the silver braid is stitched or stuck to the blue cloth without detaching the fabric from the stiffened book cover.

rusty, unless it be continually occupied: even so shall the wit of a man or a woman wax dull and unapt to do or understand any thing perfectly, unless it be always occupied upon some manner of study. Which things considered, hath moved so small a portion as God hath lent me, to prove what I could do. And therefore have I (as for essay or beginning, following the right notable saying of the proverb aforesaid) translated this little book out of French rhyme into English prose, joining the sentences together as well as the capacity of my simple wit and small learning could extend themselves. The which book is entitled or named The Mirror, or Glass of the Sinful Soul, wherein is contained, how she (beholding and contemplating what she is) doth perceive how of herself and her own strength, she can do nothing that good is, or prevaileth for her salvation, unless it be through the grace of God, whose mother, daughter, sister and wife, by the Scriptures, she proveth herself to be. Trusting also that, through his incomprehensible love, grace and mercy, she (being called from sin to repentance) doth faithfully hope to be saved. And although I know that as for my part which I have wrought in it (as well spiritual as manual) there is nothing done as it should be, nor else worthy to come in your Grace's hands, but rather all unperfect and uncorrect; yet do I trust also that, howbeit it is like a work which is but new begun and shapen, that the file of your excellent wit and godly learning, in the reading of it (if so it vouchsafe your Highness to do) shall rub out, polish and mend (or else cause to mend) the words (or rather the order of my writing) the which I know in many places to be rude and nothing done as it should be. But I hope that, after to have been in your Grace's hands, there shall be nothing in it worthy of reprehension, and that in the meanwhile no other (but your Highness only) shall read it or see it, lest my faults be known of many. Then shall they be better excused (as my confidence is in your Grace's accustomed benevolence) than if I should bestow a whole year in writing or inventing ways to excuse them.

Praying God Almighty, the Maker and Creator of all things, to grant unto your Highness the same New Year's day, a lucky and a prosperous year, with prosperous issue and continuance of many years in good health and continual joy, and all to His honour, praise and glory.

From Ashridge, this last day of the year of our Lord God 1544.

My own matchless and most kind father

The following year Elizabeth made a present for Henry, another prayer book, similar to the one for Katherine Parr. Every detail about the work suggests it was a labour of love. Elizabeth was now restored to the succession. Du Bellay's plans for her to marry a French prince had come to nothing and a scheme for her to marry the Prince of Denmark had also fallen through, but she was a dignified young lady of twelve and her father thought her a fit bride for the son of an emperor.* To her, Henry was the glorious victor of Boulogne, and it seems she stood high in his estimation. Released from her duties as Regent, Katherine had completed *Prayers and Meditations*, which had been printed by Thomas Berthelet. The royal book was an instant success, going into nineteen editions before the end of the century. The Princess translated the Queen's work into Latin, French and Italian, bound in one volume and prefaced by a Latin dedication to Henry. It is the only letter we have from Elizabeth to her father.

She bound the gift in scarlet cloth, embroidering it in silver and gold thread with Henry's initials and a monogram of 'Kateryn', K.P.'s own way of spelling her Christian name. At the corners Elizabeth sewed eight white Tudor roses, four at the front and four at the back, their leaves picked out in green silk, their centres yellow. This was her first use of the eglantine, the white rose badge of her grandmother, Elizabeth of York, which was to remain one of Elizabeth's favourite emblems. Inside the book, 117 pages of beautifully inscribed vellum testify to the care that went into preparing the present. The text is neatly set out in three four-inch rectangles. Just visible beneath the lettering are the feint lines and margins ruled by Elizabeth or her writing tutor. This time the gift was for the King. Nothing was done in a hurry and the round childish script of the previous year had developed into the fine italic hand which was to earn Elizabeth so much praise.

She was lodged again that December at Hertford Castle, which was regularly used by the royal children. A bowling alley had recently been installed there for the use of the young Prince and his companions, and Elizabeth may have watched him at play with such friends as Barnaby Fitzpatrick, and Ambrose and Robert Dudley, the sons of Viscount Lisle.† Sir John Cheke, who had retained his post as Regius Professor at Cambridge as well as acting in his advisory capacity to Edward's household, had quickly recognised Elizabeth's precocious abilities. He arranged for William Grindal, a brilliant young scholar from Lady Margaret's foundation at St John's, to become her tutor. Grindal was the star pupil of the celebrated Roger Ascham, the pioneer of the new method of pronouncing Greek which had fired all Cambridge with enthusiasm. Like Cheke and Ascham Grindal believed in the reformed religion. He joined Elizabeth's household in 1544.

---

* From October to December Bishop Gardiner was charged with negotiations to marry Elizabeth to Charles V's son, Philip, Prince of Spain (later King Philip II). The Imperialists regarded Mary as the legitimate, and Elizabeth as the illegitimate, daughter. Francis I, who had met Anne Boleyn when she accompanied Henry to France in 1532, seemed to regard Elizabeth as legitimate. Cardinal du Bellay, Archbishop of Paris, tried to negotiate for Elizabeth to marry the Duc d'Orléans, bringing Boulogne back to France as her dowry.

† Sir John Dudley was the son of Henry VII's unpopular tax-collector. Henry VIII created him Viscount Lisle. In Edward's reign he became Earl of Warwick, later Duke of Northumberland. He was Master of the Horse to Anne of Cleves and later Henry's Admiral.

The startling elegance of her Latin in the letter to Henry suggests that it may have been a joint compilation, or that the young man had lost no time in stimulating Elizabeth to remarkable new heights of attainment. The letter to Henry shows the exacting standards set for Elizabeth and Edward at an early age. It also demonstrates the rapid advancement of Elizabeth's mind in adolescence, and it sets out ideas that were to shape her thought and personality for the rest of her life. Despite conventional protestations of ignorance and humility, it is full of feeling, and I believe it demonstrates irrefutably the sincerity of Elizabeth's attitude to her father. As a piece of writing it is beautifully balanced. The nervous parentheses of the previous year have vanished. Gracious phrases find their place naturally, and the whole rhythm of the language suggests that Elizabeth knew exactly what she was doing and delighted in it. She was confident that the gift would please Henry; her extravagant praise of Katherine includes a grave little homily on the value of divine learning, and everything indicates that she was filled with a new sense of self-awareness. She was the Lady Elizabeth, heiress to the intellectual traditions of the Tudor family and with a growing understanding of what it meant to be the daughter of a king – one 'whom philosophers regard as a god upon earth'. Maybe Grindal had invented the phrase to flatter his royal patron, but it was Elizabeth who wrote it out, and unconsciously she was laying the foundations for her own deeply rooted belief in the divine origins of sovereignty. As she weathered the traumas of the following decades, it was to become a belief which no one was in a position to shake.

The title of Elizabeth's present was imposing:

℃ℨ *Prayers or meditations by which the mind may be moved to the patient endurance of all the troubles of this life, to the contempt of vain worldly prosperity and to the faithful expectation of eternal bliss, collected from several divine authors by the noble and most holy lady Katherine, Queen of England, France and Ireland, and translated from the English by the lady Elizabeth.*

To the most glorious and mighty king Henry VIII, King of England, France and Ireland, Defender of the Faith, and Supreme Head under Christ of the Church of England and Ireland for whose every happiness His Majesty's most humble daughter Elizabeth ever prays, and who she entreats to give her his blessing.

Inasmuch as the immortal mind excels the immortal body so every wise man will deem the works of the mind more highly to be esteemed and worthy of greater honour than any corporal act. As, therefore, your Majesty is of so high an excellence that none or few may be compared with you in royal and gracious attainments such that not only am I bound to you by the law of the land as my lord, by the law of nature as my lord and by divine law as my father, but as [you are] the most gracious of lords and my own matchless and most kind father so I would be bound to your Majesty by all laws and by all sorts of duties and by all means possible, and therefore I have gladly sought, as was my duty, how I might offer your Grace the best gift that my skill and industry might find.

And in this I fear only lest my green and unordered learning and the unripe childishness of my intellect may detract from the praise and commendation of a matter which intellects long steeped in arguments of theology labour upon. For nothing should be more acceptable to a king whom philosophers regard as a god on earth than the study which lifts us to heaven and renders us heavenly while on earth, and divine while yet in the flesh, and which, though we were in the toils of endless and infinite troubles, even then restores us to our happiness and felicity.

It seemed most appropriate to me that a work of such piety, a work compiled in English by the pious zeal and great industry of a glorious Queen and for that reason a work sought out by all, and by your Majesty highly esteemed, should be translated into other languages (this work which in its theme is truly worthy of a King and in its compilation worthy of a Queen) and it seemed fitting to me that this task should be undertaken by myself, your daughter and one who should be not only the imitator of your virtues but also heir to them. Whatever in this work is not mine, is worthy of the highest praise, inasmuch as the whole book is so pious in its argument, so skilful in its compilation and so well drawn up in the fittest order. But as to what is mine, if there be any error in it yet it may merit pardon on account of my ignorance, my youth, my short time of study and my goodwill, and if it be undistinguished, even though it merit no praise, yet if it be well received it will powerfully incite me to further efforts so that even as I advance in years so I shall advance also in learning and in the fear of God and so it shall come to pass that I shall worship Him ever more zealously and serve your Majesty ever more dutifully.

Wherefore I do not doubt but that your fatherly goodness and royal foresight will set no lower value on this private labour of my mind than on any other attainment and that you will feel that this holy work which is the more highly to be valued as having been compiled by the Queen your wife, may have its value ever so little enhanced by being translated by your daughter. May the King of Kings, in whose hands lie the hearts of all kings so guide your mind and protect your life that under your Majesty's rule we may live long in true piety and religion.

From Hertford, the 30th day of December 1545.

The mind I shall never be ashamed to present

Prayers and Meditations was a thoughtful gift. The Queen's book was no daring piece of reformed thinking. It was a gentle confession of personal faith, designed, as the title stated, to calm the mind in times of worldly troubles. Henry had plenty; despite the capture of Boulogne, the King had spent three times more than he intended on the French war. He had strained his relations with the Emperor almost to breaking point; he was still at war with France and with Scotland, regardless of the marriage alliance with Lennox. The French had raided the Isle of Wight, throughout the summer the Lord Admiral had been at sea with 12,000 men, and Lord Chancellor Wriothesley was at his wits' end to find subsidies. By the end of 1545 Henry VIII was very nearly bankrupt.

None of this can have been apparent to the twelve-year-old Elizabeth as she pursued her studies, diligently bent on pleasing her all-powerful father. He remained adamant in his breach with Rome, but otherwise his religious views were conservative. He continued his drive for uniformity in Church affairs in a tremendous burst of book-banning. In a proclamation of July 1546 it was declared that no one should have in their possession New Testaments translated by the early reformers, William Tyndale or Miles Coverdale, and a list of heretical writers, including Wycliff, Bale, Barnes and the innocuous Richard Tracy, was forbidden on pain of imprisonment: the 'King's Book', *A Necessary Doctrine and Erudition for any Christian Man*, contained all the knowledge an Englishman needed to get to heaven. In another proclamation he closed the London brothels. He also authorised the burning at the stake of Anne Askew, a young woman with advanced ideas about the communion service, who was condemned as a Sacramentarian.

Through 1546 Henry's health deteriorated. The ulcers on his leg grew worse. At Hampton Court he had to be winched into a wheelchair by a series of pulleys.* By the end of the year he was sinking fast and on 28 January 1547 he died. Led by Edward's uncle, Lord Hertford, the Council brought Elizabeth and Edward together before breaking the news to them. The nine-year-old King threw himself into his sister's arms, and the children wept bitterly for so many hours that all the household marvelled at such prolonged grief. Edward was taken to be crowned, while Elizabeth, subdued and depressed, remained with her stepmother. The excitement of the Coronation soon absorbed Edward, who wrote to Elizabeth that as their father was certainly in heaven they should not grieve for him. His uncle, who quickly made himself Duke of Somerset, did not allow Elizabeth to visit her brother for some time.

---

* Dr Starkey says of him: 'By later 1546 he could scarcely walk and was carried "to and fro in his galleries and chambers" in a pair of specially constructed chairs called trams, which were covered with quilted tawny velvet and embroidered with roses in Venice gold.' Dr Starkey points out that Henry could not have suffered from syphilis, as there were no prescriptions for mercury among his apothecaries' bills.

Elizabeth as Princess, holding the book of devotions bound in gold-tooled leather: 'the mind I shall never be ashamed to present.'

Shortly before Henry's death the children had been together at Hatfield, and Edward's household then moved to Hertford Castle. On 5 December he had written from Enfield:

'Change of place did not vex me so much, dearest sister, as your going from me. Now there can be nothing pleasanter than a letter from you . . . my chamberlain tells me I may hope to visit you soon, if nothing happens to either of us in the meantime.'

In a later letter he asked for her portrait. Both children had been painted in the autumn of 1546, before their father's death, and Henry's last New Year present to Edward had been portraits (or miniatures) of himself and Katherine. In a conclusive piece of re-dating Janet Arnold has linked the portrait of Elizabeth now in the royal collection at Windsor Castle with a letter formerly ascribed to the 1550s. It shows Elizabeth at thirteen, perhaps in the new dress that was ordered for her in November for the Christmas festivities. The portrait is mentioned in the inventory made for Edward in 1547 as 'a table with the picture of the Lady Elizabeth her grace with a book in her hand, her gown like crimson cloth with works'.

Elizabeth was conscious of her intellectual abilities from an early age. When Lord Chancellor Wriothesley visited her at Hertford Castle in December 1539 with greetings from Henry, he reported that the six-year-old Lady Elizabeth replied to the King's message 'with as great gravity as she had been forty years old. If she be no worse educated than she appears, she will be an honour to womanhood.'

The painter of the Windsor portrait caught this gravity exactly. Every inch the scholar, Elizabeth holds a book of devotions bound in gold-tooled leather in long, graceful fingers. On the lectern beside her another book, perhaps the Gospels, lies open. In the letter she modestly disclaims her own beauty, saying the face she 'might well blush to offer' but adding boldly, 'the mind I shall never be ashamed to present.' This theme of the mind runs through all her letters to Edward: even when the little boy wrote from Enfield to say he was missing her she replied immediately with an exhortation to him to get on with his Latin. At thirteen she had already begun to study Greek with Grindal, and was beginning to make a clear distinction between the workings of the mind, the yearnings of the heart and the aspirations of the soul. She learned also to use the mental discipline of translation as a way of turning aside from emotional stress. These habits of analysis and separation were to stand her in good stead in Mary's reign, but they were to make her formidable as a woman. Her intellectual strength was often a stumbling block in her relations with men. In the Windsor portrait pearls trim her coif, her gown, her stomacher. Pearls were the symbols of virginity: collecting them became a lifelong obsession and the acquisition of them gave her much pleasure.

ଓ Like as the richman that daily gathereth riches to riches, and to one bag of money layeth a great store till it come to infinite, so methinks your Majesty not being sufficed with many benefits and gentleness showed to me before this time, doth now increase them in asking and desiring, where you may bid and command, requiring a thing not worthy the desiring for itself, but made worthy by your highness's request. My picture, I mean, in which if the inward good mind towards your grace might as well be declared as the outward face and countenance shall be seen, I would not have tarried the commandment but prevent it, nor have been the last to grant but the first to offer it. For the face I grant I might well blush to offer, but the mind I shall never be ashamed to present. For though from the grace of the picture the colours may fade by time, may give by weather, may be spotted by chance, yet the other, nor time with her swift wings shall overtake, nor the misty clouds with their lowerings may darken, nor chance with her slippery foot may overthrow. Of this although yet the prose could not be great because occasions hath been but small, notwithstanding as a dog hath a day so may I perchance have time to declare it in deeds when now I do write them but in words. And further shall I most humbly beseech your Majesty that when you shall look on my picture you will vouchsafe to think that as you may have but the outward shadow of the body before you, so my inward mind wisheth that the body itself were oftener in your presence, howbeit because both by my so being, I think I could do your Majesty little pleasure though myself great good, and again because I see as yet not the time agreeing thereat I shall learn to follow this saying of Horace '*Feras non culpes quod vitari non potest*'. And thus I will (troubling your Majesty I fear) end with my most humble thanks. Beseeching God long to preserve you to his honour, to your comfort, to the realm's profit and to my joy.

From Hatfield this 15 day of May. Your Majesty's most humbly, sister and servant,

Elizabeth

A most cristenly lerned yonge lady

Shortly after Edward's Coronation the Queen Dowager's household moved to Chelsea, to the pretty manor house surrounded by cherry trees, lavender bushes and damask roses, which Henry had given her as part of her wedding jointure in 1544. Van der Delft, the new Imperial ambassador, commented that Katherine had 'gone back to the suburb where she belongs'. Mary, heiress to the throne under the terms of her father's will, was honourably treated by the new Council. 'Some people', Van der Delft wrote to the Queen of Hungary, 'are already beginning to call her Princess.' Scenting the strongly Protestant line the Council, led by Somerset and Cranmer, would take, Mary left Court to live mostly at Kenninghall and Hunsdon, two of the four manors her father had left her. There was at first no formal religious settlement, and she continued to say the Catholic Mass in all her houses.

Katherine married the Lord Protector's younger brother, Thomas Seymour, the Lord Admiral, newly created Baron Sudeley. She had loved him before her marriage to Henry, but even so the Court was a little taken aback by the speed with which the widowed Queen recovered from her bereavement.* Knowing Somerset would use his authority to forbid the match, the couple kept it secret until Edward's consent could be obtained. It was not easy to gain access to the nine-year-old monarch, who was at all times strictly supervised. The Admiral arranged for John Fowler, a trusted gentleman in the royal household, to prepare the ground by asking Edward whom he thought his uncle should marry. The King replied Anne of Cleves, for Henry's divorced fourth wife had remained in England, occupying a place of honour at official functions. Then with ready wit he said to Fowler, 'Nay, nay, wot you what? I would he married my sister Mary to turn her opinions.' This joke was passed back to the Admiral, who two days later came to St James's in person to ask his nephew for official permission to marry Katherine. It was readily granted and the little boy wrote in his journal: 'The Lord Seymour of Sudeley maried the Quene whose nam was Katerine,' adding with mischievous satisfaction, 'with wich mariag the Lord Protectour was much offended'.

As soon as the Protector's wife, the Duchess of Somerset, heard of Katherine's new status, she tried to claim precedence over her. The Queen Dowager invoked the Act of Succession. She remained the first lady in the land and all Henry's children continued to refer to her as 'the Queen'. She and the Duchess of Somerset became deadly rivals and an unseemly row broke out over Katherine's jewels, which she and Seymour considered her personal property, but which the Somersets tried to claim for the Crown. Elizabeth lived with Katherine variously at Hanworth, Chelsea and Sudeley Castle until the summer of 1548. All the Queen's residences were the scenes of feverish literary activity, for in the first year of the new reign the royal ladies set a high example in matters of learning and piety.

The feeling of intellectual liberation brought about by Henry's death ran like wildfire through Protestant circles. While she was Queen, Katherine had professed an irreproachable orthodoxy, but before her marriage to Henry she had gathered about her a number of advanced reformers. Some, like Miles Coverdale, had fled abroad during the later part of Henry's reign. Others paid lip-service to the King's ideas. Katherine's friends the Duchess of Suffolk and William Cecil, the brilliant young humanist who was first Secretary to Somerset and later Secretary to the Council, now persuaded the Queen to publish *Lamentation of a Sinner*, a much more

---

* Van der Delft wrote to the Emperor of a conversation with the Princess Mary: 'She then asked me what I thought about the Queen Dowager's marriage to the Lord Admiral. I answered that it appeared to me to be quite fitting since the Queen and he were of similar rank, she having been content to forget the honour she had enjoyed from the late King.' The ambassador teased Mary, saying she had had a lucky escape, as he had heard her own name linked with Seymour's. Mary 'laughed at this, saying she had never spoken to him in her life, and had only seen him once.'

Lutheran work than *Prayers and Meditations*. Her greatest achievement was supervising the translation of Erasmus's *Paraphrases of the New Testament*.

The first part of this eagerly awaited work came out on 31 January 1548 with a preface by Nicholas Udall, describing how Katherine had portioned out and collated the work. She had even persuaded Princess Mary to help translate *The Gospel of St John*. Headaches forced her to give up, so Dr Francis Malet, one of Katherine's chaplains, finished the translation, and Mary declined to put her name to it. Katherine wrote from Hanworth pointing out firmly and realistically that royal authorship would attract a wider public to study God's word. A separate preface was inserted before *St John*, praising Mary for encouraging the ignorant to 'read, hear and embrace this devout and *Catholic* paraphrase' (my italics). The book is catalogued to this day in the British Library as by Udall, Caius and Tudor.

As the exiles sped back to England to welcome the boy king as 'the new Josias', Udall captured a vivid picture of the intellectual circles in which Elizabeth now moved.

'It is now no news in England to see young damsels in noble houses and in the Courts of Princes instead of cards and other instruments of idle trifling to have continually in their hands either Psalms, Homilies and other devout meditations. . . It is now no news at all to see Queens and ladies of most high estate and progeny instead of courtly dalliance to embrace vertuous exercises of reading and writing,' he marvelled, and he told how the royal ladies and their gentlewomen gave up idle chatter 'about the moon shining in the water' in favour of 'grave and substantial talk in Greek and Latin'.

Elizabeth was too young to take part in the official work of Englishing the word of God. While her stepmother busied herself with Erasmus, she revised *The Mirror of the Sinful Soul*, turning the clumsy childish phrases she had written at eleven into more elegant prose. To a bereaved adolescent growing up in an atmosphere of religious polemic, Marguerite's poem had much to offer. It glorified those virtues of faith and charity so much preached by Henry himself. It clarified the doctrine of transubstantiation. It set forth the doctrine of works in a simple and palatable form. Above all it spoke of life as a preparation for death, and rose at the end to a moving panegyric on the blessings of the after-life. Working on it must have brought much spiritual comfort to Elizabeth as she approached her fourteenth birthday in the subdued period after her father's death. As a meditation, the poem is an ecstatic and often mystic acclamation of the benefits available to the soul through the operation of divine grace. Oppressed by its own sinfulness at the beginning of the poem, the soul rises to a state of total union with God. This is expressed in a series of family relationships; the soul becomes God's sister, daughter, mother and wife. He is brother, son, father and husband. Anyone who achieves this mystic union is so suffused with heavenly joy that it becomes apparent to the beholder. 'He maketh of me', wrote Elizabeth, 'a godly and beautiful creature.'

Much of the poem's meaning must have gone over her head at eleven, but the re-working of the translation was no childish exercise. Striking similarities of language and imagery between *The Mirror* and her later devotional writings suggest it became deeply embedded in her consciousness. The idea of life as a preparation for death occurs again and again in her writings. In a prayer written some thirty years after *The Mirror* she thanks God for granting 'even in my youth knowledge of thy truth'. Prayers were said twice daily in Katherine Parr's house, and it seems highly probable that through her constant endeavours to seek and receive guidance from an omniscient God, who could see the future, and who in strength, wisdom and policy could replace the father she had lost, Elizabeth from this time began to develop habits of prayer more becoming to a novice or a dowager than to a nubile princess.

Elizabeth, or someone very close to her, sent the new translation to John Bale. The rumbustious reformer was living in Germany. Early in Edward's reign his books, still officially banned in England, were in great demand, but while the other reformers were hurrying back, Bale had queered his own pitch. He had published from Marburg two sensational pieces of writing, *The Examynacyon of Anne Askewe* and its sequel, *The Lattre Examynacyon*. These vindicated the young woman burned as a Sacramentarian in the last months of Henry's reign and helped raise her to the status of a Protestant martyr. Carried away by his own rhetoric Bale had launched a vitriolic attack on the Lord Chancellor, Sir Thomas Wriothesley, and on Sir Richard Rich, one of Henry's chief councillors. He had also mentioned some of the Queen's ladies who had been suspected of sending money to Anne Askew when she was in prison. In short, he had offended in the very circles in which he most wished to be accepted. By the autumn of 1547 he was finishing *Illustrium Maioris Britanniae Scriptorum Summarium*, a five-part history of English literature. In need of both a patron and a pardon, Bale could not believe in his own luck when he received Elizabeth's translation.* It was manna from heaven, a personal salutation from the King's sister. How the book reached Bale, or indeed who sent it, is a mystery. It came with either a covering letter or a separate sheet of quotations chosen and written by Elizabeth herself. They accurately reflect the topics which absorbed the ladies in Katherine Parr's household. Elizabeth had quoted *Ecclesiastes*:

'There is not a more wicked head than the head of a serpent and there is no wrath above the wrath of a woman.

'But he that hath gotten a virtuous woman hath gotten a goodly possession; she is unto him an help and pillar whereupon he resteth.

'It were better to dwell with a lion and a dragon than to keep house with a wicked wife.'

---

* 'Wonderfully joyous were the learned men of our city', wrote Bale, when they beheld 'so much faith, science and experience of language. . . They could not withhold their learned hands from the publishing thereof.'

And finally: 'Yet depart not from a discreet and good woman that is fallen to thee for thy portion in the fear of the Lord for the gift of her honesty is above gold.'

In Latin she had added the first verse of the thirteenth psalm:*

'*Stultus dixit in corde suo non est Deus*' – 'the fool saith in his heart that there is no God.'

Perhaps someone with a motive for wishing Bale back in England had filched a sheet from Elizabeth's copybook, but the exiled reformer was convinced the princess had written to him herself:

'I received your noble book right fruitfully of you translated,' he assured her; 'I received also your golden sentences out of the sacred scriptures most ornately, finely and purely written with your own hand.' In a sixteen-page Preface he described Elizabeth as 'a most cristenly lerned yonge lady', exhorting her to become 'a nourishing mother to Christ's dear congregation' and elevating her as a Christian teacher above Saints Francis, Benedict, Dominic and Bruno, the great monastic founders. Elizabeth must have been delighted. Bale's view of her coincided so exactly with the blue-stocking image she had of herself at this time.

Bale printed the book from Wesel in April 1548 under the imposing title *A Godly Meditacyon of the Cristen Sowle, concernynge a love towardes God and hys Christe, compyled in Frenche by Lady Margarete Quene of Naver and aptly translated into Englysh by the ryght vertuouse Lady Elyzabeth daughter of our late souverayne, Kyng Henri VIII*. On the title page was a woodcut of Elizabeth kneeling before Christ in earnest prayer, and beneath a reminder that she was as learned in Greek as in Latin. In a Conclusion as garrulous as his Preface he told the reader: 'In four noble languages, Latin, Greek, French and Italian, wrote she unto me these clauses following which I have added to this book', and, lest anyone still doubted him, 'the written clauses are these which she wrote first with her own hand, much more finely than I could with any printing letter set them forth'.

The collaboration between the Princess and her publisher was bizarre. The Wesel press dealt almost exclusively with questionable material disapproved by the English government. Its output was racy, radical and subject to confiscation by the authorities at a moment's notice. If Elizabeth had simply wanted to get her book printed, the obvious course would have been through her stepmother, who was in constant touch with the respectable royal printers Thomas Berthelet and Edward Whitchurch. It is just possible that someone who knew Bale was engaged on the *Summarium* sent Elizabeth's book so that her name could be included in the fifth parts which dealt with contemporary English authors, but it is more commonly supposed that he printed *A Godly Meditacyon* as a means of engineering his own pardon. His Preface praised 'the faithful tutors and teachers which by their most godly instructions' had fashioned Elizabeth's youth 'into the right image of Christ', in the most extravagant terms. When the *Summarium* was finally printed, it included

---

* In the Vulgate version.

a large woodcut showing Sir John Cheke as a powerful figure standing literally behind Edward's throne. Bale insisted that Elizabeth had not quite reached her fourteenth birthday when she finished the translation. The language is more sophisticated than in the version she wrote out at eleven. It still breathes the quiet sincerity Elizabeth brought to her task:

ᛣᛉ Neither hath the eye seen nor yet the ear heard, neither yet hath it ever entered into the heart of any man, what God hath prepared for them that love him. And would he speak it no further. No truly. Yet all this that [Saint Paul] saith here is for no other purpose but to provoke us earnestly to love.

He willeth us also therein to esteem, that he neither can declare nor yet name it and so to give forth our hearts to patience and hope of that thing which never man yet could see, neither yet discern, though many through love for it have died.

O excellent gift of faith whereof so much good cometh that it can fit man to possess that thing which he cannot comprehend. Faith joined with the truth bringeth forth hope, whereby perfect charity is engendered and charity is God as thou knowest.

If we have charity then we have also God therewith. Then is God in us and we are in him. And all this cometh through the benefit of faith. For he dwelleth in all men which have true faith. Thus have we a greater treasure than we can tell of or yet any man express unto us.

Now to conclude since an Apostle as great as Saint Paul is, will speak no further of God and his inestimable love according to his righteous example and doctrine, I will hold my peace and be still, following nevertheless his teachings.

Notwithstanding yet though herein I acknowledge myself but earth and dust yet may I not fail to yield thanks unto my eternal living God for such great graces and benefits as it hath pleased him to give me.

Unto that everlasting king of heaven, immortal, invisible, incomprehensible, mighty and wise only be all honour, praise, glory magnificence and love for ever and ever.

AMEN

CHAPTER II

If your grace had not a good opinion of me

The 'cristenly lerned yonge lady' remained with Katherine Parr until a few days after Whitsunday 1548. She left after the peace of the Queen's household was disturbed by a family quarrel. It was later to assume historic proportions as a royal sex scandal, but the causes were ordinary enough. The Queen had nursed three elderly husbands through childless marriages. For her Tom Seymour was a love match. He had courted her in 1543, after the death of her second husband, Lord Latimer, and before she caught the fancy of the King. Katherine, in love perhaps for the first time in her life, speedily became pregnant. She was thirty-five, and from the moment the child kicked in her womb she was overjoyed.

'Mary Odell being abed with me had laid her hand upon my belly to feel it stir. It hath stirred these three days every morning and evening,' she wrote from Hanworth in a note to Seymour who was away on business.

Before he had aspired to marrying the Queen, the Lord Admiral had discussed the possibility of marrying Elizabeth with the Protector, who had vetoed the idea. Seymour had also made enquiries about her estate from her cofferer, Thomas Parry. This had reached the ears of Elizabeth's governess, Mrs Ashley. As Katherine's husband, Seymour was in the position of stepfather to Elizabeth, and he is mentioned in this context quite normally by Ascham; when Grindal died of the plague in 1548, Katherine and Seymour wanted Elizabeth to have a tutor called Goldsmith. Elizabeth wanted Ascham, and after a little string-pulling by Cheke, she got her way.

In her father's will Elizabeth had been left Durham Place, which had once been used by Anne Boleyn. With fine gardens sweeping down to command two reaches of the river, it would have been an ideal London home for her, midway between Somerset Place and Westminster, between the King and the Protector. A warrant was issued on 1 July 1547 to deliver £249 15s 3d to the Lord Admiral for repairs to the house. As he was also a member of the Council, he had perfectly legitimate reasons for continuing to discuss details of Elizabeth's household with Parry, but the matter was later blown out of all proportion.

The story goes that as Katherine's pregnancy advanced, Seymour began his much catalogued romps with Elizabeth. At first the Queen joined in, perhaps because they were, as Sir John Neale assumed, 'harmless frolics in an age when conventions were not exactly prim'. If a dangerous attraction had developed between her husband and her teenage stepdaughter, Katherine was sagely keeping an eye on them. Matters came to a head at Hanworth, when she came on the pair unexpectedly. Elizabeth was in Seymour's arms. 'Wherefore,' said Thomas Parry, who had the tale from Mrs Ashley, 'the Queen fell out with the Lord Admiral and with her Grace also.' The accusations and recriminations that followed must have taken place behind locked doors, for even Mrs Ashley did not know what was said. Probably Seymour blamed Elizabeth for leading him on, reminding his wife of Anne Boleyn's reputation as a coquette, since Katherine later rounded on Mrs Ashley for neglecting her duties as chaperone. The Admiral, she said, had looked in at a gallery window and seen 'my lady Elizabeth cast her arms about a man's neck'. Taxed with this new accusation, Elizabeth denied it weeping and 'bade ask all her women'. They denied it too. Mrs Ashley said the charge was impossible, for in that part of the house 'there came no man but Grindal, the lady Elizabeth's schoolmaster'.* Mrs Ashley later told Parry she thought the Queen was jealous and had made the story up.

It is difficult to sift the evidence. Most of it was given twelve months after the events, when Parry and Mrs Ashley and her husband were being cross-questioned in a treason trial. Kat Ashley testified that Seymour had been in the habit of going bare-legged in his dressing-gown into Elizabeth's bedchamber. He slapped her familiarly on the buttocks and 'would put open the bed curtains and bid her good morrow, and make as though he would come at her. And she would go farther into the bed, so that he could not come at her'. On one occasion Katherine came up to the bedchamber with her husband and they tickled Elizabeth. On another, in the garden at Hanworth, Katherine held the girl prisoner while the Admiral cut her gown in a hundred pieces. There is no account of how much giggling or merriment accompanied these proceedings, but a sinister construction has always been placed upon them. Yet when Mrs Ashley met Elizabeth returning to the house in her torn dress, she must have given a nonchalant excuse, for the good woman simply muttered: 'Well, I wish he would do you more reverence, even though he be so homely with the Queen.'

If Elizabeth, who wept easily, had felt really threatened, she would certainly have exhibited some distress. The most reasonable explanation of the dress-cutting is that it was part of some boisterous wager, otherwise Katherine Parr, who had cared for Elizabeth since she was ten years old, would scarcely have taken part. The incident has taken a lurid hold on the imaginations of Elizabeth's biographers. As early as 1740 Haynes, in collecting the Burghley Papers, added 'being of black cloth' to the description of the torn dress given in Kat Ashley's account in the State Papers. This apocryphal detail has been quoted ever since. Mumby condemned Seymour for outright debauchery; Miss Strickland, Elizabeth's nineteenth-century biographer, called him 'a bold, bad man'. More recently, Jasper Ridley supposes Seymour tore the dress to shreds 'to get a look at Elizabeth's body and her underclothes', an odd piece of voyeurism with his wife present. Elizabeth Jenkins believed the Admiral's

---

* As Alison Plowden points out, Mrs Ashley evidently considered Grindal quite unembraceable.

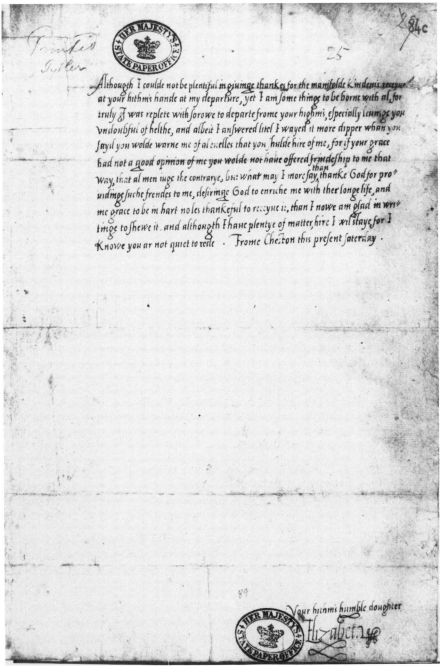

Elizabeth's letter from Sir Anthony Denny's house to Katherine

antics 'culminated in a scene of classical nightmare, that of helplessness in the power of a smiling ogre'. None of this establishes whether Elizabeth responded to Seymour's advances or indeed whether they were made in earnest or in jest. Scolded by Mrs Ashley, he had said 'God's wounds, he meant no harm by it'. What is certain is that tensions prevailed in the household from before Grindal's death in January 1548, and that scandalous stories were circulating by June or July. Either to preserve her charge's good name, or because she really believed the nubile fourteen-year-old had inflamed her husband's lusts, Katherine sent the Princess for a long summer holiday to the house of Sir Anthony Denny at Cheshunt. The Dennys had been part of the intimate royal circle when Katherine was married to Henry. From the letter she wrote immediately after leaving her stepmother, it is clear that Elizabeth had been harangued before she left on the dangers that could arise from rumour or gossip. On her own admission, she remained silent throughout the tirade, but she certainly took it in. When she reached Cheshunt she was still pondering Katherine's advice, and the contrite letter she wrote to the Queen shows she took her strictures in good part.

CB Although I could not be plentiful in giving thanks for the manifold kindness received at your highness's hand at my departure, yet I am something to be born withal for truly I was replete with sorrow to depart from your highness, especially seeing you undoubtful of health, and albeit I answered little I weighed it more deeper when you said you would warn me of all evil that you should hear of me, for if your grace had not a good opinion of me you would not have offered friendship to me that way, that all men judge the contrary, but what may I more say than thank God for providing such friends to me, desiring God to enrich me with their long life, and me grace to be in heart no less thankful to receive it, than I now am glad in writing to show it, and although I have plenty of matter, here I will stay for I know you are not quiet to read.

    From Cheston this present Saturday,
      Your highness's humble daughter,

Elizabeth

Before the end of July Katherine had written several times to Cheshunt to say she was missing Elizabeth. The Admiral had also written, sending the Queen's best wishes when she was too ill to write herself. In Elizabeth's letter of 31 July there is no hint of any rift between herself and her stepmother, nor is there any trace of the embarrassment that would have been natural if she had been caught seriously misbehaving with Seymour. She expected him to write again soon with tidings of Katherine's health. Everyone expected the baby to be a boy since it was kicking vigorously; Mrs Ashley sent greetings, the Dennys were both praying. It was thought first childbirth might be hazardous at Katherine's age, but everyone wished her well. Mary wrote from Beaulieu saying she trusted by Michaelmas 'to hear good success of your Grace's great belly', and also sending her good wishes to the Admiral. Whatever Henry's daughters thought about their stepmother's husband privately, they loved K.P. sincerely and Elizabeth's letter contains no hint of resentment:

CƷ Although your Highness's letters be most joyful to me in absence yet, considering what pain it is to you to write, your Grace being so great with child, and so sickly, your commendation were enough in my lord's letter. I much rejoice at your health, with the well liking of the country, with my humble thanks that your Grace wished me with you till I were weary of that country. Your Highness were like to be cumbered, if I should not depart till I were weary of being with you; although it were the worst soil in the world, your presence would make it pleasant. I cannot reprove my lord for not doing your commendations in his letter, for he did it; and although he had not, yet I will not complain on him, for he shall be diligent to give me knowledge from time to time how his busy child doth and if I were at his birth, no doubt I would see him beaten, for the trouble he hath put you to. Master Denny and my lady, with humble thanks, prayeth most entirely for your Grace, praying the Almighty God to send you a most lucky deliverance and my mistress* wisheth no less, giving your Highness most humble thanks for her commendations. Written with very little leisure, this last day of July.

>   Your humble daughter

>   Elizabeth

My lord, these are shameful slanders

Six weeks after Elizabeth wished Katherine a lucky deliverance, the Queen died. Seymour was with her in her last illness and a story got about that she reproached him on her death-bed for his unkindness. Their baby, a girl, did not survive infancy.† During the last months of Katherine's life the couple lived at Sudeley Castle, which they were refurbishing at great cost. A retinue of 120 ladies and gentlemen attended them, as well as a large number of servants. The King's grandmother, old Lady Seymour, was part of the household and Lady Jane Grey, who looked on the Queen and the Admiral as adopted parents, had come to live there too.‡ Seymour had paid her father, Henry Grey, Marquis of Dorset, £2,000 for her wardship, promising he

---

* Mrs Ashley.

†The baby was christened Mary. After her father's death she was looked after by Katherine Parr's friend Katherine, Duchess of Suffolk, who told Cecil she needed a state pension to maintain the baby. She wished the Marquis of Northampton would help bear the burden.

‡ Jane Grey was eleven years old when Katherine died. She was chief mourner at the Queen's funeral. On 1 October 1548 she wrote to thank Seymour for the kindness he had shown her, calling him her 'second father'.

would marry her to the King. To many it seemed that Katherine and the Admiral were setting up a rival court to the Protector's establishment at Somerset Place. Thomas Seymour has had a bad press over the years, but he spared no effort to maintain his wife in the status to which she was rightfully entitled as Dowager of England. He was a rogue and a braggart, but he appealed to Edward and Elizabeth as a man of action, one with a flair for cutting through red tape and getting things done. In his sheer flamboyance he must have reminded them a little of Henry, and he was certainly more fun than the strait-laced Protector. His chief critics were those with least idea of the costs and headaches involved in running a household which included his own mother, Henry's widow, and (until she went to Cheshunt) Henry's younger daughter and her entourage.

It was expected the Admiral would reduce his household considerably after the Queen's death, but instead of dispersing Katherine's ladies, he kept them together. This instantly fuelled rumours that he meant to renew his suit to marry Elizabeth. No concrete evidence exists as to how he proposed to accomplish this. Katherine's brother William Parr, Marquis of Northampton, said later that Seymour had told him the Lord Protector would clap him in the Tower if he went to the Lady Elizabeth, and there was no woman living that he was about to marry.* The Council, fearing he might try to repeat the ploy by which he had won Katherine, by gaining unauthorised access to Edward, doubled the night watch on the child's door.

Elizabeth was ill after Katherine's death. Somerset sent Dr Bill, the Court physician, to Cheshunt. He also promised to expedite matters relating to her lands and houses. She wrote to thank him politely, sending her greetings to the duchess.† However, nothing was done, so it was natural for Elizabeth and her cofferer, Thomas Parry, to be in touch with the Admiral again during the winter of 1548, in particular over Durham Place. Reluctantly the Somersets had allowed Katherine to keep some of the jewels Henry had given her. The Protector, spurred on by the grasping duchess, now demanded their return, claiming some had merely been lent to the Queen for a State occasion. Seymour asked Princess Mary to arbitrate by declaring which pieces belonged to the Crown. She visited his London house, Seymour Place. According to Elizabeth, he also visited Mary in the country. The Marchioness of Dorset, meanwhile, was asking for her daughter back, but the Admiral wrote to the Greys saying that to Jane he would remain 'half father and more', and that she should stay in the care of his mother at Sudeley Castle, the implication being that, since old Lady Seymour was Edward's grandmother, he would still try to make a match between

---

*Northampton implied, as did Elizabeth herself, that the prospect of a match with the admiral began as a joke, but turned into a rumour. According to the Marquis it was 'some vayne bruite'. Seymour had mentioned to Northampton that he might visit Elizabeth in the country in case he could do her any service.

†The letter to Somerset is the first instance of Elizabeth's full signature with the triple loops, and is signed 'Your assured friend to my power'. During Tyrwhitt's questioning she signed herself more ruefully 'to my litel power'. Dated 'this present Friday' but sent from 'Cheston', Elizabeth's spelling of Cheshunt, the letter would seem to have been written in the autumn of 1548.

Lady Jane and the King.* Harassed by the large number of affairs in his charge, Seymour suggested Elizabeth should discuss Durham Place herself with the Duchess of Somerset, since the lawyers were taking such an unconscionable time finalising things.† Loyal to Katherine's memory, Elizabeth replied bluntly 'In faith I will not come there, nor begin to flatter now.' Two weeks before Christmas the Admiral offered to lend her Seymour Place, fully furnished, so that she could go to Court to see the King. When Parry told her the news she was delighted, but Mrs Ashley, who had already been criticised by the duchess for allowing Elizabeth to go out on the Thames at night in a barge, suggested they should confer with Sir Anthony Denny about the propriety of the offer. He must have vetoed the idea, for there is no record that Elizabeth went to London that Christmas. She wrote to Edward in exquisite Latin from Hatfield on 2 January to apologise for not having sent a proper New Year's gift. The Lord Protector, she explained, had exonerated her because she had been ill. Mary also declined to go to Court for Christmas; the religious reforms being pushed forward by Somerset and Cranmer were anathema to her conscience. The gossips meanwhile had a field day, and the Admiral said they would be linking his name with the eleven-year-old Lady Jane next.

Rumours had now reached Hatfield that the Admiral intended to marry Elizabeth. She laughed merrily when Mrs Ashley reported this, dismissing it as 'London news'.‡ During her stay at the Dennys, however, she had matured enough to heed Katherine's last warning about refraining from behaviour that could cause gossip, and a letter was despatched to Seymour telling him to stay away.

The enmity between the two brothers continued through the last months of 1548. The Admiral swore rash oaths against the Protector and fell into black rages. According to Fowler, he was in the habit of drinking alone, and possibly this made him more than usually loose-tongued after Katherine's death. On 17 January they arrested him on a charge of high treason. He was accused of trying to abduct the King. One of the child's pet spaniels barked, raising the alarm. They lodged the Admiral in the Tower while thirty-three separate charges were drawn up against him.

He answered to three. The Council summoned an impressive body of witnesses. They accused Seymour of conspiring against the Protector's authority, scheming to marry Elizabeth, and marrying Katherine in such haste that any child she bore could have been the issue of the late King. He had also given pocket-money to Edward in a way that could be construed as a bribe to win the child's favour, although the

---

* 'My ladye, my Mother shall and will, I doubte not be as deare unto hir as though she weare hir owne Daughter and for my owne parte I shall contynewe her haulf Father and more.'

†Elizabeth was supposed to receive £3,000 a year under the terms of Henry's will. The Council scrutinised her spending down to the last pennyworth of silk on her embroiderer's bill, but matters relating to the lands and houses she inherited were not finally settled until 1550.

‡It was still a capital offence for the King's sister even to consider marriage without the full consent of the Council.

money had been given with the full knowledge of the Queen, who had deplored the way the Somersets treated her stepson.

Edward was questioned, and his evidence spoke volumes of the disparate standards which prevailed in his uncles' households. When Henry fought the French at Boulogne, Katherine had been Regent and seen to it that Edward lacked nothing. After his father's death he seldom saw her, and was subjected to a much harsher regime. The studies he could bear, but other things were irksome to the boy to whom Henry had entrusted the reception of an ambassador when he was eight years old. He was now eleven, and a king, and they treated him like an ordinary schoolboy. Man to man, he confided in the Marquis of Dorset: his uncle Somerset, he said, dealt very hardly with him in money matters, but his uncle the Lord Admiral was open-handed. Edward was striving valiantly to fulfil the kingly office in the way his father would have wished, and when Seymour teased him about his shyness and his inability to distribute largesse in the Henrician manner, the shaft went home. 'Ye ar but a very beggarly King,' the Admiral taunted, 'ye have not to play [with] or to give to your servants.'

His Tudor pride stung, the little boy plucked up courage to invent a secret post. He tore strips from his school exercises and hid notes under the carpet for Fowler to deliver to the Admiral and to the Queen's receiver. The sums varied: eleven shillings for the Lord Privy Seal's trumpeter as thanks for blowing a fanfare, similar amounts for musicians, tumblers and a bookbinder, five pounds for Jean Belmain, his French tutor, and one large gift for Sir John Cheke at New Year. At first the boy did not know how much to ask for. He consulted Seymour about the correct gratuity for Bishop Latimer, who was to preach to him at Westminster. His uncle sent £40 with word that £20 would do for the bishop. Clearly the Defender of the Faith and Supreme Head of the Church thought the Admiral a keener judge of worldly etiquette than Protector Somerset.

When it was seen how far Edward had been involved, the Council decided Elizabeth must also have consented to Seymour's plans. They sent Sir Thomas Tyrwhitt to Hatfield to question her. Thomas Parry and Mrs Ashley were taken to the Tower. A few days later Mrs Ashley was sent to the Fleet. Elizabeth cried at their arrest. 'But', wrote Tyrwhitt, 'she will not confess any practice by Mrs Ashley or the cofferer.' He tried to trick Elizabeth into an admission of guilt by relentless questioning. By 23 January 1549 he was near to defeat. 'She hath a very good wit and nothing is got out of her but by great policy,' he reported. Five days later, tiring of his methods, she wrote to the Protector herself:

CB My Lord,

   Your great gentleness and goodwill towards me, as well in this thing as in other things, I do understand, for the which even as I ought, so I do give you most humble thanks. And whereas your Lordship willeth and counselleth me, as an earnest friend, to declare what I know in this matter, and also to write what I have declared to Master Tyrwhitt, I shall most willingly do it. I declared unto him first, that, after that the Cofferer had declared unto me what my Lord Admiral answered for Allen's matter, and for Durham House, (that it was appointed to be a Mint) he told me that my Lord Admiral did offer me his house for my time being with the King's Majesty; and further said and asked me whether if the Council did consent, that I should have my Lord Admiral, whether I would consent to it or no: I answered that I would not tell him what my mind was. And I further inquired of him, what he meant to ask me that question or who bade him say so. He answered me and said, nobody bade him say so but that he perceived (as he thought) by my Lord Admiral's inquiring whether my patent were sealed or no, and debating what he spent in his house, and inquiring what was spent in my house, that he was given that way than otherwise. And as concerning Kat Ashley she never advised me to it, but said always when any talked of my marriage that she would never have me marry, neither in England nor out of England without the consent of the king's majesty, your grace's and the council's. And after the Queen was departed,* when I asked of her what news she heard from London? she answered merrily, 'They say your Grace shall have my lord Admiral and that he will shortly come to woo you. And moreover, I said unto him that the cofferer sent a letter hither, that my lord said that he would come this way as he went down into the country'.

Then I bade her write as she thought best, and bade her show it me when she had done; so she wrote that she thought it not best for fear of suspicion and so it went forth. And my lord admiral after he had heard that, asked of the cofferer why he might not come as well to me as to my sister: and then I desired Kat Ashley to write again (lest my lord might think that she knew more in it than he) that she knew nothing in it, but suspicion. And also I told Master Tyrwhitt, that to the effect of the matter, I never consented unto any such thing without the Council's consent thereto. And as for Kat Ashley and the cofferer they never told me that they would practise it.

These be the things which I both declared to Master Tyrwhitt and also whereof my conscience beareth me witness, which I would not for all earthly things offend in anything; for I know I have a soul to save, as well as other folks have, wherefor I will above all things have respect unto the same. If there be any more things which I can remember, I will either write it myself or cause Master Tyrwhitt to write it.

Master Tyrwhitt and others have told me that there goeth rumours abroad, which be greatly both against my honour and honesty (which above all other things I esteem) which be these; that I am in the Tower; and with child by my

* After Katherine's death.

lord admiral. My lord, these are shameful slanders for the which besides the great desire I have to see the King's Majesty, I shall most heartily desire your lordship that I may come to the court after your first determination that I may show myself there as I am.

Written in haste from Hatfield this 28th January

Your assured friend to my little power,

Elizabeth

Mine honour and mine honesty

Honour and honesty were the qualities Elizabeth had been brought up to value from earliest childhood. Now both were called in question. To Elizabeth it was grossly unfair: she had behaved correctly, even consulting Sir Anthony Denny, one of her father's closest friends and advisers. Now it was rumoured she was pregnant by a man she had not even received in her house. The slanders were a cause for just indignation, but a week after Elizabeth penned her reproach to Somerset, Katherine Ashley was examined in London and the bottom-slapping came inelegantly to light. They must have threatened the poor woman with torture, as she signed a confession describing early morning romps at Hanworth and Chelsea when the Queen had been alive. A copy was sent to Hatfield, where Tyrwhitt showed it to Elizabeth, reporting she was 'much abashed and half breathless' when she read it. Somerset meanwhile had written to her personally asking her to be more co-operative with Tyrwhitt. On 6 February she wrote again to the Protector, pointing out, with some hauteur, that she had already told the truth, and complaining of Tyrwhitt's methods of cross-examination.

'Whereas your Grace doth will me to credit Master Tyrwhitt, I have done so,' she objected, 'and will do so as long as he willeth me (*as he doth not*) to nothing but to that which is for mine honour and mine honesty.' The truth is that Tyrwhitt was no match for the nimble young mind that had already parsed Cicero's best legal speeches and was swift to understand where his questions were leading. Her '*as he doth not*' (my italics) drew a rebuke from Somerset, who accused her of being too self-assured. On 7 February Sir Thomas repeated he was sure she was guilty, but that she would 'in no way confess that either Mistress Ashley or Parry willed her to any practice with the Lord Admiral, either by message or writing. They all sing one song,' he grumbled. In his opinion it was collusion: they had 'set the note before'.

On 21 February Elizabeth courteously apologised for her forthright comment which had upset the Lord Protector, but again her indignation and her impatience with fools surfaced, as she pointed out that he had asked her to tell the truth. She had done so, and they had doubted her word. When Lady Tyrwhitt was appointed as her governess in place of Katherine Ashley, the Princess wept all night and lowered all day. She told Tyrwhitt she had not so demeaned herself 'that the Court need put any more mistresses upon her'. Tyrwhitt then taunted her again with the stories said to be circulating, and with tremendous dignity she asked the Council to put out a proclamation forbidding people to defame the King's sisters. To 'my very good Lord, my Lord Protector', she wrote:

ℭℬ I do understand that you do take in evil part the letters that I did write unto your Lordship. I am very sorry that you should take them so for my mind was to declare unto you plainly, because (as I write to you) you desired me to be plain with you in all things. And as concerning that point that you write, that I seem to stand in mine own wit in being so well assured of my own self, I did assure me of my self no more than I trust the truth shall try. And to say that which I knew of myself I did not think should have displeased the Council or your grace.

Elizabeth explained that her objection to Lady Tyrwhitt 'was because I thought the people will say that I deserved through my lewd demeanour to have such a one, and not that I mislike anything that your Lordship or the council shall think good. For I know that you and the council are charged with me. And seeing they make so evil reports already', she pointed out there would now be 'an increasing of their evil tongues.'

Somerset had told her that the Council would punish anyone who slandered her, but she showed an early understanding of how public opinion worked. If she reported the rumour-mongers, she foresaw

ℭℬ that should be but a breeding of an evil name of me, that I am glad to punish them, and so get the evil will of the people, which thing I would be loth to have. But if it might seem good unto your Lordship and the rest of the council to send forth a proclamation into the counties that they restrain their tongues declaring how the tales are but lies, it should make both the people think that you and the council have great regard that no such rumours should be spread of any of the King's Majesty's Sisters, as I am though unworthy, and also I should think myself to receive such friendship at your hands as you have promised me, although your Lordship hath shown me great already. Howbeit I am ashamed to ask it any more, because I see you are not so well minded thereunto. And as concerning that you say that I give folks occasion to think in refusing the good to uphold the evil, I am not of so simple understanding, nor would I have that your Grace should have so evil an opinion of me that I have so little respect to mine own honesty that I would maintain it if I had sufficient promise of the same; and so your grace shall prove me when it comes to the point. And thus I bid you farewell, desiring God always to assist you in all your affairs.

> Written in haste from Hatfield this 21 of February
> Your assured friend to my little power

Elizabeth

In the last week of February the case against the Admiral drew to a close. Only two men spoke well of him – his brother-in-law, William Parr, and Jane Grey's father, Dorset, who, despite his damning testimony concerning the King's pocket-money, staunchly added that he had heard the Admiral say that 'whosoever should go about to speak evil of the Queen, he would take his fist to their ears'.

Seymour was attainted on 27 February, Somerset being absent from the Chamber when the bill was read in the Lords. On 4 March the Master of the Rolls declared it was the King's pleasure that the Admiral should not appear before the Commons, and there was a delay of a further ten days before the King, with Somerset beside him, gave assent for his uncle's death. Elizabeth remained at Hatfield under the supervision of Lady Tyrwhitt. On 7 March she summoned up courage to write to Somerset again, having heard that the Council had followed up her suggestion of sending out a proclamation. Curiously, there is no record of this proclamation ever being made, but plainly Elizabeth was told of it and counted herself cleared. She asked to have Mrs Ashley restored. In a letter that is an endearing mixture of youthful pleading and homespun philosophy, she again marshalled her arguments in clear Ciceronian order.

ᘓ My Lord,

> I have a request to make unto your grace, which fear has made me omit till this time for two causes, the one because I saw that my request for the rumours which were spread abroad of me take so little place, which thing, when I considered, I thought I should little profit in any other suit. Howbeit now I understand that there is a proclamation for them (for the which I gave your grace and the rest of the council most humble thanks) I am the bolder to speak for another thing. And the other was because peradventure your Lordship and the rest of the Council will think that I favour her evil doings for whom I shall speak for, which is for Katherine Ashley, that it would please your grace and the rest of the council to be good unto her, which thing I do not favour her in any evil (for that I would be sorry to do) but for the considerations which follow, the which hope doth teach me in saying that I ought not to doubt, but that your grace and the rest of the council will think that I do it for three other considerations. First because that she hath been with me a long time, and many years and hath taken great labour and pain in bringing of me up in learning and honesty; and therefore I ought of very duty [to] speak for her. For Saint Gregory sayeth that we are more bound to them that bringeth us up well, than

to our parents, for our parents do that which is natural for them, that is bringeth us into this world, but our bringers up are a cause to make us live well in it. The second is because I think that whatsoever she hath done in my Lord Admiral's matter as concerning the marriage of me, she did it because, knowing him to be one of the council, she thought he would not go about any such thing without he had the council's consent. The third cause is because that it shall, and doth, make men think that I am not clear of the deed myself, but that it is pardoned in me because of my youth, because that she I loved well is in such a place, and I have at this time gone forth with it. Which I pray God be taken no other ways than it is meant.

Written in haste from Hatfield this 7th day of March.

Also I may be so bold not offending, I beseech your grace and the rest of the council to be good to master Ashley, her husband, which because he is my kinsman I would be glad he should do well.

Your assured friend to my little power,

Elizabeth

They executed Seymour on 20 March. He spent his last night in the Tower scratching letters to Mary and Elizabeth with the metal end of the lace by which he attached his hose to his doublet, since he was denied pen and ink. Tradition has it that he hid the notes in the heel of a velvet shoe for his valet to deliver. They were intercepted, however, and shown to Bishop Latimer.

There is no contemporary evidence describing Elizabeth's reaction to Seymour's execution. Five years later, when hysterical with fear and believing herself under sentence of death, she blurted out that Somerset had told her he had been persuaded that the admiral intended to murder him 'and *that* made him give his consent to the death' (my italics). If she had made the famous remark ascribed to her by many biographers, 'This day died a man of much wit and very little judgement', it would have been a wonderful epitaph and an even more wonderful testament to her sang-froid, but the source is the scurrilous seventeenth-century biographer, Grigorio Leti, a man of much invention. Romantic historians have linked Elizabeth's letter thanking Somerset for sending Dr Bill to her with the Admiral's death, and have made out a plausible case that she suffered from extreme nervous reaction, but the letter was sent from Cheshunt, which suggests a date in the late summer of 1548, *before* Seymour was arrested.

Edward showed no emotion over his uncle's death. As a precaution, however, Latimer preached a series of sermons at Court, cataloguing the Admiral's iniquities. In the Queen's time he had failed to attend daily service; he had criticised Edward's strict educational routine. 'He was, I heard say, a covetous man,' thundered the bishop, 'a horrible covetous man: I would there were no moe in Englande. He was I heard say a seditious man, a contemner of common prayer. I would there were no moe in Englande. Well he is gone. I would he had left none behind.'

Edward Seymour, 1st Duke of Somerset and Lord Protector

Sweet Sister Temperance*

Elizabeth wrote often to Edward, clear schoolgirlish letters, sometimes in English, but more usually in the elegant humanist Latin which had become a natural idiom for both of them. By her sixteenth birthday she had read all of Cicero and most of Livy. Ascham wrote to his friend John Sturmius, Rector of the Protestant university at Strasbourg, that she showed 'such dignity and gentleness as are wonderful at her age. Her mind has no womanly weakness. Her perseverance is equal to that of a man and her memory long keeps what it quickly picks up. She talks French and Italian as well as she does English, and has often talked to me readily and well in Latin, moderately in Greek. When she writes Greek and Latin nothing is more beautiful than her handwriting.' Her letters to Edward have been called sententious and dutiful, couched as they are in the respectful superlatives she considered fitting to his status, but her warm affection lights up the formal phrases.

We learn little from the letters of Elizabeth's daily life during Edward's reign, and nothing of the events that followed Seymour's death. Throughout 1549 the Protector continued to enlarge the fine buildings at Somerset Place. Either by design or by accident his engineers demolished a charnel house. Eye-witnesses watched human bones being tipped into the Thames, and this ghoulish and unhallowed procedure, combined with the signing of his own brother's death warrant, damaged his public image severely. The enclosure of sheep-land was unpopular, the debasement of the coinage had caused unrest and the religious reforms were proceeding too swiftly. Cranmer had first declared against transubstantiation in December 1548. The Book of Common Prayer was placed in many churches the following spring. A series of minor disturbances which followed this innovation were easily put down, but when Kett's rebellion broke out at Norwich, and Lord Russell was sent to quell the West Country, Somerset retreated with the King to Hampton Court, later removing him to Windsor. Edward's own recollections of this time stand out stark and vivid in his journal: 'Peple came abundantly to the house that night with al the peple at 9 or 10 a cloke at night I went to Windsore and there was watch and ward kept every night. The lordes sat in open places of London calling for gentlemen before them and declaring the causes of accusation of the Lord Protectour.'†

While an armed guard surrounded their brother, the two Princesses remained on their estates. The *coup d'état* by the London Lords leading to Somerset's fall and the re-grouping of the Council under John Dudley, Earl of Warwick and later Duke of

---

* Edward's own name for Elizabeth.

† The King went on to describe events occurring in London, where the Lords had set up levies in open spaces calling upon gentlemen to listen to the accusations against Somerset. Edward says they sent him a 'very gentle' letter to declare the Protector's faults, 'ambicion, vain glorie, entering into rashe warre in mine youth, enriching himself of my treasure, folowing his own opinion and doing al by his owne auctoritie.'

Northumberland, took place without the direct involvement of the King's sisters. On 9 October they were informed by letters that Warwick was taking over the Tower and that Edward was to be rescued from Somerset's 'cruel and greedy hands'. When Dudley appeased the Catholic party to consolidate his own position, Mary was not fooled: 'The Earl of Warwick is the most unstable man in England,' she said, and again declined to come to Court for the Christmas ceremonies.

Elizabeth knew no such caution. She adored visits to London and preserved a cordial relationship with Warwick and other members of the Council. She also remained in close contact with William Cecil, Somerset's able young secretary, who was to prove so indispensable to the new regime that he soon became Secretary of State. On 19 December 1549, Van der Delft reported to the Emperor; 'The Lady Elizabeth, sister to the King, arrived at Court the other day. She was received with great pomp and triumph and is continually with the King. It seems they have a higher opinion of her for conforming with the others and observing the new decrees than of the Lady Mary, who remains constant to the Catholic faith.' The King had been shaken by the events of the autumn, and Warwick made sure the Christmas ceremonies were cheerful and diverting for the delicate boy, now twelve years old and rapidly advancing into puberty; but amidst the merrymaking the establishment of the reformed religion moved inexorably forward. By Christmas Day Warwick had issued a statement to the bishops; the Book of Common Prayer was to be used throughout England. No one should think that since the apprehension of the Duke of Somerset 'they should have their old Latin services, their conjured bread and water'.

The new policy brought about a head-on collision with the Princess Mary. She continued to allow Mass to be celebrated in her own household, appealing to her cousin, the Emperor, who threatened England with war. Left to themselves the Council might have turned a blind eye to the heiress to the throne's private preferences, but Edward was developing an increasing sense of his responsibilities as a Christian king. An impassioned scene spoiled the dignity of Christmas at Court in 1550, when he publicly upbraided Mary for her adherence to the old ways. She burst into tears; she was his godmother, she loved him and she saw him as the pawn of an unprincipled group of men – instruments of the Devil. Seeing her so distraught, the King cried too. He let the matter rest until the end of January 1551, and then he sent her a series of stern letters urging her to accept the Protestant religion. 'If you intend to govern your faith', he wrote, 'according to the practices of what you refer to as Christendom and not according to the Anglican Church of which you are a member, you err.' He urged her to gentle conformity, ending, 'I will see my laws strictly obeyed and those who break them shall be watched and denounced.'

Elizabeth almost certainly sought to mediate between the feuding pair. Her letters to Mary at this time were light and sisterly, usually concerning neutral, domestic topics such as the exchange of a lady-in-waiting. Reports of her character suggest a blend of sweetness and strength. In addition to Ascham's praise of her dignity and gentleness, John Hooper had written to Bullinger in 1550 to commend her as a blue-stocking. Elizabeth, he said, was 'inflamed with zeal for the religion of Christ. She not only knows what true religion is, but has acquired such proficiency in Greek and Latin that she is able to defend it by the most just arguments.'

Her deep and wholly unfeigned affection for her brother, whose difficulties she understood far better than Mary could, brought certain rewards. Jehan Scheyfve, the new Imperial ambassador, who replaced Van der Delft, described her arrival at Court that memorable Christmas after Edward and Mary had fallen out:

'A few days ago the Lady Elizabeth, sister to the King, came to London with a great suite of gentlemen and ladies, escorted by one hundred of the King's horse. She was most honourably received by the Council, who acted thus', Scheyfve reasoned, 'to show the people how much glory belongs to her who has embraced the new religion and is become a very great lady.'

The rest of his letter describes the *entente* forming between Warwick and the French ambassador, who dined with Edward and Elizabeth on the Feast of the Epiphany. The King and his sister celebrated this Christian festival in high style by watching a bear-baiting after dinner, 'while the ambassador', Scheyfve noted, 'went to see Lord Warwick and they too saw the bear-baiting and talked unceasingly all the time. This Warwick is now the man who governs absolutely.' He makes no mention of how Mary spent Christmas, but of one thing Scheyfve was certain, Elizabeth knew how to twist Edward round her little finger. It was an action-packed season. Bishop Gardiner had preached about the Mass when Cranmer and the Council specifically forbade him to do so; he was to be deprived of his bishopric. The Lady Elizabeth was 'in love with a certain manor which', said Scheyfve darkly, 'she is said to be sure of acquiring.' His view of Elizabeth as an acquisitive minx was not unfounded. By March 1550, she finally obtained Durham Place, but she never lived there. It had taken the Council four years to sort out her jointure. For Warwick she was now a valuable asset to be used in foreign marriage alliances. It was in his own interest to see she was able to keep up appearances appropriate to the King's sister. Elizabeth was swift to take advantage.

Hatfield had been leased to the earl in 1549. She now exchanged some lands in Lincolnshire with him, becoming, at sixteen and a half, sole mistress of the red-brick palace she had loved since childhood, with its gentle gardens and vast park stocked with fine deer. Security of tenure, or in her words her 'patent sealed', seems to have given Elizabeth a new feeling of self-assurance, to say nothing of a taste for real estate. After Somerset's attainder, she made an even more astute deal, as we shall see, for use of Somerset Place whenever she came to London. She had indeed become a very great lady.

Mary had replied to Edward's stern letter saying her faith and her religion were 'those held by the whole of Christendom, formerly confessed by this kingdom under the late King, my father'. By March 1551 the Council tried actively to prevent her from allowing her whole household to attend Mass. Reprisals from the Emperor were a real possibility, and to strengthen the French alliance Warwick began negotiations to marry Elizabeth to the brother of the Duke of Guise. She was offered simultaneously to the King of Denmark's eldest son, and the Council also considered the son of the Duke of Florence (who was eleven years old); the second son of the Duke of Saxony; the son of the Duke of Ferrara; and Francesco d'Este, the Duke of Ferrara's brother. The Guise alliance was the most ambitious. Edward was to marry Princess Elisabeth of France and the pretty exchange of the two Elizabeths would cement the two countries against the Emperor.

None of the plans came to fruition and, pardonably, Elizabeth of England at eighteen was a little cynical on the issue of marriage. Jean Belmain gave her his translation from Greek into French of 'An Epistle of Basil the Great to St Gregory the Theologian on the Virtues of the Single Life' and, in his dedication, he teasingly outlined the difficulties of finding anything worth translating which she had not already read. In a short, powerfully worded treatise on the eremetical life, St Basil explained that marriage drew the heart away from true worship of God, focusing it on worldly cares and affairs. He also counselled temperance in all things, including diet and dress. He was preaching to the converted; Elizabeth, in this high Protestant phase, affected great simplicity of dress. She was the leader of a fashion much admired by the coterie of young Cambridge scholars who frequented Edward's Court. John Aylmer, Lady Jane Grey's tutor, describes the sensation Elizabeth caused when Mary of Guise, the Dowager of Scotland, was driven by storms to land at Portsmouth in October 1551.

Edward was fascinated by that great lady. He had been briefly betrothed to her daughter, Mary Queen of Scots, by the Treaty of Greenwich in 1543. It was also the first and only time he entertained another sovereign. His journal bursts into an excited résumé of the preparations at Hampton Court. No expense was spared: Katherine Parr's old apartments were opened up, and Northampton rode to welcome the Scottish Queen with an escort of 120 gentlemen. The King's sisters were summoned from their estates with scant time for packing finery. All the English ladies adopted new hair styles, 'frownsed and curled and double curled,' John Aylmer said, but amidst this frenzy of crimping Elizabeth 'kepte hir olde maydenly shame-fastnesse'. She must have astounded the French ladies, as she abstained completely from make-up, causing the other noblemen's wives and daughters to look 'drest and paynted like pecockes' by contrast. She also had at this time an aversion to jewellery, and Aylmer says that for seven years she never looked at the jewels her father left her and 'there came never gold nor stone upon her head tyl her sister enforced her to lay of her former sobrenes and bear her company in her glistering gaynes'.

In the meantime Elizabeth kept up her habit of giving special New Year gifts to her family. In the winter of 1548, when sickness prevented her from preparing anything, she had written to Edward from Hatfield saying she had toyed with the idea of sending something made of gold or precious stones, but had thought this would be too trifling. Her most touching New Year's present to Edward was a translation of Bernardino Ochino's *Sermon on the Nature of Christ*. Cranmer had invited Ochino to England in 1547. He was a saintly and venerable Italian monk, a former Franciscan who made friends with Peter Martyr in Naples, and who fled to Geneva after being accused of heresy by Pope Paul III. His preaching was legendary. He believed in Predestination and renounced utterly the doctrine of the Invocation of Saints. His *Prayers and Sermons* had been printed at Geneva and Basel. Anne Cooke, the learned daughter of Sir Anthony Cooke (and later mother of Sir Francis Bacon), translated five of the sermons into English in 1548. Later she translated *Fourteen Sermons of Barnardine Ochyne concernyng the predestination and election of God.** Elizabeth was not concerned with such themes. Distressed by the dissension in her own family, and deeply sensitive to Edward's insecurities, she simply searched the storehouse of her spiritual treasures and chose him the most moving and reassuring piece she knew, Sermon XII of Ochino's *Prediche*, the fire and fervency of which had been one of the chief causes of his exile. Her letter of dedication is short and to the point:

CB To the most august and most serene King Edward VI

If I should have anything at this time (Most Serene King) which it would be fitting for me to give and appropriate for your Majesty to accept, I should indeed heartily rejoice. Your Majesty deserves great and excellent things, and my mean ability can provide only so much, yet though I have little talent, and my works may be surpassed by other people's, no one can match the extent of my love and good feeling towards you. So nature decrees, your authority urges and integrity compels me to regard you with respect, since you are my sovereign, and to treat you with deepest affection, since you are my only and most dearly beloved brother.

Look upon this as a sign of greetings for a happy New Year. I respectfully offer this short oration of Bernardino Ochino to your Majesty, first written by him in Italian and translated by me into a Latin sermon. Since the subject is the nature of Christ, a matter well becoming to you who speak daily of our Lord, and who is closest of all to him in the position and dignity you have upon earth, the discussion is so pious and learned that reading it cannot fail to be useful and fruitful. And if nothing else should recommend the work, the reputation of the writer is distinguished enough, one who because of his Christian belief was driven out from his homeland and forced to lead his life among strangers in a foreign land. If anything in this work is below standard, it is my translation, which indeed is not as it should be, but simply the best of which I am capable. But let your Majesty be the judge of all those matters,

* Anne Cooke's preface to her translation of the sermons calls Ochino 'a man of great years and wonderful reputation, a man of profound learning. The most notable preacher of al Italie. Famous for the great example of hys hood lyfe. Esteemed and honoured of al Princes . . . a man of LXX yeares or thereabouts.'

through reading this my work which I commend to you, and to whom I dedicate it.

I pray God that your Majesty may see many new and happy years and grow constantly in letters and piety.

From Enfield 30th December

Your Majesty's most humble sister and servant,

Elizabeth

What followed was a sermon of great simplicity and directness, something very different from the intellectual themes which fascinated Anne Cooke. To understand Elizabeth's choice is to get to the core of that faith which sustained her throughout her life, frequently surprising her more sophisticated contemporaries by its sincerity and its strength.

'*Se una pecorella non cognosse el suo pastore,*' Ochino appealed, '*un soldato el suo capitano, un servo el suo padrone.*' If a lamb did not recognise its shepherd, a soldier his captain, a servant his master, that was a distressing state of affairs. But ignorance of Christ, the good shepherd, the best captain, the kindest lord, the true friend, the gentle spouse, the loving brother and the dear father, was a darker and more damaging kind of ignorance. The sermon is a burning exhortation to love Christ and to live by faith. Jesus came not to give laws but to bring grace. Moses was the faithful servant of God, Christ his son. Moses wrote on tablets, Jesus in the heart. 'And I say with Paul', wrote the venerable reformer, 'that Christ is the only mediator between us and the Father and that we have no need of the invocation of saints. All that the saints had was in Christ. He came to bring salvation. Christ himself preached for three years, but the spirit of Christ has lasted fifteen hundred years. He came not just to purge Sodom and Gomorrah with real fire, but to fill the whole world with divine fire.'

In choosing this direct appeal to Christ's universal humanity Elizabeth unconsciously stated what was to be her own position amidst the doctrinal issues that were to trouble the Church of England for the next half century.

CHAPTER III

Like as a shipman in stormy weather

Warwick became Duke of Northumberland on 11 October 1551. Although he never took the title of Lord Protector, he effectively ruled England for the rest of Edward's reign. Somerset was brought to trial on a trumped-up charge and sent to the Tower on 16 October. He was acquitted of treason, but sentenced to be hanged for felony on 1 December. Tried by his peers, he still had a popular following in London, and at one point a rumour got about that he had been cleared, which led to noisy demonstrations from the citizens. Northumberland used the dazzling Christmas festivities at Court to divert Edward's attention from the grisly judicial proceedings against his uncle, which it would soon be his duty to ratify. A Lord of Misrule was appointed and the Office of Revels worked overtime, devising fantastic costumes for masques and interludes. A masque of apes was followed by a pageant of the Greek worthies. Actors were dressed in painted tabards to resemble men on one side and skeletons on the other; there were tumblers and a masque of cats. A mock tournament upon hobby-horses was staged to send up the courtly jousts organised for the young lords with whom Edward shared his education.* The duke was wholly successful: the King's journal bursts into an exuberant description of a madcap battle in which his courtiers dressed up as German soldiers and Catholic friars, and of the feasting at Greenwich, which lasted until Twelfth Night, when normal State business was resumed. On 22 January Edward noted curtly: 'The Duke of Somerset had his hed cut off on Tower Hill between 8 and 9 a cloke in the morning.'

Elizabeth remained in high favour. In March she came to St James's with an escort of two hundred gentlemen on horseback, second in line to the throne, but very much the 'first lady' at Court in place of the perennially absent Mary. As she rode through London, her eye may well have lighted on the superb Italianate façade of the now vacant Somerset Place, which a year later Northumberland was to allow her to use in exchange for Durham Place.† Scheyfve noted that she was 'very honourably received'. 'The Earl of Pembroke is trying to obtain her in marriage, but she refuses her consent,' he told the Emperor. 'It is believed that the Duke of Northumberland

---

* George Ferrers, who played the Lord of Misrule, was rewarded with £50 for his twelve-day performance. On 4 January he visited London itself, delighting the citizens and diverting them from the imprisonment and imminent execution of Somerset. This supports the view that Northumberland deliberately used the Christmas festivities for political ends.

† Most of her estate had been granted to her by the summer of 1550 including Durham Place; she never fully used Somerset Place until 1555, although it was made ready for her in 1553.

has something to do with her attitude. He will not suffer the earl to make such a marriage unless for some very good reason.'

Whatever her personal views at this time, as a matrimonial prize she was still a valuable asset in Northumberland's foreign policy – too valuable to waste on William Herbert.

On 2 April 1552 there is a brief entry in Edward's journal: 'I fell sick of the measles and smallpox.' He revived during the summer, increasing his knowledge of foreign and financial affairs, and going on a happy progress through the south of England, which he described in letters to his friend Barnaby Fitzpatrick. When they reached Wilton, Pembroke, perhaps still with his aspirations fixed on the King's younger sister, gave a magnificent entertainment, and as a parting gift presented Edward with the whole of the gold plate off which the Court had dined. In September the group of schoolfellows with which Edward had been brought up since he was seven was disbanded, a preliminary to the last phase of his minority, but during the harsh winter of 1552/3 he caught cold. The journal ceases abruptly in November. The cold brought on the severe tuberculosis of which he was eventually to die. Elizabeth, deeply concerned about her brother's health, set out from Hatfield to see him. She turned back after receiving a message from Edward himself. He had evidently written to say that he was at Greenwich, where he described his lodging at some distance from the rooms of 'my Lord Marquis'. After the demise of the unreliable Seymour uncles, Katherine's brother, William Parr, seems to have been the member of the Council whom both Edward and Elizabeth felt they could most trust. He was a link with the intimate family circle they had known when the Queen and their father were alive. Elizabeth wrote immediately to say how disappointed she had been to turn back. As the letter is undated, her journey could have been made in the early spring when everyone hoped Edward would recover, or, more poignantly, some time later in the year when, wasted with disease, the boy was coughing up livid, black sputum which observers said 'smelled beyond measure'.

CȜ Like as a shipman in stormy weather plucks down the sails tarrying for better wind, so did I, most noble King, in my unfortunate chance a Thursday pluck down the high sails of my joy and comfort and do trust one day that as troublesome waves have repulsed me backward so a gentle wind will bring me forward to my haven. Two chief occasions moved me much and grieved me greatly, the one for that I doubted your Majesty's health, the other because for all my long tarrying I went without that I came for. Of the first I am relieved in a part, both that I understood of your health, and also that your Majesty's lodging is [not] far from my Lord Marquess's chamber. Of my other grief I am not eased, but the best is that whatsoever other folks will suspect, I intend not to fear your Grace's goodwill, which as I know that I never deserved to faint, so I trust will stick by me. For if your Grace's advice that I should return (whose will is a commandment) had not been, I would not have made the half of my way the end of my journey. And thus, as one desirous to hear of your Majesty's health though unfortunate to see it, I shall pray God for ever to preserve you. From Hatfield, this present Saturday.

Your Majesty's humble sister to commandment,

Elizabeth

They openly preached and set forth that my sister and I were bastards

By April 1553 the King had guessed he was dying. His fanatical wish to prevent Mary's accession led him to draw up an elaborate document, 'My Devise for the Succession'. It superseded another paper, drafted perhaps as early as January 1553. Many historians have thought Northumberland's dynastic plans, which included the betrothal in May of his fourth son, Lord Guildford Dudley, to Lady Jane Grey, granddaughter of Henry VIII's sister Mary Tudor, were part of a deliberate strategy to exclude Mary and Elizabeth from the succession, but recent research has shown that Northumberland was 'entrapped in a great conspiracy, not of his own contriving'. The prime mover was the King.

Scheyfve was out of his depth amidst the complexities of the English succession. He suspected that Northumberland, aided by the French, was planning to defeat Mary by force of arms in order to make Elizabeth Queen. On 5 May he heard a rumour that 'the Lady Elizabeth, sister of the King, is to come to town shortly; and that the Earl of Warwick, the Duke of Northumberland's eldest son, wishes to put away his wife, daughter of the late Duke of Somerset, and marry the said Elizabeth'. His suspicions increased when the Queen of France gave birth to a daughter and Elizabeth was asked to stand godmother. By June he thought Northumberland might try to poison Mary. On the 15th he reported to the Emperor that Edward could keep nothing in his stomach: for four days he had been vomiting constantly. 'The King has been attacked by a violent fever which lasted over twenty-four hours,' wrote the ambassador, 'he lives entirely on restoratives and obtains hardly any repose.' By 4 July Scheyfve heard that Edward had made a will, excluding his sisters from the succession on the grounds that they were both illegitimate because of their mothers' divorces. The will was written 'with the King's own hand'.

The Emperor was incredulous: after two decades of involvement in Mary's affairs he was willing to believe in any move the English government might make to her detriment, but he could not comprehend the logic of their proceedings against Elizabeth. He wrote loftily from Brussels:

'You, Ambassador Scheyfve, wrote that the King had declared our cousin the Princess a bastard in his will. It also seems you wish to convey that he did the same for the Lady Elizabeth, but the passage is short and rather obscure and we desire you to clear up this point in your next letters. We wish to know if the Lady Elizabeth has also been declared a bastard, and if not, what pretext has been adopted to bar her from the succession.'

Scheyfve thought that the Council had endorsed Edward's will 'rather out of fear than for any other reason'. The dying King had summoned them on 21 June to ratify the preposterous document, bequeathing the Crown to Lady Jane and her heirs male. At first the Lord Chief Justice, Lord Montague, had refused to comply, declaring such a proceeding illegal, but Edward commanded him on his allegiance. Cranmer also queried the procedure, but in the end the pale boy coughing his life out against the pillows, and passionately striving to preserve the faith in which they had instructed him, won the day. Historians have been as puzzled as the Emperor by the dubious arguments used to bar Elizabeth from the throne. She was the obvious Protestant candidate, and Edward's claim that she was only 'of the half blood' was extraordinarily weak, since she was Henry's daughter, second in line under Henry's will, the terms of which had been enshrined in statute.

William Cecil, by now Secretary of State, had hurried back to Court specifically to endorse Edward's will. Many years later he told Camden that Elizabeth had been excluded because of her own refusal to comply with Edward's ideas. Cecil held that when the proposals in the original draft of the 'Devise' were communicated to her, she had replied uprightly that her father's will gave her 'no claim or title to reign as long as her sister lived'. If Camden's story is true the irony is bitter. If Elizabeth was one of the chief supporters of the legitimacy of her sister's claim, honour and honesty had triumphed again, but she was to pay a heavy price for her integrity.

The Emperor sent a special embassy to Mary, including the famous diplomat, Simon Renard. On 3 July she received a summons to visit her brother, but, having learned of Northumberland's plans, she made instead for her manor of Kenninghall, and later retreated to Framlingham Castle, her stronghold in East Anglia. North-umberland and Lady Jane's father, now Duke of Suffolk, already had eight hundred men in livery in constant attendance, and other councillors had called up enough of their retainers to form a standing army about the capital. Edward died on 6 July. Northumberland suppressed the news for forty-eight hours, while the Council feverishly debated whether to abide by Henry's will or to embrace Edward's 'unconstitutional and grossly illegal undertaking'.* They ordered the Lord Mayor of London to proclaim Jane as Queen on 8 July.

The following day Mary wrote, reminding them of their rightful allegiance. Jane

---

* Jordan points out that up until now Northumberland had organised no conspiracy. He had scrupulously kept Mary informed of every detail of her brother's health.

Faced with the enormity of what Edward had tried to do, even Camden was lost for words, pointing out that there was no Latin expression to describe it: '*quia non germanae, sed (ut Jurisperiti nostri loquuntur)* of the halfe bloud.'

was taken by barge to the Tower for the ceremony of State Entry. Her mother carried her train. A few archers cheered; otherwise there was no sign of public rejoicing. Meanwhile the town criers had been ordered to proclaim Mary and Elizabeth bastards at every street corner. During the uproar that followed, Elizabeth remained at Hatfield, until, shire by shire, the country rose spontaneously in favour of Mary. Northumberland advanced on Mary's camp with an army of 2,000 men and there were nine days of appalling confusion. Proclamations for Queen Jane were replaced by proclamations for Queen Mary. In some towns messengers followed on each other's heels, ripping down the parchments newly posted by their rivals. On 16 July the Council ordered Bishop Ridley to preach a sermon at Paul's Cross, explaining why Jane was Queen of England.*

Messengers reached Elizabeth daily. She never forgot that time. Thirteen years later, when a deputation from the Lords and Commons came to beg her to name her own successor, it still burned in her memory. She remembered the lawyers and clerics who had supported the 'Devise', against the rights of her sister and herself, and she spat her venom at her own bishops.

'I do not marvel, though *Domini Doctores*, with you my Lords, did so use themselves therein, since after my brother's death they openly preached and set forth that my sister and I were bastards.'

On 19 July Paget and the Earls of Arundel, Shrewsbury and Pembroke approached the other members of the Council to declare their allegiance to Mary. There was a complete *volte face*. Later that day the Lord Mayor, by command of the Council, proclaimed Mary Queen in London. The people were delirious with joy. They danced and feasted all night; street parties were lit by torches and bonfires, the fountains ran with wine and the bells of the city churches rang without pause.

Elizabeth wrote immediately to congratulate her sister. Sadly the letter is lost, but its contents are known. While the whole country was milling with armed men, Henry's younger daughter, either from a keen sense of protocol, or from an equally keen concern about her own public image, wanted to know what she should wear. Should it be mourning for their brother, or something to celebrate Mary's triumph? The Queen broke camp at Framlingham and most accounts suggest that Elizabeth rode directly from Hatfield to meet her at Wanstead on 2 August, the day before the Queen entered the City in triumph. In fact Elizabeth must have gone to London first, for the diarist Henry Machyn records that on 29 July 'came riding through London my Lady Elizabeth's Grace, and through Fleet Street, and so to my Lord of Somerset's place that was, and it is now my Lady Grace's, attended with 2,000 horse with spears and bows and guns'. It seemed all Hertfordshire had joined her train and, if Machyn's count of her henchmen is accurate, Elizabeth at the end of Edward's

---

* Formerly one of Cranmer's chaplains, he became Bishop of Rochester in 1550, and on Bonner's deprivation, Bishop of London. He denied transubstantiation and ordered all the altars to be replaced by Communion tables.

reign was in a position to raise a powerful fighting force. The detail is perhaps worth noting, for it makes more sense of Mary's later behaviour towards her sister if we realise to what extent the gentle creature who signed her letters 'your assured friend to my little power' had already become a popular public figure in her own right.

She rode out of London four days later to meet the Queen. We have no details of her wardrobe; presumably if it had been mourning for Edward it would have been remarked. She was followed still by a thousand horsemen as she made her way to Wanstead. Mary welcomed her with great warmth, kissing all her ladies. Henry's daughters then rode into London together, Mary in violet velvet, her sleeves embroidered in silver and gold, Elizabeth, now heiress to the throne, taking her place immediately behind her. As they entered the city, the bells were pealing and the streets were carpeted and garlanded with flowers.

Cor Rotto

Elizabeth remained at Court through the summer and autumn of 1553. Mary had inherited the unwanted title of Supreme Head of the Church, a Protestant clergy and a Council she felt she could not trust, even though some members were her most loyal supporters. She released Stephen Gardiner from the Tower, making him her Lord Chancellor, and she begged the Emperor to let her keep Renard until after the Coronation. Two weeks after the triumphant ride into London, he told Mary that he considered Elizabeth a danger to the State, the obvious figurehead for any Protestant reaction to Mary's avowed plan to restore the Catholic religion. After nearly seventeen years of relying upon the Emperor's advice Mary was not likely to change the habits of a lifetime. Renard became her closest confidant. She listened to everything he counselled.

Dissension arose immediately over Edward's funeral. Mary, having seen him christened a Catholic, wanted him to be buried as one. Renard persuaded her that as Edward had died a heretic he was not entitled to a Catholic funeral. Eventually he was buried in Westminster Abbey according to the Protestant rite, while Mary said Mass for his soul in the Tower. Elizabeth and Anne of Cleves pointedly failed to attend Mass in the royal household. On 12 August Mary published a proclamation forbidding the use of the terms 'heretic' and 'papist'; England was to return to the forms of worship used at the end of Henry VIII's reign. The moderates breathed sighs of relief. It seemed the new Queen would steer a gentle course.

Northumberland was tried and executed, but Jane Grey and her husband were merely kept in the Tower. Jane Grey's parents, the Duke and Duchess of Suffolk, were eventually pardoned, and the Duchess, as Mary's first cousin, became one of her ladies-in-waiting. Ridley had been imprisoned for his treasonable sermon. At the end of August the Protestant Bishop Hooper was arrested and then the elderly Bishop Latimer. On 14 September Cranmer, who had tried harder than anyone to dissuade Edward from the 'Devise', was sent to the Tower. Fear and confusion reigned in the heart of every zealous Protestant, and Elizabeth was no exception. She successfully avoided the Mass until 8 September, when the Queen asked her to attend the Feast of the Nativity of the Virgin. It was an appalling trial of integrity for one who had so recently translated Ochino's sermon and recited Cranmer's Collects. In the next months her conflicting ideals were put more to the test than ever before in her life. She pointed out truthfully to Mary that she knew little of her religion. Their father had chosen her tutors; she had been educated in the new doctrines.

Mary embarked on a crash conversion programme. On 21 September she gave Elizabeth a present of a rosary of red and white coral, trimmed with gold. Two days later she told Renard, in private, that she did not trust Elizabeth. She had catechised her on transubstantiation, asking 'if she firmly believed what the Catholics had always believed concerning the Holy Sacrament', and she told Elizabeth outright that people were calling her a hypocrite, saying her conversion was from policy. Elizabeth replied that she had considered making a public declaration that she went to Mass 'because her own conscience prompted her', but the public statement was never forthcoming and Mary noticed that when Elizabeth spoke to her, she was timid and trembling. Yet Elizabeth believed implicitly in Mary's right to rule and her own duty to obey. At the Coronation she carried her sister's train and, dressed in a robe of crimson velvet trimmed with gold buttons and powdered ermine, she swore the oath of allegiance.

In the first Parliament of the reign, Katharine of Aragon's marriage was declared lawful and Elizabeth was automatically bastardised. Public humiliation followed. Chancellor Gardiner spoke against her legitimacy in the House of Lords. At Court, Henry's nieces, Lady Margaret Douglas, Countess of Lennox, and Frances Brandon, Duchess of Suffolk, were given precedence over her. Renard told Mary he believed Elizabeth had been insincere about the Coronation Oath.

The Council staunchly upheld her rights as heiress to the throne. Gardiner was against her, but her most powerful relation, Lord William Howard, the Lord Admiral, controlled the fleet, and the Earls of Arundel, Pembroke and Sussex, as well as Paget and Petre, had all faithfully served her father and wished to preserve the succession as it stood. Each day, as Mary discussed the future of England with Renard, the spectres of the past seemed to trouble her more painfully and she vented her bitterness on Elizabeth. Charles V wished Mary to marry his son Philip of Spain. As preparations for this magnificent alliance against France went forward, the Queen delved further into family history. A search was made in the Imperial archives for the Pope's letter confirming the validity of Henry's marriage to Katharine and condemning his union with Anne Boleyn. The Emperor found the original documents and sent them to Mary. They brought back memories of the indignities she had suffered in the time of Anne Boleyn. By November she told Renard that

Elizabeth would become like her mother, a woman 'who had caused great trouble in the Kingdom'.

For Elizabeth life at Court was becoming a nightmare. Overwhelmed by a sense of her own helplessness, she asked permission to retire to her own estates rather than endure the traumas of family Christmas. Many zealous Protestants had already gone into exile, among them Lady Katherine Knollys, the daughter of Anne's sister, Mary Boleyn. Elizabeth wrote to wish her cousin Godspeed. Devastated by the happenings at her sister's Court, she signed the letter 'Cor Rotto' – Broken Heart.

CB   Relieve your sorrow for your far journey with joy of your short return, and think this pilgrimage rather a proof of your friends, than a leaving of your country. The length of time and distance of place, separates not the love of friends, nor deprives not the show of good will. An old saying, when bale is lowest boot is nearest; when your need shall be most you shall find my friendship greatest. Let others promise, and I will do, in words not more in deeds as much. My power but small, my love as great as them whose gifts may tell their friendship's tale, let will supply all other want, and oft sending take the lieu of often sights. Your messenger shall not return empty, nor yet your desires unaccomplished. Lethe's flood hath here no course, good memory hath greatest stream. And to conclude, a word that hardly I can say, I am driven by need to write, farewell, it is which in one way I wish, the other way I grieve.

Your loving cousin and ready friend,

Cor Rotto

A house built on sound foundations

Mary had decided to marry Philip of Spain five weeks before Elizabeth left for Ashridge. She told Renard and four of her chief councillors that she had knelt for two hours before the Holy Sacrament praying for guidance. So much was at stake – her conscience, the future of her kingdom, the souls of her people. Next day she told Renard in private that she had always felt repugnance towards carnal desire; she would need to overcome this to be a good wife to Philip.

Mary's prayers were miraculously answered when she was filled with an inner conviction that it was the will of God for her to marry the Emperor's son. Seasoned statesmen since her father's time, Paget and Arundel were used to dealing with royal consciences. They were swift to foresee the consequences of the felicitous connivance between the Holy Spirit and their sovereign over this match, the cornerstone of the Emperor's policy to annex England to his vast dominions. Both were devoted servants of the Crown, they had helped Mary to the throne: but they had also known

Elizabeth since childhood and, anticipating that there would be French reaction, they warned her to be careful not to become involved in foreign plots. Antoine de Noailles, the French ambassador, had been dropping hints to Elizabeth since the Coronation, and Paget and Arundel realised that Renard would set spies on her. On 20 December he informed Charles of his new security arrangements. Neither he nor the Queen trusted Elizabeth an inch; special personnel had been 'set to watch what takes place in her house'.

Elizabeth was on her guard. She became very circumspect in her behaviour. Before she left Court she had an interview with Mary and, sensing the atmosphere of distrust, she asked her sister not to believe false accusations against her without first giving her the chance to clear herself. Mary, according to Elizabeth, promised to give her a fair hearing, and gave her a parting gift of a sable hood to wear against the December cold. According to Renard, Mary only granted this audience at his instigation and she could barely conceal her hatred of Elizabeth. At Court the atmosphere had become so tense that Elizabeth apparently suffered from nervous indigestion. On one occasion there was a shout of 'Treason' in the Chapel Royal; it turned out to be a false alarm, but Elizabeth asked Mary's lady-in-waiting, Susan Clarencieux, to massage her stomach.

When she arrived at Ashridge, she began to relax a little. She was on home ground and even beginning to enjoy the ironies of the situation. She was to say later that she would never break the word of a Prince, spoken in a public place; and the oath of allegiance was in one sense her salvation, for the Parliament which legitimised Mary re-established the Mass as the legal form of worship in England. Under the new regime, whatever her private thoughts, she was simply 'rendering unto Caesar', by reciting in public the devotions prescribed by the State. As her sense of equilibrium returned, she realised that if she was to obey the letter of the law, she might at least do so at the Queen's expense. On arrival at Ashridge, which in their grandfather's day had been a monastery, she virtuously sent to her sister for copes and chasubles for the Catholic priests whom she had taken down to Hertfordshire in lieu of her former chaplains. If she had to listen to the prayers of Popish priests, and to provide their stipends, Mary could at least pay for their vestments.

On 2 January Philip's cousin, Count Egmont, arrived to complete Mary's marriage negotiations. The Londoners pelted him with snowballs as he rode through the street, for there was much opposition in the country to the Spanish match. Elizabeth fully understood this when she wrote dutifully to congratulate Mary on the finalising of the negotiations, and to thank her for her New Year's gift. The original letter is lost, but thanks to the vigilance of Renard's spies and de Noailles' counter-espionage, a copy survived. Translated into French and back into English, it is a little stilted, but the tone and details ring true. Elizabeth had caught 'flu at Ashridge; she apologised for not having written earlier to thank Mary for her New Year present. She was utterly phlegmatic about the marriage with Philip. Eight years earlier, as part of one of Henry's more complex schemes to ally with the greatest house in Europe, she herself had been suggested as a bride for Philip, while Mary was to marry the Emperor. Charles had politely declined on the grounds that, at that date, *both* Henry's daughters were illegitimate. Now the irony was complete.

ᚼ Although by neglect of my duty, most noble Queen, I might be reprehended for not having sent your Highness any news of myself, since I left Court, yet I trust that your Grace, of your noble nature and inclination, will forgive me and attribute this failing to its true causes. I have been troubled, since arriving at my house, with such a cold and headache that I have never felt their equal, and especially during the last three weeks I have had no respite because of the pain in my head and in my arms. I have several times had occasion to offer your Highness my humble thanks for having sent to ask after my health and for the plate you gave me, but I now have an even more compelling reason to do so, for you have been pleased not only to write me a letter with your own hand, which I know is tedious for you, but also to tell me of the conclusion of your marriage and of the articles to accompany it. This is a deep and weighty matter, but I have no doubt it will redound to the glory of God, the repose of your Majesty and the safety and preservation of your Kingdoms. There is one thing that ought to be considered even before these three points and without which nothing can prosper: *quia frustra enim nititur decretum hominum contra voluntatem divinam*; but as you, Madame, are sure about that, I doubt not that your will shall be made the instrument of His, so that the issues may be good. For a house built on a sound foundation can only stand firm, whereas one built on the sand may soon be wrecked by light winds and sudden tempests. And as I know of no one more bound by duty and inclination to wish your Highness all prosperity than myself, so no one shall be found, though comparisons be odious, more ready to pray to God for you, or more sincere in wishing you greatness.

Therefore Madam, fearing to importune your Majesty, I will commend you to the Creator's keeping and finish this letter.

I come in no traitor

On the memorable August day that Mary and Elizabeth rode into London in triumph Mary had released four prisoners from the Tower: Gardiner, the old Duke of Norfolk, the Lord Protector's widow, the Duchess of Somerset, and Edward Courtenay, a great-grandson of Edward IV and last of the Yorkist line. Courtenay had lived in the Tower since he was twelve years old, when his father had been imprisoned by Henry VIII. He had been brought up a Catholic. Mary restored him in blood, granting him the title Earl of Devon. She made his mother, Gertrude, Marchioness of Exeter, one of her ladies-in-waiting. It was suggested that Mary should marry Courtenay and Gardiner, who had known him in the Tower, was strongly in favour of the idea until Mary said she really could not be expected to marry a man because a bishop had made friends with him in prison. During the winter of 1553 she discussed the idea of marrying Elizabeth to Courtenay with Renard and several senior councillors. Elizabeth's preferences do not seem to have been considered, but the plan was widely publicised. The Emperor was not in favour of the project, and it was shelved amid the more important preparations for Mary's wedding.

The strong popular resentment at the idea of the Queen marrying a foreigner had not abated. While Elizabeth was at Ashridge, Sir Thomas Wyatt, a gentleman of Kent, led a rebellion against the Spanish match. He marched to London at the head of 7,000 men who assembled menacingly at Southwark. Mary showed great courage. She rode to the Guildhall where she made a magnificent speech to the Londoners. She was their Queen, wedded to the realm at the time of her Coronation, and she vowed the Coronation Ring should never come off her finger. She told her subjects that she loved them as 'naturally as the mother loves the child', reflecting perhaps her own apprehensions when she commented that she had never yet been a mother. But she ended rousingly, 'I doubt not but that we shall give these rebels a short and speedy overthrow.' Popular rumour had it that 25,000 Londoners declared for Mary that day, which improved government morale considerably, since there had already been a rising led by Sir Peter Carew in the West Country.

Mary ordered the gunners in the Tower not to fire on Southwark, and Wyatt marched round the city walls, entering by Knightsbridge, which was then a separate hamlet. Lord Pembroke was ready for him with a troop of men on the high ground (which has since been flattened to form Oxford Street). There was skirmishing at Ludgate and in Hyde Park, but eventually Wyatt was captured and brought to Whitehall, where Mary sat watching at a window of the gatehouse: she had refused even to go to safety in the Tower. Wyatt was charged with treason for plotting to overthrow the Queen and to set Elizabeth and Courtenay on the throne. Courtenay was sent back to prison and Elizabeth was summoned from Ashridge.

It was a miserable winter; the Emperor's ambassadors had commented in one of their despatches that they were astonished by the timing of the rebellion:

'The season is too early yet for a popular rising and this cold damp weather is not usually selected by the English for insurrections.'

Elizabeth was still ill. Her doctors told Mary she should not be moved from Ashridge, but Mary believed she was play-acting to save her skin and commanded that she should be brought to London in a litter. The Queen was in a new and pitiless mood. She gave orders for Jane Grey and Guildford Dudley to be executed, although they had had no part in the rising. The Marquis of Northampton was put in the Tower purely on suspicion, and the Duke of Suffolk, who had tried to raise a separate revolt in the Midlands, was betrayed by his own gamekeeper, when discovered hiding on his estates. He was sent to London and beheaded. One hundred and twenty rebels were put to death, their remains being strung from gibbets throughout the city. A further 400, with halters about their necks, knelt and asked Mary for pardon, which was granted, principally because the London prisons were too full to take any more suspects. Wyatt himself exonerated Elizabeth from the scaffold, but it was alleged Elizabeth had been in contact with him before he died, and Francis Lord Russell, son of the Lord Privy Seal, revealed during cross-questioning that he had delivered a letter from Wyatt to Elizabeth's household. Gardiner's spies had also found a copy of a letter Elizabeth had written to Mary in the French Ambassador's postbag.

Because of her illness Elizabeth travelled slowly, taking five days to accomplish the thirty-five-mile journey from Ashridge to London. She arrived on 23 February with a great company of her own people and an escort of the Queen's, and she caused a sensation by throwing back the curtains of her litter, so that the Londoners could see how sick she was. Her complexion was deathly pale and she lay propped against pillows in a white gown. Renard was convinced she had led a loose life and was pregnant.

The Queen's escort brought the doleful procession past Somerset House to St James's, where Mary kept her sister under guard for a month, allowing her six of her ladies, two gentlemen and four servants. The rest of Elizabeth's entourage was sent ignominiously to find lodgings in the town. She entreated Mary to remember her promise to allow her an audience but, bitter and anxious since her own wedding plans were now postponed, Mary decided to confine her to the Tower. The Council argued against the plan, pointing out that Elizabeth was still heiress to the throne. Mary asked if any of them were prepared to keep her under arrest on their own estates. They were not. Gardiner was campaigning for Parliament to meet in Oxford, where he was arranging for a disputation at which the three Protestant bishops, Latimer, Ridley and Cranmer, should be examined on questions of doctrine. It was a foregone conclusion that they would be condemned as heretics and burned, even though the legislation providing for this had been repealed and would have to be renewed. He wanted Mary to remove the Court to Windsor, arguing that Elizabeth should be imprisoned as a matter of public safety, since there was no knowing what might happen if she was left at St James's, a figure of popular sympathy among the Londoners.*

On 16 March the Earl of Sussex and another peer, probably the Marquis of Winchester, came to take her to the Tower. She believed that her life depended on gaining a personal interview with her sister. In Edward's reign they had both suffered enough at the hands of councillors, and she could not believe the Queen would deny

---

* One of Renard's most comprehensive despatches. He had even grasped that one of the disadvantages of Gardiner's idea was that the London merchants would object because of the money they would lose if Parliament was held elsewhere, as Members whose spending power was considerable would be billeted out of town.

her the right to speak with her. She called for pen and paper to write to Mary. As the hysteria mounted inside her, she remembered the Admiral and a sorrowful comment of Somerset's – that his brother would never have been executed had they met before the trial. While Elizabeth was writing the tide of the Thames rose, so that her barge could not have passed under London Bridge. She drew diagonal lines freehand over the bottom half of the paper, so that no one could add a forged postscript. Then she added a separate line begging Mary to send a reply. Her journey was postponed by one day.

When the Queen heard what had happened, she was incensed; such a thing would not have been allowed to happen in her father's time. She raged helplessly at Sussex; she only wished that Henry VIII might come to life again for a month. The following day, Palm Sunday, Elizabeth was rowed in a covered barge to the Water Gate of the Tower with her six ladies-in-waiting and a gentleman usher. It was four weeks since Jane Grey's execution, and Elizabeth knew that somewhere in the great fortress her own mother lay headless and buried. Tradition has it that when the barge reached its mooring place she sat down on the damp stone steps, refusing to go in and crying, 'I pray you all good friends and fellows, bear me witness that I come in no traitor, but as true a woman to the Queen's Majesty as any is now living.' Eventually the gentleman usher burst into tears and Elizabeth, scolding him for his weakness, roused herself and went through the gate. A detachment of Yeoman Warders, who should have been her gaolers, fell on their knees before her shouting, 'God save your Grace.'

ଓ If any ever did try this old saying, that a King's word was more than another man's oath, I most humbly beseech your Majesty to verify it in me, and to remember your last promise and my last demand that I be not condemned without answer and due proof, which it seems that now I am, for without cause proved, I am by your Council from you commanded to go to the Tower, a place more wonted for a false traitor than a true subject. Which, though I know I desire it not, yet in the face of all this realm appears that it is proved, which I pray God I may die the shamefullest death that ever any died, afore I may mean any such thing. And to this present hour I protest afore God (who shall Know my truth, whatsoever malice shall devise), that I never practised, counselled, nor consented to anything that might be prejudicial to your person any way, or dangerous to the state by any means. And therefore I humbly beseech your Majesty to let me answer afore yourself, and not suffer me to trust to your Councillors. Yea, and that afore I go to the Tower (if it be possible) if not, afore I be further condemned. Howbeit, I trust assuredly your Highness will give me leave to do it afore I go, for that thus shamefully I may not be cried out on, as now I shall be yea, and that without cause. Let conscience move your Highness to take some better way with me, than to make me be condemned in all men's sight afore my desert [is made] known. Also, I most humbly beseech your Highness to pardon this my boldness, which innocency procures me to do,

The Tower Letter: written in Elizabeth's own hand when she was in great danger

together with hope of your kindness, which of truth will not see me cast away without desert, which what it is, I would desire no more of God, but that you truly knew. Which thing I think and believe you shall never by report know, unless by yourself you hear.

I have heard in my time of many cast away for want of coming to the presence of their Prince, and in late days I heard my lord of Somerset say, that if his brother had been suffered to speak with him he had never suffered, but persuasions were made to him so great, that he was brought in belief that he could not live safely, if the Admiral lived, and that made him give consent to the death, though these persons are not to be compared to your Majesty. Yet I pray God the like evil persuasions persuade not one sister against another, and all for that they have heard false report and the truth not known. Therefore once again with humbleness of my heart because I am not suffered to bow the knees of my body I humbly crave to speak with your Highness, which I would not be so bold to desire, if I knew not myself most clear, as I know myself most true. And as for the traitor, Wyatt, he might peradventure write [i.e. have written] me a letter, but on my faith I never received any from him, and as for the copy of my letter sent to the French King, I pray God confound me eternally if ever I sent him word, message, token, or letter by any means, and to this my truth I will stand in to my death.

I humbly crave but only one word of answer from yourself.

Your Highness's most faithful subject, that hath been from the beginning, and will be to my end.

Elizabeth

CHAPTER IV

Much suspected

Mary married Philip in Winchester Cathedral on 25 July 1554. He had landed in England five days earlier, after delays of nearly a month which almost made Mary ill with nervous anxiety. Immediately the Spanish ships were sighted off the Needles Elizabeth's great-uncle, Lord William Howard, the Lord Admiral, was sent to escort them into Southampton Water. His ships had been waiting for so long that Howard complained his sailors had been 'devoured by vermin'. They were also unpaid. No English admiral had ever put up with all he had gone through, he grumbled, and he would not do it again, even if he were given the whole realm.

There was still much opposition to the Spanish match. Faction in the Council had reached a high point. Renard believed the Earl of Arundel planned to marry his son to Elizabeth and make a bid for the throne; Paget was in league with Arundel, and in touch with the French. Gardiner mistrusted Paget; Renard mistrusted everybody, and someone managed to send further shivers down the ambassador's spine by suggesting the Admiral might desert to the French, taking the navy with him. The Venetian ambassador, who was in a position to view things more calmly, merely pointed out in his despatches that the Prince was supposed to be carrying 3,000,000 ducats, some of which was destined to pay the Emperor's armies in the Netherlands, and that Howard was stationed to prevent pirates attacking the treasure ships. Philip was finally brought ashore by barge, and immediately made a good impression by his affable manners. Mary had sent an escort of a hundred archers dressed in Spanish livery, and also a white charger upon which her bridegroom could enter the ancient capital of Arthurian romance.* As the Prince rode towards Winchester he cut a handsome figure, until an English downpour soaked him to the skin, ruining his richly embroidered clothes. His progress through the dripping lanes was further slowed by relays of pages arriving from Mary, bearing gifts and messages.

The Queen was lodged in Gardiner's palace, while Philip was taken to the mayor's house. As a wedding present the Emperor had made his son King of Naples, so that he should be a worthy consort for the Queen. This was announced when the couple met formally on 24 July. The Queen and her ladies were arrayed in violet velvet and Philip wore a cloak of the same colour, fringed with silver. He greeted Mary by

---

* Philip's own household was not landed immediately and a separate one had been arranged for him by the English, so that at first there was confusion; the Spaniards complained they had nothing to do and spent their time looking at the tourist sights, including a round table said to have been used by King Arthur.

kissing her on the mouth in the English fashion, while his courtiers caused a great stir by kissing all the ladies' hands in the Spanish manner. The following day, before the wedding ceremony, the heralds announced the new title in the cathedral, also proclaiming Philip King of England. As Gardiner intoned the nuptial Mass, Mary never took her eyes from the Holy Sacrament.

Philip's first marriage, to the Infanta Maria Manuela of Portugal, had been celebrated with much gaiety at Salamanca in 1543, when he was a youth of seventeen. Charles had thought it prudent then to write to his son before the wedding, counselling sexual restraint even in marriage, for the Emperor believed excess might endanger the Prince's health. Philip had nevertheless fallen in love with his beautiful young wife, who had died giving birth to his only son, Don Carlos. If he felt misgivings, that July afternoon in the English cathedral, over marrying a woman of thirty-eight, eleven years his senior, they were well concealed.* The King and Queen left the altar hand in hand, Mary radiantly happy in cloth of gold, Philip all in white. They banqueted until 6 PM and then led the dancing. A little before 9 o'clock the bishops blessed the marriage bed according to English custom and the courtiers retired, leaving the couple to consummate their union. 'What happened that night, only they know,' wrote a gallant member of the Spanish entourage. 'If they give us a son our joy will be complete.' Others were less charitable, describing Mary as flabby, 'older than we had been led to expect', 'a perfect saint, who dresses badly' and from Ruy Gomez, Prince of Eboli and one of Philip's closest companions, the stinging observation: 'It would take God himself to drain this cup.'

Elizabeth was not present at her sister's wedding. She remained two months in the Tower and was then sent to Woodstock, where she was kept under house arrest for nearly a year. Wyatt had been executed on 11 April, when Elizabeth and Courtenay were already in the Tower. Despite his speech exonerating them both, the Council continued to cross-examine them. The most that could be proved against Elizabeth was misprision, failure to report treason which she had known to be taking place. During the rebellion Wyatt had advised her to move to Donnington, one of her houses which could be easily fortified. Elizabeth claimed she did not know she owned such a house, and asked if she was not free to come and go to her own houses at all times. It was alleged she knew of Wyatt's letter, even though she had not replied to it, and this she never tried to deny, but she was said to have sent a verbal message to the rebel leader by Sir William Saintlow, thanking Wyatt for his

---

* In his biography, *Philip II*, Professor Geoffrey Parker says 'Philip II was simply not interested in women, either for their companionship or for their sexual charms. If he felt lust at all strongly, he seems to have kept it, like the rest of his emotions, under strict control.' In fact Philip seems to have adored his third wife Elisabeth of Valois, both as a sexual partner and as a companion. He wrote warm, affectionate letters to his daughters, and always treated Mary Tudor with respect and gentleness. Peter Pierson puts forward an opposite view of Philip's sexuality, and offers an intriguing glimpse of him as a youth of seventeen, riding out eagerly to get a sight of his first bride as she arrived from Portugal.

goodwill and saying non-committally that she would do as she should see cause, when the time came.

It was upon this casual remark that the case against Elizabeth turned, and it was to cost her her freedom for over a year. When Mary was banished from her father's Court and harassed by her brother's councillors on account of her Masses, she had intrigued continually with the Spanish ambassadors, planning even to flee the country. Nothing would convince her that Elizabeth was innocent. The suspicion that the celebrated letter destined for the French King was part of an elaborate plot remained lodged in the Queen's mind. Gardiner insisted he had seen a copy of the letter, when de Noailles' postbag was impounded. Challenged to produce it, the bishop said it had been destroyed when the rebels were encamped at Southwark and had ransacked the library of Lambeth Palace. Renard and Gardiner wanted Elizabeth executed, or at least sent on a long visit to the Court of Mary of Hungary, Regent of the Netherlands, or safely married off to Philip's cousin, Emmanuel Philibert, the Duke of Savoy. Much of de Noailles' correspondence was devoted to reporting the progress of these plans. At the time of her own accession, when Elizabeth offered heartfelt thanks to God for her safe deliverance, she was to look back on Renard and Gardiner as the 'greedy and raging lions' who had plotted her destruction.

She was allowed six ladies in the Tower, three of the Queen's and three of her own, also two grooms and the gentleman usher who had accompanied her in the barge on Palm Sunday. She was permitted to walk along the leads of the Tower, a narrow passageway between the Beauchamp Tower and the Bell Tower, but she was kept under strict surveillance and was not allowed to communicate with other prisoners. In Foxe's *Book of Martyrs*, a popular story tells of the child of one of the warders, who used to bring her flowers every day, until the authorities got hold of the idea that he might be smuggling notes in the posies. He was threatened with a whipping if he went to her again, and called to her through a grille, 'Mistress, I may bring you no more flowers.'

A great fuss was made about her food. After she had been in the Tower for one day her own gentlemen arrived with her dinner. The constable said she must be served, like other prisoners, from the lieutenant's table. Although Lord Chandos would probably have furnished her with a perfectly appropriate diet, this was considered a scandalous insult to the heiress to the throne. Appeals were immediately lodged with the Council, and the Admiral took up cudgels on his niece's behalf. In the end she was allowed her own cook, butler, cellarer and servants of the wardrobe and pantry, but Sir John Gage, the Lord Chamberlain, had to come with them daily to check nothing was hidden among the dishes and hampers. The loyalty of Elizabeth's household in keeping up this routine for two months meant much coming and going in the vicinity of the Tower, so that details of her treatment were widely circulated, arousing much sympathy among the Londoners. When she was released on 20 May, the gunners in the steelyards fired off a spontaneous salute as her barge passed down the Thames.

Elizabeth left the Tower in the custody of Sir Henry Bedingfeld, a Norfolk gentleman whose father had been in charge of Katharine of Aragon during her imprisonment in Kimbolton Castle. She was badly frightened when she arrived at Richmond and found the palace surrounded by guards. She believed she was being taken to a place of execution. Instead she went to Windsor, where she was lodged, not in the castle, but ignominiously in the dean's house. Her journey into Oxfordshire turned into a triumphal progress; the details have been related many times. At Thame she was 'very princely entertained' by Lord Williams, the High Sheriff of the County, who gave a banquet in her honour, while Sir Henry grunted his disgust. At Rycote housewives threw cakes and biscuits into her litter, until it was so laden with presents she had to beg them to stop. At Woburn a farm labourer climbed a hill to get a sight of her. Bedingfeld discovered he was an ardent Protestant, and wrote to Mary to say the local populace were 'not good and whole in matters of religion'.

Although Elizabeth was forbidden writing materials, the period at Woodstock is well documented. Mary sent a memorandum to Bedingfeld on 21 May 1554 with precise instructions on how her sister was to be treated: she was to be detained until 'certain matters' had been more thoroughly investigated. She was not to walk in the garden without Sir Henry in attendance, or to converse with any suspected persons. Nor was she to receive any 'message, letter or token to or from any manner of person'. Bedingfeld obeyed his instructions scrupulously, reporting back regularly to the Council, so that many of Elizabeth's comments are preserved verbatim. When she called him her gaoler, he begged her on his knees to regard him as her 'officer'. 'From such officers', she said, 'good Lord deliver me.' Her own entourage remained supportive. She was not allowed to see Mrs Ashley, but Parry set up his household accounts department at the Bull Inn in Woodstock. To Bedingfeld's consternation, it quickly became a general meeting place for Elizabeth's friends. De Noailles sent a servant with a present of apples, to try to get a verbal message to her, but he was unsuccessful. Sir Henry was so zealous in preventing her from speaking with strangers that one of her gentlemen, wanting to make her laugh, carried a goat into the house and solemnly told Bedingfeld that it had been seen carrying on a conversation with her Grace, as she walked in the garden. He had brought it before Sir Henry in case it was a Welshman in disguise.

On 12 June Elizabeth begged to be allowed to write to Mary. Bedingfeld referred to the Council and evidently the request was granted, for although no letter survives, Mary showed one to Renard. He reported indignantly that Elizabeth was full of self-justification; her letter was, he complained, 'as bold as anything I have ever seen'. She addressed Mary, not as 'Highness' or 'Majesty', but merely as 'you'. Amidst the high drama of the wedding preparations, the Queen fired off yet another memorandum to Bedingfeld:

'Our pleasure is that we shall not hereafter be molested any more with her disguised and colourable letters.' The Queen was sorry to suspect her own sister, but as it 'appeared that copies of her secret letters to us were found in a packet of the

French ambassador and that divers of the most notable traitors made their chief account upon her, we can hardly be brought to think they would have presumed to do so, except they had more certain knowledge of her favour towards their unnatural conspiracy than is yet confessed by her'.

Elizabeth seethed with rage. The Queen's Majesty might think her letters colourable, she told Bedingfeld sarcastically, but 'I must say for myself that it was the plain truth'. It was perhaps at this point in her detention that, denied pen and ink, she ground the famous inscription onto a window pane with a diamond ring.

> *Much suspected by me*
> *Nothing proved can be, quoth Elizabeth prisoner*

In a worse case than the worst prisoners in Newgate

On 3 July Bedingfeld again wrote to the Council. Elizabeth had called him to her, while she was walking in the garden that rainy morning.

'I remember yesterday', she said, 'you utterly refused to write on my behalf to my lords of the Council, and therefore if you continue in that mind still, I shall be in a worse case than the worst prisoners in Newgate, for they are never gainsaid in the time of their imprisonment by one friend or another to have their cause opened and sued for, and this is and shall be such a conclusion to me that I must needs continue this life without all worldly hope, wholly resting in the truth of my cause, which will be opened before God, arming myself against whatsoever shall happen, to remain the Queen's true subject, as I have done during my life. It waxes wet and therefore I will depart to my lodging again.'

The rest of Bedingfeld's letter worries away over the situation at the Bull. He particularly suspected one Verney, who had been seen speaking with William Crudge, a servant of the late Duke of Suffolk. 'If there be any practice of ill within England, this Verney is privy to it,' he warned the Council. 'Parry, her Cofferer, lies at the same sign of the Bull, a marvellous colourable place to practise in.' Besides about forty servants in Parry's own livery, Elizabeth's people were continually coming and going. 'Many more', complained Sir Henry, 'than have cause to repair there for any provision.'

By the end of the month Elizabeth was losing heart. Even Bedingfeld pitied her. He wrote to the Council 'to beseech your Lordships to consider her woeful case'. She was again begging to be allowed to see the Queen. On 15 August he told them she had complained during her afternoon walk. Her comment gives us a vivid glimpse of the interminable and depressing procedures available in Tudor England to one who had incurred the Sovereign's displeasure, or fallen foul of the law.

'I have very slow speed in the answer of any of my suits,' she confided, 'and I know it is ever so when there is not one appointed to give daily attendance in suit making for answer, and therefore I pray you let me send a servant of my own to whom I will give a message in your own hearing that he shall do by my command, and this I think is not against the order and service appointed unto you.'

On another occasion she went to confession, took communion and swore to Bedingfeld and one of the Queen's ladies before the Holy Sacrament that she had never done or intended to do anything that was perilous to the Queen or the realm. Perhaps this softened Mary's heart, but by now she was too absorbed in her own affairs to pay attention to her sister's plight.

After their State Entry into London, the King and Queen settled at Hampton Court, where they were giving their fullest attention to the important matter of begetting an heir. It was probably the happiest time of Mary's life. She had fallen head over heels in love with her husband, and he treated her with great respect, lightening the burden of government by helping with decision making, and offering intelligent suggestions for the reform of the Council. The English lords were pleased to receive Spanish pensions, which met some of the heavy expenses of attendance at Court. Council meetings were held in Latin, so that the King-Consort could more easily get to grips with the thorny issues of English politics. With the possibility that Mary would bear children, her sister seemed less of a threat.

On 15 September Elizabeth gained permission to write another letter to her sister. It has not survived, but the story of its composition offers a vignette of Elizabeth at her most feminine and most prevaricating. Bedingfeld sent her an inkstand, five pens, two sheets of fine writing paper and one sheet of rough paper, all of which he gave to Mistress Norton, one of the Queen's most trusted ladies-in-waiting, on a Monday morning. Having stormed for nearly three months for the writing materials, Elizabeth did not use them on Monday, having developed a headache. On Tuesday morning she washed her hair. Finally on Tuesday afternoon she sent for Bedingfeld, to say that she never wrote to the Council except through a secretary, so she asked Sir Henry to write the letter for her. In the end a suitable message was composed and conveyed to the Lord Treasurer and the Lord Chamberlain by Verney. Bedingfeld then took away the pens and paper, carefully noting that one of the pens was missing; we never learn whether it was broken, or whether Mistress Norton was ordered to search Elizabeth's belongings in case she had secreted it about her person.

During October it was discovered that Elizabeth was still saying the Litany in English. Mary wrote from Westminster: her sister 'should stand content with the service used in our own Chapel and throughout our realm, and no more to use the said suffrages and Litany in English, but in Latin according to the ancient and laudable custom of the Church'. Elizabeth meekly explained that she had been using the only service book she had been allowed to keep, an English prayer book dating from Henry VIII's reign. It had been given to her in the Tower by Lady Anne Grey, one of her attendants until she was withdrawn to wait on the Queen at the royal wedding. It must have been an innocuous publication, for Bedingfeld had made a great to-do when she first arrived at Woodstock and had asked for an English translation of the Bible. Parry had sent her Cicero and the Psalms, and these she was allowed to keep, but only after an exchange of letters with the Council.

By November her health had declined. Dr Owen and Dr Wendy were sent from Court to bleed her. Mary was preoccupied with affairs of State and Bedingfeld was in great distress as the Council had sent no money to pay the soldiers who guarded Woodstock day and night. He had to settle some of the charges out of his own pocket. At one point he even conferred with Parry, who was still controlling Elizabeth's accounts from the Bull. A perfectly practical request went to the Council for a change of abode, for the winter weather had made the country roads impassable, so that it was difficult to get supplies to what was then a remote part of Oxfordshire. There is a widely held tradition that at this point in the story Elizabeth consoled herself with the *Epistles of St Paul*. A small volume bound in black cloth, and embroidered with silver and gold thread, still exists in the Bodleian Library with an inscription on the flyleaf, in what is claimed to be Elizabeth's hand:

☙ *August*
> I walk many times into the pleasant fields of the holy scriptures, where I pluck up the goodly green herbs of sentences by pruning: eat them by reading, chew them by using and lay them up at length in the high seat of memory by gathering them together: that so having tasted thy sweetness I may the less perceive the bitterness of this miserable life.

The embroidery includes the device of a heart with a flower growing through it and the inscription ELEVA SURSU[M] COR. Beneath the flower stem is stitched IBI UBI. On either side of the heart initials were embroidered – on the left side an E and on the right side the initial has worn away. Thomas Warton, who examined the book during, or before, 1772, when he wrote his *Life of Sir Thomas Pope*, thought the worn initial was a C, and surmised the letters stood for ELIZABETHA CAPTIVA. This romantic supposition has held good for over two centuries.

Alas, when carefully examined under strong electric light, the missing initial can be seen in outline; it was R, not C. This suggests the book really did belong to Elizabeth I, and the fine embroidery is similar to that on the covers of the volumes described earlier in this work. The English translation of St Paul has, however, been identified as Laurence Tomson's, and his version of the New Testament was not printed in England until 1576, so the captive princess cannot have read it at Woodstock. It is a pity to explode such a pretty myth, since all the embroidered Latin mottoes, such as VICIT OMNIA PERTINAX VIRTUS, fit in perfectly with what we understand of her mood at this time. As is well known to readers of the *Book of Martyrs*, while taking her solitary exercise in the walled garden Elizabeth once heard a milkmaid singing in Woodstock Park, and commented that the girl's life was merrier than her own, since she was free to come and go as she pleased. Happily there is no documentary evidence for or against the milkmaid, so we must hope Foxe's story is true.

Kept a great while from you, desolately alone

It was Mary's deepest wish that England should be reunited with Rome, as an integral part of that European Christendom which had existed before her father meddled with notions of royal supremacy. She had been in communication with Pope Julius III since her accession, also with her cousin, Reginald Pole, a man of rank and letters living in Italy and an influential voice at Rome.

At the beginning of Mary's reign, although he had been a cardinal since 1536, Pole was still in deacon's orders. Before Mary made it clear that she was determined to accept the Emperor's choice of Philip, it was even suggested by some members of the Council, who were eager for her to take an English husband, that she might marry Pole. A nephew of Edward IV, he was the son of Mary's godmother, the old Countess of Salisbury, whom Henry had persecuted with horrifying cruelty. The cardinal had lived in exile for nearly two decades on account of his outspoken criticism of Henry's divorce from Katharine of Aragon.

In 1533, after the King married Anne Boleyn, the countess, who was Mary's governess, refused to give up the Princess's jewels to the new Queen. Out of loyalty to Katharine she continued to serve Mary, at her own expense, when the girl was in disgrace for her refusal to acknowledge either Anne or the royal supremacy. Lady Salisbury and her sons, Lord Montague and Sir Geoffrey Pole, were received back at Court after Anne's execution, but in 1537 Reginald published *Pro Ecclesiasticae Unitatis Defensione*, an attack on the break with Rome which so enraged Henry that the cardinal feared he might try to have him assassinated. He was accused of treason and attainted in his absence. In order to keep her own position, Margaret Pole, who was like a second mother to Mary, pretended to be shocked by her son's book, but after the Northern Rebellion she was imprisoned with great savagery, and in 1541, amid the reprisals following Sir John Neville's rising in Yorkshire, she was executed. She was given no chance to defend herself legally and her death was particularly horrible, as an inexperienced executioner hacked her neck and shoulders with many blows.

There is also a story that Pole's younger brother Geoffrey had been tortured until he betrayed Montague, who was executed in 1538. Geoffrey was set free. He was said to be demented with guilt at causing his brother's death and he fled to Italy, where Reginald was living in Viterbo. All the Pole family were devoted to Katharine of Aragon. They saw Anne Boleyn as the prime cause of Henry's decline from a Catholic monarch to a bloodthirsty tyrant.

Kept a great while from you, desolately alone

When the Pope learned of Mary's intention to restore Catholicism in England, he appointed Pole his legate. The cardinal urged Mary to deal with religious affairs immediately, but a complex situation developed in April 1554, when Parliament debated the re-enactment of the heresy statutes. The House of Lords objected to the possible restoration of the monastic lands, and made it clear to Mary that they would only agree to accept the Pope's authority in return for guarantees that their property would remain intact. The common lawyers, also, took exception to Mary's plan to re-establish the legatine courts. The Emperor believed the marriage should take precedence over the formal reconciliation with Rome. He was unenthusiastic about the prospect of Pole's intervention in English affairs, believing Philip should first establish himself as King of England. He detained him in the Netherlands on various pretexts and the cardinal was kept busy with the peace negotiations between France and Spain.* In November he at last arrived in England to heal the schism and absolve the realm.

Mary believed herself pregnant. The King and Queen confided only in their intimate friends. Ruy Gomez knew as early as 2 October. Renard had heard a story on 18 September from one of the Queen's doctors, but so many rumours were circulating that even he did not know which to believe. He was still unsure as he started his despatch to the Emperor on 23 November, but as he sat dictating the news was made official. He added a postscript in his own hand, a jubilant bulletin on the Queen's fecundity: not only was her womb swollen, the state of her breasts showed she was pregnant.

On 27 November the Council informed Bishop Bonner that the Queen had conceived. The succession to the throne was therefore certain and the news was to be proclaimed all over London. Three days later Pole addressed the Lords, Commons and clergy in Parliament. He outlined England's long connection with the Holy See, referring to the English Reformation as 'innovations' springing from the root of avarice, and from Henry VIII's lust and carnal affection, which had confounded all laws both human and divine. He mentioned Northumberland's attempt to conspire against Mary, reminding them all that it was a miracle that God had preserved her, 'a virgin, helpless, naked and unarmed', to reign over them. The Lords and Commons knelt to ask forgiveness for their error in breaking away from the Holy See. Mary later claimed that at the moment Pole arrived she felt the pious child leap in her womb. The following day Philip wrote to the Pope to describe the return of the country to the Catholic faith. Within three weeks Parliament had re-enacted the old heresy laws; anyone openly professing the Protestant religion could be burned at the stake.

Elizabeth was left languishing at Woodstock, a figure of diminishing importance, as Mary awaited her confinement. It was not until 17 April that the Queen ordered

* Renard wrote of him, 'the Right Reverend Legate who between ourselves may be a learned and most virtuous prelate of holy life, but is not good at negotiating.'

her sister's release. She was brought to Hampton Court still ignominiously guarded by Bedingfeld. Some members of the Council thought she should be sent immediately to the Court of Mary of Hungary, but Philip believed it best she should remain in England until after the Queen's baby was born. If Mary Tudor died in childbirth it would serve Habsburg interests better if Elizabeth succeeded, than for the throne of England to go to the Scottish claimant, Mary Stuart, who had just become engaged to the Dauphin. Suddenly Elizabeth had a powerful new ally in her own brother-in-law.

It was some time before she was allowed an audience with Mary, and Gardiner, Arundel, Shrewsbury and Petre visited her first to try to persuade her to make a formal submission to the Queen.

'My lords, I am glad to see you,' she greeted them, 'for methinks I have been kept a great while from you, desolately alone.'

At first she was kept in seclusion, but eventually Mary received her. It was the first time the sisters had met since Elizabeth left Court in the winter of 1553.

'You stiffly still persevere in your truth,' said Mary acidly. 'Belike you will not confess, but that you have been wrongfully punished.'

'I must not say so, if it please your Majesty, to you,' came the level reply. 'I have borne the burden and must bear it', and then, more humanly, 'I humbly beseech your Majesty to have a good opinion of me.'

On 30 April a rumour got about that Mary had given birth to a son; bonfires were lit in London and the bells pealed until it was realised a mistake had been made. Dr Weston, the Dean of Westminster, composed a prayer for the children of Westminster School to recite morning and evening for the Queen's safe delivery, for the dangers to mother and child for a woman of Mary's age were fully recognised; the Westminster boys prayed that the Queen might 'bring forth a child in body beautiful and comely in mind'.*

The eyes of all Europe were fixed on the drama at the English Court. Already the French ambassador had heard from a lady of the bedchamber that the chief midwife had doubts. Apart from her swollen womb, Mary had none of the usual symptoms of pregnancy. The Venetian ambassador thought it would end in wind. The Protestants made coarse jokes, claiming the whole affair was a Catholic plot to pass off a supposititious heir on the kingdom, and to deprive Elizabeth of her rightful inheritance. Crowds gathered daily at Hampton Court hoping for an announcement. There were constant religious processions. Elizabeth sewed a layette.† Philip waited uneasily, concealing his humiliation, as the tragic farce of Mary's false pregnancy was played out. Nothing was said; no announcement was made to the

---

* Dr Weston's prayer suggests there may have been some knowledge in the sixteenth century of the causes of Down's Syndrome.

† Oral tradition at Hever Castle, where there is a full set of baby clothes which Elizabeth is supposed to have made.

crowd outside the palace, or to the lords and ladies who had come from all over the country to attend the royal birth.

On 3 August the Court moved to Oatlands, so that the Queen could re-emerge into public life with least embarrassment. At the end of the month Philip left to visit his father. The Emperor was preparing to retire to his monastery at Yuste. His son was at last to take over his great inheritance in Spain and the Netherlands, while his brother Ferdinand, King of the Romans, was to take the title of Holy Roman Emperor. On 29 September Licentiate Games, ambassador to Ferdinand, wrote from Brussels, 'As there is no hope of fruit from the English marriage, discussions are going on everywhere about the consort to be given to Elizabeth, who is and will continue to be lawful heir unless the King and Queen have issue.'

Elizabeth remained at Court, outwardly conforming to the Catholic religion. After Philip's departure she accompanied her sister to Greenwich, where the Queen had re-established the Friars Observant. Mary set a high example over the return of monastic land, setting up houses at Westminster, Sion and Sheen, but there was to be no fulfilment of that early vision shared by herself and Pole at the beginning of the reign. A full-scale return to the position of the 1520s would have been impossible. The Crown's revenues were scarcely enough to cover the administration and defence of the country as it was. Mary could not have survived without the funds that her father had so impiously directed into the royal exchequer. She plunged herself into a routine of prayer and fasting, waiting only for Philip's return. Elizabeth remained with her until October, when she at last gained permission to go to her own estates. Later that month Ridley and Latimer were burned in Oxford; soon Cranmer, her own godfather, would follow.

Throughout all this time Elizabeth experienced a sense of her own miraculous preservation, and a strengthening of her own religious faith. She had been absent from Hatfield and Ashridge for almost two years. Dispassionately she set about putting her own houses in order, the veil of discretion slipping only once as she penned a note to William Paulet, Marquis of Winchester, the old Lord Treasurer who had served her father and her brother, and who in her own reign would hold office until his death in 1572. It was almost the only time she ventured to criticise Mary openly, or to comment on her own eighteen-month ordeal as a prisoner of state, and it was a *cri de coeur* which rings eloquently down the centuries – no one had ever been so badly treated by their own family.

℃ My Lord,

With my hearty commendations I do most heartily desire you to further the Desires of my last letters that thereby the health of my mind and sickness may be the rather restored and as you were constrained to come the first unto me in the entry of my troubles so would I wish your self to be now the last that should freely end this same.

And for this my Lord I will most heartily thank you. And as you would I should assure myself of your Lordship's good will and friendship. For I evermore desire you that of myself and my own things and doings mine own words may stand in most credit with you and all my Lords for in the earth, my Lord, none of my state hath been and yet is, more misused with them of mine own family than myself. As knoweth God who judgeth all. And whom I pray to keep you.

At Ashridge this 29th day of October,

Your assured friend to my little power

Elizabeth

Anatomies of hearts

As soon as Elizabeth was re-established at Hatfield, Ascham, who was Latin secretary to the Queen despite his Protestant views and known friendship with Cheke in the previous reign, was recalled to his post as tutor. Elizabeth resumed her daily readings in Latin and Greek. The familiar mental discipline helped her regain her composure and ward off that 'sickness of mind' of which she had written to Paulet. Her household was still kept under careful scrutiny, for Mary never again fully trusted Elizabeth.

In the spring of 1556 Castiglione, her Italian tutor, was arrested for seditious behaviour, set free, and then arrested again. On the second occasion Katherine Ashley went with him to the Tower. A coffer full of Protestant tracts had been found in her bedchamber. Mary wrote to comfort Elizabeth in June 1556, assuring her of her goodwill and sending her a ring to show she was not personally suspected. She was however to be supervised; a new governess replaced Mrs Ashley, who was forbidden to go near Elizabeth, and on 16 June Giovanni Michiel, the Venetian ambassador, wrote to the Doge to say that Sir Thomas Pope, 'a rich and grave gentleman of good name', had been appointed as her governor. He was an urbane and scholarly man, much preoccupied at this time by his new foundation at Oxford, Trinity College, about which Elizabeth asked lively and intelligent questions. It was Michiel's opinion that she might be said to be 'in ward and custody though in such decorous and honourable form', as was becoming to her position as heiress to the throne. He records that Pope's custody lasted from June to October 1556, but Pope's biographer, Thomas Warton, suggests he was at Hatfield for a longer period, mentioning that on Shrove Tuesday 1556 he arranged a masque at his own expense to amuse Elizabeth. She was serenaded by twelve minstrels, while forty-six lords and ladies dressed in crimson satin embroidered with gold and pearls took part. There was a tournament, a banquet of seventy dishes and a play about Holofernes; but the Queen objected, requiring Sir Thomas to take his duties more seriously.

In August an impostor named Cleobury pretended to be Courtenay. At Yaxley in Sussex he proclaimed Elizabeth Queen and her 'beloved bedfellow', Lord Courtenay, King. Elizabeth wrote a long and loyal letter to Mary, expressing her sorrow that her name had once again been used in a plot of which she had no cognisance. Amidst the Latin quotations and circumlocutions, one metaphor stands out powerfully. Elizabeth wished there were surgeons 'for making anatomies of hearts', meaning she wished the Queen could see fully into hers. Clearly she was still troubled by the fact that Mary distrusted her, and once again her frustration at not being believed echoes through the centuries.

 C3 When I revolve in mind most noble Queen the old love of Paynims to their Prince and the reverent fear of Romans to their Senate, I can but muse for my part and blush for theirs to see the rebellious hearts and devilish intentions of Christians in name, but these in deed towards their anointed King. Which men if they had feared God though they could not have loved the state, they should for dread of their own plague have refrained from that wickedness which their bounden duty to your Majesty hath not restrained. But when I call to remembrance that the devil, *tamquam leo rugiens circumiit quaerens quem devorare potest*, I do the less marvel though he has gotten such novices into his professed house as vessels (without God's grace) more apt to serve his palace than fit to inhabit English land, I am the bolder to call them his imps, for that Saint Paul saith *seditiosi filii sunt diaboli*, and since I have so good a buckler, I fear the less to enter into their judgement.

Of this I assure your Majesty though it be my part above the rest to bewail such things though my name had not been in them. Yet it vexes me too much that the devil owes me such a hate as to put me in any part of his mischievous instigations, when as I profess him my foe, that is all Christians' enemy, so wish I, he had some other way invented to spite me. But since it has pleased God thus to bewray their malice before they finish their purpose, I most humbly thank him both that he has ever thus preserved your Majesty through his aid, much like a lamb from the horn of Basan's bulls; and also stirs up the hearts of your loving subjects to resist them and deliver you to his honour and their shame, the intelligence of which proceeding from your Majesty deserves more humble thanks than with my pen I can render, which as infinite I will leave to number.

And amongst earthly things I chiefly wish this, that there were as good surgeons for making anatomies of hearts that might show my thoughts to your Majesty as there are expert physicians of the bodies able to express the inward griefs of their maladies to their patient. For then I doubt not but know well that whatsoever others should suggest by malice, yet your Majesty should be sure by knowledge so that the more such misty clouds obfuscate the clear light of my truth, the more my tried thoughts should glister to the dimming of their hidden malice. But since wishes are vain and desires often false I must crave that my deeds may supply that [which] my thoughts cannot declare, and they be not misdeemed there as the facts have been so well tried. And like as I have been your faithful subject from the beginning of your reign, so shall no wicked person cause me to change to the end of my life. And thus I commit your Majesty to God's tuition, who I beseech long time to preserve, ending with this new remembrance of my old suit more for that it should not be forgotten than for that I think it not remembered.

   From Hatfield this present Sunday the second day of August.

   Your Majesty's obedient subject and humble sister,

Elizabeth

To the Queen's most Excellent Majesty.

Though I were offered to the greatest prince of all Europe

At the end of November 1556 Elizabeth arrived in London with a touch of her old style. She rode to Somerset Place with an escort of 200 horsemen and visited both Mary and Cardinal Pole. Courtenay had died in Padua in September. This cleared the field for Philip to put renewed pressure on Mary to persuade Elizabeth into a marriage with the Duke of Savoy. Various schemes had been suggested in the interests of preserving the Tudor-Habsburg alliance. Before the Emperor retired to his monastery they had included a proposal that Elizabeth should marry the Archduke Ferdinand, the son of Charles's brother, the King of the Romans, and more preposterously that she should wait for Philip's eleven-year-old son Don Carlos to grow up: it was not then known that the Spanish Infante had paranoid tendencies, bordering on madness. Drawn into war with France by Pope Paul IV's determination to expel the Habsburg armies from Italy, Philip had every motive for wishing to cement the English alliance, even though the terms of his own marriage with Mary expressly stated that England was not to be drawn into any war which Spain might be fighting with her hereditary enemies. Mary sought vainly to please her husband by beseeching Elizabeth to accept Emmanuel Philibert; but on 3 December Elizabeth withdrew to Hatfield with a great company of servants 'all in red, guarded with velvet', leaving the matter she had come to discuss characteristically unresolved.

   In March 1557 Philip returned to England. He had two main objectives to enlist England's aid in his war against France, and to marry Elizabeth to Emmanuel Philibert. Philip seems to have done everything in his power to encourage Mary to overcome her hostility to Elizabeth, despite the many dark hints thrown out by the Venetian ambassador that the Queen hated her half-sister and would stop at nothing to get her barred from the succession. Outwardly their relationship was impeccable.

Mary visited Hatfield and was entertained with a varied programme, including a play, a bear-baiting, and the singing of Maximilian Poynes, a famous boy soprano, who was accompanied by Elizabeth herself on the virginals. Mary gave a sumptuous garden party at Richmond, and Elizabeth sailed down the Thames in a barge garlanded with flowers to picnic in a pavilion embroidered with lilies and pome-granates.

During the spring of 1557 Philip invited his cousins, the two Spanish Duchesses of Parma and Lorraine, to England in the hope that they would convince Elizabeth of Emmanuel Philibert's charms. The ladies arrived at Westminster at the end of March and stayed with the King and Queen at Greenwich; but they left a month later and by 21 May the French King was rather gleefully commenting on their return to Spain with their mission unaccomplished. Towards the end of April 1557 Michiel had been transferred from London to Paris. He made a long report to the Doge and Senate at the end of his term in England, which includes a perceptive description of Elizabeth at twenty-three, and some trenchant observations on her bearing at Mary's Court. The Queen, he claimed, regarded her as 'the illegitimate child of a criminal, who was punished as a public strumpet': however, he approved of her fluent command of Italian and thought her:

CB Proud and haughty, as although she knows she was born of such a mother, she nevertheless does not consider herself of inferior degree to the Queen, whom she equals in self-esteem; nor does she believe herself less legitimate than her Majesty, alleging in her own favour that her mother would never cohabit with the King unless by way of marriage, with the authority of the Church, and the intervention of the Primate of England; so that even if deceived, having as a subject acted with good faith, the fact cannot have invalidated her mother's marriage nor her own birth, she having been born under that same faith . . . She prides herself on her father and glories in him; everybody saying that she also resembles him more than the Queen does and he therefore always liked her and had her brought up in the same way as the Queen.

Michiel estimated Elizabeth's income at 10,000 scudi: 'She now lives upon this settlement from her father, but is always in debt, and would be much more so did she not steadily restrain herself to avoid any increase of the Queen's hatred and anger, either by increasing the number of gentlemen servants of her household, or by adding to her expenditure in any other way; and here I may add that there is not a lord or gentleman in the kingdom who has failed, and continues endeavouring to enter her service himself or to place one of his sons or brothers in it, such being the love and affection borne her.' Her poverty, he said, incited 'a tacit compassion' and 'yet greater affection, as it seems strange and vexatious to everybody that being the daughter of a King she should be treated and acknowledged so sparingly'. In short, Elizabeth was of the stuff from which fairy-tale heroines are made, and at the time of the

Queen's pregnancy Michiel observed that she 'contrived to ingratiate herself with all the Spaniards and especially with the King, that ever since no one has favoured her more than he does'.

One of Michiel's duties in Paris was to attend the wedding of Mary Stuart and the Dauphin, a glittering occasion which delighted the French because their Kings had previously married abroad, bringing their wives home with them. 'On the same night the consummation took place,' Michiel recorded, 'the bride having completed her fifteenth year and the bridegroom being fourteen years old.' They were required to produce issue to assure the future of the Franco-Scottish alliance. The union of these two young people, coupled with Mary Stuart's claim to the English throne, spurred Philip, who had left England on 6 July 1557 and was based in Brussels, to press Emmanuel Philibert's suit. Matters came to a head when an ambassador arrived from Gustavas Vasa, King of Sweden, with a suggestion that Elizabeth should marry his son, Prince Erik. Ignorant of English etiquette, the Swedish ambassador went straight to Hatfield and proposed by proxy to Elizabeth herself. She prudently informed the Queen, who sent Sir Thomas Pope straight to Hatfield to ascertain Elizabeth's preferences. Despite Mary's hope that she was pregnant after Philip's short stay, the King cannot have held out much hope, so the continuation of the alliance with England rested wholly upon preserving his amity with Elizabeth. Sir Thomas arrived at Hatfield on 26 April, ostensibly to find out how Elizabeth felt about Prince Erik's proposal. He wrote at once to the Queen, so we probably have here a verbatim account of the interview:

CB Master Pope,

I require you after my most humble commendations to the Queen's Majesty to render unto the same like thanks that it pleased her highness of her goodness to conceive so well of my answer made to the same Messenger and herewithal of her princely consideration with such speed to commend you by your letters to signify the same unto me, who before remained wonderfully perplexed, fearing that her Majesty might mistake the same, for which her goodness I acknowledge myself bound to honour, serve, love and obey her highness, during my life requiring you also to say unto her Majesty that in the King my brother's time, there was offered me a very honourable marriage, or two, and ambassadors sent to treat with me touching the same, whereupon I made my humble suit unto his highness (as some of honour yet living can be testimonies) that it would like the same to give me leave with his grace's favour to remain in that estate I was [in], which of all others best liked and pleased me. And in good faith I pray you say unto her highness, I am even at this present of the same mind and so intend to continue, with her Majesty's favour. Assuring her highness I so well like this estate, as I persuade unto myself there is not any kind of life comparable unto it. And as concerning my liking the said motion made by the said messenger, I beseech you, say unto her majesty, that to my remembrance I never heard of this matter before this time and that I so well like both the message and the messenger, as I shall most humbly pray God upon my knees that from henceforth I never hear of the one, nor the other. Assure you that if it should eftsoons repair unto me I would forbear to speed him. And were there nothing else to move me to mislike the motion other than that his master would attempt the same without making the Queen's Majesty privy thereunto, it were cause sufficient.

Pope reported that at this point in the tirade he was bold enough to enquire if she might not be well content to marry if some honourable match offered. He received a foretaste of the magnificently prevaricating reply that she was to give again and again in the next decade, when pressed by her own Council and Commons. The language is startlingly similar to the speeches she was soon to make to the first and second Parliaments of her reign.

CB What I shall do hereafter I know not, but I assure you upon my truth and fidelity, and as God be merciful unto me, I am not at this present [time] otherwise minded than I have declared unto you, no, though I were offered to the greatest prince of all Europe. And yet percase the Queen's Majesty may perceive this my answer rather to proceed of a maidenly shamefastness than upon any certain determination.

CHAPTER V

Whensoever time and power may serve

Calais was lost on 7 January 1558. It had been an English possession for over two hundred years, and was of immense strategic and commercial importance. The blow to national pride was severe, the blow to Anglo-Spanish relations even worse. The English blamed the Spaniards for not coming to their aid, for Philip had an army less than twenty miles away at Gravelines which could easily have been mobilised. The Spaniards thought the English negligent, as they had been warned that the French might attack, but they had taken no adequate precautions. If Holinshed, writing twenty years after the event, is to be trusted, the defeat was a bitter blow to Mary Tudor, who said shortly before her final illness,

'When I am dead and opened, you will find Calais lying in my heart.'

Philip had left for the Netherlands in July 1557 with ten thousand English soldiers. No such force had crossed the Channel since Henry VIII had embarked for Boulogne. The combined English and Habsburg armies invaded France from the north-east, winning a decisive battle at St Quentin in Picardy on 10 August. This was partly due to the able generalship of Emmanuel Philibert. *Te Deum* was offered thankfully in London, where religious processions of a more sombre nature had become a regular sight, as the burning of heretics increased with Mary's ardent desire to purge her realm from Protestant error. As early as February 1555 Renard had been alarmed by the severity of the persecutions. He wrote to the Emperor, warning him that the Spaniards would be blamed for a policy which in his view emanated from the zeal of Gardiner, Pole and Mary herself. In March 1555 one of Philip's chaplains, Alonso de Castro, preached a sermon at Court condemning religious persecution, but Mary saw herself as the saviour of men's souls. She would purge with earthly fire to save her people from eternal damnation.

Although the burnings could not stop the spread of heresy, and the Protestants continued to hold secret prayer meetings, the outcome of St Quentin seemed to Mary and a 'handful of priests in white rochets' to be linked with her attempt to root out heresy. In a literally-minded age, victory in battle was a sign of God's favour. Henry II withdrew the French forces. He was facing bankruptcy, and Philip's own resources were severely strained by maintaining such large armies. At St Quentin he had put forty thousand men in the field. As the autumn of 1557 approached, both sides prepared to go into winter quarters according to the time-honoured rules of European warfare.

Mary spent Christmas at Greenwich that year. On 22 December Lord Grey, commander of the fortress at Guisnes, the largest stronghold apart from Calais itself on the twenty-five-mile strip of coast which belonged to England, wrote to the Council, having heard a rumour that the French were planning an advance. He requested immediate reinforcements. On 29 December Lord Wentworth, the Governor of Calais, wrote that he thought he was strong enough to hold the town. In the midst of the Christmas festivities the Privy Council did not treat Grey's request seriously enough. On the 31st the French commander, the powerful Duke of Guise, brother of the Regent of Scotland and uncle of Mary Stuart, the future Dauphine, invaded the Marches of Calais.

Guise moved his troops forward in small detachments, so that the size of the advance was not fully perceived until it was too late. By 3 January only Calais and Guisnes held out. Guise commanded some twenty thousand troops. Lord Wentworth had a garrison of two thousand. On 2 January Mary ordered the levying of as many men as possible to go to the relief of her commanders. On the 7th, unaware that Wentworth had already surrendered, she wrote to the Lords-Lieutenant of every shire, urging them immediately to raise men for the succour of 'Calais, the chief jewel of the realm'. The expedition had almost taken on the significance of a Crusade. The English soldiers were to be clothed in white coats with red crosses, and the Queen was very sorry when these were not ready in time.

On 9 January she ordered the vice-admiral, Sir William Woodhouse, to repair to the Narrow Seas with as many ships as he could requisition, 'the French King having besieged the town of Calais'. The Earl of Rutland had in fact got as far as Dover with a force of some two thousand men. He did not cross the Channel, however, and the Council heard on the 13th that a storm had damaged the fleet. The French had already taken Lord Wentworth and his garrison prisoners, but the news seems to have taken some time to reach England. On the 19th Lord Admiral Howard was ordered to repair the fleet, and it was not until 28 January that the Queen, 'Calais being lost', gave orders for Sir Thomas Cheyne to keep Dover garrisoned, but to send home the men who were to have gone to help Wentworth and Grey. We have no record of how Elizabeth reacted to the devastating news. She must have sent messages of condolence to Mary, but none have come to light.

Philip sent Count Feria, one of his most trusted diplomats, to England at the end of January, ostensibly to discuss plans for the recovery of Calais. The discussions continued through February and March. On 13 February Lord Clinton replaced Howard as Lord Admiral. He had served with distinction under Edward, and he and Paget believed it might be possible to recapture the lost territory, but the prevailing opinion in the Council was that England could not afford to continue the war. Calais could only be recovered if Philip would fund the operation. All available English troops were needed to man the Scottish border, and defend the coast in case the Danes and the Hanseatic towns should attack. Feria was shocked by the mood of despondency. He continued to press Paget and Clinton to organise the recapture of Calais, and wrote to Philip on 1 May urging him to make Mary raise an army, 'for when the English see that your Majesties are determined to avenge the insult of Calais,' he assured the King, 'they will help.' 'No prince', he added philosophically, 'ever begins a war with all the money he is going to need to finish it.'

At the beginning of Mary's reign, she had confidently believed that the Habsburg alliance would bring wealth to England. By the middle of 1557 inflation was worse than ever recorded. A working man's wage is generally quoted as having risen from fourpence a day to sevenpence. Beef however was fourpence a pound, eggs had risen to a startling price of two for a penny, so that a dozen would account for almost the whole of a man's daily pay. John Ponet, the former Bishop of Winchester, who had fled abroad at the end of Edward's reign, wrote a forceful pamphlet, *A Short Treatise of Politic Power*, in which he described the people of England being 'driven of hunger to grind acorns for bread meal, and to drink water instead of ale'. At Court the Spanish pensions with which Philip had hoped to buy the loyalty of Mary's leading councillors were mostly twelve months in arrears by the beginning of 1558, although Feria reminded Philip to keep up those which he considered most vital, in particular to the Admirals, Lord William Howard, and later Clinton.

After Philip's short stay in the summer of 1557 Mary desperately longed to be pregnant, although it was obvious to most of those who were close to her that she was past the age of child-bearing. This time she did not announce the news, as, she said, she wished to be absolutely certain that she was not mistaken. Her ladies reported no swollen womb, or rounding of the breasts, but Mary clung pathetically to the notion that she was with child. In March 1558 she added a codicil to her will in the belief that there would be a last-minute miracle, or that Philip would return to solace her and produce the longed-for heir. The Crown was to go, she directed, to the 'heirs, issue and fruit of my body according to the laws of the realm'. Philip was to be guardian both of the heir and the realm. It was eight months since the King had left her and, although he did not realise that Mary was soon to die, he certainly did not share her hope of issue.

By May, Mary Tudor was a sick woman. Abstemious and hard-working all her life she was, at forty-two, careworn and prematurely aged. Philip's departure, the loss of Calais and her failure to produce an heir to carry on the work she had accomplished in bringing England back to the Catholic religion were the causes of severe depression. Feria commented that she was given to frequent outbursts of weeping. She continued to observe all the fasts in the church calendar, which probably added to the deterioration of her health. She also stubbornly refused to recognise her sister as her successor. Philip had instructed Feria to ingratiate himself with Elizabeth, and he visited her in June, two months after Mary Stuart's marriage to the Dauphin and Elizabeth's refusal to consider either Erik of Sweden or Emmanuel Philibert as suitors.

The count reported that she was 'much pleased, and I also, for reasons I will tell your Majesty, when I arrive over there'. He went to join Philip in the Netherlands in July, but by October Mary was seriously ill, probably with cancer of the ovaries. uneasy at the prospect of Mary Stuart's claim being pressed by the French, Philip sent his confessor, Francisco Bernardo de Fresneda, to try to persuade his wife to accept Elizabeth as lawful heiress to the English Crown. According to Jane Dormer, one of Mary's ladies who later married Feria, the Queen was outraged, calling her sister a bastard, the daughter of an adulteress, and more likely to be Mark Smeaton's child than Henry VIII's. Later that month Charles V died, and three weeks afterwards his sister, Mary of Hungary, died too. Cardinal Pole was sick with a quartan ague at Lambeth, and as Mary Tudor lay dying at Whitehall, they sent messages of comfort to each other. When he realised how ill she was, Philip sent his own physician, Dr Nuñez, to England. He also sent Feria on a second mission, this time with specific instructions that he was to establish full diplomatic contact with Elizabeth, whom Mary at last acknowledged as her heir.

Feria arrived in London on 9 November at midday. The Queen was happy to see him, but he thought she had only a few more days to live. As soon as it was known that Mary was dying, every family of note sent representatives to Hatfield to offer their services to Elizabeth. The Hertfordshire roads were nearly impassable, and Surian, the Venetian ambassador with King Philip, heard that 'many personages of the Kingdom flocked to the house of Miladi Elizabeth, the crowd constantly increasing with great frequency'. She had retreated to the house of her neighbour, Sir John Brocket, which was where Feria visited her on 10 November. In the event of any military necessity arising, Brocket Hall seems to have been ear-marked as an operational headquarters, for despite Elizabeth's tremendous popularity, it was by no means certain that she could expect to take over peacefully. There is evidence that she was quite prepared to make a show of force: Thomas Markham reminded her, many years later, that at the time of Mary's death he had been in charge of three hundred foot soldiers at Berwick-upon-Tweed, and he had received instructions from Thomas Parry that they were to be marched down to Brocket Hall. Offers of assistance were arriving daily and Elizabeth was obviously kept busy dictating instructions, memoranda and swift thank-you notes to an overworked secretary, whose calligraphy deteriorated under the strain.

One such note, dated Brocket Hall, 28 October 1553, is preserved in the British Library. The secretary had scribbled with such haste that the writing is barely legible. It is a thank-you letter for an offer of service, and there is no indication to whom it is addressed, but in the top left-hand corner in Elizabeth's most careful handwriting is added, 'Your very loving friend Elizabeth.'

This winning personal touch may have caused the recipient to treasure the scrap of paper for many years, but what is chiefly interesting is that three weeks before her accession either Elizabeth, or the secretary, had already slipped into the idiom more usually reserved for a reigning sovereign. The note is written throughout in the royal plural.

C♋ Our right hearty commendations.

We have thought good to address these few lines unto you to render like thanks for your gentleness and the readiness and endeavour of your good will to do unto us all the pleasure you can, which we sufficiently understand. You may well assure yourself that we neither do, nor can, forget the same. Whensoever time and power may serve, you shall well find upon promise at our hands, God willing, to whom we remember yourself.

To make a good account to Almighty God

Two remarkable documents relating to the three weeks preceding Elizabeth's accession, when Mary lay dying and Philip was still King of England, survive in the Spanish archive at Simancas. They are a letter written intermittently between early November and 4 December by Philip to his sister Joanna, Princess Dowager of Portugal and Regent of Spain, and Feria's own despatch, which he finished on 14 November, after his visit to Elizabeth at Brocket Hall and immediately after hearing Mary Tudor had received Extreme Unction. Philip has frequently been described as coldly impassive, too well schooled by his early mentor Zuniga ever to let real feelings break through the façade of princely dignity, but in the letter to Joanna, begun just after their father died, he gave vent to a rare outburst of emotion.

'When this [Charles's death] had happened, came the death of the Queen of Hungary, my aunt. You may imagine what a state I am in. It seems to me that everything is being taken from me at once. Blessed be the Lord for what he does! One must say nothing but accept his will . . . The Queen, my wife has been ill; and although she has recovered somewhat, her infirmities are such that grave fears must be entertained on her score, as a physician I sent to her with Count Feria writes to me. All these happenings are perplexing to me.'

He was worried about the government of the Netherlands and pondering '. . . on what I must do in England, in the event either of the Queen's survival or her death, for these are questions of the greatest importance on which the welfare of my realms depends. I will say nothing of my own peace and quiet, which matters little in this connection.'

He went on to write of the proposed peace with France. It was not to be completed until the Treaty of Câteau Cambrésis the following year, but preliminary negotiations were already under way. The French, Philip complained, were changeable and they 'had tried to snatch every possible advantage. They are so far determined not to give back Calais.'

Philip felt a profound responsibility towards England. He in no way wished to relinquish his hold over a territory which linked the Habsburg dominions in Spain and the Netherlands so conveniently, but in the raw time of grief after Charles's death he revealed to Joanna that he was aware of his failings as King of England, and that he felt partly to blame for the loss of Calais.

'I have been unwilling to consider any solution without the English, for to do so would be a very heavy load for me to carry. To conclude peace without the return of Calais would make the whole kingdom of England rise in indignation against me, although they lost the place by their own fault when I had warned them the French were going to attack, and had offered them reinforcements many days before the attack took place. But as England went to war on my account, I am obliged to pay great attention to this matter. If God were to call the Queen, it would be especially necessary to keep the English satisfied for many reasons . . .'

This thought had also occurred to Philip's beautiful young sister-in-law, as she waited on her estate at Hatfield for the moment when she could exploit the unpopularity of the Spaniards to her own advantage. Philip probably liked Elizabeth. It was well known that he had interceded for her when Mary's rage against her was at its height. He also recognised her acumen and may have hoped that she would accept Feria as an adviser on European affairs, as Mary had accepted Renard.

On his arrival at Brocket Hall, the count was invited to dine with Elizabeth. Lady Clinton, the Admiral's wife, was present. Probably the company drank quite a lot, since Feria wrote that during the meal 'we laughed and enjoyed ourselves a great deal'. Elizabeth then sent most people out of the room, except for two or three ladies, who spoke only English. Together she and Feria pored over the instructions written in Philip's own hand. She promised to maintain good relations with him, while Feria repeated Philip's promise that he would always be her good friend, touching on the ancient amity between England and Burgundy, and elaborating on why she should consider the King as her true brother.

'I gave her to understand', he wrote, 'that it was your Majesty who had procured her recent recognition as the Queen's sister and successor, and not the Queen or the Council, and this was something your Majesty had been trying to secure for some time, as she no doubt realised, for it was common knowledge in the whole kingdom; and I condemned the Queen and the Council severely.' He then tried to draw Elizabeth out by talking innocuously about general topics. Nor did he have to try hard, for either Elizabeth was carried away by her own sense of elation, or she had drunk enough at dinner to throw caution to the winds.

The ambassador was taken aback by her frankness. He wrote:

'She is a very vain and clever woman. She must have been thoroughly schooled in the manner in which her father conducted his affairs, and I am very much afraid that she will not be well disposed in matters of religion, for I see her inclined to govern through men, who are believed to be heretics, and I am told that all the women around her definitely are . . . She puts great store by the people who put her in her present position, and she will not acknowledge that your Majesty or the nobility of this realm had any part in it, although, as she herself says, they have all sent her assurances of their loyalty . . . There is not a heretic or traitor in all the kingdom, who has not joyfully raised himself from the grave to come to her side. She is determined to be governed by no one.'

Feria sent Philip a detailed list of the councillors he believed Elizabeth would retain: Archbishop Heath, the Lord Chancellor; Paget and Petre; Sir John Mason, the Treasurer of the Chamber; Dr Nicholas Wotton, the chief negotiator at Câteau Cambrésis; Lord Admiral Clinton, and her own great-uncle, Lord William Howard. He named Lord Grey, who had been taken prisoner by the French after his defence of Guisnes, and he noted that she did not get on well with the Earls of Arundel and Pembroke, nor with Thomas Thirlby, the Bishop of Ely. She also disliked the two councillors who had been sent to fetch her from Ashridge when she was ill in February 1554, Lord Edward Hastings and Sir Thomas Cornwallis. 'With Boxall', he wrote, 'her relations are worse, and with the cardinal worst of all. I fear she will cause his downfall.'

The ambassador counselled Elizabeth not to display a desire for revenge or anger against anyone, and for a few moments it seemed that the interview would take on the colour of the early conversations between Mary and Renard, the practised European diplomat advising the frail, feminine and politically naïve Princess. Elizabeth's nerves must have been strung to breaking point for, giving sudden vent to her frustration, she told Feria all she wanted to do was to make the councillors who had wronged her admit they had done so. Then, she explained, she would pardon them.

Feria found her honesty unnerving. He believed she would favour the Earl of Bedford; Lord Robert Dudley; Sir Nicholas Throckmorton; Peter Carew, imprisoned for his part in the 1554 rebellion, but redeemed in Mary's eyes by his gallant conduct at St Quentin. He also mentioned John Harington, a former retainer of Thomas Seymour, and he told Philip that it was a foregone conclusion that Cecil would be appointed Secretary of State. The count then related how he had turned the conversation to the question of the Spanish pensions. Philip was still King of England. He had given orders as a matter of course for those in receipt of his funds to serve Elizabeth loyally, so the ambassador was caught completely off balance when she asked sharply for a list of the pensioners, 'in order to decide whether it was right or not that they should be receiving money from your Majesty'. This shed an entirely new light on the future relations between England and Spain. Feria pretended not to notice Elizabeth's hostile tone, saying he would give her a list of the pensioners so that she could decide who should be added, and who left out.

The interview began to develop into a comedy of wits. Elizabeth grumbled that she had never had anything but the £3,000 a year her father had left her in 1546 to survive on, and Feria sweetly turned the tables by saying that she should have brought the matter to Philip's attention earlier. They then spoke of the jewels which Mary had given to Philip at the time of the wedding. Elizabeth assumed a tone of authority but the count regained the upper hand by gently pointing out that Philip had given

Mary far grander presents than she had given him. The jewels included the gold and enamel insignia of the Order of the Garter, which were heavily encrusted with gem stones. They had been left in a treasure chest at Whitehall. Philip later offered them as a present, which cut down the diplomatic haggling and saved the need for them to be sent to Brussels or Madrid under naval and military escort.

After all these preliminaries had been disposed of, Feria turned to the main topic of his visit. Although peace negotiations had been started with the French, he assured Elizabeth that Philip would not conclude them until the English were satisfied. She showed her relief and the count wrote that 'she made it very clear' that she would have the commissioners 'beheaded if they made peace without Calais'. There was a little more sparring over Emmanuel Philibert and the question of Philip's popularity in the country, then Feria asked outright what he should do when Mary died. He thought he should go to Elizabeth, wherever she might be. She told him to wait until he was sent for.

After a brief description of his visit to Cardinal Pole, and a report of a conversation with Paget, who had declined to discuss the topic of Elizabeth's marriage, muttering that he had arranged Mary's and got little thanks for it, Feria spelled out Philip's position to him with considerable misgivings:

'Four years ago your Majesty could have disposed of Madam Elizabeth by marrying her off to someone of your own choosing. Now she will marry whomsoever she desires and your Majesty has no power to influence her decision . . . Madam Elizabeth already sees herself as the next Queen, and having come to the conclusion, that she would have succeeded, even if your Majesty and the Queen had opposed it, she does not feel indebted to your Majesty in this matter. It is impossible to persuade her otherwise than that the kingdom will not consent to anything else, and would take up arms on her behalf. A great offence has been done to your Majesty by the Queen our lady's acceptance of her, as both sister and successor.'

He guessed that Elizabeth intended to conclude the peace with France, and then to maintain good relations with both Spain and France, 'without tying herself to either party'. He recommended that Philip should get her to stop the pensions, and then offer them secretly to those who resented their cessation, thus buying a valuable espionage network. Feria ended the despatch on 14 November, twenty-four hours after Mary had received the Sacrament of Extreme Unction.

The Queen died on 17 November. Cardinal Pole died twelve hours later. Elizabeth had moved back to Hatfield, and she is supposed to have been standing under an oak tree in the park when the messengers came to her carrying Mary's Coronation Ring. She knelt on the grass and spoke the opening words of Psalm 118, '*A domino factum est et mirabile in oculis nostris.*' There were three days of conventional mourning, during which Archbishop Heath announced Elizabeth's accession in London and the Council members rode to Hatfield, where there was scarcely space to accommodate them all. On 20 November they assembled in the Great Hall, together with all the other nobles who had come to do homage. If any were present who had made private arrangements with Feria for the renewal of their Spanish pensions, they must have squirmed inwardly as she formally appointed William Cecil Secretary of State.

'I give you this charge,' she said, 'that you shall be of my Privy Council and content yourself to take pains for me and my realm. This judgement I have of you, that you will not be corrupted with any manner of gift and that you will be faithful to the State, and that without respect of my private will, you will give me that counsel that you think best: and, if you shall know anything necessary to be declared to me of secrecy, you shall show it to myself only and assure yourself I will not fail to keep taciturnity therein. And therefore herewith I charge you.'

Then she turned to the great company before her and with the utmost simplicity, pledged herself to be their Queen.

CB My Lords, the law of nature moveth me to sorrow for my sister: the burden that is fallen upon me maketh me amazed, and yet, considering I am God's creature, ordained to obey his appointment, I will thereto yield, requiring from the bottom of my heart, that I may have assistance of his grace, to be the minister of his heavenly will in this office now committed to me. And as I am but one body naturally considered, though by his permission, a body politic to govern, so I shall require you all, my Lords (chiefly you of the Nobility every one in his degree and power), to be assistant to me, that I with my ruling, and you with your service, may make a good account to Almighty God, and leave some comfort to our posterity in earth.

I mean to direct all mine actions by good advice and counsel, and therefore at this present, considering that divers of you be of the ancient nobility having your beginnings and estates of my progenitors, Kings of this realm, and thereby ought in honour to have the more natural care for the maintaining of my estate and this commonwealth. Some others have been of long experience in governance and ennobled by my father of noble memory, my brother and my late sister to bear office. The rest of you being upon special trust lately called to her service only, and for your service considered and rewarded.

My meaning is to require of you all nothing more but faithful hearts, in such service as from time to time shall be in your powers towards the preservation of me and this commonwealth. And for counsel and advice I shall accept you of my nobility and such others of you the rest as in consultation, I shall think meet, and shortly appoint; to the which also with their advice I will join to their aid and for ease of their burden, others meet for my service. And they which I shall not appoint, let them not think the same for any disability in them, but for that I consider a multitude doth make rather disorder and confusion than good counsel, and of my good will you shall not doubt, using yourselves as appertaineth to good and loving subjects.

That I should continue your good Lady and Queen

It was a reassuring speech; it made no promises, it told no lies, but it gave Elizabeth and Cecil the time they needed to get the machinery of government under control, and to assess the dependability of the Marian councillors they wished to retain in office. The next three days were filled with intensive business meetings. Parry was knighted and made Controller of the Household. It was his immediate responsibility to get everyone safely to London. Among those who came to do homage at Hatfield, a splendidly caparisoned figure rode into the picture with consummate timing. Lord Robert Dudley had been one of the childhood companions of Edward VI. He had also been a prisoner in the Tower at the same time as Elizabeth. He was married to Amy Robsart, and both Elizabeth and Edward had been guests at his wedding. Dudley was made Master of the Horse; his talents were put to use at once, organising the State Entry into London. The cavalcade of over a thousand people left Hatfield on 23 November. Elizabeth, and as many of the household as could be accommodated, stayed at Lord North's house at the Barbican until the Palace of Whitehall could be made ready. On 28 November she made her triumphal entry into the City. The Londoners gave her a rapturous welcome with gun salutes, fanfares of trumpets and speeches of praise, as she rode first to the Tower, and then to Somerset Place, where she remained until 23 December, when she moved to Whitehall for Christmas.

The new government had no wish to deal with controversial religious questions until the Queen was safely crowned. Mary was buried with full Catholic rites on 14 December. Preaching the funeral oration, John White, the Bishop of Winchester, predicted accurately that religious disturbance would be inevitable. 'The wolves', he said, 'be coming out of Geneva and other places in Germany.' They had already sent ahead 'their books full of pestilent doctrines, blasphemy and heresy to infect the people'. It was reported that when Elizabeth received letters of congratulation from Bullinger and Peter Martyr, whose writings she had read so eagerly in Edward's reign, she wept with relief.

However, she did nothing precipitate. In the Accession Proclamation the 'etcetera', which Mary had used instead of the distasteful title 'Supreme Head', was left ambiguously in place. This may not have been as significant as is sometimes suggested. Heath, as Lord Chancellor, had read out the Proclamation at Westminster. Even if Cecil had tried to revive the Edwardian style, it is unlikely that Heath would have countenanced it and, as Archbishop of York, he was automatically senior prelate after Pole's death. The title was amended on 15 January, the day of the Coronation, to an even more ambiguous 'Defender of the true ancient and Catholic Faith'. On 27 December a proclamation was issued forbidding all unlicensed preaching. The Epistles and Gospels, the Ten Commandments, the Creed and the Lord's Prayer could be said in English, but otherwise the Latin Mass was still the only legal service in the land.

On Christmas Day, in her own chapel at Whitehall, Elizabeth asked Owen Oglethorpe, the Bishop of Carlisle, to refrain from elevating the host. It was a testimony to his courage that he refused to comply, and she, to show her displeasure, walked out of the Mass as soon as the Gospel was finished. Often interpreted as her way of 'giving a sign' to the Protestants of her intention to revert to the Edwardian service, the incident was more probably the release of five years' pent up spiritual anguish. She was Queen in her own country, and on Christmas morning she could not worship her maker in the clear, pure way of her girlhood. What to Mary had always been the supreme moment of mystic union with the power of God was to Elizabeth a piece of irrelevant mummery. The impatient gesture, which two months previously would have been enough to get any man or woman in England burned at the stake, hardened the bishops' opposition to her, and in their eyes branded her as a Sacramentarian. It was with the greatest reluctance that Oglethorpe agreed to crown her. The Archbishop of York had refused outright.

On the eve of the Coronation she made the traditional procession through London. There were shows and pageants at every turn in the route, and Elizabeth, whose sense of theatre was at its peak, responded to them all. As she left the Tower, she paused before getting into her chariot to offer up a spontaneous prayer:

'O Lord Almighty and Everlasting God, I give thee most hearty thanks that thou hast been so merciful unto me to spare me to behold this joyful day. And I acknowledge that thou hast dealt as wonderfully and as mercifully with me as thou didst with thy true and faithful servant Daniel, thy prophet whom thou delivered out of the den from the cruelty of the greedy and raging lions. Even so was I overwhelmed and only by thee delivered. To thee therefore only be thanks honour and praise forever. Amen.'

It was the first of many such prayers she was to make at moments of heightened emotion throughout her reign. Cynics may think she played to the gallery, never missing an opportunity to advance her own propaganda, but this is to misunderstand the well-spring of Elizabeth's nature. Despite the sophistication of her upbringing, she retained a natural inner simplicity and had a happy gift of suiting words and images to the occasion. Her hearers must have been delighted by the reference to the miraculous escape of the prophet Daniel. Furthermore the menagerie in the Tower which boasted real lions enhanced the aptitude of the comparison.*

The procession moved off and the Londoners roared their approval. At Fenchurch the crowd made such a noise that they drowned the words of the child who was to welcome Elizabeth on behalf of the whole City. She called for silence and listened

---

* Letter from Annibale Litolfi, an Italian traveller: 'On entering the Tower there is a seraglio in which from grandeur they keep lions, and tigers and cat lions.'

to the doggerel verses with 'a perpetual attentiveness in her face' and 'a marvellous change of look as the child's words touched her person'. At Gracechurch Street three stages towered above each other supporting figures of Henry VII, Elizabeth of York, Henry VIII, Anne Boleyn and Elizabeth herself. The whole pageant was decorated with red and white roses, and in case anyone had missed the point, an inscription proclaimed 'the uniting of the Two Houses of Lancaster and York'. The citizens felt no qualms about her descent. At Cheapside there was a tableau of Father Time and his daughter Truth. 'Time,' quipped Elizabeth, 'ay and time hath brought me hither.'

Ranulph Cholmely, the Recorder of London, presented her with a purse of crimson satin, containing 1,000 gold marks. She made an impromptu speech:

'I thank my Lord Mayor, his brethren and you all. And whereas your request is that I should continue your good lady and Queen, be ye ensured that I will be as good unto you as ever Queen was unto her people. No will in me can lack, neither do I trust shall there lack any power. And persuade yourselves that for the safety and quietness of you all I will not spare if need be to spend my blood. God thank you all.'

At Little Conduit, a child was holding a book. Anticipating its presentation Elizabeth sent Sir John Perrot forward to receive it, until it was explained that the climax of the action was to be when the book, an English Bible, was lowered down to her from the pageant on a silken thong. She moved her chariot closer and when the descent had been safely engineered, she held the book aloft, kissed it and laid it on her breast. All was theatre: 'So that if a man should say well, he could not better term the city of London', wrote one observer, 'than a stage wherein was showed the wonderful spectacle of a noble hearted princess toward her most loving people.'

There were six pageants in all, mostly following themes from the Old Testament or the popular morality plays. Il Schifanoya, a minor Italian diplomat writing to the Castellan of Mantua, was quick to catch their intensely Protestant significance. The second pageant, he reported, had 'a very extravagant inscription, purporting that hitherto religion had been misunderstood and misdirected and that now it will proceed on a better footing'. An enthroned Queen dominated the pageant, surrounded on one side by 'many persons clad in various fashions with labels inscribed *Religio pura; Justicia gubernandi; Intelligentia; Sapientia; Prudentia; Timor Dei*. On the other side, hinting I believe at the past, were Ignorance, Superstition, Hypocrisy, Vain Glory, Simulation, Rebellion and Idolatry.'*

Time and Truth were mounted on an open stage with scenery painted to represent a cragged and barren landscape on the north side, with a withered tree and the legend '*Ruinosa Respublica*', while on the south side there was a fair, fresh green meadow, 'full of flowers and beauty', with a sign to explain that it was '*Respublica bene instituta*'.†

---

* Il Schifanoya picked up the political significance of the Time/Truth pageant immediately. 'The whole implied in their tongue that the withered mount was the past state, and the green one the present and that time for gathering the fruits of truth was come.'

† The anonymous author of *The Passage of our dread Sovereign Lady* pamphlet described the *Ruinosa Respublica* and the *Respublica bene instituta* scene more diplomatically. Significantly the pamphlet was published

The fifth pageant showed Deborah dispensing justice, and the sixth explained the other five. It has been suggested that the verse spoken by the many children who took part was the 'poetry of Bottom the weaver', but only the English translations were naïve.

The guilds and citizens had spared no expense; the inscriptions painted on the stages and wagons were in best municipal Latin. At St Paul's one of the schoolboys spoke a Latin oration with great sophistication, comparing Elizabeth to Plato's philosopher kings. When the child had finished he kissed the parchment on which his speech was written and handed it to her reverently. She took it 'most gently', remembering perhaps how at thirteen she had herself penned the Latin preface for her father – 'a King whom philosophers regard as a god upon earth'.

The Coronation took place the next day on a crisp winter morning with a hint of snow in the air. The City went wild with enthusiasm. In a gown of cloth of gold she sat in a chariot draped with crimson velvet over which four knights held a canopy. She wore her hair as her mother had done twenty-five years earlier, unbraided and hanging loosely about her shoulders, which were covered with a cape of finest ermine. The 'chariot' was a litter supported by two sturdy mules, and open-sided so that the spectators could get the best possible view. Lord Robert Dudley rode immediately behind her leading a white palfrey, while his brother Lord Ambrose and Lord Giles Paulet led the mules. There must have been exacting rehearsals, for the canopy bearers had to synchronise their movements precisely with that of the mules, so that the two sections did not part company. As the procession reached Westminster Abbey, the crowd surged forward to grab pieces of the purple carpet upon which Elizabeth had walked, nearly upsetting the young Duchess of Norfolk who carried her train, and leaving the other court ladies to gather up the hems of their fine gowns and drag them across the gravel as best they could.

A book of sketches showing the order of the procession survives in the Egerton Manuscript. It was obviously made as an official plan of the proceedings, either by someone at the College of Arms, or by someone from the Lord Marshal's department, and it was to act as a guide for all those taking part. The sketches show the procession from the Tower to Whitehall, and the one from the palace to the Abbey. A plan of the Abbey is included, showing the layout for the ceremony, including the cushions for the anointing, the dais for the crowning and the kneeling stool from which the Queen would say her prayers.

Margaret Douglas, Countess of Lennox, who as Margaret of Scotland's daughter was next in blood, was expected to bear Elizabeth's train, but if Il Schifanoya's account is accurate, there was a last-minute change of plan, and the Duchess of Norfolk was chosen instead. After the anointing, the Queen was to withdraw into

---

on 23 January, the date on which Parliament was originally scheduled to begin. This perhaps suggests that it had quasi-official approval, or that the author and the printer R. Tothill hoped for a wide circulation among the Members.

a traverse, or private closet, to the right of St Edward's Chapel, where her ladies would divest her of the white garments she had worn in case the oil spilled, reclothing her in the purple velvet Coronation robes. It has been suggested that Elizabeth might have withdrawn into the traverse to avoid the moment when Oglethorpe elevated the host. This is to discount Il Schifanoya's assertion that Mass was celebrated at the Abbey by her own chaplain, because she had already fallen out with the bishops who would not omit the elevation. The Epistle and Gospel, he said, were recited in English and thereafter Oglethorpe carried out the Coronation 'according to the Roman ceremonial neither altering or omitting anything'.

Il Schifanoya seems to have been present at the ceremony. He noted the buffet set in the Abbey itself with 140 gold and silver drinking vessels, and he gave a vivid account of the moment when the bishop asked the congregation if they wanted Elizabeth as their Queen: 'Whereupon they all shouted "Yes"; and the organs, fifes, trumpets and drums playing, the bells also ringing, it seemed as if the world would come to an end.'

The Italian clearly considered himself a great expert on ceremonial matters. As Elizabeth came out of the Abbey holding the orb and the sceptre, she smiled so much at the crowds that he thought she 'exceeded the bounds of gravity and decorum'.

The banquet took place in Westminster Hall. The Duke of Norfolk as Lord Marshal, and the Earl of Arundel, who was the Lord Steward, rode about the hall in medieval fashion on finely caparisoned horses, excluding anyone who was not officially invited. The duke had taken off his coronet and was in silver tissue. The earl wore cloth of gold and carried a silver staff, and on that day took precedence over the duke. All the peers and peeresses kept their coronets on, except at one moment when Elizabeth stood up and drank their healths, thanking them for the trouble they had taken. Il Schifanoya did not think much of the music, having heard better in Italy, but the English guests were less critical and the banqueting went on until one in the morning.

CHAPTER VI

A marble stone shall declare that a Queen lived and died a virgin

In retrospect the famous words which Elizabeth asked Sir John Mason, the Member for Hampshire, to deliver to the House of Commons, when they asked her to marry, sound prophetic. At the time they were uttered they were dismissed as a piece of feminine coquetry, wrapped up in royal rhetoric. Parliament was convened for 23 January 1559. Elizabeth, who had confirmed everybody's opinion of her youth and frivolity by holding Court daily and dancing until late into the night, went down with a cold. On account of her ill-health and the appalling weather, the official opening was postponed until the 25th. As the Members battled along the snow-covered roads to the capital, the patriotic author of the pamphlet describing the Queen's triumphant passage through the city before the Coronation briskly turned his work in to the printer. It went into three editions. As it quoted all the sage verses the Londoners had emblazoned on the pageants, it combined the virtues of a popular souvenir with those of an effective piece of Protestant propaganda. The first issue on 23 January must in part have been aimed at all those gentlemen from distant shires who had not been present when Elizabeth made her flamboyant gesture to the reformers by holding aloft the English Bible presented to her at Little Conduit. Sir John Neale has pointed out that there was no attempt to pack the Parliament. Mary had summoned her House of Commons by indicating to the mayors and sheriffs which names the Council thought suitable for election. It seems this was not the method adopted in December 1558. Elizabeth and Cecil wanted a free election as a means of determining the balance of religious feeling in the country, so that they could decide what sort of settlement would be most workable.

The Queen arrived at Westminster in a State procession equal to that on the day of the Coronation. She wore a crimson velvet robe lined with ermine and a golden cap embroidered with pearls. The peers, forty-six in all, wore their Coronation robes. The procession included all Elizabeth's ladies on horseback, their gowns flashing with jewels, and a full complement of foot-soldiers, heralds, trumpeters and knights-at-arms, their scarlet liveries newly embellished with 'E.R.' in gold braid. When the Queen reached the Abbey, she was welcomed by Abbot Feckenham in his pontifical robes. As prior of the recently restored Benedictines he was followed by a procession of monks carrying lighted candles. 'Away with those tapers,' Elizabeth commanded contemptuously, 'for we see very well.' To the Catholics it was a gesture of scandalous impiety. Candles, reviled by the reformers, were symbols of faith. She was also on hallowed ground, and Queen Mary's grave, newly made near the tomb of Edward the Confessor, was still surmounted by the wax effigies of ascending angels used at her funeral.

There was worse to come. As the Queen took her seat by the High Altar, Dr Richard Cox, formerly her brother's tutor and councillor, mounted the pulpit to begin a vehement sermon against the monks for the part they had played in supporting the burning of the heretics. A married man newly returned from exile, he was used to holding forth in the energetic style of the continental reformers. He preached for an hour and a half, while the peers, still in their coronets, remained standing on the Abbey's flagged pavements, the Protestants among them presumably paying silent tribute to friends and fellow statesmen who had perished in the flames. God had given Elizabeth this dignity, Cox reminded them, that she might no longer allow or tolerate such practices as had been restored by Philip and Mary. He exhorted her to destroy the images of the saints, to purify the churches of idolatry, and to dissolve again those monasteries which her sister had endowed.

In this highly-charged atmosphere Elizabeth opened her first Parliament. The issues to be thrashed out were put clearly by Sir Nicholas Bacon, who as Lord Keeper opened the session instead of the Lord Chancellor, Archbishop Heath (his fate, since his refusal to officiate at the Coronation, still hung in the balance). There were three points to be discussed: the establishing 'of an uniform order of religion', a review of all such statutes as might be 'contrary or hurtful to the commonwealth', and lastly the raising of a subsidy for the war against Scotland and France, which, despite the protracted negotiations at Cercamp, had not yet formally ended. When he came to the matter of the war the Lord Keeper was almost overcome by his own rhetoric. He could not see how 'a good true Englishman' could consider the situation without mixed emotions of joy and sorrow. Joy, he emphasised, because Elizabeth was a Princess who would 'never be so wedded to her own will and fantasy' that she would let it override her concern for her people (which he implied was what Mary had done by involving them in the war in the first place), and sorrow for the peril which had come to the realm on account of it. He laid before them the matter which hurt most:

'Could there have happened to this Imperial Crown a greater loss in honour, strength, and treasure than to lose that piece, Calais I mean, which was in the beginning so nobly won and hath of long time so honourably and politically in all ages and times and against all attempts both of force and treason been defended and kept?' he asked. 'Did not the keeping of this breed fear to our mightiest enemies and make our faint friends most assured?' England's whole reputation was at stake; the sea coasts were now open to piracy; there had been great loss of 'divers valiant gentlemen'; there were 'incredible sums of money owing at this present and in honour due to be paid', and worst of all there was 'biting interest to be answered for the forbearing of this debt'. Then he dismissed them to their separate Houses to deliberate as best they might, how to remedy 'the necessity and need of this ragged and torn state', which because of misgovernance by the previous regime compelled its new ruler to ask them for a subsidy.

The matter uppermost in Englishmen's minds was, strangely, not Calais. There was something even more urgent. It was the need to get Elizabeth married, and preferably not to a foreigner. On Saturday 4 February a motion was carried in the Commons that she should be requested to marry as soon as possible for the sake of the succession. The following Monday a delegation from the Commons went to present their petition to her. On Friday the 10th she sent John Mason to them with her reply. Despite the existence of several manuscript versions, she must originally have spoken extempore in the presence of several councillors, among them Paulet, the old Marquis of Winchester, to whom she addressed her aside in the first part of the speech. Once when someone asked how he had survived in office for four reigns, he replied that he was made of willow, not oak. During Mary's time Renard had called him the richest man in England; he had entertained Philip and Mary at his house at Basing during their wedding progress, but as the brief note after her imprisonment at Woodstock shows, he had never lost touch with Elizabeth, whom he had known since childhood, and he had watched her evade the proposals made in her brother's reign, and more recently witnessed her 'escape' from Emmanuel Philibert.

CB As I have good cause, so do I give you all my hearty thanks for the good zeal and loving care you seem to have, as well towards me as to the whole state of your country. Your petition I perceive consisteth of three parts and my answer to the same shall depend of two.

And to the first part I may say unto you that from my years of understanding since I first had consideration of myself to be born a servitor of almighty God, I happily chose this kind of life in which I yet live, which I assure you for my own part hath hitherto best contented myself and I trust hath been most acceptable to God. From the which, if either ambition of high estate offered to me in marriage by the pleasure and appointment of my prince whereof I have some records in this presence (as you our Lord Treasurer well know); or if the eschewing of the danger of my enemies or the avoiding of the peril of death, whose messenger or rather continual watchman, the prince's indignation, was not a little time daily before my eyes (by whose means although I know or justly may suspect, yet I will not now utter, or if the whole cause were in my sister herself, I will not now burden her therewith, because I will not charge the dead): if any of these, I say, could have drawn or dissuaded me from this kind of life, I had not now remained in this estate wherein you see me. But so constant have I always continued in this determination, although my youth and words may seem to some hardly to agree together, yet is it most true that at this day I stand free from any other meaning that either I have had in times past or have at this present; with which trade of life I am so thoroughly acquainted that I trust

God, who hath hitherto therein preserved and led me by the hand, will not now of his goodness suffer me to go alone.

For the other part, the manner of your petition I do well like of and take in good part, because that it is simple and containeth no limitation of place or person. If it had been otherwise, I must needs have misliked it very much and thought it in you a very great presumption, being unfitting and altogether unmeet for you to require them that may command or those to appoint whose parts are to desire, or such to bind and limit whose duties are to obey, or to take upon you to draw my love to your likings or frame my will to your fantasies; for a guerdon constrained and a gift freely given can never agree together. Nevertheless if any of you be in suspect, that whensoever it may please God to incline my heart to another kind of life, you may well assure yourselves my meaning is not to do or determine anything wherewith the realm may or shall have just cause to be discontented. And therefore put that clean out of your heads. For I assure you – what credit my assurances may have with you I cannot tell, but what credit it shall deserve to have the sequel shall declare – I will never in that matter conclude anything that shall be prejudicial to the realm, for the weal, good and safety whereof I will never shun to spend my life. And whomsoever my chance shall be to light upon, I trust he shall be as careful for the realm and you – I will not say as myself, because I cannot so certainly determine of any other; but at the least ways, by my goodwill and desire he shall be such as shall be as careful for the preservation of the realm and you as myself. And albeit it might please almighty God to continue me still in this mind to live out of the state of marriage, yet it is not to be feared but He will so work in my heart and in your wisdoms as good provision by his help may be made in convenient time, whereby the realm shall not remain destitute of an heir. That may be a fit governor, and peradventure more beneficial to the realm than such offspring as may come of me. For although I be never so careful of your well doings and mind ever so to be, yet may my issue grow out of kind and become perhaps ungracious. And in the end this shall be for me sufficient, that a marble stone shall declare that a Queen, having reigned such a time, lived and died a virgin.

And here I end, and take your coming unto me in good part, and give unto you all eftsoons my hearty thanks, more yet for your zeal and good meaning than for your petition.

Romish pastors

During the Christmas festivities at Court there had been a good deal of irreverent merry-making, including a performance by mummers on Twelfth Night in which figures with crows' heads were dressed as cardinals, asses as bishops and wolves as abbots. It was watched, Il Schifanoya recorded, by the Queen. Such buffoonery had been allowable in the officially Protestant milieu of Edward's court. Elizabeth's position was more delicate. Philip had proposed marriage to his sister-in-law on 10 January, and with the peace negotiations with France still in progress, Elizabeth could not afford to offend him.

The fervently Protestant feeling of the Londoners, however, was undisguised. After the opening of Parliament Il Schifanoya reported a thriving trade in what we would call fringe theatre. Impromptu plays 'in derision of the Catholic faith, of the church, of the clergy and of religion', he wrote, were being performed and advertised 'by placards posted at the corners of the streets'. The authors and players invited people 'to the taverns to see the representations, taking money from their audience'. Other rogues and vagabonds were robbing the churches at night, breaking windows and stealing the altar plate. Several London churches had followed the new form of service adopted in the Chapel Royal, omitting all mention of the Virgin Mary and the saints, and eliminating references to the Pope and the prayers for the dead. Candles and crucifixes were however in use at Court. This was a great source of worry to the returning reformers, who plied Bullinger and Peter Martyr with letters begging them to intervene personally against such Popish superstition.* On St George's Day the procession of the Order of the Garter took place without the traditional silver and gold crucifixes. Elizabeth asked what had become of them and was told they had been removed to the Tower for safekeeping, being of such precious metal.

In short, there was anything but uniformity. The Spanish and Venetian envoys sent home, alternately, reports of the new services and gleeful bulletins of parishes which adhered to the old Mass. The Act which by the end of the session finally established the third Book of Common Prayer, so often regarded as a triumph of gentle compromise, was hammered out in an atmosphere of stormy debate.

Five bishoprics were vacant at the time of Mary's death; Pole's decease had created a sixth. As Archbishop of York, Heath was technically the leading cleric in the land. In the last weeks of Mary's reign he had conferred several times with Cecil, and indicated his willingness to continue in office as Lord Chancellor. His attitude over the Coronation after Elizabeth had made plain her views on the elevation of the host had of course altered the position, but as Parliament tackled the religious settlement, he spoke out fearlessly on the royal supremacy. He asked the House of Lords to consider 'what this supremacy is and whether it doth consist in spiritual government or temporal. If in temporal,' he continued, 'what further authority can this House give unto her Highness than she hath already?' If the supremacy was to cover spiritual

---

* Feria got hold of a rumour that Peter Martyr, Bernardino Ochino (who must have been in his eighties) and Calvin were coming to England. He was particulary fierce about Elizabeth's lady-in-waiting, Anne Bacon, the Lord Keeper's wife, formerly Anne Cooke, Feria called her 'a tiresome blue-stocking.

government, then he queried whether the House of Lords could grant such powers, and whether Elizabeth, as a woman, could receive them. St Paul had said no woman could be an apostle, shepherd, doctor or preacher; it could therefore reasonably be supposed that a woman could not be supreme head of the Church. A further breach with Rome would cause the English bishops 'by leaping out of Peter's ship' to exclude themselves from taking part in general councils of the Church. They would no longer be able to voice an opinion in matters affecting European Christianity. They would be 'overwhelmed and drowned in the waters of schism'.

It was considered fair comment, and no immediate action was taken against Heath for saying what he thought. On 18 March the bill abolishing the Papal Supremacy and restoring the Henrician and Edwardian position was passed. In the Lords it got through by thirty-three votes to twelve, all the bishops voting against it. It was left to the lawyers to invent for Elizabeth the ingenious title 'Supreme Governor' of the Church in England, thus covering an exigency undreamed of by St Paul. On 22 March, in Holy Week, the Queen issued a proclamation that on Easter Sunday communion was to be administered in both kinds, as it had been in the time of Edward VI.

The news that peace had been concluded between England, France, and Spain at Câteau Cambrésis reached London a few days before Elizabeth adjourned Parliament for Easter. She had been forced to give in over Calais; the French were to have it for eight years and to return it to England on 2 April 1567. Philip was to marry Elisabeth of Valois, Henry II's daughter, which caused the Queen of England to comment wryly that her brother-in-law could not have been very much in love with her, if he could not wait for four months while she changed her mind after her first refusal.

With the supremacy established, and peace between England and France assured, Elizabeth could proceed less cautiously in religious affairs. The uniformity debate continued through April. A public disputation was held in Westminster Abbey on 31 March. There was a heated session after which John Whyte, Bishop of Winchester and Thomas Watson, Bishop of Lincoln were committed to the Tower. Abbot Feckenham bravely tackled the innovations in the communion service in his speech to the Lords in the last week of April. He described the development of Cranmer's ideas, how he had first affirmed the real presence of Christ in the eucharist, but 'very shortly after he did set forth another book wherein he did most shamefully deny the same'. The Edwardian divines, intimated the abbot, had been so unsure of their own position that they had set forth 'these plain words of Christ (*Hoc corpus meum*)', which so troubled their wits that they later amended their statement 'with a little piece of paper clapt over the aforesaid words, wherein was written the verb substantive (*est*).' The English and German writers were so confused in their beliefs, he claimed, that 'this religion which by them is set forth can be no constant and stayed religion'. He then spoke of the havoc that was going on in the London churches. 'I shall desire your honours to consider the sudden mutation of the subjects of this realm since the death of good Queen Mary.' The people then had been law-abiding, not openly disobeying royal proclamations; there had been no 'spoiling of churches, plucking down of altars and most blasphemously treading the sacrament under their feet and hanging up of the knave of clubs in the place thereof'. He was tactful and loyal, laying the blame not on 'our most sovereign and dear Lady Queen Elizabeth' but rather on 'the preachers and scaffold players of this new religion' who, notwithstanding Elizabeth's godly proclamations and virtuous example, were turning everything upside down.

In the same week that Feckenham put his views to the Lords, the Commons introduced a bill to expel all friars, monks, nuns and hospitallers from England, assigning their revenues to the Queen, while the 'scaffold players' put on a particularly virulent satire involving Philip and Mary and Pole. The Act of Uniformity was passed by both Houses, the bishops voting against it to a man, and on 16 May, eight days after the Parliament ended, a proclamation was issued banning the performance of all interludes and unlicensed plays until All Hallow-tide. It was one thing to legislate for uniformity in religion, backed up by a system of fines and imprisonment for those who refused to take the oath affirming the Queen's supremacy, it was quite another to enforce it. If Elizabeth was to appoint Protestant bishops in the place of the deprived Catholics, she first had to arrange for their consecration. A list of all the bishoprics in England and Wales with their revenues, and a list of clergymen who would be eligible to fill the vacant sees, was compiled in May. Cecil wrote himself a memorandum that dangers were 'growing within the realm for lack of good government ecclesiastical'.

Elizabeth seems to have decided on Matthew Parker for her new Archbishop of Canterbury in the summer of 1559. On 19 July she appointed a commission to see that the Act of Uniformity was obeyed. The letters patent establishing it refer to 'Matthew Parker nominated Archbishop of Canterbury' and 'Edmund Grindal nominated Bishop of London'. Others included Sir Francis Knollys, Sir Thomas Smith, Dr William Bill, Ambrose Cave, Walter Haddon and several courtiers with no ecclesiastical pretensions: a quorum of six of them was empowered to restore ecclesiastical order and to stop 'false rumours tales and seditious slanders' against the new laws. They could also stop seditious books and fine improperly dressed clergy. Someone prepared Cecil a short paper on the correct form of ordination for an Archbishop of Canterbury, at which another archbishop and several bishops were required to officiate. In the margin Cecil wrote 'There is no Archbishop, nor four bishops now to be had', adding in Latin: 'Wherefore a search must be made.' Although Anthony Kitchin, the Bishop of Llandaff, was persuaded to agree to the Oath of Supremacy, four Edwardian bishops had to be brought out of retirement before Parker could be consecrated and he had to remain 'Archbishop elect' until the week before Christmas, when William Barlow, John Scory, Miles Coverdale and John Hodge finally installed him at Lambeth.

For Elizabeth the clash with the Marian bishops was frustrating, after the initial success of the Coronation and her first Parliament. No documentary evidence remains to support the magnificent letter Strype attributes to her in *Annals of the Reformation*. He claims five of the deprived Catholic bishops wrote to Elizabeth on 4 December begging her not to embrace the new 'schisms and heresies'. The bishops' letter is supposed to have been read in Council at Greenwich. unfortunately the Council register for the period is lost, and no foreign ambassador verifies whether Elizabeth was at Greenwich on that date. Strype alleges that she dictated the following reply:

CB Sirs,

As to your entreaty for us to listen to you we waive it; yet do return you this our answer. Our realm and subjects have been long wanderers, walking astray, whilst they were under the tuition of Romish pastors, who advised them to own a wolf for their head (in lieu of a careful shepherd) whose inventions, heresies and schisms be so numerous, that the flock of Christ have fed on poisonous shrubs for want of wholesome pastures. And whereas you hit us and our subjects in the teeth that the Romish Church first planted the Catholic faith within our realm, the records and chronicles of our realm testify the contrary; and your own Romish idolatry maketh you liars; witness the ancient monument of Gildas unto which both foreign and domestic have gone in pilgrimage there to offer. This author testifieth Joseph of Arimathea to be the first preacher of the word of God within our realms. Long after that, when Austin came from Rome, this our realm had bishops and priests therein, as is well known to the learned of our realm by woeful experience, how your church entered therein by blood; they being martyrs for Christ and put to death because they denied Rome's usurped authority.

As for our father being withdrawn from the supremacy of Rome by schismatical and heretical counsels and advisers; who we pray advised him more or flattered him than you good Mr Heath, when you were Bishop of Rochester? And than you Mr Bonner when you were archdeacon? And you Mr Turberville? Nay further, who was more an adviser of our father than your great Stephen Gardiner, when he lived? Are ye not then those schismatics and heretics? If so, suspend your evil censures. Recollect, was it our sister's conscience made her so averse to our father and brother's actions as to undo what they had perfected? Or was it not you, or such like advisers that dissuaded her and stirred her up against us and other of the subjects?

She cited the example of St Athanasius, who had once been excommunicated, and pointed out that they acknowledged his creed.

CB Dare any of you say he is a schismatic? Surely ye be not so audacious. Therefore as ye acknowledge his creed, it shows he was no schismatic. If Athanasius withstood Rome for her then heresies, then others may safely separate themselves from your church and not be schismatics.

We give you warning that for the future we hear no more of this kind, lest you provoke us to execute those penalties enacted for the punishing of our resisters, which out of our clemency we have foreborne.

E.R. Greenwich 6 December, 1559

We highly commend this single life

Matrimonially Elizabeth was the best prize in Europe. Although her treasury was empty because of the war with France, England's strategic importance, with its control of the routes from the North Sea to Europe and from Spain to the Low Countries, made her a bride worth coveting. Philip's proposal, conveyed by Feria on 10 January, long before the completion of the negotiations at Câteau Cambrésis, was perfectly sincere. Elizabeth would have to change her religious views, and a Papal dispensation would be required for him to marry his late wife's sister, but no one on the European side saw these as serious objections. Elizabeth was a woman and she needed military protection and a husband to share the burdens of government; Feria thought she would be committing political suicide if she turned down the powerful Habsburg alliance. No one seemed to take into account Englishmen's dislike of foreign domination, or Elizabeth's own determination to restore the religion in which she had been brought up, the establishment of which her father and brother had perfected. On the Continent the uniquely English form of worship which affirmed Christ but denied the Pope and the obligation to pay taxes to him, and admitted a communion service but left it to the individual conscience to decide on the degree to which Christ was or was not present in the sacrament, was imperfectly understood.

On 1 February Paolo Tiepolo, the Venetian ambassador at Philip's Court, wrote to the Doge and Senate;

'Concerning the marriage, it is said to be referred to the will of King Philip and that the Queen has given it clearly to be understood that she is content to have him for a husband, which is also desired and solicited by the chief personages of the kingdom.'

They expected, Tiepolo thought, further Spanish pensions 'such as his Majesty gave them in like manner in the time of the other Queen'. He was distressed to hear that the Coronation had been conducted without the elevation of the host. Throughout February Elizabeth kept up the diplomatic game of pretending she might accept Philip, and by all accounts she enjoyed every moment of it. On one occasion she sweetly asked the ambassador to explain how she could marry her sister's husband without dishonouring her father's memory, since he had been so scrupulous in divorcing Katharine of Aragon because she had been married to his brother Arthur.

After the announcement of Philip's betrothal to Elisabeth of Valois, he still showed a genuine regard for his sister-in-law, writing to her in his own hand. Apart from her great-uncle Lord William Howard, and Katherine Parr's brother, the Marquis of Northampton, who after her father's death had had something of an avuncular status, Elizabeth had no older male relations. To Philip, since he had saved her life in her sister's reign, it seemed the most natural thing in the world to feel that he was 'family'. Feria, whenever he wrote of Elizabeth's marriage, implied it was entirely within the King of Spain's gift. He fully expected Elizabeth to confer with him as Mary had with Renard, and was very disappointed when he was not assigned rooms in the palace. Philip's initial proposal of 10 January had been realistic and gravely thought out. Marrying Elizabeth would seem like 'entering upon a perpetual war with France', for Mary Stuart and her husband Francis had already indicated their intention of treating Mary's claim seriously by quartering their arms with those of England. This annoyed Elizabeth intensely. For Philip, to support her would be almost like taking up a knightly challenge. He fully realised, he wrote to Feria, that she was 'not sound in matters of religion'; she must ask secret absolution of the Pope before Philip could commit himself, but as a service to God, and in order to keep the country which he and Mary Tudor had brought back to the Papal fold securely Catholic, the King was prepared to overlook these disadvantages.

He never once questioned his ability to achieve the proposed ends, simply assuming that as Elizabeth was younger than her sister and would obviously produce an heir to keep England safely within the Habsburg dominions, marriage would cure all the rest. Such matters were in the hands of God. When she refused him he was not offended. He wrote on 23 March that he was very sorry such a marriage could not be arranged, as he had greatly desired it, and 'the public weal demanded it'. The same objects, however, could be achieved by good friendship. Feria should assure her that he would co-operate in any way he could towards the good government of her realm and 'render her any service in the matter of her marriage'. He replaced Feria by the worldly Bishop of Aquila, Alvaro de Quadra, who arrived in London on 30 March, the day before the great disputation was to begin in Westminster Abbey. Feria himself married Jane Dormer, one of Mary's ladies-in-waiting, and after the couple left England their household in Spain became a centre for disaffected English Catholics.

Elizabeth had already refused the King of Denmark's offer of marriage. At the beginning of April, Erik of Sweden, who as Crown Prince had proposed in Mary's reign, renewed his suit. She commented that his first proposal had been made to her when she was plain Lady Elizabeth; he must now propose to her as a King to a Queen. He sent a costly present of tapestries and fine ermine and the following autumn the Duke of Finland came to woo her on his brother's behalf. Simultaneously the Duke of Saxony proposed and Philip's uncle, the Holy Roman Emperor, offered a choice of his two sons, the Archdukes Ferdinand and Charles.

Ferdinand was known to be an ardent Catholic, so zealous that even de Quadra made fun of him. He soon dropped out of the running. Elizabeth told the Imperial ambassador that she would prefer to meet Charles in person. Portrait painters could not always be trusted. She avoided mention of the disaster in her father's time over Holbein's flattering picture of Anne of Cleves, but said forthrightly that Philip must have cursed all portrait painters when he had set eyes on her sister. We can probably deduce from this remark that Moro's mannish representation of Mary, which finally came to rest in the Prado, was closer to the truth than the pictures painted of her by the English and Dutch artists. Philip backed his cousin's suit enthusiastically. If Elizabeth were to marry the Archduke, he wrote to Feria, 'his Caesarian Majesty will hold her as a daughter and will then aid her with all the power of the Empire'. Another advantage was that his cousin 'having no states of his own would always be with her and would help her to bear the government of her kingdom'. This was something Philip could not have promised, owing to the extensive dominions he had to control. But 'by reason of her husband being of our blood and of so near kin she would be more feared and esteemed by her own subjects and will have all the protection she may require'.

Elizabeth listened to what everybody had to say; then on 5 June at Westminster she summoned Cecil and Ascham, and together they composed a long, courteous Latin reply to the Emperor. She realised that the match would enhance her dignity, she acknowledged it from her inmost soul, and she expressed her warmest thanks for the Emperor's benevolence:

'When however we reflect upon the question of this marriage and eagerly ask our heart, we find that we have no wish to give up solitude and our single life, but prefer with God's help to abide therein of our free determination.'

Five weeks later, during a tournament to celebrate Philip's marriage to Elisabeth of Valois, the King of France died, so that Mary Stuart and her husband became King and Queen. Suddenly the Imperial protection and Philip's friendship were worth a great deal diplomatically. Elizabeth set out to prolong the Archduke's courtship for as long as she could, using it, as Neale observed, 'as a kind of insurance policy'. De Quadra spent as much time trying to further the match as the Emperor's ambassadors, Count von Helffenstein and Baron von Breuner. When their hopes flagged Elizabeth set herself to revive them. When she met von Breuner rowing on the Thames, she invited him into the Lord Chamberlain's barge. Next day she asked him aboard her own boat, letting him take the helm, and playing the lute to him. If she was to marry Charles, she wanted to meet him: did the Emperor think she was trying to make a laughing stock of him? If that was the way they felt, it was better Charles should not come. De Quadra found her no easier to deal with than Feria had. On 27 December he wrote a letter to his predecessor. 'I think she must have a hundred thousand devils in her . . . notwithstanding that she is forever telling me she yearns to be a nun and pass her time in a cell praying.'

Elizabeth revelled in the whole business of courtship. It was a game, and one at which she excelled. She loved the rich gifts that were showered upon her, the flattery and the protestations of the various envoys striving to outdo each other. In October 1559 de Quadra wrote that there were ten or twelve ambassadors competing simultaneously for her favour. She loved arranging parties for the diplomatic visitors, and gave a magnificent reception at Whitehall to celebrate the peace with France. The piazza under the long gallery was draped with silver and gold brocade and hung with fresh flowers. When Elizabeth entered for supper, she came through a door made entirely of roses. All her courtiers were encouraged to take part in the duties of official entertaining, in order to defray her own expenses. Shortly before the Coronation Feria reported that the Earl of Arundel had given 2,000 crowns' worth of jewels to the Queen's ladies. He was trying to oust Paulet as Lord Treasurer, but only succeeded in buying himself the office of Lord Steward.

Of the English suitors, Arundel and Sir William Pickering were tipped as favourites. Feria's last despatch reported the arrival of Pickering on Ascension Day. He had been England's ambassador to France for a brief spell during Edward's reign, and had subsequently travelled extensively in France and Italy. Elizabeth received him privately two days after his return, and remained closeted with him for four or five hours. 'In London', wrote Feria, 'they are giving 25 to 100 that he will be King.' He had followed Pickering's progress keenly since 14 December 1558, when his name had first been mentioned by the Court gossips. He warned de Quadra to keep an eye on him. The bishop's vigilance was rewarded when Pickering offended Arundel by passing through Elizabeth's private apartments on his way to the Chapel Royal. His place, as a mere knight, was in the Presence Chamber. Pickering called the earl 'an impudent discourteous knave', but refused to fight him on the grounds that Arundel was the weaker. He took to dining alone with musicians playing to him, but there is no evidence that Elizabeth ever considered him seriously as a suitor. Arundel's only recommendation, apart from his noble lineage, was that he was rich. Elizabeth had leased him Nonsuch, the fantastic palace that Henry VIII built in emulation of the châteaux of the Loire. The earl entertained her there for five days in August, giving a banquet that lasted until three in the morning. It had cost him a fortune, but had not noticeably advanced his cause, which perhaps explains his jealousy of Pickering.

In July Erik of Sweden announced that he would come in person. His brother, the Duke of Finland, was showering everybody with gifts. The English courtiers took the gifts, but laughed heartlessly behind his back at his outlandish ways. In August 1560 Erik set out. He was turned back by fierce winds, which Elizabeth unhesitatingly regarded as a sign of God's protection. undeterred, the Swedish King made another attempt, but a further storm damaged his fleet. He wrote to tell Elizabeth that at her first summons he would rush through armies of foes to protect

Erik XIV of Sweden: the portrait was painted especially for Elizabeth

Elizabeth I: the portrait she had painted for Erik

her. Alarmed by his ardour, she wrote to him explaining that she had never felt passion of the kind he described, and entreating him not to get carried away by his own imagination.

C8 Most Serene Prince Our Very Dear Cousin,

A letter truly yours both in the writing and sentiment was given us on 30 December by your very dear brother, the Duke of Finland. And while we perceive therefrom that the zeal and love of your mind towards us is not diminished, yet in part we are grieved that we cannot gratify your Serene Highness with the same kind of affection. And that indeed does not happen because we doubt in any way of your love and honour, but, as often we have testified both in words and writing, that we have never yet conceived a feeling of that kind of affection towards anyone. We therefore beg your Serene Highness again and again that you be pleased to set a limit to your love, that it advance not beyond the laws of friendship for the present nor disregard them in the future. And we in our turn shall take care that whatever can be required for the holy preservation of friendship between Princes we will always perform towards your Serene Highness. It seems strange for your Serene Highness to write that you understand from your brother and your ambassadors that we have entirely determined not to marry an absent husband; and that we will give you no certain reply until we shall have seen your person.

We certainly think that if God ever direct our heart to consideration of marriage we shall never accept or choose any absent husband how powerful and wealthy a Prince soever. But that we are not to give you an answer until we have seen your person is so far from the thing itself that we never even considered such a thing. But I have always given both to your brother, who is certainly a most excellent prince and deservedly very dear to us, and also to your ambassador likewise the same answer with scarcely any variation of the words, that we do not conceive in our heart to take a husband, but highly commend this single life, and hope that your Serene Highness will no longer spend time in waiting for us.

She went on to praise the Duke of Finland's skill and zeal as a proxy. If Erik himself had come to England he could not have wooed Elizabeth with more ardour and sincerity. 'Nothing', Elizabeth assured the King, could have been added 'to his zeal, or carefulness, or counsel, or advice', and she wrote thus with her own hand and mind, without summoning any of her Council, she insisted, because she understood that to be Erik's own wish. England and Sweden must continue in friendship and do everything that would be 'convenient and safe for the subjects of us both'. And she ended fervently,

C3 God keep your Serene Highness for many years in good health and safety. From our Palace at Westminster, 25 February
Your Serene Highness' sister and cousin,

Elizabeth

At this point an afterthought struck her. She realised Erik's professions of passion were quite immoderate, and passion she had studied with Ascham quite dispassionately in the writings of Plato. If he could imagine himself so much in love, he could imagine himself rejected and humiliated. He might even take reprisals. Elizabeth added a well-thought-out postscript.

'Concerning your coming, however earnest your desire yet we dare not approve the plan, since nothing but expectation can happen to your Serene Highness in this business: and indeed we very greatly fear lest your love, which is now so great, might be turned to another alien feeling, which would not be so pleasing to your Serene Highness, and to us also would be very grievous.'

She has broken her neck

The intrepid Swedish King set out again for England in 1561, although by then the whole of Europe knew that Elizabeth was in love with her Master of the Horse. Accidents of fortune and affairs of State had brought Elizabeth Tudor and Robert Dudley into each other's orbit throughout their lives. Before either of them was born, his grandfather Edmund Dudley had been her grandfather's tax collector, executed by Henry VIII as a move to win popular favour as soon as he came to the throne. Despite being the son of an attainted traitor, John Dudley rose as Earl of Warwick to be Edward's leading councillor and when, as Duke of Northumberland, he was overthrown and executed for treason, his five sons followed him to the Tower. After Mary had executed Jane Grey and Guildford Dudley in the reprisals following Wyatt's rebellion, John, Ambrose, Robert and Henry remained confined in the Beauchamp Tower. Shortly afterwards Elizabeth was imprisoned in the adjacent Bell Tower. Robert, like Elizabeth, felt he owed his life to Philip's intervention. When he was released he and his brothers mustered enough men to join the King's expedition to St Quentin. Robert was made Master of the Ordnance; Henry was killed by a French cannon ball.

At a more personal level, Robert had been one of Edward's school-fellows. He had not shared lessons with Elizabeth, but they had been taught by the same tutors. The twelve-year-old Edward, who was one of the guests at Dudley's wedding to Amy Robsart, left a peerless description in his journal, omitting all mention of the nuptials, but telling how afterwards some of the young men tilted at a live goose tied to a post.

When the King lay dying, Robert and his brother-in-law, Henry Sidney, took it in turns to keep vigil in the boy's sick-room. Later, when Elizabeth was in financial difficulty in Mary's reign, Robert had sold lands to help her, at a time when he was still struggling to reverse the fortunes of his own family. It was a kindness she never forgot. His appointment as Master of the Horse in the first week of her reign was a natural one. His older brother, John, had held the office in her brother's reign, and Robert had been Master of the Buckhounds. Robert was a good judge of horseflesh, an excellent huntsman, a celebrated contestant in the tilt yard, and having been brought up all his life at Court, he was an expert on royal ceremonial. He looked splendid in processions in the green and white Tudor colours, four sets of which were part of his official equipment. Having no town house of his own at the beginning of the reign, he was also entitled to rooms in the palace.

The first recorded gossip about the intimacy between the Queen and Dudley was in Feria's letter to Philip of 18 April 1559. Shortly to return to Spain, the ambassador, who had never succeeded himself in obtaining rooms at Court, and who had complained of this several times to Cecil, wrote grudgingly, 'During the last few days Lord Robert has come so much into favour that he does whatever he likes with affairs.'

He revealed that Elizabeth visited Dudley in his chamber night and day, including the information which everyone close to Elizabeth already knew Robert's wife had 'a malady in one of her breasts'. This was her principal reason for not attending Court as part of the close circle which surrounded the Queen and included Robert's brother Ambrose and his sister Lady Mary, who was married to Sir Henry Sidney. If, as is usually supposed, Amy Dudley's illness was cancer, Tudor medicine could not save her, and as an invalid it was best that she should remain peacefully in the country. She lived at Cumnor Place in Oxfordshire, a house the Dudleys had leased from a Mr Owen. She had borne Robert no heirs, and for this reason, when the natural affection between Elizabeth and Dudley became an obvious physical attraction, it was probably looked on indulgently by their closest acquaintances. Protected by the code of chivalry, the conventions of courtly love, and the continuous attendance of Elizabeth's maids-of-honour, there seemed no opportunity for an adulterous affair.

On 23 April Elizabeth made Dudley a Knight of the Garter, along with the Duke of Norfolk and the Earl of Rutland. It was only five years since his father had been executed and attainted, so a few eyebrows were raised. By 29 April Feria reported that people were saying openly that the Queen was in love with Lord Robert and would not let him leave her side. By 4 May Tiepolo had picked up the rumours and sent them winging across Italy: Lord Robert was 'a very handsome young man to whom the Queen evinces such affection and inclination, that many persons believe that if his wife, who has been ailing for some time, were to die, the Queen might easily take him for her husband.'

Tales of a royal romance have a tendency to get out of hand. By midsummer de

Quadra wrote to Philip: 'She has just given £12,000 to Lord Robert as an aid towards his expenses.' He was in fact supposed to use part of it for buying the Queen Irish bloodstock, but by the autumn, even though Elizabeth was still in the midst of negotiations to marry the archduke, it was widely assumed on the continent that Dudley had become her lover. At Whitehall, his rooms on the ground floor were damp because of their proximity to the river. She had his suite moved to the first floor, next to her own apartments. Kat Ashley was distraught. She warned her mistress of the scandal which abounded. Elizabeth pointed out that the rumours were ridiculous. She asked how she and Dudley could possibly be lovers when she was surrounded by ladies-in-waiting at all hours of the day and night. Then, in the manner of one caught in the conflict between love and duty, she added petulantly that if ever she had the will or found pleasure 'in such a dishonourable life', she knew of no one who could forbid her.

De Quadra reported all gossip to Philip and the Duchess of Parma. Since it was well known that Arundel loathed Dudley, the Queen and Mary Sidney, presumably for a joke, fed the ambassador a rumour that the earl intended to give a banquet and to poison Lord Robert. De Quadra fell hook, line and sinker, and sent the story off in his next despatch. It was of course pure fantasy. If Elizabeth had suspected any such thing she would have placed Arundel under instant arrest. By 12 November von Breuner, who was sharing a house with de Quadra, told the Emperor it was said that Milord Robert 'seeks means to poison his wife', after which it was confidently expected Elizabeth would marry him. De Quadra, meanwhile, had written to the Duchess of Parma to say the Duke of Norfolk spoke openly of Elizabeth's 'lightness and bad government'. He too was planning to kill Lord Robert. 'People are ashamed', hinted the bishop, 'of what is going on.' There is no evidence that anything was going on, although Elizabeth clearly adored Dudley and the young people enjoyed provoking the ambassador.

Scottish affairs reached a crisis the following spring, and Cecil went north in July to negotiate the Treaty of Edinburgh. When he returned, triumphant, he found that Elizabeth had abandoned statecraft for a summer of pure pleasure. She went hunting and hawking, riding and dancing. Cecil saw the attraction between Robert and Elizabeth as something that could undo his handiwork. He grumbled to de Quadra that he foresaw 'the ruin of the realm through Robert's intimacy with the Queen, who surrendered all affairs to him and meant to marry him'. Cecil said he was thinking of resigning even if he was sent to the Tower. He also repeated the old rumour that Robert was thinking of killing his wife. Two days after this extraordinary outburst the news reached Court that Amy Dudley had fallen down a staircase at Cumnor Place on 8 September. Elizabeth seemed almost dumb with shock. 'She has broken her neck,' she told de Quadra.

CHAPTER VII

As should neither touch his honesty nor her honour

The coroner's court returned a verdict of accidental death. The matter was independently investigated and tried by an ordinary jury. No special representatives were sent from the Privy Council. It was recorded that on Sunday, 8 September, all the members of the household at Cumnor Place had gone to Abingdon Fair, except for Amy Dudley, her friend Mrs Odingsells and old Mrs Owen, whose son William owned the house. Cumnor Place was a rambling fourteenth-century manor built round a courtyard. Part of it was rented by Robert's friend, Anthony Forster, and his family, who lived in one wing. Forster acted as steward to the Dudleys, who were not in a strong position financially as they were still recovering from the attainder of the previous reign.* Amy had moved to Cumnor at the end of 1559, an arrangement which was probably intended as a temporary measure, but which suited everyone concerned. The elderly Mrs Owen had her own apartments above the great hall and Amy's adjoined these. The old lady had her son's tenants for company, and the ailing Lady Dudley was not overburdened by the cares of managing a large estate while her husband was absent at Court. Elizabeth had given Robert a small house at Kew, which he could use as an independent base for his exacting duties as Master of the Horse at London and Windsor. There is no record of any estrangement between Amy and Robert; she lived the life of a country gentlewoman, surrounded by loving and protective friends whose own affairs were linked with the fortunes of her brilliant, but busy husband.

On the morning of Abingdon Fair Lady Dudley had announced her intention of dining with Mrs Owen. That afternoon she must have fallen on her way back from the old lady's apartments. She could have slipped through drowsiness, pain, or even a little too much to drink. When the rest of the household returned they found her dead at the foot of a staircase. Modern medical knowledge indicates that the cancer would have spread through Amy's body, making her bones so brittle that a fall could easily have broken her neck. She had obviously been in pain for many months, and it emerged during the enquiry that her maid, Pinto, told Sir Thomas Blount, a member of Dudley's household, that she had heard her mistress 'pray to God to

---

* Robert's mother Jane, Duchess of Northumberland, died in comparative poverty, after the attainder of Mary's reign. She was allowed the use of the duke's house in Chelsea and stuff to furnish it, but the lands the family had owned at Edward's death were all forfeit to the Crown.

deliver her from desperation'. Blount thought that Amy might have attempted suicide, but Pinto had replied sharply to his insinuation, 'No, good Mr Blount, do not judge so of my words; if you should so gather, I am sorry I said so much.' Blount himself had been despatched from Windsor on a separate errand. On the road he met Bowes, a servant who had been sent from Cumnor to tell the news to Lord Robert at Windsor. Blount rode on towards Cumnor, but before he got there he stopped at an inn in Abingdon. He quizzed the landlord concerning local opinion. The man spoke highly of Forster. He said he thought Amy's death must have been an accident, because 'it chanced at that honest gentleman's house. His great honesty doth much curb the evil thoughts of the people.'

Elizabeth sent Dudley away from Windsor to Kew, where he remained until after the inquest. Wild rumours circulated. Some said he had killed his wife; others that he had been in collusion with Anthony Forster to do away with her. One report claimed she had been stabbed with a poniard. The English Court was a hotbed of gossip. In France Mary Stuart pronounced her memorable judgement: 'The Queen of England is going to marry her horsekeeper.' Cecil went to visit Robert at Kew, perhaps with condolences, perhaps with personal messages from Elizabeth. Dudley seemed completely bewildered. He wrote to Cecil, whom de Quadra always described as Lord Robert's worst enemy, plainly touched by the great friendship he had shown. 'I pray you let me hear from you what you think best for me to do,' he entreated. 'I am sorry so sudden chance should breed me so great a change, for methinks I am here all the while as it were in a dream, and too far from the place I am bound to be.'

As soon as the coroner's verdict was known Elizabeth recalled Robert to Windsor. The Court was ordered into mourning, and remained subdued until mid-October. Amy's funeral took place in Oxford. It was a splendid affair with the Queen's friend, Lady Norris, as chief mourner. Many years later it was alleged that the preacher, Francis Babington, the Master of Balliol, had made a slip of the tongue during the funeral sermon, referring to Amy as 'this lady so pitifully slain'.

Although Robert was officially cleared, the gossip continued. Sir Nicholas Throckmorton, Elizabeth's ambassador in France, had a particularly embarrassing time. On 10 October he wrote three letters to London. A horse, which Dudley must have arranged to be shipped before the scandal erupted, had just arrived. Throckmorton thanked him for the present, and wrote an ordinary letter of condolence. To Cecil he commented rather cautiously that he had heard of Amy Dudley's 'strange death', for he knew that anything he said to the secretary would be repeated to the Queen. Later that day he wrote to the Marquis of Northampton, a close friend to whom he could unburden himself. He wished he were dead, or anywhere but Paris, so that he might not hear the 'dishonourable and naughty reports' that were going about. He was at his wits' end, he told Northampton. Everyone was reviling the Protestant religion. 'What religion is this,' the French were asking, 'that a subject shall kill his wife, and the Prince not only bear withal but marry with him?' The ambassador's heart bled; he believed the slanderous stories that he kept hearing would lead to a war. William Parr, as an elder statesman with a quasi-avuncular relationship with the Queen, might be able to say more to her than Cecil.

Henry Killigrew's letter from London crossed with the ambassador's packet.

'I cannot imagine what rumours they be you hear there,' he wrote, 'unless such as were here of the death of my lady Dudley for that she brake her neck down a pair of stairs, which I protest unto you was done only by the hand of God to my knowledge.'

Five days later the Court came out of mourning and settled itself to speculate at regular intervals on the likelihood that Elizabeth and Robert would marry. When she was told of the malicious rumours in France, she said that 'the matter had been tried in the country and found to be contrary to that which was reported and that it fell out as should neither touch his honesty nor her honour'.

Those closest to Elizabeth were in no doubt that she was in love with Dudley. It seemed to some that the hand of God had indeed miraculously intervened to make it possible for her to marry, and for her to marry an Englishman. Henry and Mary Sidney almost certainly thought like Killigrew. Cecil must have been dumbfounded, remembering his earlier bitter remark to de Quadra. He wished Lord Robert in Paradise, he had said petulantly. It is a common enough human experience to predict something in malice or in jest, but it is always a little shattering if the prediction comes true. Cecil, a Tudor lawyer whose sister-in-law had written a book about predestination, must have felt unnerved.

Elizabeth was in a quandary; her heart coursed one way, her head another, and probably it was one of the few times in her life when prayer was of no avail. She was in a position to exercise free will. To remove herself from the European marriage market was to lose bargaining power. To marry a subject would be to bring herself to the level of the Duchess of Somerset, who after the Protector's death had married a Mr Newdigate, and the Duchess of Suffolk who married her steward, Adrian Stokes. Did Philip want her to emulate these ladies, Elizabeth asked de Quadra? She was apparently joking, but after the traumas of her alleged illegitimacy, she was always defensive about matters of status. As Henry's daughter, Queen of England, and sister-in-law to the King of Spain, she was still a fit bride for the Emperor's son. On a purely practical level, there was also the possibility of the Earl of Arran, now officially heir to Mary Stuart's throne, whom the Scots Lords were urging her to marry. It was a scheme with much potential.

In addition to these considerations, Robert's father had died an attainted traitor. Elizabeth's indecision took many forms. In October 1560 she drew up a patent to make Robert an earl, then publicly humiliated him by cutting it to pieces. Diplomatic relations with Spain were strained over Elizabeth's treatment of English Catholics who wished to leave the country. One of Feria's parting requests had been that she would grant passports to monks and nuns who wished to continue in their vocation. By December she would not even give leave for Mistress Clarencieux, Mary

Tudor's lady-in-waiting, or old Lady Dormer, grandmother to the Countess of Feria, to go abroad.

In January Henry Sidney approached de Quadra, suggesting that if Philip would use his influence to encourage the match with his brother-in-law, Lord Robert would be under such an obligation that he would 'behave like one of Philip's own vassals'. De Quadra replied loftily that what he had heard about the relationship was 'of such a character' that he had hardly dared write two lines about it to Philip. Nor had the Queen or Lord Robert ever said a word that he could write. At this Sidney sprang boldly to Dudley's defence. He saw no reason, he said, 'why de Quadra should hesitate to write. Although it was a love affair yet the object of it was marriage and there was nothing illicit about it, or such as could not be set right' by Philip's approval. De Quadra pointed out to Sidney that although Robert had been cleared of any murder charge, many people did not believe in his innocence. Sir Henry was forced to admit that this was a real difficulty. 'Even preachers in the pulpits discoursed on the matter in a way that was prejudicial to Elizabeth's honour.' On Midsummer Day 1561 the ambassador was invited aboard the Queen's barge to watch a water pageant on the Thames. He has left us a vivid picture of the Queen and Dudley at their merriest.

'She, Robert, and I being alone on the gallery, they began joking, which she likes to do much better than talking about business. They went so far with their jokes that Lord Robert told her that if she liked I could be the minister to perform the act of marriage, and she, nothing loth to hear it, said she was not sure whether I knew enough English.'

At a coarser level, Mother Dove of Brentford said Elizabeth was already pregnant, and drunken Burley of Totnes was up before the magistrate for saying Lord Robert 'did swive the Queen'.

In the midst of this emotionally turbulent phase, the heiress to the throne managed to get herself pregnant. Lady Katherine Grey, sister to Lady Jane and daughter of Frances Brandon, Duchess of Suffolk, was the granddaughter of Henry VIII's younger sister, Mary. Henry's will excluded the issue of his elder sister, Margaret of Scotland, from whom Mary Stuart was descended. The Greys were therefore first in the line of succession.

Elizabeth inclined to the argument that Lady Katherine's claim was forfeit on account of her father's treason in Mary Tudor's time. She was also suspected of intriguing with the Spaniards. Cecil believed he had uncovered a plot to marry her to Philip's son, Don Carlos, and both Feria and de Quadra mentioned her regularly in despatches. Lady Katherine fell in love with Lord Hertford, son of the late Duke of Somerset. Encouraged by the Duchess of Suffolk, she married Hertford in secret; the duchess then died, and the only other responsible witness to her daughter's marriage seems to have been Hertford's sister, Lady Jane Seymour. Lady Jane died in March 1561. Elizabeth gave her a State funeral in Westminster Abbey and sent Hertford on a diplomatic mission to France. When Lady Katherine, who must have conceived in either December or January, discovered her plight, she turned to Lady Saintlow,* one of Elizabeth's shrewdest ladies-in-waiting, for advice. Lady Saintlow, who had a talent for self-preservation, declined to get involved. Lady Katherine was already in disfavour for having spoken very arrogant and unseemly words in the hearing of the Queen.

In due course Elizabeth learned what had happened. Lady Katherine was arrested and Lord Hertford's mother, the Duchess of Somerset, was sent for. On 22 August she swore she had no knowledge of her son's marriage, and she hoped 'the wilfulness of her unruly child' would not diminish the Queen's favour. This was the woman who twelve years earlier had dared to dispute precedence with the widowed Katherine Parr, and who had claimed Kat Ashley was not a fit person to be governess to the Lady Elizabeth. Nobody could find the priest who had married the Hertfords. Four days after the duchess was questioned Cecil wrote to Throckmorton, 'The Lady Katherine is in the Tower and near the time of delivery of her child. Nobody', he added drily, 'can appear privy to the marriage, nor to the love, but maids, or women going for maids'.

Hertford confessed paternity and was himself put in the Tower. Legally it was still a capital offence to marry any member of the royal family without the sovereign's consent, under the 1536 Act which had so offended Chapuys. Hertford was luckier than Lord Thomas Howard, who had lost his head for paying court to Lady Margaret Douglas before she became Countess of Lennox. Elizabeth eventually persuaded Matthew Parker to declare the Hertfords' marriage void, which meant their child was illegitimate, but first she ordered a thorough enquiry, hinting to Sir Edward Warner, the Lieutenant of the Tower, that he might even threaten Lady Saintlow with torture to make her tell the truth.

C03 To the Lieutenant of the Tower

Our pleasure is that ye shall, as by our commandment examine the Lady Catherine very straitly, how many hath been privy to the love betwixt the Earl of Hertford and her from the beginning; and let her certainly understand that she shall have no manner of favour except she will show the truth, not only what ladies or gentlewomen of this Court were thereto privy, but also what lords and gentlemen: for it doth now appear that sundry personages have dealt therein; and when it shall appear more manifestly, it shall increase our indignation against her, if she will forbear to utter it.

We earnestly require you to show your diligence in this. Ye shall also send

---

* Later to be known as Bess of Hardwick. Her first three husbands, Robert Barlow, Sir William Cavendish and Sir William Saintlow, all left her large properties, including the manor of Chatsworth. As Lady Saintlow she was one of Elizabeth's maids-of-honour in Mary's reign, and is mentioned by Sir John Harington's father in the poem in *Nugae Antiquae*. She built Hardwick Hall 1591-7 when married to her fourth and last husband, the Earl of Shrewsbury.

to Alderman Lodge secretly for Saintlow, and shall put her in awe of divers matters confessed by the Lady Catherine and so also deal with her, that she may confess to you all her knowledge in the same matters. It is certain that there hath been great practices and purposes and since the death of the Lady Jane, she hath been most privy. And as ye shall see occasion, so ye may keep Saintlow two or three nights more or less, and let her be returned to Lodge's or kept still with you, as ye shall think meet. We have signed a licence for your absence but we would that ye should forbear a fortnight, and not to depart, until also our pleasure be further signified.

17 August, 1561

There was much sympathy for the young Hertfords, and shortly after their baby was born they managed to conceive another child in the precincts of the Tower. Both the babies were boys. Elizabeth was so angry that she had Lady Katherine placed under house arrest with her uncle, Lord John Grey, as custodian. Hertford remained in the Tower and the unfortunate young people never met again. She died in 1568, after which Hertford was released.

Katherine's sister, Lady Mary Grey, was very small; according to some reports she was a dwarf. She married the Queen's Serjeant Porter, Thomas Keys, who was immensely tall. When Elizabeth discovered this match, she sent Keys to the Fleet Prison and put Lady Mary under house arrest like her sister. The Greys' only offence was that the dangerous blood royal flowed in their veins. Elizabeth's own experiences as heiress to the throne during Mary's reign had left her with fears about the succession that were bordering on paranoia. Keys eventually died in prison in 1571; Mary Grey survived him by seven years. The Queen tried to get Grindal, the Bishop of London, to declare the marriage void like the Hertfords', but she was not successful.

In the knot of friendship

On 31 August 1559 the Marquis of Winchester had drawn up a weighty document, 'The Lord Treasurer's Memorial upon the Affairs of Scotland'. 'The best worldly felicity that Scotland can have', it declared, 'is either to continue in perpetual peace with England or to be made one monarchy with it. If the first be sought then Scotland must not be subject to the appointments of France, which being an ancient enemy with England seeks always to make Scotland an instrument to exercise their malice against her.'

During the short reign of Francis II, Mary Stuart, as Queen of France, continued to quarter her arms with those of England, emphasising the loss of Calais and underlining the validity of Mary's claim to the English throne. When it was pointed out to Elizabeth that *she* used the arms of France, she retorted furiously that everyone knew the leopards and lilies on her arms dated back to the time of Edward III; England had held territory in France since time immemorial. Mary Stuart's quartering was a gratuitous insult. Mary explained that she had agreed to the quartering at the insistence of her father-in-law, Henry II.

When Francis died on 6 December 1560, his ten-year-old brother, Charles IX, became King. Mary Stuart's relations, the all-powerful Guises, left Court to return to their own estates, and Catherine de' Medici, the Queen Mother, was made Regent. In Scotland, meanwhile, Mary's mother, Mary of Guise, who had acted as Regent since her daughter's childhood, had negotiated first the Treaty of Upsetlington with Elizabeth, and later the Treaty of Edinburgh.

By the Treaty of Upsetlington Elizabeth had sworn not to aid the Scottish rebels, those militant Lords of the Congregation who seized power from the Regent and, urged on by the fiery John Knox, established the Protestant religion. Within a few weeks of signing it, Elizabeth was sending money to the rebels. She met secretly with James Hamilton, Earl of Arran, whom the Scots lords made heir to their throne, and whom they urged her to marry. She also allowed her Admiral, Sir William Winter, to blockade the Firth of Forth. He captured the ships sent to supply munitions to the French army which had gone to the aid of the Regent. Elizabeth accomplished all this while maintaining apparently friendly relations with both Mary of Guise and the French ambassador.

By March 1560, an English army had marched into Scotland. It was repulsed by the Regent's troops at Leith with terrible loss of English lives. Elizabeth sent Cecil to Scotland, where he negotiated the Treaty of Edinburgh. Francis and Mary were to relinquish their use of the English arms. Elizabeth's title was to be formally recognised by the French, while the French forces were to withdraw unconditionally from Scotland. Mary of Guise died on 11 June before the treaty was finally settled, and the sixteen-year-old Francis II refused point blank to ratify the agreement made by his late mother-in-law.

The French decided after Francis's death to return Mary Stuart to her own kingdom, which she had not visited for twelve years. She had been brought up a Catholic, and in their reforming zeal the Scottish lords viewed her arrival with mixed feelings. To say Mass in Scotland was punishable, after the third offence, with death. Mary asked Elizabeth for a safe-conduct to travel through England. Elizabeth refused this until Mary should ratify the Treaty of Edinburgh. Mary set sail for Scotland instead of going overland. Her retinue included three Guise uncles, Claude de Lorraine, Duke of Aumale; René de Lorraine, Marquis d'Elboeuf; and Louis de Lorraine, Grand Prior of the Order of Malta. Mary had set out without the escort of ships fitting for a widowed Queen of France; the illustrious company travelled in two vessels through waters known to be infested with pirates, and patrolled by the English fleet. It was rumoured that Elizabeth's ships might try to capture Mary.

John Knox, who had written several times to Elizabeth and Cecil explaining that his notorious book, *The First Blast of the Trumpet against the Monstrous Regiment of Women*, was not aimed at her, wrote again on 6 August in a state of high excitement. He had heard Mary Stuart intended to get his book banned, or at least 'confuted by the censure of the learned in divers realms'. He was not, he explained to Elizabeth, a Sacramentarian 'desirous of innovations'. On 15 August Maitland of Lethington, one of the Scottish gentlemen awaiting Mary's arrival, wrote to Cecil to say he had heard that Elizabeth had refused a passport to her cousin, even though it had been courteously requested. 'It passes my dull capacity to imagine what this sudden enterprise means,' he objected. Elizabeth relented and despatched the safe-conduct, which reached Scotland four days after Mary's homecoming. She had landed unexpectedly on 19 August at 10 o'clock in the morning, before a welcoming party could be arranged.

Thomas Randolph, Elizabeth's representative in Scotland, wrote immediately to Throckmorton. Mary went four days without attending Mass, he reported, but on the Sunday after her arrival it was celebrated by a French priest in her private chapel. She had great personal charm and the Scots lords were uncertain how to behave, torn between their religion and their allegiance to the captivating young Queen. Knox preached a sermon in the town, which was as well attended as ever. One nobleman, the Earl of Cassilis, had enthusiastically gone to hear Knox preach on Sunday, and attended Mass in the royal chapel on Monday. 'It is said he has repented it,' wrote Randolph, 'and this is but Tuesday.' He reported the arrival of two Catholic bishops, 'both in long gowns and tippets with hats upon their heads', but added that they 'scarce dare put their noses out of doors' for fear of being attacked. The priest who celebrated Mass in the royal chapel was almost trembling when he raised the monstrance.

The Scots lords demanded that Mary should make peace with England, that she should have Protestant councillors, and that she should enrich the Crown with Abbey lands. She was nineteen years old, and since the age of eight had known the delights and luxuries of the French Court. She had been pampered and adored. She loved fine clothes, music and dancing; she was accustomed both to watch and to take part in ballets and masques of incomparable elegance. The people of Edinburgh had prepared her a fearsome welcome. When she made her formal entry into the capital, a child of six stepped out of a globe painted to represent heaven to hand her a Bible, a Psalter and the keys of the city. Other pageants told Old Testament stories of God's wrath against idolaters. Lord Huntly, according to Randolph, had to suppress one fervently Protestant tableau, which represented a priest being burned at the stake.

Elizabeth sent Sir Peter Mewetas to congratulate Mary on her safe arrival. She also entertained the Guise uncles, who passed through England on their way home. Shortly before Mary had disembarked, Elizabeth sent her a letter saying she understood from Mary's envoy, M. de St Colme, that her reason for refusing to ratify the Treaty of Edinburgh had been her wish to discuss it with her Council. Elizabeth pointed out sharply that she wanted deeds, not words.

CB We assure you your answer is no satisfaction, we only require performance of your promise, whereto you are bound by your seal and hand – in your own power as Queen of Scotland which yourself in words confess, concluded by your late husband's and your own ambassadors, to which your own nobility and people were privy, and without which no amity can continue. Yet seeing by report of the bringer, that you mean forthwith on coming home to follow the advice of your Council there, we suspend our conceit of all unkindness, and assure you we be fully resolved on performance thereof, to unite in sure amity and live with you in the knot of friendship, as we are that of nature and blood. And herein we are so earnestly determined, that if the contrary follow (which God forbid) the world shall see the occasion to be in you, not in us; as the story witnesseth the like of the King your father our uncle, whom evil councillors advised against meeting our father at York to conclude a perpetual bond; whereof we know witnesses remain with us, and some (we think) with you. For the report that we had sent our admiral and navy to impeach your passage; your servants know its falseness, and that we have only 2 or 3 small barques at sea to apprehend certain Scottish pirates haunting our seas under pretence of letters of marque; whereto we were almost compelled by the complaint of the Spanish ambassador. On this matter we earnestly require your consideration at coming to your realm – the rather for respect that should be betwixt Scotland, our realm, France, Spain and the House of Burgundy. Recommending us to you with a request not to neglect these our friendly and sisterly offers of friendship, which before God we mean and intend to accomplish.

Under our signet. Hevingham, 16 August, 3rd year of our reign

To lend credence to the idea that English ships had only been patrolling Scottish waters because Philip was insisting she should keep her seas clear of pirates, Elizabeth wrote again to Mary on 25 August. She asked for the extradition of three notable buccaneers, Marychurch, Whitehead and Johnson, who were all English subjects. Mary should 'make straight order to apprehend them', since the Kings of Spain and Portugal were always complaining about pirates, 'some English' but, she sniffed, 'most Scots'.

Our right to Calais

There were now two unmarried Queens in one island. Several of Elizabeth's suitors transferred their attentions to the younger, prettier Scottish Queen, since the English one remained adamantly virginal. Mary created her half-brother, Lord James Stuart, Earl of Moray. Under his leadership Scotland continued firmly Protestant, although Mary asked her uncle, the Duke of Guise, to assure the Pope that she would do everything in her power to further the Catholic cause. There were frequent incidents involving attacks on priests; candles were stolen, altars vandalised. The Earl of Arran was a ringleader in such escapades and Randolph wrote to Cecil that Mary hated him. John Knox reduced her to tears, but according to the ambassador they were tears of rage, not sorrow. She asked Knox 'to use more meekness in his sermons'. Otherwise she remained perfectly tactful towards her Protestant subjects.

On 17 September Elizabeth again demanded the ratification of the Treaty of Edinburgh. Mary replied that it was 'fitter for none to live in peace than for women: I desire it with all my heart,' she told Randolph. One day in October she drew him aside confidentially in her garden, after a Council meeting, and Professed herself eager to visit England. She was delighted that Elizabeth had received the Guise uncles at her Court. She asked for a licence to send English horses to her friends in France. She longed to have the Queen of England's picture, but by November an exasperated letter arrived from Elizabeth:

'We only require the ratification of the treaty passed by your hand. When princesses treat openly by assembly of ambassadors, the world, especially the subjects of both, judge the amity not sound, but shaken or crazed.'

It was decided that the two Queens should meet. Cecil and Maitland were instructed to arrange matters. In February 1562 Mary, still awaiting Elizabeth's portrait, said to Maitland, 'It will do me good to have it, but it will not content my heart until I have both seen her and spoken with her.'

The Guise uncles also desired concord between England and Scotland, but in March 1562 followers of the Duke of Guise led an attack on a Protestant congregation in France. Catherine de' Medici had tried to appease the powerful Protestant party headed by Jeanne d'Albret, Queen of Navarre, the Prince de Condé and Admiral Coligny, with promises of religious toleration. In Paris, however, where the Protestants had been nicknamed 'Huguenots', religious tension often flared into violent brawling. Fighting broke out at Montpelier when the Huguenots held an open air prayer meeting. Soon France was in a state of civil war.

Throckmorton advised Elizabeth to ally with Condé, for by her intervention in Scotland and the swift establishment of the reformed religion in her own country, she was already a heroine in the eyes of Protestant Europe. Elizabeth's councillors urged her unanimously to postpone the meeting with Mary until the outcome of the French war was known. She defiantly arranged to meet Mary in York 'or some such convenient place', but in July the French situation deteriorated. Protestants in England were so stirred by the stories of Catholic atrocities in France that by the autumn Elizabeth agreed to help Condé.

She sent a force of 6,000 men into Normandy, justifying her action in a magnificently feminine letter to Philip of Spain. She had been 'much troubled and perplexed from the beginning of these divisions in France,' she confided. She felt 'great compassion to see the young King, our brother, so abused by his subjects'. She thought the French war might cause 'an universal trouble to the rest of Christendom', and the Duke of Guise and his party were dealing in a hostile manner with her merchants and subjects resident in France. Then she turned to the old grievance:

'And thereupon we could not forget how they were the very parties that evicted Calais from this crown; a matter of continual grief to this realm, and of glory to them. Neither could we forget how hardly by their means we were dealt withal at the conclusion of the peace at Casteau in Cambresis where you, the Duke of Savoy and others having restitution of possessions, our right (notwithstanding your good will to the contrary) was deferred to the end of certain years without restitution of anything.'

There followed a list of outrages perpetrated by the Guise family, including 'publishing of arms and such like', while 'a treaty which was concluded by the French King and Queen was unjustly and unhonourably denied (and so remaineth until this day) contrary to the several promises and solemn covenants of the said French King and Queen, their niece'. Elizabeth explained that her army would do 'no injury or violence' to Charles IX, but she wished 'to save to our realm in this convenient time our right to Calais with surety, which manifestly we see by their proceedings they mean not to deliver'.

During the course of the war the Duke of Guise was assassinated. Randolph reported from Scotland that Mary was 'marvellous sad, her ladies shedding tears like showers of rain'. Eventually Condé was taken prisoner and Catherine de' Medici negotiated peace. The Catholics and Huguenots then united to drive out the English, who were garrisoned at Le Havre. Elizabeth ordered the Earl of Warwick to hold on to the town. She wanted Calais back. Plague broke out; the English soldiers were dying at the rate of five hundred a week. By the end of July Elizabeth was obliged to surrender. She made peace at the expense of Calais, losing even her right to the restitution proposed by the Treaty of Câteau Cambrésis. It was a bitter lesson in the realities of war.

Three weeks before the surrender of Le Havre she wrote to Warwick. She was earnestly determined, she said, 'to go through with all things that any wise shall concern the defence of that town against all violence and force that can be devised by the enemy. And considering the substance thereof dependeth upon three principal things, men, money and victual, we are resolved, and have already put in execution that there shall be no lack of any of them. And we pray you to notify unto all our good servants and subjects, the gentlemen and captains there, that we take it no small augmentation to the honour of our Crown and Realm, and specially to our nation, that they have hitherto so manfully and skilfully acquitted themselves.'

The letter was written on 4 July and Elizabeth still believed that by the straight defence' of Le Havre 'against the whole force of France this our nation shall recover the ancient fame which heretofore it had, and of late with the loss of Calais lost also. This our opinion we pray you to communicate to our subject there.'

In her own hand she added a postscript to Ambrose:

C3 My dear Warwick, if your honour and my desire could accord with the loss of the needfulest finger I keep, God help me so in my most need, as I would gladly lose that one joint for your safe abode with me; but since I cannot that I would, I will do that I may, and will rather drink in an ashen cup than you or yours should not be succoured both by sea and land, yea, and that with all speed possible, and let this my scribbling hand witness it to them all.

Yours as my own,

E.R.

The second Parliament of the reign was summoned for 11 January 1563. Bad weather again caused the opening to be put off for a day. The principal business was expected to be the raising of a subsidy for the war with France, and reform of certain outdated laws. The previous autumn there had been an outbreak of smallpox. The Queen had been feverish and decided to take a bath, which was widely regarded as a health cure. She went out immediately afterwards and developed a temperature. A German doctor diagnosed the illness as smallpox. Elizabeth was outraged and refused to believe him. Five days later she was almost delirious. The doctors sent for Cecil, telling him the Queen was about to die.

The Privy Council were summoned to Hampton Court to discuss whether her successor should be Lord Huntingdon, who was of Plantagenet descent, or Lady Katherine Grey, who was still in the Tower. No one mentioned Mary Queen of Scots. Elizabeth, believing she was about to die, ordered them to appoint Dudley Lord Protector of the Realm. She swore, with God as her witness, that they had never been lovers, and in the same breath commanded that a legacy of £500 a year should be given to Robert's body-servant. The German doctor, who had considered himself insulted, was brought back at sword point. According to one story he wrapped the Queen in a length of scarlet cloth and gave her a potion which brought out the spots. She recovered quickly and was not permanently disfigured by the pock marks, but Robert's sister Lady Mary Sidney, who nursed her through the disease, was marked for life. Once more Elizabeth was deeply beholden to the Dudley family.

She had come close to death, and, had she died that autumn of 1562, the country would have been left with no certain successor. By the time Parliament met both Lords and Commons were clamouring for her to name a successor. A deputation from the Commons visited her at Whitehall. The Catholics, they claimed, were waiting for an opportunity 'to advance some title under which they may renew their late unspeakable cruelty'.

Sir Ralph Sadler prepared a speech full of trenchant arguments against Mary Stuart's claim. He was 'a mere natural Englishman' and he did not relish the idea of being 'subject to a foreign prince, a prince of a strange nation': 'And for the Queen of Scots, though she were indeed next heir in blood to the Queen's Majesty, yet being a stranger by the laws of the realm, as I understand she cannot inherit in England.' Lady Katherine, meanwhile, although still in the Tower, gave birth to her second son just ten days after the Commons presented their petition.

Elizabeth deferred her reply until the subsidy bill was through, contenting herself with telling the Commons that though after her death they might have 'many stepdames, yet shall you never have a more natural mother than I mean to be unto you all'. She was more impatient with the Lords, informing them they ought to know better than to meddle in such matters. According to de Quadra she told them she was still young enough to bear children and the marks they saw on her face were not wrinkles but smallpox scars. On 10 April at the close of the session she gave them her answer, daring them to doubt her word, promising them in ambiguous language that she would marry in due course, and informing them that if any thought she had taken a vow of celibacy they were completely mistaken.

'Since there can be no duer debt than Princes' word,' she said, it was important for her to keep hers 'unspotted'. She fully understood the value of credit in the mercantile world, and she did not wish them to doubt her word.

CB Therefore [she said] I will answer give. And this it is: The two petitions that you presented me in many words expressed, contained these two things in sum as of your cares the greatest: my marriage and my successor. Of which two the last I think is best to be touched, and of the other a silent thought may serve; for I had thought it had been so desired as none other tree's blossoms should have been minded or hope of my fruit had been denied you. And by the way, if any here doubt that I am as it were by vow or determination bent never to trade that life, put out that heresy; your belief is awry; for as I think it best for a private woman, so do I strive with myself to think it not meet for a prince. And if I can bend my will to your need I will not resist such a mind. But to the last, think not that you had needed this desire if I had seen a time so ripe to be denounced. The greatness of the cause therefore and need of your returns, doth make me say that which I think the wise may easily guess: that as a short time for so long a continuance ought not to pass by rote, as many telleth tales, even so, as cause by conference with the learned shall show the matter worthy utterance for your behoofs, so shall I more gladly pursue your good after my days than with my prayers be a means to linger my living thread. And this much more than I had thought will I add for your comfort; I have good record in this place that other means than you mentioned have been thought of, perchance for your good as much and for my surety no less, which if presently could conveniently have been executed, had not been deferred. But I hope I shall die in quiet with *nunc dimittis*, which cannot be without I see some glimpse of your following surety after my graved bones.

CHAPTER VIII

One mistress but no master

In the summer of 1564 the Queen went on one of the most dazzling progresses of her reign. She arrived in Cambridge on the afternoon of 5 August, preceded by a contingent of trumpeters and accompanied by a vast train of richly dressed lords and ladies. She was magnificently elegant in a gown of black velvet, the proper garb for a Renaissance princess. Her hair was held in place by a net embroidered with pearls and precious stones, and she wore a hat spangled with gold and topped with 'a bush of fine feathers'. Sir William Cecil, Chancellor of the University, was waiting at the city gate, sitting on a little black nag, sternly checking that the scholars obeyed his orders by first welcoming the Queen and then returning to their college in an orderly manner.

Elizabeth stayed for five days; she would have remained longer if the town had not run out of beer. She marvelled at the beauty of King's College Chapel where she heard the choir sing. She attended Latin plays and a disputation in St Mary's Church. She visited most of the colleges: Trinity, endowed by her father, St John's founded by her illustrious great-grandmother, Lady Margaret Beaufort. She saw Trinity Hall, Gonville and Caius, Pembroke, Magdalen, Benet College, Christ's College and Peter House, where she praised Sir Walter Mildmay's son, who made a 'neat and trim oration'. Everywhere she rode, she stopped to speak graciously in Latin to the scholars. No expense had been spared; the stage erected in King's was thought too small for the Court ladies to sit around in comfort. A new one was built in the chapel.

Elizabeth enjoyed herself enormously. She was given many presents, books bound in red velvet in Greek, Latin and Hebrew, four pairs of the double gloves for which Cambridge was famous, and six boxes of sweets and comfits, sent specially from London. Her courtiers were all presented with two pairs of gloves and the traditional gifts of marchpane and sugar loaves. In St Mary's Church the Duke of Norfolk and Lord Robert teased the Queen to address the scholars in Latin. She said if she might speak her mind in English, she would not stick at the matter, but Cecil told her nothing might be said openly to the university in English. She bade him speak for her, since he was the Chancellor and supposed to voice the Queen's opinion. He replied that he was the Chancellor of the university, not *her* Chancellor. Then Richard Cox, raised to the dignity of Bishop of Ely but in Elizabeth's eyes still Edward's old Latin tutor, the pedagogue who knew how perfectly she had mastered Ascham's method of double translation as a girl, said that three words from *her* mouth would be enough. To their delight she spoke extempore: '*Etsi feminilis pudor, clarissima academia,*' she began. 'Although that womanly shamefacedness, most celebrated university and most faithful subjects, might well determine me from delivering this my unlaboured speech and oration before so great an assembly of the learned, yet the intercession of my nobles and my own good will towards the university have prevailed with me to say something. And I am persuaded to this thing by two motives; the first is the increase of good letters, which I much desire, and with the most earnest wishes pray for; the other is as I hear all your expectations.' She went on for a further ten periods of mellifluous Latin, at which the scholars 'marvellously astonished' roared '*Vivat Regina*'. Elizabeth replied with a graceful pun, '*Taceat Regina*'. She left on 10 August, stopping for dinner at Cox's house at Stanton.

The success of the visit was partly due to Cecil's careful arrangements, but while he was Chancellor of the university, Dudley was its High Steward. In the feverish weeks preceding the Queen's visit it was to Lord Robert that the flustered heads of colleges turned, to ask if their arrangements would meet with approval. On 27 July he wrote reassuringly to the Vice Chancellor, 'Knowing how far her Highness doth esteem good will above any other gifts, let this persuade you that nothing can be with better will done by you than it will be graciously accepted of her', and he promised to come early on the day of the Queen's visit to see if there was anything he could do to help.

Elizabeth's nickname for Dudley was 'Eyes'. He signed private letters to her with the symbol $\overline{OO}$. There was a double meaning in the name in which she delighted. He was her 'eyes' in the sense that he kept watch, but also in another sense. Included in the Renaissance ideal of love as a union of two souls is the concept that love enters in through the eyes, the windows of the soul. In the fourth book of *The Courtier*, Cardinal Bembo, discoursing on the difference between sensual and spiritual love, advises the Courtier to lay aside 'the blind judgement of the senses and enjoy with his eyes, the brightness, the comeliness, the loving sparkles, laughters, gestures and all other pleasant furnitures of beauty – so shall he with most dainty food feed the soul.' With her grounding in Divinity it was perhaps easier for Elizabeth to accept the limitations of the higher love than for Robert.

The great beauty of the Queen's cryptic speech to the Parliament of 1563 lay in the fact that she had not stated *whom* she intended to marry. Cecil was left free to pursue his negotiations for a marriage with the Archduke Charles, Lord Robert, when his arduous duties as Master of the Horse left him time, could continue to scheme for his own advancement. In 1562 as an opening gambit in his campaign to settle the succession Dudley had brought the tragedy *Gorboduc*, which had been performed the previous year at the Temple, to Court. Its message was obvious: England, left without an heir after the untimely death of Ferrex and Pollex, the two Princes of the blood, falls into civil war. Thomas Norton, one of the joint authors of *Gorboduc* and a client of Dudley's, was the first to start the agitation in the Lower House for Elizabeth to marry. Sir Geoffrey Elton has demonstrated that this was then successfully manipulated by the councillors into the great hue and cry over the succession. Dudley was also the patron of Alexander Nowell, the Dean of St Paul's, who before the session began delivered a tremendous homily on the Queen's duty to beget an heir. Elizabeth was fully aware that Robert would have liked to be King of England, but for the moment she saw no good reason to change the *status quo*. Protective, informal, laughing and relaxed, Dudley had a unique gift for making the Queen herself relax. It was an infinitely preferable situation for her to be able to turn to a dependable friend, rather than to suffer the domination of an unwanted foreign husband. Moralists complained frequently because the favourite had apartments next to the Queen's in all her principal residences, but it was the Master of the Horse who had charge of Elizabeth's travelling arrangements, so it was necessary that he was always on hand to see that things went smoothly. Socially and domestically he fulfilled the role of a consort already. He hosted parties and he helped her arrange them. She told Guzman de Silva, without irony, that had Robert been a King's son she would indeed have married him. After the Cambridge progress, his advancement moved swiftly and before the end of the year she made him Chancellor of the university of Oxford.

Elizabeth went there on progress in 1566, repeating her Cambridge triumph by addressing the scholars in Greek, although this time she delivered a prepared oration. During a performance of *Palamon and Arcite* a stage collapsed, fatally injuring three students. The Queen sent her doctor to attend them. The play was postponed on account of the tragedy, but took place the following day. A cry of hounds had been arranged to enhance Theseus' entrance, and the scene was so convincing that some foolish youths, believing a real hunt was in progress, began hallooing from the windows. Elizabeth was enchanted, but such were the traumas of the production that the play's theme has gone almost unremarked. Two suitors contend for the hand of Theseus' ward, the fair Emily: Palamon the brother of a King, and Arcite, who is nobly born but not a Prince. Arcite wins her but dies, leaving Emily to wed the socially superior Palamon. Leicester had brought some actors from Gray's Inn to perform at Whitehall the previous spring. Their play had included a dialogue in which Juno praised marriage and Diana chastity, while Jupiter arbitrated in favour of matrimony. Elizabeth turned to de Silva during the performance, saying 'This is all against me.' Leicester had chosen the Whitehall piece; as Chancellor of Oxford he would also have chosen, or approved the choice of, *Palamon and Arcite*.

Its theme was peculiarly apposite. The death of the Emperor had brought negotiations for Elizabeth to marry the Archduke Charles to a halt. His older brother became Emperor and in the spring of 1565 plans for the Habsburg match got under way again. Cecil worked strenuously to promote it, as did the Archduke's envoy, Baron von Breuner. The Earl of Sussex was sent to Vienna and the greater part of 1565 and 1566 was spent in discussions about the Archduke's religion, whether he could be sent over for inspection, and if so which government would pay the expenses. Both parties appeared to be trying to fix suitable terms. In the midst of the negotiations Catherine de' Medici panicked over the idea of an Anglo-Habsburg alliance. She offered Elizabeth Charles IX, who was nearly fifteen. The Queen was twenty-nine. She told de Silva that she would not make the world laugh by letting them see at the church door 'an old woman and a child'. This said, she pretended to be interested in Catherine's proposal. The French would stop at nothing to prevent a rapprochement between England and the Habsburgs, and du Foix, their ambassador, categorically told de Silva that on New Year's Night 1566 Elizabeth slept with Lord Leicester.

It was not a likely story, although there was a disturbing intimacy between the couple which gave rise to continuous speculation that they were lovers in the fullest sense. He was wont to come into her bedchamber and hand her her shift early in the morning, but her ladies were always present. In March 1565 when Leicester was playing tennis with the Duke of Norfolk, the earl snatched Elizabeth's handkerchief out of her hand to mop his sweating brow. The duke raged at Leicester's presumption, and the handkerchief-snatching eventually led to the Court dividing into two camps, Norfolk's followers wearing yellow favours and Leicester's blue. Before things had reached this juncture, the earl took de Silva riding one morning in Windsor park. On the way back they skirted some woods, stopping beside the Queen's lodging. Leicester's fool began shouting so loudly that Elizabeth came to the window, *déshabillée*. During 1565 the relationship between the Queen and her favourite was fraught with emotional tension. In a row over a man of Leicester's who had been refused entrance to the Presence Chamber, Elizabeth is said to have screamed, 'God's death, my Lord, I will have here one mistress but no master.'

Yonder long lad

When the Queen assured the 1563 Parliament that she had taken no vows of celibacy she was twenty-seven by Tudor standards already on the way to middle age. Mary Stuart was twenty-one. Widowed for three years, and with Scotland for her dowry, she did not lack suitors. Her Protestant councillors had eagerly put forward the Kings of Sweden and Denmark. Her Guise uncle, the Cardinal of Lorraine, favoured the Archduke Charles, while Catherine de' Medici had offered her the King of France, then thirteen and nearing the age at which his brother had married her. Mary preferred what seemed to her the most magnificent match of all, Philip's son, Don Carlos. She had a high notion of her own dignity, and having been Queen of France she liked the idea of one day becoming Queen of Spain. The Infante's behavioural oddities were still being put down to the wildness of youth. He had not yet reached that stage of insanity at which he was to tell his valet to eat his shoes, after which he threw the unfortunate man out of the window. Philip hesitated over the match for other reasons. After his own experiences as King of England, he must have doubted the wisdom of shipping his heir off to a country as unstable as Scotland, with its history of clan feuds and insurrections. A *canard* was also circulating through the courts of Europe that Mary had poisoned Francis II.

As Sir Ralph Sadler had pointed out to the Lower House, no right-thinking Englishman would want to see Mary Stuart on Elizabeth's throne. She had not yet acquired that notoriety with which successive parliaments were to charge her, but she was, quite simply, a Scot, and this made the other claimant, Lady Katherine Grey, who had been born in the realm, a more attractive proposition. But for as long as the English succession remained unsettled, Elizabeth could dangle the possibility before the Scots that she might some day make Mary her heir. As this decision would involve removing the obstacle of Henry VIII's will which excluded the descendants of his sister Margaret, it was hinted that any scheme to legalise Mary's claim would depend upon her marrying with Elizabeth's approbation. Her tone towards her cousin was often that of a rather bossy elder sister, and she began to behave as though she had charge of Mary's wardship. The Countess of Lennox intrigued continually to marry her eldest son Henry, Lord Darnley, to Mary. A handsome youth of eighteen, Darnley had his own place in the line of succession to the thrones of England and Scotland through his descent from Margaret Tudor, although only by her second marriage to the Earl of Angus. Theoretically, however, the Darnley match would strengthen Mary's claim. At the beginning of Elizabeth's reign the ambitious Countess had spent a short time in the Tower, and a condition of her release had been that she would drop the idea of marrying her son to the Scottish Queen. By 1564 she was at liberty and living at the English Court. Elizabeth suggested Mary should restore lands which the Lennoxes had lost in the wars between England and Scotland. In the autumn of 1564 Lennox went to Edinburgh for the formal ceremony of restitution. He requested Elizabeth's permission for his son to join him. It was refused.

Elizabeth meanwhile had put forward a preposterous scheme of her own for Mary Stuart to marry Dudley. It began as a joke, and was intended to pay him back for deliberately inciting the House of Commons against her in the spring of 1563. The Scottish laird, Maitland of Lethington, had been sent to England as Mary's envoy with secret instructions to confer with de Quadra about a Spanish match. He was to alarm Philip by hinting that Mary might really take up Catherine de' Medici's suggestion of marrying the young French King. Elizabeth learned what was going on. She told Maitland that if his mistress wished to marry 'safely and happily', she would find her a husband who would ensure that she did both. This was Lord Robert 'in whom nature had implanted so many graces that, if she wished to marry, she would prefer him to all the princes in the world.'

Maitland returned the banter, saying Elizabeth should marry Robert herself and when she died, leave Mary heiress to her kingdom and her husband. To everyone's astonishment Elizabeth pursued the idea, apparently seriously, for the next two years. Mary was not at all amused to be matched with a man whom she considered to be of markedly inferior rank, and whom half Europe regarded as Elizabeth's paramour. Elizabeth kept up the charade, however, creating Robert Earl of Leicester, ostensibly to show that she was serious in her offer, and was raising him in rank to make him a more suitable husband for Mary. During the investiture she leaned down to tickle his neck in full view of the French and Spanish ambassadors.* Whether this was a deliberate gesture to demonstrate that he was her creature, or whether her sense of fun simply overcame her, is uncertain. Sir James Melville, Mary's representative, was present. When Elizabeth arrived for the ceremony she was preceded by the tall figure of Henry Darnley bearing the sword of state in its pearl-studded scabbard. As the new Earl of Leicester rose to his feet, resplendent in his coronet and scarlet mantle, Elizabeth asked Melville what he thought of her creation. The ambassador replied politely and the Queen, pointing at Darnley, remarked laughingly, 'And yet you like better of yonder long lad', implying she had full knowledge of any plot being hatched by the Lennoxes. Dudley took as his motto *'Droit et loyal'*, which epitomised everything Elizabeth expected from a trusty and well-beloved servant of the Crown. A few days after the ceremony the Queen took Sir James Melville into her bedchamber to show him some treasures she kept locked in a cabinet. One was a miniature of Mary, another was of Leicester. Elizabeth unwrapped it from a piece of paper on which was written 'My Lord's picture'. Melville suggested she should send it to Mary but Elizabeth said she could not spare it; she had no copy. Despite this coy scene implying Elizabeth and Leicester were sweethearts, Melville continued to take her proposal seriously. Elizabeth said archly that nothing could be better for the two kingdoms than that Mary should marry one whom she favoured and loved 'as a brother'.

Leicester had no desire to marry Mary Stuart. He wrote to her saying the whole idea was a diplomatic ploy of Elizabeth's to keep the Queen of Scotland from marrying other suitors. In February 1565 Darnley was allowed to join his father. Leicester was among those who counselled Elizabeth to let him go. Mary had spent a great deal of her young life in mourning. Her mother, her father-in-law, and her first husband had all died within the space of two years, quickly followed by her favourite uncle, the Duke of Guise. She had behaved with great dignity in her widowhood, accepting the vast cultural differences between the French and Scottish courts, and enduring John Knox's endless criticism of her elegance and her liking for music and dancing. When she set eyes on her handsome English cousin, tall as she was herself and, on first acquaintance, well trained in courtly behaviour, she fell in love. The couple met first at Wemyss Castle, where they danced a galliard together, and an ecstatic Mary told Melville that her cousin was 'the properest and best proportioned long man' she had ever seen. Randolph cautiously reserved judgement; 'A great number wish him well, others doubt him,' he wrote to Cecil.

---

* The tickling is decorously omitted from the official report of the proceedings.

Mary immediately went ahead with wedding plans. Elizabeth was outraged. She imprisoned the Countess of Lennox again, and when Melville arrived with letters from her husband, the unfortunate woman was not even allowed to receive them. A full Catholic wedding took place at Holyrood House on 29 July 1565. Darnley was given the title 'King Henry', but he was not granted the Crown Matrimonial, which would have given him equal rights with Mary. He quickly alienated many Scottish nobles by his arrogant behaviour. Mary's half-brother, Moray, rebelled. With a pistol at her saddle and accompanied by Darnley in gilded tilt armour, Mary rode at the head of her army, chasing the rebel earl from Edinburgh to Glasgow. He escaped over the border, causing acute embarrassment to Elizabeth. After this dashing beginning the marriage deteriorated, although Mary's physical passion lasted long enough for her to conceive a child. She travelled to Linlithgow in December, Randolph reporting that she was definitely pregnant.

The royal couple were often apart; the King went hunting and hawking, while Mary continued to shoulder the serious business of government. To prevent delays Darnley's signature was made into a seal for stamping official documents. This was given to Mary's secretary, David Riccio. The little Italian had come to Scotland in the suite of the Duke of Savoy. Mary, lacking a bass singer for a quartet, employed him as a musician. Later he became her secretary. Gossip-mongers alleged he was something more. Darnley was frequently drunk; hawking and hunting gave way to roisterous and unkingly behaviour in the streets of Edinburgh. Mary's ardour cooled swiftly. She lost respect for her husband, placing more and more trust in the base-born Riccio, even offending Maitland, who had been her principal secretary since the reign began. Darnley conspired with a group of Protestant lords to kill the Italian. Someone had persuaded him that Riccio's position was an affront to his honour. On March 9, headed by the ghastly figure of Patrick, Lord Ruthven, clad in a steel helmet with his armour showing beneath his cloak, the assassins burst into a private supper party in Mary's apartments, dragged the terrified secretary out of the room and murdered him in the antechamber. Fifty-six stab wounds were discovered on the body, and while Mary did not actually witness the murder, she could hear Riccio's voice shouting in a mixture of French and Italian, '*Justizia, justizia, sauvez moi, Madame.*'

A faithful cousin and friend

Mary's biographer, Antonia Fraser, argues that the Queen believed the conspirators intended to kill her that night. Mary was six months pregnant, and a loaded pistol was pointed at her stomach. She managed to persuade Darnley that his accomplices meant also to kill him. They escaped together down a back staircase of Holyrood

House and rode twenty miles to the Castle of Dunbar, where Mary dictated a letter to Elizabeth. She told how the conspirators had occupied her house. They had 'taken our most special servant in our own presence and thereafter holden our proper persons captive treasonably whereby we were constrained to escape straitly about midnight, out of our Palace of Holyrood House to the place where we are for the present, in the greatest danger for our lives and evil estate that ever princes on earth stood in.' She implored Elizabeth to help her and apologised for not writing in her own hand, adding, 'but of truth we are so tired and ill at ease, what through riding twenty-five miles in five hours of the night'. The letter is written in broad Scots and dated 15 March. It is a testimony to Mary's own popularity that nine days later she was able to re-enter the city of Edinburgh victoriously at the head of some eight thousand men. She was lodged in the castle, which was thought to be safer than Holyrood House, and on 19 June 1566 gave birth to her son, James. Elizabeth was invited to be godmother. She sent the Earl of Bedford north with a magnificent golden font. Melville, writing many years later, alleged that his brother, Sir Robert, told him that when Elizabeth heard of James's birth she cried in anguish, 'The Queen of Scotland is mother of a fair son, and I am but a barren stock.' She was dancing when they brought her the news and sat down heavy with shock, leaning her head on her hand. By the time Melville had his audience she was cheerful and smiling again.

After a short convalescence Mary began to discuss with her councillors what should be done about Darnley. Divorce was not considered a possible solution. It would have bastardised the baby prince. Darnley fell ill, officially with smallpox, although it seems more probable that he had syphilis, which would explain Mary's utter repugnance. Anxious to retain the dignity of the Crown, she visited him to hush up the scandal, and lodged him in a small house at Kirk o' Field in Edinburgh not far from the city wall. It stood on a hill, and the official reason for the King staying there was that it had healthy air. One of Mary's ablest supporters since the murder of Riccio was James Hepburn, Earl of Bothwell. He was a confirmed womaniser who had recently married Lady Jean Gordon, the wealthy sister of the Earl of Huntly. Bothwell undertook to dispose of the King. It is not certain whether Mary knew what was planned. She stayed some nights at Kirk o' Field, playing cards with her sick husband, with whom she now appeared to be on good terms. On 9 February she went to Holyrood to attend a wedding feast.

At two o'clock the following morning a violent explosion blew Kirk o' Field to pieces. Darnley's body was found in the garden. He had apparently tried to escape in his nightshirt. Beside him, also dead, lay his servant Taylor. A doublet, a dagger, a chair and a piece of rope were all in the vicinity. There was reported to have been no mark on either body, but it seems fairly certain that they had been strangled. One of Bothwell's henchmen, a Captain William Blackadder, the first person to rush into the street, was promptly arrested, although he later swore he had been drinking at a friend's house. Mary was awakened at Holyrood by the blast. She sent messengers to find out what had happened. Bothwell was the prime suspect. Elizabeth urged Mary to order an instant enquiry.

CB Madam,

My ears have been so astounded and my heart so frightened to hear of the horrible and abominable murder of your former husband, our mutual cousin, that I have scarcely spirit to write; yet I cannot conceal that I grieve more for you than for him. I should not do the office of a faithful cousin and friend, if I did not urge you to preserve your honour, rather than look through your fingers at revenge on those who have done you that pleasure as most people say. I advise you so to take this matter to heart, that you may show the world what a noble Princess and loyal woman you are. I write thus vehemently not that I doubt, but for affection. As for the three matters communicated by Melville, I understand your wish to please me, and that you will grant the request by Lord Bedford in my name to ratify the treaty made six or seven years ago. I will not trouble you about other matters, referring you to the report of this gentleman.

Westminster, 24 February 1567

Charged with the murder of your late husband

Although Bothwell was the main suspect, and obscene graffiti accusing him appeared on the Edinburgh tolbooth, Mary took no immediate steps to bring him to justice. Both Elizabeth and Catherine de' Medici urged her to prosecute the murderers immediately and vengefully, in order to proclaim her own innocence in the eyes of the people. In London a distraught Margaret Lennox was taken from the Tower and lodged compassionately at the house of Sir Richard Sackville. De Silva reported that the wretched woman believed that Mary had 'had some hand in the business' and that it was a 'revenge for her Italian secretary'. He also observed that Elizabeth had the keys taken from the locks in the doors of her own chambers.

In Edinburgh there was a show trial. Bothwell was charged, not by the Crown, but by the sorrowing Earl of Lennox, who did not even dare to appear, since the town was seething with Bothwell's supporters. The proceedings lasted from noon until seven in the evening. The Court Recorder wrote that Bothwell 'was made clean of the said slaughter, albeit that it was heavily murmured that he was guilty thereof'. On 24 April, less than three months after the murder, Mary was abducted by Bothwell as she rode with a small escort from Stirling to Edinburgh. She had been to see her baby son. Bothwell took her, apparently with her consent, to Dunbar Castle, where she had taken refuge with Darnley after Riccio's murder. It seems probable she was so depressed and exhausted that, believing herself once more in danger, she simply allowed this resolute man to take charge. It was said that he raped her, and that this explains their hurried marriage according to Protestant rites, twelve days after Bothwell's contrived divorce from Lady Jean.

Antonia Fraser has demonstrated why Mary, in a state of nervous collapse, seemed at this point to lose control of her destiny in the series of events which led to her surrender at Carberry Hill. Despite the scene being set for a pitched battle, Mary and Bothwell flying the lion rampant of Scotland and the cross of St Andrew, and the renegade nobles who had gathered to oppose them under a fearful banner portraying the corpse of Darnley with the motto 'Judge and avenge my cause, oh Lord', neither side wished to fight. The French ambassador, du Croc, rode between the two parties bearing messages. Bothwell challenged the confederate lords, some of them his former supporters, to send out a champion to fight him in single combat. Mary, trusting in a peaceful solution, gave herself up to her nobles, believing that the whole matter could be settled in Parliament. She was taken back to Edinburgh in clothes caked with mud, while the rebel soldiers shouted 'Burn the whore, kill her, drown her.' Subsequently they conducted her to the grim fortress of Lochleven, utterly degraded.

Elizabeth, who had not realised the fullness of Mary's plight, sat dictating her opinions from her summer palace of Richmond.

Cʒ Madam,

It has been always held in friendship that prosperity provideth, but adversity proveth friends, wherefore we comfort you with these few words. We understand by your trusty servant Robert Melville of your estate and as much as could be said for your marriage. To be plain with you our grief has not been small thereat: for how could a worse choice be made for your honour than in such haste to marry a subject who, besides other notorious lacks, public fame has charged with the murder of your late husband, besides touching yourself in some part, though we trust in that behalf falsely! And with what peril have you married him, that hath another lawful wife nor any children betwixt you legitimate?

Thus you see our opinion plainly, and we are heartily sorry we can conceive no better, what colourable reasons soever we have heard of your servant to induce us otherwise. We are earnestly bent to do everything in our power to procure the punishment of that murder against any subject you have, how dear soever you should hold him, and next thereto to be careful how your son the prince may be preserved to the comfort of you and your realm.

For your comfort in such your present adversity, as we hear you are in, we are determined to do all in our power for your honour and safety and to send with all speed one of our trusty servants not only to understand your state, but thereon so to deal with your nobility and people, as they shall find you not to lack our friendship and power for the preservation of your honour in quietness. And upon knowledge had, what shall be further right to be done for your comfort and for the tranquillity of your Realm we will omit no time to further the same as you shall and will see, and so we recommend ourselves to you good sister in as effectual a manner as heretofore we were accustomed.

I will marry as soon as I can conveniently

During 1566 Leicester began a flirtation with Lady Hereford. He was encouraged by Throckmorton, who advised him to test the strength of Elizabeth's affection. Better known as Lettice Knollys, Lady Hereford was the Queen's first cousin. She was voluptuously beautiful.* Elizabeth retaliated by flirting with Sir Thomas Heneage. When Leicester and Elizabeth made up their quarrel, they both shed tears. All this suggests a good deal of emotional tension. No one wanted to force the Queen to come to a decision, but the realm needed an heir, and among Cecil's private memoranda was a paper weighing up the relative merits of Leicester and the Archduke. Under the heading 'In birth', Cecil had written for Charles, 'Nephew and brother of an Emperor. An Archduke born.' By Leicester he wrote, 'Born of a knight, his grandfather but a squire. An Earl made.' under 'Wealth' Cecil estimated the Archduke at 3,000 ducats a year; beside Leicester he wrote 'All of the Queen and in debt'. He recorded that Charles's father, the Emperor Ferdinand, had been 'blessed with multitudes of children'; by Leicester he wrote '*Nuptiae steriles*'.

Leicester's position was slightly unfair, for as long as the earl was the object of the Queen's affections, he could not embark on a second marriage, but he was a man with healthy appetites. He also wanted an heir. His position was the more intolerable, since every public demonstration of Elizabeth's love and favour earned him more enemies at Court. Everyone held him responsible for the Queen's spinsterhood. If he pursued his own suit honourably, Norfolk, Sussex and Cecil condemned him as vilely ambitious. If he remained near Elizabeth in a state of permanently suspended desire, he came in for the lion's share of her nervous outbursts and hysterical tantrums. Cecil believed these would cease automatically as soon as she bore children. The doctors saw no reason why she should not (although Dr Huick had frightened her by suggesting she might not have an easy delivery). She appeared once more to be tormented by indecision, and she told de Silva that she feared the Archduke might not want to marry her. If this should be the case, she would be in a very delicate position, since she might then marry Lord Robert, who would feel she had chosen him as a last resort. All this was passed on to Philip in the same despatch as the

* De Silva called Lettice 'one of the best-looking ladies of the Court'.

French ambassador's story that the Queen and the earl had slept together on New Year's night.

Robert was so despondent that early in 1566 he gained permission to leave Court for a time to see to his affairs 'as other men do'. He was away three months and would have stayed longer if he had been allowed. He had clearly resigned himself to the idea of the Austrian marriage. In February he wrote to Cecil, 'I pray God she may proceed therein as may bring both content to herself and comfort to all. Surely there can be nothing shall so well settle her in good estate as this way (I mean her marriage) with whomsoever it shall please it to put her mind to like and honour.' Reading between the lines, Robert was as exhausted as anyone by Elizabeth's tenacious hold on her virginity.

When the Parliament which had been called in 1563 met for its second session on 30 September 1566, negotiations for the Austrian marriage were still in progress. In Elizabeth's view these were the concern of the Council. The House of Commons saw the matter differently. Despite her promise, their Queen was still unmarried. The first business before the House should have been the subsidy bill, but instead there was a spontaneous and often rowdy debate on the succession. Elizabeth sent in councillor after councillor to stop it. She promised that she really intended to marry. The Commons had decided, however, to petition her on the succession, and they persuaded the Lords to join them. A committee was appointed to draft the matter.

Elizabeth was really angry. Her private life was her affair. She felt her secret instructions to diplomats and months of patient negotiating were in danger of being overturned by grown men behaving like schoolboys. Some members of the Council came to her in the Privy Chamber. She turned vehemently upon them. She called the Duke of Norfolk a traitor; she told Pembroke he talked like a swaggering soldier. She pointed out that the Marquis of Northampton's matrimonial problems were such a scandal it had required an Act of Parliament to establish his marriage. Let him look to his own affairs instead of mincing words with her. As for Leicester, he was a false friend. She had thought if all the world abandoned her, he would not. He offered to die at her feet. That, she raged, had nothing to do with the matter. Cecil thought it might be best to prorogue Parliament, 'because presently it seemeth very uncomfortable to the Queen's Majesty to hear of this at this time. It is hoped that God will direct her heart to think more comfortably hereof.'

Elizabeth did not wish to endanger the subsidy. On 5 November she forestalled the threatened petition by summoning a delegation from both Houses to Whitehall, thirty from the Lords, thirty from the Commons. Her own corrected draft of the opening sentences she intended to speak survives, as does the final version reported by one of the delegates. In the end she required no notes. She was magnificent. She attacked Edward Bell, who had raised the subject in the Commons, and she drowned them in her oratory, showing that November afternoon how completely she had absorbed the techniques of the classical masters.

In the first place, she said, if they had considered the gravity of the matter, they would have stuck to the proper procedures:

'But those unbridled persons whose heads were never snaffled by the rider did rashly enter into it in the common house, a public place; where Mr Bell with his accomplices alleged that they were natural Englishmen and were bound to their country which they saw must needs perish and come to confusion unless some order were taken for the limitation of the succession of the crown.'

The Lords, she added scornfully, had thrown in their lot, 'seduced and of simplicity' assenting. They had been rash; they should have given more thought to the importance of the matter. But in the Upper House 'two bishops with their long orations sought to persuade you also with solemn matter'. Working herself into a frenzy of sarcasm she went on, 'As though you, my Lords, had not known that when my breath did fail me I had been dead unto you, and that then, dying without issue, what a danger it were to the whole state; which you had not known before they told it you. And so it was easily to be seen *quo oratio tendit*. For those that should be stops and stays of this great good and avoiding of so many dangers.'

She turned back to the Commons, bitterly mocking the hapless Bell:

'Was I not born in the realm? Were my parents born in any foreign country? Is not my kingdom here? Whom have I oppressed? Whom have I enriched to other's harm? What turmoil have I made in this commonwealth that I should be suspected to have no regard to the same? How have I governed since my reign? I will be tried by envy itself. I need not to use many words, for my deeds do try me.

'Well, the matter whereof they would have made their petition (as I am informed) consisteth in two points: in my marriage, and in the limitations of the succession of the crown, wherein my marriage was first placed, as for manners' sake. I did send them answer by my council, I would marry (although of mine own disposition I was not inclined thereunto) but that was not accepted nor credited, although spoken by their Prince.

'I will never break the word of a prince spoken in a public place, for my honour's sake. And therefore I say again, I will marry as soon as I can conveniently, if God take not him away with whom I mind to marry, or myself, or else some other great let happen. I can say no more except the party were present. And I hope to have children, otherwise I would never marry. A strange order of petitioners that will make a request and cannot be otherwise assured but by the prince's word, and yet will not believe it when it is spoken.

'The second point was for the limitation of the succession of the crown, wherein was nothing said for my safety, but only for themselves. A strange thing that the foot should direct the head in so weighty a cause', a cause, she pointed out, to which she had given careful consideration since it concerned her more nearly than it concerned them.

'I am sure there was not one of them that ever was a second person, as I have been and have tasted of the practices against my sister, who I would to God were alive again. I had great occasion to hearken to their motions for whom some of them are of the common house.'

She forebore to name those who had plotted against the Crown in Mary's reign, contenting herself with:

'And were it not for my honour, their knavery should be known. There were occasions in me at that time, I stood in danger of my life, my sister was so incensed against me. I did differ from her in religion and I was sought for divers ways. And so shall never be my successor. I have conferred with those that are well learned, and have asked their opinions touching the limitation of succession.' The lawyers, she said, had been silent; they understood the legal complications but 'they could not tell what to say considering the great peril to the realm.'

As for those who thought they knew better: 'They would have twelve or fourteen limited in succession and the more the better. And those shall be of such uprightness and so divine, as in them shall be divinity itself. Kings were wont to honour philosophers, but if I had such I would honour them as angels that should have such piety in them that they would not seek where they are the second to be the first, and where the third to be the second and so forth. It is said I am no divine. Indeed I studied nothing else but divinity till I came to the crown; and then I gave myself to the study of that which was meet for government, and am not ignorant of stories wherein appeareth what hath fallen out for ambition of kingdoms – as in Spain, Naples, Portugal and at home; and what cocking hath been between the father and the son for the same. You would have a limitation of succession. Truly if reason did not subdue will in me, I would cause you to deal in it, so pleasant a thing it should be unto me. But I stay it for your benefit. For if you should have liberty to treat of it, there be so many competitors – some kinsfolk, some servants, and some tenants; some would speak for their master, and some for their mistress, and every man for his friend – that it would be an occasion of a greater charge than a subsidy. And if my will did not yield to reason, it should be that thing I would gladliest desire to see you deal in it.'

And still she had not finished. She accused them of errors; she accused them of 'lack of good foresight'; and then she turned on the bishops with withering scorn:

'I do not marvel, though *Domini Doctores*, with you my Lords, did so use themselves therein, since after my brother's death they openly preached and set forth that my sister and I were bastards. Well, I wish not the death of any man, but only this I desire, that they which have been the practisers herein may before their deaths repent the same, and show some open confession of their fault, whereby the scabbed sheep may be known from the whole. As for my own part I care not for death, for all men are mortal; and though I be a woman yet I have as good a courage answerable to my place as ever my father had. I am your anointed Queen. I will never be by violence constrained to do anything. I thank God I am indeed endowed with such qualities that if I were turned out of the realm in my petticoat I were able to live in any place in Christendom.

'Your petition is to deal in the limitation of the succession. At this present it is not convenient, nor never shall be without some peril unto you, and certain danger unto me. But as soon as there may be a convenient time and that it may be done with least peril unto you, although never without great danger unto me, I will deal therein for your safety and offer it unto you as your prince and head without request. For it is monstrous that the feet should direct the head.'

She told the Lord Chief Justice to deliver this message to the House of Lords, and Cecil to inform the Commons. It took Cecil three drafts to word the matter diplomatically enough for it to bear repeating.

I love so evil counterfeiting

The speech to the two select committees was not the end of the matter. The House of Commons began to discuss the question of its ancient privileges and the money bill was again delayed. Elizabeth had learned early in the session that the Commons meant to use it against her, threatening to withhold the subsidy if she did not declare a successor, until she silenced them with her tirade. When the subsidy, which was to be paid in three parts, was finally agreed, she remitted the third part. Someone misconstrued the gracious gesture as a sign of feminine weakness, and when the act granting the subsidy was drafted there was an attempt to slip into the preamble a promise on the Queen's part to marry, which could later have been used to force her hand. After eight years of Cecil's tuition Elizabeth, who scrutinised government papers with care, was not likely to be fooled. When she spotted the offending clause, she scrawled over the draft in blazing fury:

'I know no reason why any my private answers to the realm should serve for prologue to a subsidies book. Neither yet do I understand why such audacity should be used to make, without my licence, an act of my words like lawyers' books, which nowadays go to the wire-drawers to make subtle doings more plain. Is there no hold of my speech without an act compel me to confirm? Shall my princely consent be turned to strengthen my words that be not of themselves substantives? I say no more at this time; but if these fellows were well answered and paid with lawful coin, there would be fewer counterfeits among them.'

Money was on Elizabeth's mind. It was not the first time that she had likened those who practised deceitfulness of any kind to the coin-clippers and currency forgers who were a perennial problem to the realm.* In her speech at the end of the session, the same metaphor occurs.

* Several proclamations refer to Elizabeth's determination to make the currency sound and to restore faith in the coinage. One, referring to the introduction of the new 3d and 6d pieces of 'fine sterling silver', is of

'I love so evil counterfeiting and hate so much dissimulation', she said, 'that I may not suffer you to depart without that my admonitions may show your harm and cause you shun unseen peril.' The definitions were clear in Elizabeth's mind. Secrecy over whom she would marry or name as her successor was for the safety of the realm. Prying into these matters by the House of Commons was a breach of government security. Doubting her word, the word of a Prince, was an offence highly distasteful to Almighty God. Attempts to restrain her or influence her policy were dissimulation or underhand dealing. They were points of view from which she never wavered. So passionately did she feel about the issues raised by the members of the 1566 Parliament, that she addressed them herself. There was no hard and fast tradition that the sovereign should close Parliament with a personal appearance. The Lord Keeper had already spoken on her behalf. But just as her father had been moved that Christmas Eve in 1545 to rebuke the members for their lack of charity towards each other, so she was moved to remind them who was in charge. 'Prince's words', she said, were 'better printed in the hearer's memory' than those spoken by her commandment.

There followed a long harangue on her prerogatives. 'Two visors' had blinded their eyes, 'succession and liberties'. Such a weighty cause should not have been discussed 'in so public a place'. It had been a 'lewd endeavour' which would make people think she was behaving irresponsibly over the succession, and this was not the case. 'As to liberties,' she continued, 'God forbid that your liberty should make my bondage, or that your lawful liberties should anyways have been infringed', and in this vein she went on, scolding them, cajoling them, forgiving them and finally completely turning the tables with expressions of love and thanks. Their love alone, she said, had made her 'heavy burden light, and a kingdom's care but easy carriage'. She warned them 'never to tempt too far a prince's patience', and so dismissed them with 'you return with your Prince's grace; whose care for you, doubt you not to be such as she shall not need a remembrancer for your weal'.

They left for their counties, some under the impression she would marry the Archduke, and others believing it would be Lord Leicester, who had been notably absent when she made her speech in the Presence Chamber with its cryptic explanations that she could say no more until her future husband stood beside her.

---

particular interest. Rewards were frequently offered for information leading to the detection of anyone melting down foreign coin to forge illicit money.

CHAPTER IX

They have no warrant nor authority

The succession remained unsettled, but while the English Parliament was pleading with Elizabeth to marry, the golden font despatched with the Earl of Bedford had arrived safely at its destination. On 17 December 1566 Prince James was christened with full Catholic ritual at Stirling Castle. Darnley was at this point still King of Scotland, but he did not attend the ceremony.* The Comte de Brienne stood proxy godfather for the King of France, the French ambassador for the Duke of Savoy, and the Countess of Argyll for the baby's Protestant godmother, the Queen of England. There were fireworks and Court masques. Queen Mary had arrayed her noblemen, 'some in cloth of silver, some in cloth of gold', and even the puritanical Earl of Bedford let the young gentlemen in his train join the dancing. Seven months later, his father dead, his mother imprisoned and deposed, the one-year-old infant was declared King of Scotland with his uncle Moray for Regent. When Elizabeth heard the full extent of Mary's plight she was horrified. The Scots lords had forced their Queen to sign a document of abdication, threatening her life if she did not. Elizabeth's wrath rings down the ages:

'They have no warrant nor authority by the law of God or man to be as superiors, judges or vindicators over their prince and sovereign, howsoever they do gather or conceive matter of disorder against her.'†

She sent Throckmorton to Scotland, but he was not allowed to visit Mary at Loch Leven, although he managed to get messages to her. His ostensible mission was to suggest that James should be brought up in England as Elizabeth's ward, in the same way that Margaret Douglas, his Lennox grandmother, had been at Henry VIII's Court. Elizabeth's original plan was that Mary should divorce Bothwell and be restored to her throne by the English, in return for which she was, of course, to ratify the Treaty of Edinburgh. When Throckmorton arrived Mary was pregnant and Bothwell still at liberty trying to raise an army. If Mary had divorced him, she would have bastardised the unborn twins of which she later miscarried. Elizabeth declared herself ready to go to war on her cousin's behalf, although Cecil pointed out that if

---

* There was no particular reason why a King should attend a royal infant's christening. Henry VIII did not attend Edward's, although the baby's sisters did. Edward was brought afterwards to the King's presence in a solemn procession.

† The original draft is corrected in Cecil's hand; the letter must have been a joint compilation between himself and Elizabeth. It rolls to a crescendo quoting scripture, Roman Law and Civil Law. Seditious ballads had already appeared in England justifying the deposition of a Sovereign.

she did so, the Scots lords might put Mary to death on the spot. Elizabeth's enemies would then have been able to say this was her real objective.

On 2 May, after less than a year's captivity, Mary escaped from Loch Leven. She managed to raise an army but her troops were defeated at Langside. She fled to England, crossing the Solway in a fishing boat, wearing borrowed clothes and with a small band of loyal followers. Lord Scrope, the Governor of Carlisle, was away, but Richard Lowther, his deputy, arrived with a troop of four hundred men who escorted Mary to the castle. He gallantly bought her a length of black velvet with which to make a gown. She was confident that within a month she would be back in Scotland at the head of an army. If the English did not help her, she was certain the French would. Elizabeth, who throughout her cousin's troubles in Scotland had supported her as an anointed Queen, now found her a grave embarrassment. Cecil believed that if Mary came to Court, she would be a focus for English Catholics. The Scots lords might also ally with the French. Mary was kept in the north in the custody of landowners whom Elizabeth could trust. She was taken from Carlisle to Bolton Castle in Wensleydale and placed under the surveillance of Elizabeth's cousin, Sir Francis Knollys. He fell under her spell even while trying to convert her to the Protestant religion. Mary wrote over twenty letters to Elizabeth begging her to let her come to her Court, or to meet her in person.* When Leicester was suspected of Amy Robsart's murder, Elizabeth had insisted he must submit himself to the common law of England, and he had been detained at his house at Kew until he was cleared. It was declared that Mary must go through the same process. It would be very prejudicial to Elizabeth's honour to receive at Court one who had been publicly accused of the murder of her own husband, especially when that husband happened to be Elizabeth's kinsman. Mary must wait until she was cleared of all complicity in the crime.

An enquiry was set up at York at the beginning of October 1568. Its aim was to consider the conduct of Moray and his party. Elizabeth hoped by this means to mediate in such a way that Mary would eventually be restored to her throne. Moray was determined to prove Mary guilty of murder. The findings were inconclusive, and Elizabeth ordered that the enquiry be transferred to Westminster.

Moray then produced fresh evidence, the celebrated 'Casket Letters'. On 7 December a small gilded casket, about a foot long and decorated with 'F', the initial of Mary's first husband Francis II, surmounted by a royal crown, was produced at the tribunal. Its contents were supposed to be letters Mary had written before Darnley's death to Bothwell. They were intended to prove that Mary and he had been lovers before the murder. Mary swore the letters were forgeries, and the point

---

* 'Over twenty' is the expression adopted by several historians. I have counted over twenty in one volume of the Cotton MS alone. There were so many that Elizabeth could scarcely answer them. In one reply dated 20 February 1569 she wrote, 'In your letter I note a heap of confused thought, earnestly and curiously uttered to express your fear.' Elizabeth believed that the fear was caused by Mary's 'own guiltiness'. Cecil, who acted as go-between, deftly crossed out 'guiltiness' and substituted 'doings'.

has been debated ever since.* Distressed by the new allegations, Elizabeth wrote to Mary saying she would keep an open mind, but she asked for a direct answer on certain points, since Mary's own commissioners had refused to give complete answers, alleging their Queen had commanded them not to do so. Elizabeth was sending the commissioners back to Mary with a full report of the proceedings, adding sympathetically:

'We have been very sorry of long time for your mishaps and great troubles, so find we our sorrows now double in beholding such things as are produced to prove yourself cause of all the same; and our grief herein is also increased in that we did not think at any time to have seen or heard such matters of so great appearance and moment to charge and condemn you. Nevertheless both in friendship, nature and justice we are moved to cover these matters and stay our judgement, and not gather any sense thereof to your prejudice before we may hear of your direct answer thereunto.'

Elizabeth advised her 'as one Prince and near cousin regarding another, not to forbear from answering'.

'We are heartily sorry and dismayed to find such matter of your charge, so shall we be as heartily glad and well content to hear of sufficient matter for your discharge.'

She sent the letter by the Bishop of Ross, commending him to Mary very highly. She said he had 'not only faithfully and wisely, but also carefully and dutifully for your honour and weal behaved himself, and both privately and publicly'. Elizabeth wished Mary had 'many such devoted, discreet servants. For in our judgement we think ye have not any that in loyalty and faithfulness can overmatch him. And this we are the bolder to write, considering we take it the best trial of a good servant to be in adversity, out of which we wish you to be delivered by the justification of your innocency. And so trusting to hear shortly from you we make an end.' [Hampton Court, 21 December 1568.]

Throughout Mary's trial Elizabeth had communicated with her only through Cecil, although before it she had always written with her own hand. The Hampton Court letter was written by a secretary, but the Queen signed it 'Your good sister and cousin, Elizabeth', writing her signature with an extra measure of the loops and flourishes she affected, almost as though she were trying to convey some mitigating message of hope to Mary. One of the flourishes beneath the 'E' even appears to be the knot of true love, or true friendship, with which she decorated the embroidered prayer books in her youth.

---

* Antonia Fraser discusses the topic thoroughly, offering much evidence that the letters were forged. She believes 'The long letter written from Glasgow from the Queen of Scots to the Earl of Bothwell' was written to the Earl of Moray. Her argument turns on the fact that Mary compares Darnley's bad breath with that of 'your uncle'; Bothwell had no uncles.

A disordered, unhonourable and dangerous practice

Mary's commissioners did not produce the fresh evidence Elizabeth hoped would clear her. The deposed Scottish Queen quickly became a figurehead for the Catholic cause in England, just as Cecil had predicted. At the time of the York enquiry there was a plan for her to divorce Bothwell, who had fled to Denmark, and to marry the Duke of Norfolk. Officially the idea was dropped, but later Mary revived it without Elizabeth's sanction. She began to correspond secretly with Norfolk, and they made a formal exchange of love tokens, he sending her a fine diamond and she sending her miniature in a gold frame. Anglo-Spanish relations had deteriorated through a series of incidents starting with the appointment of Dr John Man, Dean of Gloucester and Warden of Merton, as English ambassador in Madrid in 1566. A thoroughgoing Protestant, he had made the mistake of referring to the Pope as 'a canting little monk'.

In 1568 Philip expelled him, and Elizabeth appointed no new ambassador in Spain. At the same time Philip withdrew the likeable Don Guzman de Silva, sending Don Geurau de Spes to England. An inveterate schemer, he completely misjudged the character of Elizabeth's councillors and entered into secret negotiations with Mary. Philip's Protestant subjects had rebelled in the Netherlands, where the Duke of Alva was in command. Elizabeth seized some Spanish treasure ships carrying bullion to Alva. A loan from Genoese bankers, the bullion was not technically Philip's until it reached its destination. The Queen appropriated the loan and then gained the approval of the banking house which had sent it. De Spes recommended Alva to seize English ships in the Flemish ports and, as Philip was receiving English Catholics in Spain and many Englishmen were in sympathy with the revolt in the Netherlands, amity between the two countries had declined.

The conservative peers in Elizabeth's Council blamed Cecil for leading the country into an undesirable situation. They believed Mary should marry Norfolk, that she should be recognised as Elizabeth's successor, that England should stop helping the Huguenots in France, restore Philip's treasure and regain the friendship of Spain. Although the diverted treasure was Italian, the sailors who manned the ships were Spanish. One hundred and fifty of them were interned in the Bridewell Prison. The Spanish ambassador naturally complained, and was placed under house arrest. When he was released he began to intrigue with prominent English Catholics, particularly with the two powerful northern earls, Northumberland and Westmorland. The plan was to raise a rebellion in the north, release Mary Stuart from captivity, overthrow Elizabeth and restore the Catholic faith. Elizabeth raised an army of twenty-eight thousand men under the command of the Earl of Sussex. She had given Norfolk an opportunity to confess his dealings with Mary, but he left Court and retired to his own estates, pleading illness. Elizabeth told him to come in a litter. By 11 October he was in the Tower. Four weeks later the Northern Rebels entered Durham

Cathedral, tore up the Bible, overturned the communion table and set up altars to restore the Mass. Mary Stuart, who was lodged at Tutbury Castle, was removed to Coventry. Sussex's men routed the earls, who by 20 December had fled over the Border, leaving only Northumberland's cousin, Leonard Dacres, to be reckoned with. He was chased over the Border in February by Elizabeth's cousin, Lord Hunsdon.

The reprisals were severe; six hundred men were hanged as a result of the Northern Rebellion. It has been argued that Mary herself disapproved of the rising, and that the Bishop of Ross later testified that she had tried to dissuade Northumberland. This was not Elizabeth's view of the matter. On 26 October, two weeks after she had committed Norfolk to the Tower, she sent a long letter to Sir Henry Norris, her ambassador in Paris, asking him to relate the details of what had happened to Charles IX and Catherine de' Medici. An eight-page draft survives, a remarkable document in which Elizabeth clearly tells her side of the story.

The French ambassador had been pleading Mary's cause in England. Norris, said Elizabeth, did not need to relate 'the misfortune of the Queen of Scots to have her husband foully murdered who indeed was our nearest kinsman by the King on our father's side'; nor did he need to tell the sordid tale of how 'the principal murderer was by her also further married and maintained (in certain tyranny) against the states of her realm, who sought, as they allege, to have her delivered from such an abominable husband and the country from such a tyrant'. Charles and Catherine knew all that from their own ambassador, but Elizabeth commanded:

CB This we would should be known to the King and all that bear her any favour, that by our own means only her life was saved in her captivity, and since her flying into this our realm she hath been honourably used and entertained and attended upon by noble personages, and such hath been our natural compassion towards her in this her affliction that we utterly secluded and set apart all such just causes as she had given us of sundry offences whereof some were notorious to the whole world to be such as in no age hath been betwixt any princes remitted touching the right of our Crown.

Norris was to tell of the trial at York. Mary's commissioners had entered into 'a bitter accusation of her subjects', but shortly after the proceedings had begun, Elizabeth was sorry to relate that justice had also been sought by 'the father and mother of her husband murdered, whose mother, namely the Lady Margaret attending upon us in our Court, was daughter to our aunt the Scottish Queen, our father's sister's daughter, and sister also to the King of Scots.'

The Lennoxes wanted Mary tried for murder.* Elizabeth claimed, 'such circum-

---

* Elizabeth forgave the Lennoxes for allowing the Darnley marriage almost immediately after the murder.

stances were produced to argue her guilty', and she confided in Charles and Catherine that she had wished the commissioners had not entered on such a rash course. Mary had been disappointed too. She had commanded her commissioners 'not to proceed any further, willing them to return to her that she might send some of them to Scotland to confer with others'. She had promised Elizabeth that they would return with further evidence. They had left in January and, as Elizabeth understood, they had conferred with Moray and his party in March. Elizabeth declared herself 'very desirous' that both Mary and her subjects 'might come to some accord by any manner of means. But yet of that attempt no good event ensued, but a continuance of troubles and so we forebore to intermeddle any further therein'.

None of Mary's commissioners had returned until the end of April. Then the Bishop of Ross had arrived, 'to solicit us again to be a means to make some end and specially to help the Queen to be restored without making any mention of the matter of the murder of her husband, or any other part of the rest of the heinous crimes, whereunto we were very inclinable.' Elizabeth had assured the bishop that she was 'fully determined, to see Mary restored, but while she was 'earnestly travailing' on her behalf, 'it pleased Almighty God, who always assisteth them that direct their actions in his fear and in simplicity of good meaning, to cause to be discovered unto us, a disordered, unhonourable and dangerous practice, which had been very covertly begun by her ministers 6 or 7 months before, when her cause was first begun to be heard at York.'

Mary had pestered Elizabeth 'with frequent letters, tears and messages', assuring her 'she would never seek nor use any means to be helped but by us, nor would attempt anything in our realm, but by our advice'. Elizabeth had trusted Mary, but during the meeting at York some of her ministers 'entered into a practice for marriage of her with the Duke of Norfolk intending, as it now appeareth, by means of this fancy to have all things suppressed that had been produced against her and an end made of her private purpose with regard to us.'* All this, Elizabeth explained, was 'secretly and cunningly handled' without her own knowledge, before the York proceedings were moved to Westminster.

Antonia Fraser suggests Mary thought Elizabeth knew of such a plan a little before the proceedings opened at York. Elizabeth's letter, however, sheds even more light on the tangled intrigues. The plotters, she insisted, had even got Moray to assent to the plan for a marriage between Mary and Norfolk, by threatening the Regent with assassination. He had gone back to Scotland, having almost been murdered on the

---

In June 1567 a family conference took place at Richmond. Lady Margaret stayed the night. Elizabeth ordered the restoration of all the estates she had confiscated at the time of the Darnley marriage. De Silva said: 'She seems very sorry for their troubles.'

* Endorsed 'From the Queen to Norris sent by Harcourt'. The draft is corrected in Cecil's hand; the corrections show clearly how his precise legal phrasing differed from Elizabeth's more emotionally direct style. The letter is not as long as the one written to Norris three months later, but it is an original MS and the indignation comes fresh off the page!

way, but had been told that Elizabeth was 'secretly content' about the Norfolk marriage and that she intended not only to restore Mary to her kingdom, but also to declare her heir to the English throne. 'And', continued Elizabeth indignantly, 'in this sort when we never had a thought of any such matter, she did also by secret messages assure sundry of her part in Scotland that this marriage should take place within a few days.'

'You may say', she instructed Norris, 'we have willed you briefly to declare her dealing to abuse us . . . And you may say to the Queen Mother, because her experience by years serveth her to judge of such matters better than her son, that in this so long a practice, begun in October and not to us known before August, there were many particular devices which now are to us sufficiently known.' The marriage had merely been the first of Mary's plans. Elizabeth was 'right sorry, yea half ashamed, to have been thus misused by her, who we have so benefited by saving of her life'.

Norris should further tell the King and Queen that whatever they had been told about Mary's custody, since she had complained 'of her strait keeping and that she hath some lords attending upon her, who she liketh not', was not true. Elizabeth had thought fit to appoint the Earl of Huntingdon to help Lord Shrewsbury in his task because Mary corrupted anyone who came in contact with her. Huntingdon was a man of 'discretion and integrity' and Mary disliked him because 'the practice intended both for her marriage and her escape' was now 'broken'. And if any more false information reached France concerning Mary Stuart, she ordered Norris to 'pray the King to suspend his judgement betwixt us and her until our answer thereto shall be given'.

To defer this execution

The Scots were divided into two parties, the King's Lords who supported the Regent Moray, and the Queen's Lords, who wished to see Mary restored. In January 1570 Moray was assassinated. France and Spain were pressing Elizabeth to release Mary and help her regain her throne. By February the Pope had excommunicated Elizabeth in a bull which absolved her Catholic subjects from their allegiance. Largely as a result of Elizabeth's support, the Earl of Lennox, James's grandfather, was chosen as the new Regent. Lennox was a Catholic; his wife remained at the English Court as an unofficial hostage. Dumbarton Castle, which commanded the Clyde estuary, was in the hands of the Queen's Lords. It was the ideal point for the French to land with an army, and from which to mount an invasion for the restoration of Mary Stuart. In April 1571 it was captured in a dawn raid by the King's Lords. Lennox arranged for Archbishop Hamilton to be hanged in his episcopal vestments for his complicity in Darnley's murder. This caused further blood feuds, leading to the murder of Lennox himself at Stirling Castle.

Elizabeth appointed the Earl of Mar as Regent. Negotiations for Mary's return had just got under way when the English government discovered another plot against Elizabeth. Roberto Ridolfi, an Italian banker based in London, tried to organise a scheme by which Philip's general, the Duke of Alva, was to invade England from the Netherlands. Catholicism was to be restored in both England and Scotland. Norfolk had been released from the Tower, but he was still under surveillance. Foolishly he continued to intrigue with Mary and the Spanish ambassador, although he had given undertakings not to do so when he left the Tower. Cecil, who had been created Lord Burghley, discovered the details of the plot. De Spes was called before the council and ordered to leave the country. On 16 January the Duke of Norfolk was tried for treason in Westminster Hall. The trial lasted from eight in the morning to eight at night. He was found guilty, but Elizabeth shrank from the idea of ordering his execution. He was her blood relation, and England's only duke. He was to have been beheaded on 21 January 1572. Elizabeth deferred matters. In February she signed another warrant, but then countermanded it. Burghley remonstrated with her. On 9 April she signed a third warrant. Two days later at two in the morning she sent Burghley a note written with her own hand.

CB My Lord,

Methinks that I am more beholden to the hinder part of my head than well dare trust the forwards side of the same, and therefore sent the Lieutenant and the S., as you know best, the order to defer this execution till they hear farther. And that this may be done, I doubt nothing without curiosity of my further warrant, for that their rash determination upon a very unfit day, was countermanded by your considerate admonition. The causes that move me to this are not now to be expressed, lest an irrevocable deed be in the meanwhile committed. If they will needs a warrant, let this suffice, all written with my own hand.

Your most loving sovereign,

Elizabeth R

Honour and conscience forbid!

Norfolk was executed on 2 June 1572 after a great deal of pressure from Parliament. The House of Commons demanded unanimously that Elizabeth should punish Mary too. 'Cut off her head and the duke's,' they urged. It made nonsense of the laws of England if the chief conspirators in the Ridolfi Plot were seen to be able to act with impunity. Peter Wentworth, the ebullient member for Lillingstone Lovell,

Robert Dudley, Earl of Leicester, by Federigo Zuccaro (British Museum)

called Mary a notorious whore. A joint committee for both Houses discussed the matter for several days. The bishops joined in the hue and cry, listing Mary's sins, 'adulteries, murders, conspiracies, treasons, blasphemies'. The Commons devised two bills against Mary: one to execute her for high treason and another to deny her any right of succession to the English throne. Elizabeth refused to consider the first, but said she would think about the second. In Council she pointed out that Mary had originally come to England for refuge:

'Can I put to death the bird that, to escape the pursuit of the hawk, has fled to my feet for protection? Honour and conscience forbid!'

Although she would not execute Mary, she let it be known that her policy had changed, and that she no longer intended to restore her to the throne. She formally recognised her godson as King of Scotland. The Papal bull and the cooling of Anglo-Spanish relations drove Elizabeth to seek alliance with France. Catherine de' Medici believed it was high time the Virgin Queen took the idea of marriage seriously. Herself the mother of ten children, seven of whom survived infancy, and three of whom successively were to be Kings of France, she had married the future Henry II when she was fourteen years old. For a great deal of her life as Queen of France she had been overshadowed by the powerful personality of Henry's dazzling mistress, Diane de Poitiers. Her attitude to marriage was entirely pragmatic; she regarded Elizabeth's aversion with deep cynicism. In January 1571 Catherine had proposed that Elizabeth should marry Charles IX's brother, Henry, Duke of Anjou. Sir Francis Walsingham was sent to Paris shortly after the publication of the papal bull. In March Catherine was taking the negotiations seriously, but by July 1571 they were foundering over the question of the Duke's religion. Elizabeth wanted to impose the same terms that had served four years previously for the Archduke Charles, including the stipulation that her consort should publicly attend Protestant services.

In April 1572 England and France signed the Treaty of Blois. It was proposed that Elizabeth should marry not Anjou, but his brother Francis, Duke of Alençon, who was exactly half Elizabeth's age. Catherine sent the Duke of Montmorency to ratify the treaty.* He had been a great success with Elizabeth when England and France had made peace in May 1559. He made much of Alençon's good qualities, but Elizabeth, who was so fastidious in matters of male beauty that she had once rejected an applicant for the post of Yeoman of the Guard because he had a tooth missing, wanted to know what her suitor looked like. It was commonly rumoured that Alençon was extremely ugly, with a face disfigured by smallpox.

The summer progress of 1572 was a long one; Elizabeth's courtiers were particularly eager to soothe her after the unpleasantness of Norfolk's execution. On 23 July the Queen was staying at Burghley's house, Theobalds. She wrote to Walsingham

---

* Elizabeth gave a banquet at Whitehall to celebrate the treaty. Leicester, charged with most of the arrangements, described it as 'the greatest that was in my remembrance'.

that 'considering the youngness of the years of the Duke of Alençon compared to ours', she could hardly be expected to take the proposal seriously. However, she had sent Lord Clinton to France to inspect Alençon personally for, she said, 'such was the importancy of our own subjects of all estates to have us marry'. When Lord Clinton returned, she told Walsingham, they had discussed Alençon's personal appearance in detail. Clinton had reported well of the young man's character, but 'as to his visage and favour everybody doth declare the same to be far inferior and that specially for the blemishes that the smallpox hath wrought therein so as his young years considered, the doubtfulness of the liking of his favour joined therewith we cannot indeed bring our mind to like this offer'. She also feared public opinion, 'whereby the absurdity that in the general opinion of the world might grow to commend this our choice after so many refusals of others of great worthiness'. Elizabeth's fortieth birthday was two months away; age had become a sensitive issue.

Two days later, relaxing in the pleasant atmosphere of her summer progress, she reconsidered the idea. The long train of ladies and gentlemen, bags and baggage, had reached Sir Nicholas Bacon's house at Gorhambury. The Lord Keeper had finished building it in 1568. He was a family man. By his first wife he had had six children. His second wife, Elizabeth's hostess on this occasion, was Anne Cooke, the daughter of Sir Anthony and sister of Burghley's wife, Mildred. The Lord Keeper had two sons by his second marriage, Anthony, who was fourteen at the time of Elizabeth's visit, and Francis Bacon, who was twelve. Away from the cares of London, Elizabeth wrote again to Walsingham. She would like to see the proposed bridegroom for herself.

'In marriage, when the persons are to think one of the other, nothing doth so much rule both parties as to have their own opinions satisfied.'

She would leave it to Charles and Catherine to work out the details of the visit, but if Alençon would come to see her in person, she would gladly receive him. She stressed only one thing, 'the desire we have to deal *plainly* in this matter'.

Sadly there are no details of Elizabeth's stay at Gorhambury, as the rest of the account of this progress is taken up by her more sensational visit to Warwick Castle. The Warwicks had arranged many entertainments, including a country dance in the courtyard and a magnificent firework display, which included a mock battle in which wildfire shot about the surface of the river. It set fire to some houses in the town, burning down the home of an elderly couple. The courtiers raised £25 12s 8d for them and Elizabeth expressed great sympathy and relief that they were unharmed. By 22 August she was at Leicester's still unfinished home, Kenilworth. Burghley, stricken with gout had accompanied the progress in his litter. That evening he noted in his diary that he had spoken with de la Mothe Fénelon, the French ambassador, who had also accompanied the progress. Burghley thought the French match seemed very unlikely, although in his eyes such a match would be for the benefit of all Christendom, since it was proposed that Charles IX should send help to the Protestants in the Netherlands, and that Alençon might become their leader.

A thing very repugnant, and contrary to itself

While Elizabeth was on progress, the French Court was celebrating the marriage of Catherine's daughter, Marguerite de Valois, with Henry, the Protestant King of Navarre. Admiral Coligny, the Huguenot leader, was in Paris for the wedding. On the morning of 22 August 1572 he was returning from the Louvre to his house, when he was shot in the hand. The King was indignant and announced that whoever was responsible would be punished. The Huguenots spoke of attacking the Catholics in revenge. Amid the general panic which followed the incident, Catherine gave orders on 23 August, St Bartholomew's Eve, for the city to be cleared of Huguenots. The King reluctantly sanctioned the order and there followed the appalling slaughter known as the Massacre of St Bartholomew.

Mary Stuart's cousin, the Duke of Guise, was invited to avenge his father's assassination. He stood by while a Swiss guard murdered the wounded Coligny in his bedchamber. The Paris mob joined the fray, and the killing went on for two days. The newly-married King of Navarre and the Prince of Condé were taken prisoner. Walsingham heard the screams and shots from his house at St Germain des Prés, just across the river. His despatch did not reach Elizabeth until 3 September. By then Protestant refugees were pouring into London and the Channel ports with tales of horror and bloodshed.

Elizabeth was utterly sickened. She wept to hear the news and refused to receive de la Mothe Fénelon in her presence. At the end of September she wrote to Walsingham to say she had at last given audience to the ambassador on 22 September. It had seemed very strange, 'because we had heard before of the daily murdering of those of the Religion there in France, at Paris and at Orleans, as also at Lyons and Rouen, and divers other places and cities of that Realm, all the which was said to be done by the King's appointment and commandment.'

She ordered Walsingham to demand an audience with the King and the Queen Mother:

'And you may say, as touching any worthy punishment executed upon his own subjects, we have not to deal therein, but if they have worthily suffered, we are sorry for their evil doings. But yet the King to destroy and utterly root out of his Realm all those of that Religion that we profess, and to desire us in marriage for his brother, must needs seem unto us at the first a thing very repugnant, and contrary to itself, specially having confirmed that liberty in them of the Religion by an edict of his, perpetual and irrevocable; of the which to whom the liberty was granted, if any were partakers of any evil conspiracies against him, surely a great part of them must needs be ignorant, and ignorant of any evil fact or thought against him, especially women and innocent children, who, we do understand, are not yet spared. And therefore if that Religion of itself be odious unto him that he thinks he must root out all the professors of it, how should we think his brother a fit husband for us, or how should we think that the love may grow, continue and increase betwixt his brother and us, which ought to be betwixt the husband and wife?'

Such a massacre, and at a wedding feast, was to Elizabeth redolent of the methods used by the petty princes of the city states in the old barbarous days when France and Spain had battled over Italy. She was certain that Catherine de' Medici was responsible, and she bade Walsingham enquire discreetly whether Charles IX was himself 'inclined and bent to all these cruelties', or whether he had been 'overruled' by his dominant mother. The Huguenots still held the town of La Rochelle. They had begged Elizabeth for aid. She refused it, but English privateers and English Protestants were sending supplies and munitions. La Rochelle resisted for four and a half months, after which the Huguenots were able to negotiate rights to worship in certain Protestant towns. They called Elizabeth 'Defender of the Christian Faith', although she had sent no official help.

By December Charles and Catherine were assuring Elizabeth they wished to continue the friendship with England. Monsieur de Mauvissière was sent to London as Ambassador Extraordinary, and the excommunicated Protestant Queen was invited to be godmother to yet another Catholic infant, Charles's daughter, whose grandfather, Maximilian II, was the Holy Roman Emperor. Catherine continued to offer Alençon as a bridegroom. Elizabeth was scandalised. She wished to continue the alliance but she was sorry to hear of the King's part in 'the great slaughter made in France of Noblemen and Gentlemen, unconvicted and untried'.

The excuse given for the massacre was that the Huguenots had plotted treason; 'whether it was true or false' did not concern Elizabeth, but she had been deeply distressed, 'that they were not brought to answer by law and to judgement before they were executed.' This was 'a terrible and dangerous example'. She had expected Charles to be 'more humane and noble', but when more was added unto it, 'that women, children, maids, young infants and sucking babes were at the same time murdered and cast into the river; and that the liberty of execution was given to the vilest and basest sort of the popular, without punishment or revenge of such cruelty done by law, upon those cruel murderers of such innocents: this increased our grief and sorrow in our good Brother's behalf'.

Those of the Reformed Religion were 'either driven to fly or die, or to recant or lose their offices', and as Elizabeth herself professed that reformed religion it seemed 'very strange both to us and to all other that our good Brother should require us to be Godmother to his dear child, we being of that Religion which he doth now persecute and cannot abide within his Realm,' wrote the Queen.

Despite these objections she would still stand godmother 'wishing that these spiritual alliances may be to our comforts and conservation of the amity begun betwixt us'. But she could not come to a decision on the marriage.

Princely pleasures

For New Year 1572 Leicester gave Elizabeth a golden bracelet studded with rubies and diamonds. When she took it out of its purple velvet case, lined with green velvet, she found a tiny clock had been mounted in the gold. It was one of the earliest wrist-watches. The following year he gave her a golden collar with two large emeralds and four rubies, set off by a scintillating collection of smaller rubies and diamonds. When she was forty, thickening a little at the waist and with her red-gold hair helped with close curled hairpieces, he gave her a fan of white feathers, its handle made of gold and decorated with the bear from his coat of arms and the lion from hers. Twelve months later he chose her a doublet of white satin, ornamented with goldsmith's work. It fastened over her breasts with eighteen clasps, covered with diamonds and rubies. In 1578 the earl's present still came at the head of the list of New Year's gifts. It was, as usual, lavish and costly, but it was less personal than in previous years – a clock set ornately in gold.

It is not known at exactly what point in his long, intensely public courtship of Elizabeth the Master of the Horse began to sleep with Lettice Knollys. As Lady Hereford she had flirted with the earl in 1566. At that time, despite negotiations for a marriage with the Archduke, Leicester had not quite lost hope that Elizabeth would marry him. His older brother Ambrose had no children, and Dudley seriously believed that the privations Elizabeth's love forced upon him would 'be the cause almost of the ruin of my own house. For there is no likelihood that any of our bodies of men kind are like to have heirs,' he wrote sadly. 'My brother you see long married and not like to have children. It resteth so now in myself.' If he married he would lose the favour that he valued above everything. But the price seemed sometimes intolerable. There was nothing in the world that he would not give 'to be in hope of leaving some children behind me, being now the last of our house. But yet the cause being as it is, I must content myself.'

Some time in the early seventies Leicester had begun an affair with one of the Ladies of the Bedchamber, Lady Sheffield. Widowed in 1568, she and her sister, Lady Frances Howard, were both reported as being in love with him. These ladies were the daughters of Elizabeth's great-uncle, Lord William Howard, the former Lord Admiral, and it was commonly rumoured that the Queen did not approve and had set spies to find out what was going on. In 1573 Lady Sheffield became pregnant and in May Leicester went through a form of marriage ceremony with her, witnessed by his physician, Dr Julio.*

---

* The validity of this marriage has frequently been contested. Leicester's will left Kenilworth to his son, which implied he did not consider him base-born. In 1604, after Elizabeth's death, the Sidneys inherited the Warwick title, since Ambrose had no heirs. They tried to claim Leicester's title too, but Sir Robert Dudley, Leicester's son, contested this in the Star Chamber. However, he never succeeded in proving his parents' marriage.

They had one son, Robert, whose existence Leicester never tried to conceal. His uncle, the Earl of Warwick, and Sir Henry Lee were the boy's godfathers. Leicester took care of his education, and in 1588 he went to Christ Church.

Elizabeth made no fuss about the base-born son, but the marriage was kept entirely secret. Probably Lady Sheffield feared for her liberty, knowing a spell in the Tower would be her lot if the Queen learned what had happened. She lived quietly at Esher but had herself served as a countess in her private apartments. Fearing servants' gossip, Leicester drew the line at this. When he became involved with Lettice, Leicester treated Lady Sheffield very badly, offering her a pension of £700 to hush up their affair. When she refused this, he told her that the marriage had never been valid. This occurred in 1578, and it is widely assumed that Lettice and Leicester had by then been lovers for several years.

Lettice's husband, Walter Devereux, Viscount Hereford, was a soldier. He had fought with distinction at the time of the Northern Rebellion and was made Earl of Essex on 4 May 1572 and a Knight of the Garter on 17 June of the same year. Leicester was not only present at the ceremony but deputised for the Queen, so that he actually received Essex into the Order. In 1573 Essex was serving in Ireland at the head of a colonising force. He returned to England in 1575 and according to the Spanish ambassador he fell out with Leicester at Court, '*it being well known that Dudley had seduced his wife*' (my italics). The ambassador even reported that he had two children by her. Apart from this one piece of gossip there seems to be no contemporary evidence of an adulterous liaison between Leicester and Lettice before Essex's death. The orders of chivalry were valued highly and it would have been a shocking breach of the code of honour if Leicester had seduced the wife of a brother knight. It is more likely that Leicester started his serious pursuit of the voluptuously beautiful Lettice after the death of her husband in September 1576.

The summer progress of 1575 was dedicated to Diana, the chaste goddess of the hunt. Briefly, during Edward's reign, Kenilworth Castle in Warwickshire had belonged to Robert's father, Northumberland. Elizabeth had given it to Leicester in 1563 in that ardent period of their love when her whole person was said to glow with desire whenever she was near him. He had spent ten years turning Kenilworth from a medieval fortress into a Tudor palace. It had a square Norman keep which Leicester modernised with large windows. He made a little forecourt and built a gatehouse with octagonal turrets and tall mullioned windows. He also laid out a pleasure garden with a large fountain of white marble, embellished with sea gods and naked nymphs, which profoundly disturbed Robert Laneham, door-keeper of the Privy Council Chamber, who was unused to such sophistication.* Laneham accompanied the progress, describing its wonders. To the west 'lay a goodly chase vast, wide, large and full of red deer and other stately game for hunting'.

---

* Of the marble fountain Laneham wrote, 'Here were things might inflame any mind after too long looking'.

Elizabeth and her entourage arrived at Kenilworth at eight in the evening on 9 July. The castle was blazing with lights like a palace in a fairytale. When the Queen appeared at the gates, a Sybil dressed in silken robes spoke welcoming verses, predicting the continuance of peace and prosperity. That they were more stirring than elegant did not mar the occasion:

> *The rage of War bound fast in chains*
> *Shall never stir nor more,*
> *But peace shall govern all your days,*
> *Increasing subjects' love.*
> *You shall be called the Prince of peace,*
> *Peace shall be your shield*
> *So that your eyes shall never see*
> *The broils of bloody field.*

Hercules, the Porter, appeared next for a comic interlude, complaining of all the noise and stamping made by her Majesty's train. Then, as Elizabeth reached the lake, a floating island lit with torches came towards her, bearing a boy actor, dressed in flowing silks as the Lady of the Lake. He told the story of the castle, mingling historical fact with Arthurian romance and a high moral allegory. The drawbridge was decorated with pillars hung with cornucopiae to symbolise all earthly luxuries. Branches of apples and cherries vied with cages of live birds, salvers of salmon and oysters and red and white grapes 'gracified' with vine leaves and poised beside silver flagons of wine. On the last pillars there were musical instruments and, finally, two great staves, made all of silver like the ragged staff of the Dudley arms, which were hung with armour in token that Leicester would lay down his life for the Queen.

For nineteen pleasure-filled days she stayed at Kenilworth. There was feasting and dancing, fireworks on the lake, a banquet at which Robert Laneham noted three hundred dishes, and a rustic wedding followed by a morris dance. The bride, he said, was about thirty and smelled foul, but she was so excited at the prospect of dancing before the Queen that she put on airs as though she were as beautiful as her bridesmaids. All through the visit there were magic surprises. Figures of classical antiquity alternated with the characters of Arthurian legend. The Lady of the Lake was delivered from her prison, into which she had been forced by the inordinate lust of the magician Merlin. As the Queen returned from hunting, she spied a mermaid in the lake with an eighteen-foot tail. Neptune, Triton and Proteus appeared in a water pageant on the back of a floating dolphin within which was concealed a consort of musicians. The men of Coventry performed a play about the Danish invasion.

There were few hitches but of course sometimes arrangements had to be modified because of the weather. The Lady of the Lake was to have been rescued in a mock battle, which the Queen was to have watched from a torchlit barge; this was cancelled, as was the masque about Diana and her favourite nymph, Zabeta, which involved Juno and Iris, the goddess of the rainbow. At the end of the visit Leicester commissioned its author, George Gascoigne, to spring from a thicket in the costume of Sylvanus, the god of the woods. He ran beside the Queen's palfrey reciting farewell verses, and she had to bring the horse to a standstill for fear the poet might run out of breath.

After Kenilworth, Elizabeth visited the Earl of Essex's manor at Chartley, where Lettice played hostess. It makes a pretty story to assume that Leicester's private courtship of the countess began while he was publicly fêting Elizabeth in her role as the chaste Diana. A number of biographers and the guides at Kenilworth Castle hold fast to the theory, but there is no evidence apart from the Spanish ambassador's *canard*.

CHAPTER X

If I were a milkmaid with a pail on my arm

⅍ Boy Jack,

I have made a clerk write fair my poor words for thine use, as it cannot be such striplings have entrance into Parliament Assemblies as yet. Ponder them in thy hours of leisure and play with them till they enter thine understanding, so shalt thou hereafter perchance find some good fruits hereof when thy godmother is out of remembrance, and I do this because thy father was ready to serve us in trouble and thrall.

Few youths of fourteen can have had quite the surprise young John Harington must have felt when this note arrived from his royal godmother with a copy of her speech to the Parliament of 1576. He was still a schoolboy at Eton when she sent it to him. His father, Sir John Harington, had been a gentleman at Henry VIII's Court, and had later entered the service of Thomas Seymour. On one occasion he carried a message to Elizabeth from the Admiral. In 1554 he and his wife, Isabella Markham, were imprisoned in the Tower on suspicion simply because they were known to sympathise with Elizabeth. Harington was a man of unswerving loyalties, who strenuously defended the Admiral's reputation long after he was dead. The Haringtons seem to have remained in the Tower as long as Elizabeth, and since she never forgot a kindness, or an injury sustained on her behalf, she was particularly fond of them, standing godmother when their son John was born in 1561.

She was obviously impressed by the boy's wit and intelligence, though she later scolded him for his bawdy sense of humour. When as a young man he made an English translation of the twenty-eighth book of *Orlando Furioso* (a blue novel in its time), she sent him away from Court for corrupting the maids-of-honour, making him translate the whole of Ariosto's poem as a penance, which he did, retaining the original *ottava rima*.* Perhaps as a schoolboy he was bold and precocious enough to request a copy of the Queen's celebrated speech, or maybe she sent it to him on a sudden whim while staying at Windsor. Elizabeth was clearly intensely proud of her 'poor words', which created a great stir when they were first uttered.

Technically the Parliament which assembled on 8 February was the fourth in

---

* The twenty-eighth book of *Orlando Furioso* tells the tale of Fiametta, a concubine shared by two travellers, one of whom is a King. Both men are married; Fiametta consorts with her true love while they are asleep. In the end they provide her with a dowry so that she can marry him.

Elizabeth's reign, the 1571–2 Parliament having been prorogued. There was no formal opening, although the session began with the excitements of Peter Wentworth's defence of the principle of Free Speech. The patriotic member from Lillingstone Lovell was disturbed by the many 'rumours and messages' said to come from Elizabeth herself. He believed the Queen was in favour of the Commons' ancient liberty to say what they thought, but the Privy Council saw the matter differently, construing Wentworth's views as an attack on the Crown. He was examined by a committee and sent to the Tower. The 1576 Parliament had been called for the usual reason – to raise a subsidy, and after Wentworth's sensational outburst it settled down to business.

Sir Walter Mildmay, founder of Emmanuel College, Cambridge, who was Chancellor of the Exchequer, praised the Queen for her fiscal policy, which had delivered the kingdom from its 'great and weighty' debt dating from the end of Henry VIII's reign. The subsidy bill was swiftly passed and members turned to other matters. Ecclesiastical discipline was criticised; a statute of apparel discussed; bills on salt marshes and forests were mooted, and another attempt was made to petition the Queen to marry and produce an heir, although she was by now forty-two. In thirty-one days the Commons dealt with over a hundred bills. Peter Wentworth was released from the Tower, and a lively bid by the Commons to bring up again the matter of their liberties was quashed by the Lords, now virtually dominated by Burghley. He had become Lord Treasurer on the death of the old Marquis of Winchester, who had remained in office until his ninety-seventh year, living (it was rumoured) to see the birth of over a hundred great-grandchildren. As a result of Cecil's elevation, the Secretary's office was divided between Sir Francis Walsingham and Sir Thomas Smith.

Walsingham, Leicester and Sir Francis Knollys were all in different ways supporters of the Puritan movement, which had gained strength in the seventies. Sir John Neale's view that there was by this time organised Puritan pressure in Parliament has recently been modified. In several counties, however, 'Prophesyings' or prayer meetings were being held. Leicester and his brother Warwick supported these, but Elizabeth disliked anything that deviated from the established church services, as breaches of uniformity. She wanted to see the end of the Prophesyings, and as early as 1574 she had ordered Matthew Parker to suppress them. The archbishop died in the spring of 1576. In December Elizabeth summoned his successor, Edmund Grindal, telling him to see to it that the meetings were stamped out. Grindal could not find it in his heart to condemn them, and said so, whereat Elizabeth suspended him. This outright clash between the Supreme Governor of the Church of England and its Primate had not come to pass when Parliament assembled, but by the spring of 1575 Elizabeth's views on religion were clear. She wanted uniformity. The session should have ended on 14 March, but the Queen adjourned proceedings until the following day. At 3 PM on the 15th Lord Keeper Bacon began to make the conventional closing speech. The Queen had given her assent to thirty-seven bills.

Everyone was waiting for Sir Nicholas to finish and for Elizabeth to make her formal procession out of the Parliament Chamber.

Suddenly the Queen stopped the Lord Keeper and began a long speech of her own. Neale called it 'replete with wisdom, obscurity and literary artifice', but this is unjust. It was a review of her reign and an expression of relief that there had been no repetition of the unseemly clashes of 1572 when the feet had tried to guide the head. She also outlined much of her own philosophy of life, her determination to live in the present moment and not to look too far into the future. Although this principle alarmed her councillors, it was the fundamental reason behind many of Elizabeth's famous hesitations. She summarised her pragmatism in one unforgettable phrase: 'in being, not in seeming, we may wish the best'. Her words were far from obscure to her original audience. In this speech more than in any of her previous parliamentary speeches, Elizabeth seemed really to open her heart to her subjects, taking them warmly into her confidence as she told them of the cares of government.

Thomas Cromwell, the Commons' diarist, wrote that after the Queen stopped the Lord Keeper, 'the greatest company went forth'.* This has been taken as meaning that when the Queen began speaking, the members were already streaming away out of the Chamber. Cromwell himself could not hear the speech, 'scant one word of twenty', which suggests that the Commons did not go out of the House, but rather that they surged forward towards the bar which separated them from the Lords. Cromwell himself must have been at the back of the throng. The Earl of Shrewsbury's sons who were nearer the front of the crowd must have heard better, for they wrote to their father that Elizabeth made 'a very eloquent and grave oration'. She began with a gentle jibe at the Prophesyings, where interpretation of the Gospel counted for more than the word of God and, consciously or unconsciously, she echoed her father's famous speech on uniformity. Then followed a hint to those who habitually misrepresented her sayings, to get them right. This was perhaps directed at those very rumour-mongers of whom Peter Wentworth had complained, or perhaps at the four unfortunate clerks to the House of Lords, who as commoners in such an august assembly were obliged to record the proceedings kneeling for hours at a stretch. Small wonder that by the time a copy of the speech was made for John Harington it had to be written out fair.

CƐ Do I see God's most sacred word and text of holy writ drawn to so diverse senses be it never so precisely taught [asked Elizabeth] and shall I hope that my speech can pass forth through so many ears without mistaking, where so many ripe and diverse wits do oftener bend to construe, than to attain the true and perfect understanding? If any look for eloquence, I shall deceive their hope. If some

---

* Sir Geoffrey Elton suggests Thomas Cromwell had in fact been instructed to take notes of the proceedings by Burghley, who now sat in the Upper House.

think I can match their gifts that spake before, they hold an open heresy, I cannot satisfy their longing thirsts.

The humour may be a little heavy for modern taste, but she was teasing the previous speakers. The point she wanted to make was that she never ceased from 'that restless care' which she was ever bestowing in matters of government. To praise her own endeavours would be to detract 'from the divine providence' which had protected her throughout her reign. She could not receive the commendation for what was only due to God's eternal glory. She began to reiterate the points made earlier by the Speaker; her chiefest blessing had been her subjects' love:

CB One special favour yet must I needs confess I have good cause to vaunt of: that whereas variety and love of change is ever so rife in servants to their masters, in children to their parents, and in private friends one to another – as though for one year, or perhaps for two, can content themselves to hold their course upright, yet after by mistrust, or doubt of worse, they are dissevered, and in time wax weary of their wonted liking – yet still I find that assured zeal among my faithful subjects to my especial comfort which was first declared.

Can a Prince that of necessity must discontent a number to delight and please a few (because the greatest part are oft not best inclined) continue a long time without great offence, much mischief or common grudge? Or haps it often that princes' actions are taken in so good part and favourably interpreted? No, no, my lords. How great my fortune is in this respect I were ingrate if I should not acknowledge. And as for those rare and special benefits which have many years followed and accompanied my happy reign, I attribute to God alone the prince of rule and count myself no better than his hand maid, rather brought up in a school to abide the ferula than traded in a kingdom to support the sceptre.

She turned to those who criticised her foreign or religious policy. Had she not founded a Protestant State, when she could more simply have allowed the Marian settlement to continue, accepting Philip as a husband and continuing the alliance with Spain:

CB If policy had been preferred before truth, would I, trow you, even at the first beginning of my rule have turned upside down so great affairs or entered into tossing of the great waves and billows of the world that might, if I had sought my ease have harboured and cast anchor in most seeming security? It cannot be denied [she went on] but worldly wisdom rather bade me knit and match myself in league and fast alliance with great princes to purchase friends on every side by worldly means.

165

Elizabeth on her throne in the House of Lords:
in the centre are the four kneeling clerks, writing shorthand

Anyone could have seen that that was the obvious course, but Elizabeth had chosen a higher path.

Ꮟᏸ All these means of leagues, alliances and foreign strengths, I quite forsook [she reminded them] and gave myself to seek for truth without respect, reposing my chief stay in God's most mighty grace. Thus I began, thus I did proceed, and thus I hope to end. These seventeen years God hath prospered and protected you with good success under my direction, and I doubt not but the same maintaining hand will guide you still and bring you to ripeness of perfection. Consider yourselves the bitter storms and perils of your neighbours, the true cause whereof I will not attribute to princes (God forbid, I should) since these misfortunes may proceed as well from sins among the people.

She was aware of her own shortcomings and she had no intention of blaming others. Let all men bear their private faults, she advised. 'My own have weight enough for me to answer for. The best way therefore, I suppose, for you and me is by some humble prayers to crave of God, that not in weening, but in perfect weight, in being not in seeming, we may wish the best.'

From this homespun piece of philosophy she moved to their wish that she should marry, and this time there were no pretences. She spoke openly of her preference for celibacy.

Ꮟᏸ I must confess my own mislike so much to strive against the matter, as if I were a milkmaid with a pail on my arm – whereby my private person might be little set by – I would not forsake that single state to match with the greatest monarch of the world. Not that I do condemn the double knot or judge amiss of such as forced by necessity cannot dispose themselves to other life, but this I wish that none were driven to change but such as could not keep within the bounds of honesty.

As for the succession:

Ꮟᏸ I know I am but mortal and so therewhilst prepare myself for death, whensoever it shall please God to send it; as if others would endeavour to perform the like, it could not be so bitter unto many as it hath been counted. My experience teacheth me to be no fonder of these vain delights than reason would, neither further to delight in things uncertain than may seem convenient. But let good heed be taken lest that reaching too far after future good you peril not the present, or begin to quarrel or fall together by the ears by dispute before it may be well decided who shall wear my Crown.

Perhaps they thought she was indifferent to the future, since when these points were settled, she would no longer be with them. Only she could tell them who would succeed her, but they should not misunderstand her reluctance to discuss it. She was not trying to deceive them:

CB I intend it not [she protested]; my brains be too thin to carry so tough a matter. Although I trust God will not in such haste cut off my days, but according to your own deserts and my desire I may provide some good way for your security. And thus as one that yieldeth you more thanks, both for your zeal to myself and service in this parliament, than now my tongue can utter, I recommend you to the assured guard and best keeping of the Almighty, who will preserve you safe I trust, in all felicity.

Excessive and terrible shedding of Christian blood

Although Elizabeth was in sympathy with the Protestant cause, she disliked the idea of helping subjects who had rebelled against their Prince. In the early days of the Protestant resistance in the Netherlands she had allowed the Dutch privateers, 'the Sea Beggars', to use English ports. At the end of 1572, when she was seeking rapprochement with Philip, after three years of strained relations between England and Spain, she closed her ports to the Sea Beggars. As a direct result of this the Dutch leader, William of Orange, was forced to seek his own centre of operations. The Dutch captured Brill, and the whole country rose in revolt against Spanish domination.

The Duke of Alva besieged Haarlem for seven months, starving out the garrison and hanging the 1,600 soldiers who survived, but William still controlled the waterways and he was able to cut off Alva's supply lines. Philip recalled Alva in 1574, making Don Luis de Requesens governor. To Elizabeth's fury the Sea Beggars frequently attacked English ships. She threatened to form an alliance against them with Philip, the Emperor and the German princes. Requesens died of a fever and Philip decided to send his own half-brother, Don John of Austria, the victor of Lepanto and in the eyes of many the greatest soldier in all Christendom, to suppress the revolt. In January 1576 the Dutch Protestants had again asked Elizabeth for help. She did not wish to get involved in a war against Spain, but she offered to negotiate on their behalf and sent envoys to Philip. Shortly before Don John arrived to take up his command, the Spanish soldiers in the Netherlands took the law into their own hands, sacking the town of Antwerp, which as an important trading centre had managed to remain neutral. On 19 and 20 October the Spaniards began firing on the town from an adjacent fort. The gates of Antwerp had always proudly been left open for free trade, but the Spaniards thought they could cut off the supplies brought up the river by William of Orange's ships. The Spanish attack proper began on 2 November. The estates levied a garrison of 3,000 infantry and some 800 horse. On 30 November the gates were shut. George Gascoigne, the poet who had run beside Elizabeth's palfrey as she left Kenilworth, was in Antwerp on private business. He found himself besieged in what today would be called the 'English consulate'.

Detachments of Spanish soldiers arrived from all over the Netherlands, including some 2,000 infantrymen who had mutinied because they had not been paid. The Spanish forces soon numbered 5,000 and they surprised the garrison by entering the town from the south-west. Trenches had been dug inside the walls but the Spaniards swiftly crossed them, slaughtering all who stood in their way.

Accounts of the ensuing massacre may have been exaggerated. Gascoigne claimed that when the dead were counted it was found that 17,000 men, women and children had been killed. He published his own eye-witness account, he said, to correct the many wild stories which were flying about. He was horrified by the barbarous cruelty of the Spaniards, but he could not help admiring their discipline. 'A pitiful massacre,' he wrote, 'though God gave victory to the Spaniards, and surely, as their valiance was to be much commended.'

The attack was so swift that many people did not realise what had happened. Gascoigne was dining in 'the English house' when the Spaniards started setting fire to some buildings. He went to the exchange and the main market place to see what was happening and was swept up in the mob running away from the battle. He was knocked over backwards and says the crowd 'ran over my belly and face long time before I could recover on foot. At last when I was up I looked on every side and seeing them run so fast began thus to bethink me, "What in God's name do I here, which have no interest in this action? Since they who came to defend this town are content to leave it." ' He was then knocked over by a crowd streaming in the other direction, this time the crowd trampling on his back. He struggled up and ran with them, eventually regaining the English consulate and persuading them to barricade the gates.

Ten days after the town had been taken the Spaniards were still slaughtering and spoiling.

'They neither spared age nor sex,' he lamented, 'they slew great numbers of young children, . . . and women more than fourscore years of age.'

Heaps of carcasses lay by every trench, sometimes piled six feet high. The German mercenaries were found roasted alive in their plate armour.

Gascoigne escaped on 12 November, after nearly being killed in mistake for a Walloon. He was back in England by the 25th and immediately had his own account, The Spoyle of Antwerp, printed. Although it appears to have gone into only one edition, it was widely read. Elizabeth held an emergency Council meeting; she advised all her subjects to remove their goods from the city, although from Gascoigne's account nothing was left. The Spanish agent in London, Antonio de Guaras, who was later arrested, wrote: 'She and her Council desire to expel the Spaniards from Flanders, more than the Flemings themselves.'

The Queen sent John Smith to Madrid with letters to Philip offering her services to mediate between him and his subjects in the Netherlands. Philip thanked her politely but refused the offer. By the time Don John arrived in the Netherlands the provinces had united in a fresh alliance, prompted by the excesses at Antwerp. Alençon was now Dauphin of France. His brother Charles IX had died, and Anjou became King, Alençon taking the title Duke of Anjou.* He was known to favour the Huguenots, and the States invited him to become their leader. Elizabeth, horrified by the idea of French influence in the Low Countries, promptly lent the Dutch £20,000, promising she would guarantee a further £100,000. Philip meantime was helping the Catholics against Elizabeth in Ireland, and the Pope was encouraging Don John to lead an Enterprise against England. Philip had gone bankrupt in 1575; neither he nor Elizabeth wanted war. In December 1577 she wrote to him again offering to mediate, moved, she said, by:

CS the sorrow we feel for the calamities and miserable events which have befallen your Serenity's Netherlands, the excessive and terrible shedding of Christian blood, and our desire in all sincerity to promote your honour and advantage.

As the destruction and desolation of dominion hinders kings themselves from founding their power and glory on the opulence of prosperous citizens [she wrote, commenting acidly on the decline of the Antwerp trade] so is it unworthy of the regal office and dignity to judge harshly those who love and strive for us.

She hoped that she would arouse in Philip 'the same compassion' for his subjects which she felt for them, and she wished 'to testify how sincerely and straightforwardly we desire to act'. She ended her letter with a reminder of the trust that had once been between them:

CS We beg very affectionately that all suspicions may be banished from between us, if any such have been raised by the arts of wicked men with the object of destroying that close friendship which we enjoyed in our earlier years.
From our Palace of Hampton Court, 20 December 1577.

Elizabeth

This was to her brother-in-law, the man who had once intervened to save her life. She sent the letter to Philip by Thomas Wilkes, Secretary to the Council. The King was put out that she had not used a nobleman of high rank to bear the message, but Elizabeth had already begun to adopt a policy of choosing the best man for the job.

---

* Although Alençon was now Duke of Anjou, most people continued to call him Alençon. Presumably this was to avoid confusion with his brother. Both Philip II and Lord Burghley refer to Francis as 'Alençon'. Very few contemporaries call him 'The Dauphin', although he is frequently known by his proper title of 'Monsieur'.

In her view Wilkes was in a position to understand and explain competently the correspondence that had gone on between herself and the States.

I must get married

Philip sent Don Bernardino de Mendoza to London with detailed instructions on how to behave towards Elizabeth. He was to tell her that nothing would make him 'relinquish the determination we have adopted to bring our subjects back again to obedience'. He told Mendoza he hoped to have Elizabeth 'on our side and that as a friend and sister she will turn her arms as she promises to do, to our support'.

Mendoza was the first Spanish ambassador since the expulsion of de Spes after the Ridolfi Plot. The Queen received him on 16 March 1578. He had arrived a few days earlier, just in time to learn that she had raised the £100,000 promised to the Dutch through Fugger's Bank. Her credit was the best in Europe; to raise such a sum was a vindication of that careful fiscal policy which Sir Walter Mildmay had commended in the 1576 Parliament. It was not however a propitious beginning to the new phase in Anglo-Spanish relations. England needed a defence alliance and Henry III, who had wooed Elizabeth as Duke of Anjou, proposed a revival of the courtship between his brother Francis, formerly Duke of Alençon, now Duke of Anjou and, since Henry was childless, Dauphin of France. Elizabeth was forty-five and the irrepressible Francis was exactly half her age. Although nominally a Catholic he was known to sympathise with the Prince of Condé and the King of Navarre and in 1574, when Charles IX lay dying, Catherine had shut her younger son up in the Louvre to check his intrigues. A Captain Leighton, whom Elizabeth had sent to Paris, managed to communicate with Francis, who let it be known he was in fear of his life. Perhaps this offered a romantic parallel with Elizabeth's own situation in Mary's reign and aroused her sympathy. By 1578 Alençon had escaped his domineering mother's influence and was very much in the forefront of international affairs. He took an army to the Low Countries, but he did not fare well and by the end of the year withdrew to France. Alençon was not only in need of a wife, he was in need of a backer. Everyone wished to see the re-establishment of peaceful trading conditions in the Netherlands. Shortly after the Sack of Antwerp Don John had signed the Pacification of Ghent with the States. Both he and William of Orange tried to make it work, but neither side trusted the other. In September 1578 Don John fell sick with a fever and his death on 1 October brought a halt to the Pope's plan for an invasion of England.

Elizabeth and her suitor pursued their love games energetically. On 5 January 1579 Anjou's special friend and envoy, Jean de Simier, Baron de St Marc, arrived in England. He met Elizabeth on the 11th and she immediately nicknamed him her

Monkey. Mendoza noted the Frenchman had brought with him 10 or 12,000 crowns' worth of jewels to give away. Philip was not impressed: 'I have always looked upon the idea of a marriage between the Queen and Alençon as a mere invention,' he wrote loftily. 'This is evident from the present position of the affair, as he is already reconciled with his brother.'

The Most Catholic King clearly regarded the Dauphin's escapade in the Netherlands as something undertaken in a fit of youthful pique. Nevertheless Anjou announced his intention of going to England. Elizabeth was entranced. After nearly twenty-one years of begging, entreating, and praying for her to marry, the astonished members of her Council were suddenly presented with the spectacle of their Prince, the sage virgin who had been likened to Deborah in her wisdom, and Diana in her chastity, behaving like a lovesick girl of seventeen. The modern explanation might be that Elizabeth was reaching the menopause and experiencing violent changes of mood and fierce surges of sexual desire. It is not an argument which would have commended itself to Lord Burghley. At the end of March 1579 he made two memoranda on the same day. In the first, he detected the hand of God intervening to provide for the English succession; 'The public peace of the realm' had always seemed to depend on Elizabeth marrying 'some person meet for her contentation'. The choice should be left to the Queen herself; there had been very many offers.

'Yet none', the Lord Treasurer reasoned, 'hath taken effect. The very true causes thereof are to be referred to God's will without imputation to any certain known cause. If it now pleases God to incline her Majesty's heart to yield to give ear to this motion of the Duke of Alençon, and upon sight of him accept this offer of marriage, it is to be allowed of all good subjects as a marriage ordained by Almighty God.'

It was not for Lord Burghley to question the divine providence. If all things were to work together for the best possible end, Elizabeth might fall in love with Alençon, the marriage yield issue, Henry III might die childless, England could regain Calais, and the two countries might yet be united in a great and ultimately Protestant dynasty, which would safeguard them for ever against the might of Spain. He did not commit this scheme to paper, but it must certainly have crossed his mind. So perhaps had the spectre of Elizabeth's menopause – but if that was the case he banished it firmly.

Under the heading 'Apparent reasons to dissuade her Majesty from this marriage', he noted that she was forty-five years old, which he thought might 'yield occasion to doubt either her conception or her good delivery'. The Queen's doctors, however, were optimistic and Burghley appeared to regard Elizabeth's constitution as indestructible. Despite her forty-five years she had 'no lack of natural functions in those things that properly belong to the procreation of children, but contrariwise by judgement of physicians that know her estate in those things, and by the opinion of women, being most acquainted with her Majesty's body in such things as properly appertain to show probability of her aptness to have children even at this day'. Many women, he reasoned, 'have had and have still, children when they are past the years her Majesty hath'. He crisply dismissed the problem of Alençon's religion. There was only one difficulty which seemed insurmountable: 'Marriage with a stranger, especially with a prince of power, may procure misliking to the realm, for that naturally this realm as commonly all realms do, mislikes strangers.'

The Council debated the marriage through March and April; Sussex and Burghley were for it, Walsingham and Leicester against, but the majority of the Council fell out with Simier when he demanded that Alençon should have equal shares with Elizabeth in the administration, and they decided to a man that he could only be crowned if Parliament did not object. He also demanded an income for life of 'threescore thousand pounds', Elizabeth wrote to Sir Amyas Paulet, her ambassador in Paris. In the same letter she insisted he should come in person:

'A Duke of Anjou would do no hurt to his honour by visiting the Queen of England, whatever the result of his journey might be.'

If the French had been treating 'with a Princess who was ugly or otherwise unsuited to him', Elizabeth could have understood his delay, 'but seeing the graces which God has bestowed on us,' she wrote to Paulet, 'we deem ourselves worthy of a prince as great as Monsieur.'

On 14 May Mendoza wrote to Philip that the Queen had ordered members of the Council 'to give their individual opinions on the marriage with Alençon, which papers she read whilst staying at Leicester's house at Wanstead'. The councillors then discussed the matter again, but most of them still objected to the new terms Simier was demanding, and he flounced out of the conference to lay his grievances before the Queen. 'She was very melancholy,' Mendoza remarked, and she burst out: 'They need not think it is going to end this way; I must get married.' If Elizabeth was acting, she was certainly throwing herself wholeheartedly into the role. Burghley believed in her sincerity, so did Leicester. He was reported as having prostrated himself at her feet, begging her not to meet the Frenchman. He also put it about that Simier had been giving her love potions.

A matter which is so hard for Englishmen to bear

Alençon himself arrived in August. His visit was supposed to be a secret, but the Countess of Derby and a daughter of the Earl of Bedford gossiped so much that Elizabeth confined them to their quarters. The whole point of the secrecy was to ensure that if either of the parties disliked the other they could withdraw from the negotiations without loss of dignity. Simier had been laying siege to the Queen's affections since January, stealing love trophies to send to his master – on one occasion her handkerchief and on another, more coyly, her nightcap. These tactics were widely condemned as an 'unmanlike, unprincelike, French kind of wooing', but not by the Queen: she revelled in the Frenchman's attentions. They brought an entirely new measure of sophistication to the game of courtly love which, in one form or another, had been played by those around her since her childhood. Simier had been assigned a pavilion in the gardens of Greenwich Palace, where the duke was able to stay incognito. He arrived early one morning before anyone was awake and Simier put him to bed, writing Elizabeth a suggestive little note, wishing to God she was between the sheets with his master.

At dusk she slipped out of the palace with only one lady and they supped with Simier and the duke. It was a great success. Elizabeth had preserved a remarkably youthful appearance and Alençon was both witty and well-mannered. He was not handsome, but certainly not as bad-looking as she had been led to believe, and, if Hilliard's miniature is accurate, the pock marks had not disfigured his face. Elizabeth nicknamed him her Frog and the affair began to take on a fairytale glamour. On Sunday 23 August there was a grand ball at which Alençon, from a hiding place behind the arras, admired Elizabeth's dancing. Everyone knew he was there; Mendoza reported that she spent the whole evening waving to him. Lord Leicester, he told Philip, 'was in great grief'. Letters then arrived from France to say Monsieur's best friend, Bussy d'Amboise, had been killed in a duel. The duke left immediately for France, post-horses and a royal ship being placed at his disposal. He loved Elizabeth absolutely, he declared, writing her three letters from Dover, one from aboard *The Scout*, and three more from Boulogne. If he thought he would never see her again, he would not want to go on living for another quarter of an hour. He tied his letters with pink silk ribbon.

The idea of a French match was creating a furore in the kingdom. John Stubbs, a barrister from Lincoln's Inn, wrote a pamphlet, *The Discovery of a Gaping Gulf, wherein England is like to be swallowed by another French marriage, if the Lord forbid not the banns by letting her Majesty see the sin and punishment thereof.* He was passionately devoted to the Queen, but he expressed Englishmen's fears in language that was crudely direct. It would be 'exceedingly dangerous for her Majesty at these years to have her first child'. It was suspicious that the French should seek this match 'at the uttermost time of hope to have issue'. Clearly that malevolent nation wanted the Queen to conceive and die in childbirth. Not one in a thousand young men sought to marry older women without ulterior motives. 'How can we think otherwise in a young prince, heir apparent of France?' asked Stubbs. 'It is quite contrary to his young appetites, which will otherwise have their desires.' Furthermore, as a Frenchman, Alençon might have the pox.

Elizabeth was furious. On 27 September she issued a proclamation against 'such fanatical divinations'. They were nothing but 'forged lies against a prince of royal blood, as Monsieur the French King's brother'. There had also been 'dishonest railing speeches and taunts against his principal minister and ambassador attending here'. She gave orders for Stubbs and his bookseller, Page, to have their right hands cut off. Stubbs thought he might die from loss of blood, since so many veins would be opened. He asked all the people to pray for him, protesting his loyalty to God and the Queen. As the hand came off, he fainted away. Page suffered more courageously, saying he had left on the block 'the hand of a true Englishman'.

Leicester's nephew, Sir Philip Sidney, also wrote against the marriage. His protest was only circulated in manuscript and the penalty was lighter: he was sent away from Court for a year, and occupied his time gracefully by beginning to write *Arcadia*. His protest against the marriage, however, was designed for a more influential public than Stubbs's pamphlet. Sidney had been at the French Court and in the Netherlands. Like Stubbs, he pointed out that it would be difficult for Englishmen to trust Alençon when his brother had authorised the Massacre of St Bartholomew. More interestingly, he dismissed the duke, whom he had met, as a warlike adventurer, 'having Alexander's image in his head, but perchance ill painted'. The description was to prove frighteningly accurate; Alençon had his own charisma, but he was not a very good soldier. Sidney phrased things more elegantly than Stubbs. 'There was never monarch held in more precious reckoning of her people,' he assured Elizabeth, ending, 'No, no, most excellent Lady, do not raze out the impression you have made in such a multitude of hearts and let not the scum of such vile minds bear any witness against your subjects' devotion.'

On 2 October the Council met for an emergency session, Lord Burghley himself taking the minutes. They debated all through the 7th and during the morning of the 8th. In the afternoon a deputation went to Elizabeth to know her pleasure. She understood they were distressed by the question of Monsieur's religion, but she marvelled 'that any person would think so slenderly for her as that she would not for God's cause, for herself, her surety and her people have so strait regard thereto, as none ought to make that such a doubt as for it to forbear marriage and to have the Crown settled in her child.'

This seemed to conclude the matter. 'The Lord Chancellor, the Lord Treasurer, the Lord Admiral, Sussex, Leicester, Lord Hunsdon, Mr Treasurer, the Lord President, Mr Vice Chamberlain, Mr Secretary Wilson, Sir Peter Sadler and Sir Walter Mildmay came all to her Majesty and by mouth of the Lord Chancellor offered their services in furtherance of the marriage.' Then she changed her mind, capitulating suddenly to all their previous persuasions. Mendoza gave many detailed accounts of her reactions in the next few weeks. She was very sad, she had really wanted to marry Alençon and to have children. She was particularly bitter against Walsingham, who had been one of the chief opponents of the marriage. Shortly after the October Council meetings she wrote to Alençon to say it was better that they should remain 'faithful friends' than that they should fall out over religion.

'You realise, my dearest, that the greatest difficulties lie in making our people rejoice and approve. The public practice of the Roman Religion so sticks in their hearts. I beg you to consider this deeply, as a matter which is so hard for Englishmen to bear that it passes all imagination. For my part I confess there is no prince in the world to whom I think myself more bound, nor with whom I would rather pass the years of my life, both for your rare virtues and sweet nature.' She signed it 'with my commendations to my dearest Frog'.

Unfortunately this letter crossed with one Alençon had written to say he now had his mother's blessing, and his brother's permission for the marriage. He pressed an emerald (worth 400 crowns, the Spanish ambassador noted) into the sealing wax.

Scylla and Charybdis

What lay behind Elizabeth's extraordinary *volte face*? Why was she so bitter? Had she after twenty-one years of calculated celibacy become infatuated by the one suitor who had taken the trouble to cross the seas and visit her in person? Or was she, three years after her emphatic speech to the Parliament of 1576, overwhelmed by the simple human craving to have a child of her own, and to see the line of Henry VIII established in perpetuity?

The explanation that fits best is a tenuous linking of two stories. Leicester married Lettice in a private ceremony in the spring of 1578. She was pregnant but her child did not survive. On 21 September, probably just before it was born, and almost certainly at the instigation of her father, Sir Francis Knollys, there was a further ceremony at Wanstead attended by Knollys himself, Ambrose Dudley and the Earl of Pembroke. Lettice eventually bore a son at the end of 1579, Robert, Baron Denbigh, adored by both his parents, and nicknamed the Noble Imp. According to Camden the secret of Leicester's marriage was kept until the autumn of 1579, when Simier told the Queen that Leicester was married to revenge himself on the earl for trying to wreck the negotiations for Elizabeth to marry Alençon. Camden says Simier hoped 'to remove Leicester out of his Place and Favour with the Queen'. The traditional version of the story has Elizabeth in a fearful rage, commanding Leicester not to stir out of the Castle of Greenwich. Camden says she would have locked the earl up in the Tower had not Sussex dissuaded her. Almost all subsequent biographers tell this story, embroidered in some form or other with dissertations on the noble nature of Sussex.

The extraordinary thing about Camden's story is that the full details never seem to have reached Mendoza's ears. If Elizabeth had put Leicester under house arrest and threatened him with imprisonment it would surely have been so sensational that everyone would have known, but the ambassador's only reference to Leicester's marriage is in a letter to Philip of 13 January 1580. He wrote to tell the King that Alençon was taking the idea of marrying Elizabeth so seriously, that he was already thinking of his image as King of England. He had written to Elizabeth from France asking her to release Stubbs and Page, that he might make a better impression on the English and be thought a merciful Prince. He was sorry the men had had their hands cut off; he was also sorry that Elizabeth was 'not showing so much favour as formerly to the Earl of Leicester'. This was the letter Alençon sealed with the emerald, the symbol of keeping faith and honouring vows. 'The French ambassador', continued Mendoza, 'had high words with Leicester the other day about his trying to persuade him to confess to the Queen that he was married, as Simier and the ambassador had assured her.'

This indicates that as late as January 1580 Elizabeth either did not know that Leicester was secretly married, or that she was trying not to believe the monstrous story Simier and the French ambassador, de Mauvissière, had told her. Leicester's biographer, Derek Wilson, suggests a different sequence of events. He believes Robert confessed his involvement with Lettice to Elizabeth as early as April 1578. He supports his theory by quoting a despatch of Mendoza's concerning a cancelled audience. This story is really the stuff of Shakespeare's plots. According to Mendoza, Elizabeth was walking in a garden when she found a letter, which had been thrown in at a doorway. After reading it she went straight to Leicester's house and stayed until 10 o'clock at night, sending a message to Mendoza that she was unwell. Leicester then went to Buxton to take the waters, missing much of the summer progress. Wilson quotes a letter from Sir Christopher Hatton to Leicester saying that the Queen was 'in continual melancholy' since he had gone away. 'She dreameth of marriage that might seem injurious to her.' This suggests Elizabeth had more than an inkling of what was going on. A third story related in Nichols' *Progresses* describes Elizabeth and the French ambassador attending Robert and Lettice's wedding banquet. Nichols gives his source as Thomas Churchyard's account of the 1578 progress.* But Churchyard says no such thing; he comments that the progress ended at Wanstead and that Leicester, who was now back from Buxton, gave a banquet for the Guard. He gives a date for the Queen's arrival at Wanstead, which would have been only a few days after the September wedding. This would have given time for the pregnant countess to be hustled off the premises.

If we assume Elizabeth had some idea of what was afoot, either that Lettice was pregnant, that the couple were indeed married, or, most hurtful of all, that Leicester was in love with Lettice in a way that he had not been with Elizabeth, then her behaviour towards Alençon, and in particular her anguished cry of May 1579, 'I must get married', make more sense. The determined gaiety with which she threw herself into the affair with the Dauphin is more plausible as the manifestation of a hurt ego than as the desperate infatuation of an ageing spinster; and hurt her ego was. She never forgave Lettice, and she lost no opportunity to insult her. Leicester was not allowed to bring his wife to Court. In 1583, when Elizabeth heard of a plan to match his stepdaughter, Lady Dorothy Devereux, with the young King of

---

* Thomas Churchyard says the progress ended at 'my Lord of Leicester's house where, to knit up all, the goodcheer was revived, not only with making a great Feast to the Queen and the French Ambassador, but also in feasting solemnly at several times the whole Guard.'

Scotland, she called Lettice a she-wolf, vowing she would expose her for the bad woman she really was through all the Courts of Christendom and prove her husband a cuckold.

The following year the couple spent a few days hunting at Burghley's house, Theobalds. Leicester's thank-you letter suggests the full measure of Lettice's ostracism. He is almost pathetically grateful that Burghley had dealt 'so friendly and honourably with my poor wife. For truly my lord, in all reason she is hardly dealt with. God must only help it with her Majesty for which my lord you shall be assured to find us most thankful to the uttermost of our powers.'

The vendetta did not end even when Leicester died. Elizabeth made Lettice pay back every penny he owed to the Crown. The countess sold jewellery to raise £50,000 and the Queen snatched back estates she had given him.

Alençon's affection was a salve to Elizabeth's wounded feelings. Although by the autumn of 1579 she had inwardly decided against going through with the marriage, she was genuinely fond of the duke, and for his part he had no intention of letting such a prize slip through his fingers. At the end of February 1580 Mendoza reported a private conversation between Elizabeth, Burghley and the Archbishop of York.

'My lord, here I am between Scylla and Charybdis,' Elizabeth said. 'Alençon has agreed to all the terms I sent him and he is asking me to tell him when I wish him to come and marry me. If I do not marry him, I do not know whether he will remain friendly with me. And if I do, I shall not be able to govern the country with the freedom and security that I have hitherto enjoyed. What shall I do?'

Burghley told her, patiently, that if it was her pleasure to marry she should do so, no harm would come to the country; but if she did not intend to marry, 'she ought to undeceive Alençon at once'.

Elizabeth replied: 'That is not the opinion of the rest of the Council, but that I should keep him in correspondence.' According to Mendoza, Burghley told her 'that those who tricked princes, tricked themselves'.

They have thought me no fool

Catherine de' Medici had set her heart on the Alençon marriage. Elizabeth thought it would be more desirable to forget the marriage, but keep the alliance. The French Queen Mother, guessing that Elizabeth was about to glide out of the affair, took a firm line – no marriage, no alliance. For Elizabeth the alliance was increasingly important. Politically she was beset by dangers. English Catholics were leniently treated by comparison with Protestants in Philip's realms. The punishment for celebrating Mass was more often a fine than imprisonment.

Seminary priests began to arrive in England from William Allen's 'College of

Martyrs' at Douai. Their mission was to save souls and to administer the sacraments to those families who had no contact with a priest. Some of the older Catholic families, particularly in the north, maintained chaplains, heavily disguised as Latin or Italian tutors. Priest-holes and secret passages were built, and panelled recesses were let into walls, where altars, candles and chalices could be hidden at a moment's notice. In 1580 two Jesuits, Edmund Campion and Robert Parsons, arrived in England. Parsons later escaped to France, but Campion, after administering the sacraments for some months, was arrested and tortured. In an attempt to make him name families who were secret Catholics he was racked until his joints were dislocated. Elizabeth herself examined him at Leicester House; she would probably have liked to save him, for when he was a young man she had listened appreciatively to his brilliant dissertation at Oxford on the moon and the tides. She is said to have asked him what Catholics called 'the Bloody Question': if the Pope organised an invasion against England to overthrow the Queen, on which side would you fight? Campion replied: 'I would do as God should give me grace.' The reply was too equivocal; in December 1581 he was hanged, drawn and quartered.

Elizabeth had offended Philip by giving support to Dom Antonio, one of the many claimants to the disputed Portuguese succession. At one point he made his headquarters at Baynard's Castle, just east of Blackfriars. The Portuguese nobles, after the death of their Cardinal King, favoured the Duchess of Braganza, but Philip, in a massive display of military strength, stepped in and annexed the country, enforcing his own claim. In the Netherlands his nephew, the Duke of Parma, a soldier almost as redoubtable as Don John, had arrived to take over as governor. He immediately began a series of reprisals known as 'the Spanish Fury'. For England and France, therefore, there were advantages for both sides in keeping up the pretence that the marriage between Elizabeth and Alençon would take place. Whether Philip Sidney's view that the Dauphin was no Alexander was true or not, Elizabeth could rely on her suitor to be a thorn in the King of Spain's side. For his part, his credit stood higher as prospective King of England.

Burghley had told her that if she did not wish to marry him she should undeceive him, but she had decided to 'keep him in correspondence'. Throughout 1580 and 1581 she poured out letters to him. Most of them are difficult to date accurately, as she wrote in her own hand, never putting the year. Many of the first drafts are preserved at Hatfield among the Cecil Papers, scribbled in Elizabeth's excellent French and her execrable 'running hand'. Writing to Monsieur began as a diplomatic ploy, but it was also an outlet for her tangled emotions. Two themes dominate the letters: her deep appreciation of his constancy, which she said was '*un clair rocher*' amidst life's storms and tempests, and her concern over the delays in the marriage negotiations, which she always blamed on the French. He sent her a golden flower with a frog perched on its petals, and with his miniature inside. She sent him constant assurances that their souls were meant to be united, but she was not sure when.

In the spring of 1581 Alençon's envoy, the Sieur de Marchaumont, arrived with a posy of flowers which Monsieur had picked himself. She wrote effusively to thank him 'for the sweet flowers plucked by the hand with the little fingers, which I bless a million times, promising you that no present was ever carried so carefully, for the leaves were still as green as when they were freshly picked, a vibrant token of your affection, and I hope there shall never be any just cause for it to wither'.

Politically she did not trust the French an inch: the lesson of Câteau Cambrésis, when France and Spain had made peace to her detriment, was never forgotten. In the summer of 1580 the Dutch States had offered Alençon the sovereignty of the Low Countries. Parma by this time had recaptured the southern provinces for Spain and Elizabeth knew that if Alençon accepted the leadership of the Protestant States, it would mean more fighting, more money, and from her coffers. Even before the news of the Dutch offer was confirmed, she wrote to Sir Edward Stafford, who was in Paris negotiating the long-drawn-out marriage treaty. A copy of her letter found its way to the Lord Chamberlain's department and has survived among the papers of Sir Christopher Hatton.

CB Stafford,

There is even now another accident fallen out, of no small consequence to this realm. I am sure the States have accorded to the demands of Monsieur, and do present him the sovereignty of all the Low Countries. Suppose now, how this may make our people think well of him and of me to bring them to the possession of such neighbours? Oh Stafford, I think not myself well used, and so tell Monsieur that I am made a stranger to myself; who he must be if this matter take place? In my name show him how impertinent it is for this season to bring to the ears of our people so untimely news. God forbid that the banns of our nuptial feast should be savoured with the sauce of our subjects' wealth. Oh what may they think of me, that for any glory of mine own would procure the ruin of my land? Hitherto they have thought me no fool; let me not live the longer the worse. The end crowneth the work.

Elizabeth was disconcerted to have heard the news of the Dutch offer, before any despatch reached her from Alençon himself.

CB I am sorry that the common posts of London can afford me surer news than the inhabitants of Tours will yield me. Let it please Monsieur to suspend his answers unto them till he send some unto me of quality and of trust to communicate and concur with that I may think good for both our honours. For I assure him, it shall too much blot his fame if he deal otherwise, not only in my sight, to whom it hath pleased him to promise more than that, but especially to all the world, that be overseers of his actions. Let him never procure her harm whose love he seeks to win. My mortal foe can wish me no greater loss than England's hate. Neither should death be less welcome unto me than such a mishap betide me. You see how nearly this matter wringeth me. Use it accordingly. If it please him the deputies may have the charge of this matter joined with the other two that were aforementioned. I dare not assure Monsieur how this great matter will end until I be assured what way he will take with the Low Countries for rather will I never meddle with marriage than have such a bad covenant added to my part. Shall it be ever found true that Queen Elizabeth hath solemnised the perpetual harm of England under the glorious title of marriage with Francis, heir of France? No, no it shall never be.

Monsieur would probably ask Stafford, 'Why should not the Low Countries be governed by the in-dwellers of that country as they were wont', but under his own sovereignty instead of 'that of the King of Spain?' Elizabeth's answer was:

CB The case is too far different, since the one is far off by seas' distance, and the other near upon the continent. We willingly will not repose our whole trust so far on the French nation as we will give them in pawn all our fortune, and afterwards stand to their discretion. I hope I shall not live in that hour.

In haste your sovereign, Elizabeth

Where delights be snares, where dangers be imminent

At the end of September 1580 there was a further rupture in the diplomatic relations between England and Spain. Francis Drake returned from the New World with unheard-of plunder, having waylaid King Philip's treasure fleet. The original investors in the voyage had included Leicester, Walsingham, Hatton and the Queen herself. Before Drake had set out in the autumn of 1577, she had sent him an embroidered sea-cap, and a green silk scarf embroidered with the words 'The Lord guide and preserve thee until the end'. His ships had included the *Elizabeth*, captained by John Wynter, and the expedition had set off without the knowledge of the Lord Treasurer.

Officially it was to have been a voyage of exploration: rumour now had it that investors would have a return of £47 for every £1 they had put into the venture. There was a crisis in the Council; Burghley, Sussex and Secretary Wilson believed the treasure should be returned to Philip. Leicester, Hatton and Walsingham refused to sign the order for the restitution of the plunder. Burghley and Sussex pointed out that anyone who shared in it would be receiving stolen property. Elizabeth coolly suggested Drake should bring interesting souvenirs of his voyage to London. Mendoza screamed for the thief to be punished, but she retorted that she could not possibly condemn the corsair if she did not first question him.

Drake loaded his treasure onto packhorses and set out for Richmond Palace, where he spent six hours closeted with the Queen. Mendoza pressed for a return of the stolen bullion, but Elizabeth turned on him in blazing fury, demanding an apology from Philip for his interference in Ireland and his ill-treatment of her Protestant subjects in trading matters. Drake was sent back to Plymouth and told he could keep £10,000 of his booty and distribute a similar sum among his associates. The rest was to be placed in safe-keeping in the Tower, until a decision could be reached about its restitution. Burghley and Sussex refused to touch a single ducat. On New Year's Day at Court Elizabeth wore a crown Drake had given her containing five magnificent Peruvian emeralds. Mendoza continued to demand audiences, but he was told Elizabeth was busy. In April 1581 the famous scene took place aboard the *Golden Hind*, which lay at Deptford. After a magnificent banquet, the like of which had never been seen since Henry VIII's day, Elizabeth, accompanied by Alençon's envoy, inspected the ship. The King of Spain, she said, had asked for Drake's head, and raising a golden sword of state, she teased as if to strike it off herself. Then, passing the sword to de Marchaumont, she ordered him to knight Francis Drake, thus neatly drawing the French into the proceedings. During the tour of inspection Elizabeth's garter became loose. When de Marchaumont asked for it to add to Alençon's peculiar collection of souvenirs, she pointed out that she had nothing else to hold up her hose, and stooped significantly to re-adjust it. Later she gave it to the envoy for Monsieur.

At the end of April the French commissioners arrived to complete the marriage treaty. A special banqueting-house had been erected in the gardens at Whitehall to receive them. It was made of canvas, painted to look like stone, with 292 glass windows, so that it was a cross between a marquee and a greenhouse. The heat generated was said to be overwhelming, but the roof was painted to resemble the heavens with suns and stars, and the royal arms had been moved there and newly gilded. Some of the Spanish treasure had gone into paying for it, and Mendoza continued to press for restitution.

Elizabeth received the French delegation in a gown of gold tissue; the magnificence of the occasion seemed to indicate the marriage would really take place, even though the bride would be forty-eight before the wedding. After the feasting the envoys went to visit Lord Burghley to talk business. Once again the negotiations foundered, as the English pressed for a treaty, the French for a marriage. In October Alençon himself arrived. Elizabeth did everything she could to prevent him from coming, but his mother and brother, fearful that the duke's operations in the Low Countries would plunge France into war with Spain, were entreating him to withdraw. Henry III had even forbidden Frenchmen to enlist in his brother's army. England seemed to be Monsieur's only hope. Burghley had warned Elizabeth that those who tricked Princes deserved to be tricked themselves. She had used Alençon mercilessly to buy time, gambling on the hope that the French would agree to a treaty without insisting on the marriage. It was now up to her to save his honour. There followed some moments of high theatre, when Elizabeth publicly kissed the duke in the gallery at Whitehall, and the couple exchanged rings, which was tantamount to an official engagement.

Elizabeth told the French ambassador, de Mauvissière: 'You may write this to the King, that the Duke of Alençon shall be my husband.'

Burghley was in bed with gout: 'Blessed be the Lord that this business has at last reached a point where the Queen has done all she can,' he said. Mendoza wrote tartly to Philip that she had been negotiating for three years, and if she had really wished to marry, 'she would not have wasted time'. He was finally granted his audience to discuss the restitution of the treasure. She received him at Richmond, lecturing him on the law of nations and demanding an apology from Philip for his interference in Ireland. Mendoza lost his temper; perhaps if his words carried no weight, they should try cannon.

'She told me', wrote Don Bernardino, 'I need not think to threaten and frighten her for if I did she would put me in a place where I could not say a word.'

Her even tone convinced him she meant what she said. She lent Alençon a further £30,000, demanding that his brother should also finance the campaign. He finally left England at the end of February 1582, the Queen herself accompanying him to Canterbury. They continued their ardent correspondence through 1582, Elizabeth remarking that she would give a million pounds to see her Frog swimming in the Thames again. He was pitiably afraid that she would make him the laughing-stock of Europe. His letters begged her to pray for him. It would not be long before he paid her back her loan, he assured her, then she must fulfil her promise to make him her lawful husband. She wrote a sonnet, 'On Monsieur's Departure', recording her ambivalence in an elegant Petrarchan imitation, ending with the couplet,

I am and am not, freeze, and yet I burn
Since from myself, my other self I turn.

More significantly, and more sincerely, she compiled a miniature prayer book for her private use. The two English prayers, composed at some time between her first meeting with Alençon in 1579 and his death in 1584, are perhaps the most beautiful of all Elizabeth's writings. They are not well known, and no one has succeeded in dating exactly the little book known as 'Queen Elizabeth's Book of Devotions'. The original measured two inches by three; it was covered in shagreen binding with a jewelled clasp. It passed from James II to the Duke of Berwick, through Horace Walpole to the Duchess of Portland. It went for £106 1s on 24 May 1786 at the duchess's sale, where the buyer was Queen Charlotte. It was later owned by the Dowager Duchess of Leeds and in 1884 came into the possession of J. W. Whitehead. In 1893 Whitehead made forty autotype copies of the original, which was subsequently lost. One of the copies survives in the British Museum, but no one appears to know what has happened to the remaining thirty-nine. The book appears

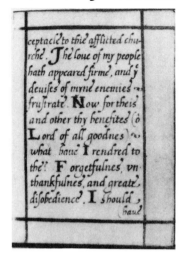

One of the English prayers
from 'Queen Elizabeth's Book
of Devotions', written in
Elizabeth's tiny script

to be in Elizabeth's own handwriting and, in the two English prayers, it compares with the fine italic script she used in the book for her father, written when she was twelve years old. Although she used an abominable scrawl for drafting letters and official documents, she was proud of her good eyesight and she was still capable of producing the beautiful handwriting which won her such praise in her youth.

There are six prayers in the book, two in English, one in Italian, one in French, one in Latin and one in Greek. Different scripts were used for the different languages, and at the front and back of the book are miniatures of Elizabeth and Alençon by Nicholas Hilliard. In the facsimiles these portraits are in sepia-tint monochrome, but Whitehead described them as 'on a gold ground with fleurs de lys' which can just be discerned in the autotype. The heads themselves are in oval gold frames each decorated with eight Tudor roses, and presumably in the originals the heads themselves are silhouetted against Hilliard's famous blue background.* In 1970 an enlarged version of the facsimile was published by Adam Fox and Canon Hodges, who point out that Elizabeth refers to ordinary sinners with a small 's' and herself as 'a Sinner'. The sincerity of the two English prayers is deeply compelling, but their tone suggests they were composed at different times. The size of the book and the description of its original binding suggest Elizabeth carried it about with her, probably attached to a jewelled girdle, when Alençon went to the wars, or possibly after his death as a *memento mori*. In the first English Prayer she thanks God for

---

* Whitehead exhibited the original in 1902 at the Fine Arts Society. Sir Roy Strong considers the miniature of Elizabeth to be one of the finest ever painted. Even the sepia-tint autotype captures her features; they are not at all serene, and the whole painting has a sense of nervous unease. In 1923 F. W. Chamberlain reproduced the miniatures in his book *The Sayings of Queen Elizabeth I*, making a clumsy attempt to colour them. They bear no resemblance to Whitehead's descriptions of the originals.

having preserved her through so many perils, echoing what she said to the Parliament of 1576, that Englishmen should count their blessings for her peaceful reign.

Cঃৈ O most Glorious King and Creator of the whole world to whom all things be subject both in heaven and earth and all best Princes most gladly obey. Hear the most humble voice of thy handmaid in this only happy to be so accepted. How exceeding is thy goodness and how great mine offences. Of nothing hast thou made me not a worm but a Creature according to thine own image, heaping all the blessings upon me that men on earth hold most happy. Drawing my blood from Kings and my bringing up in virtue; giving me that more is even in my youth knowledge of thy truth and in times of most danger most gracious deliverance, pulling me from the prison to the palace, and placing me as Sovereign Princess over the people of England. And above all this making me (though a weak woman) yet thy instrument to set forth the glorious Gospel of thy dear Son Christ Jesus. THUS in these last and worst days of the world when wars and seditions with grievous persecutions have vexed almost all Kings and Countries round about me, my reign hath been peaceable and my Realm a receptacle to thy afflicted church. The love of my people hath appeared firm and the devises of mine enemies frustrate. Now for these and others thy benefits (O Lord of all goodness) what have I rendered to thee? Forgetfulness, unthankfulness and great disobedience. I should have magnified thee. I should have prayed unto thee. I have forgotten thee, I should have served thee, I have sinned gainst thee. THIS is my case. Then where is my hope? If thou Lord wilt be extreme to mark what is done amiss who may abide it. But thou art gracious and merciful, long suffering and of great goodness, not delighting in the death of a Sinner. Thou seest whereof I came of corrupt seed, what I am, a most frail substance, where I live in the world full of wickedness; where delights be snares, where dangers be imminent, where sin reigneth and death abideth. THIS is my state. Now where is my comfort? In the depth of misery I know no help (O Lord) but the height of thy mercy who hast sent thine only Son into the world to save sinners. This God of my life and life of my soul, the King of all comfort is my only refuge. For his sake therefore to whom thou hast given all power and wilt deny no petition hear my prayers. Turn thy face from my sins (O Lord) and thine eyes to thy handiwork. Create a clean heart and review a right spirit within me. Order my steps in thy word that no wickedness have dominion over me, make me obedient to thy will and delight in thy law. Grant me grace to live godly and to govern justly; that so living to please thee and reigning to serve thee, I may ever glorify thee, the Father of all goodness and mercy. To whom with thy dear son my only Saviour and the Holy Ghost my Sanctifier, three persons and one God; be all praise dominion and power, world without end. AMEN.

In 'The Book of Devotions', the termagant Princess who flared at her councillors and ordered her subjects' hands cut off becomes again the gentle soul who prayed for her father at the Siege of Boulogne, reciting Katherine Parr's prayer for English armies to gain victory 'with small effusion of Christian blood'. In the French prayer Elizabeth again thanks God for her peaceful reign, when her nearest neighbours have experienced 'the evils of a bloody war and thy poor persecuted children have found with us both peace and a secure home'.

This would seem to be a reference to the Huguenots, many of whom had settled in England after the Massacre of St Bartholomew. In the second English Prayer the tone is very different. She asks God to grant her the strength and wisdom to preserve the Gospel and rule her State.

CB So teach me, I humbly beseech thee, thy word and so strengthen me with thy grace that I may feed thy people with a faithful and true heart and rule them prudently with power.

I acknowledge oh my King without thee my seat unsure, my Kingdom tottering, my life uncertain, I see all things in this life subject to mutability, nothing to continue still at one stay, but fear and trembling, hunger and thirst, cold and heat, weakness and faintness, sorrow and sickness doth ever more oppress mankind. I hear how oft times untimely death doth carry away the mightiest and greatest personages. I have learned out of thy holy word that horrible judgement is nigh unto them which walk not after thy will, and the mighty swerving from thy law shall be mightily tormented. Therefore since all things in this world, both heaven and earth shall pass and perish and thy word alone endureth for ever, engraft oh most gracious Lord Christ, this thy word of grace and life so in my heart that from henceforth I neither follow after feigned comforts in worldly power neither distract my mind to transitory pleasures, nor occupy my thoughts in vain delights, but yet carefully seeking thee where thou showest thyself in thy word, I may surely find thee to my comfort and everlastingly enjoy thee to my salvation.

CHAPTER XI

I find no consolation

Alençon died at Château Thierry in France on 10 June 1584. His campaign in the Netherlands had been undistinguished. As the despatches arrived from the Low Countries Elizabeth must have been reminded uncomfortably of Philip Sidney's comment, that Monsieur was a man with Alexander's image in his head, 'but perchance ill painted'. In command at last of a combined army of French and English troops, the devout young man went to pray for victory. He and his officers openly attended Catholic masses in Antwerp, creating considerable ill-feeling among the Dutch Protestants they had come to liberate.

Squabbles in the town council irritated Alençon so much that he tried to gain control of the city by an underhand coup. He rode out of Antwerp with a cavalry escort, but when the city gates were opened to let him pass, an army of French soldiers rode into the town shouting '*Vive la Messe*'. The citizens resisted, and seven or eight hundred men were killed on each side in the ensuing skirmishes. The Dutch linked this piece of treachery with the Massacre of St Bartholomew, announcing they would no longer accept Monsieur as their leader. In the English regiment commanded by Sir John Norris, the soldiers sympathised so much with the local people that spontaneously they helped to defend the Scheldt against the French. It was all Norris could do to prevent the extreme Protestants in his ranks from attacking them.

Alençon ordered the English to remain in their own camp, while Parma offered an amnesty to the States, promising to drive the perfidious French out of the Low Countries if only the people would accept King Philip's lawful sovereignty. The southern provinces, which were Catholic, had few objections, but since Parma's offer did not include religious toleration, the Protestant States fought on. Elizabeth wrote encouragingly to Alençon, who tried to dismiss the Antwerp affair as a mistake made by one of his colonels, but as the campaign progressed she found it difficult to conceal her distaste. William of Orange and Elizabeth tried to hold the French alliance together. Meanwhile Parma's armies advanced from the south, capturing Eindhoven, Zutphen, Nieuport and Dunkirk, making the possibility of a Spanish attack on England seem infinitely more likely. At the end of the summer Alençon made one more approach to Elizabeth. She wrote to him on 10 September 1583 with some asperity:

'My God, Monsieur, are you quite mad? You seem to believe that the means of keeping our friends is to weaken them. Is the King, your brother, so feeble a Prince that he cannot defend you without another neighbour, who has enough on her back?'

Nevertheless she wept inconsolably ten months later to hear her Frog Prince had

Elizabeth in black, with a diaphanous silver shawl, as described by the German traveller von Wedel (p.189)

died of a fever. The French ambassador believed she was acting, but she had thrown herself so energetically into the task of keeping Alençon in correspondence that she had become genuinely fond of him, and she sustained the role of a heartbroken fiancée convincingly. There was a measure of sincerity amidst the extravagant phrases in which she expressed her sympathy to Catherine de' Medici:

'Although you were his mother, you have several other children,' she wrote, 'but for myself I find no consolation, if it be not death in which I hope we shall be re-united. Madame, if you could see the image of my heart you would see there the picture of a body without a soul, but I will not trouble you with sorrows for you have too many of your own. I will turn a great part of my love for him to the King my good brother and you, assuring you that you will find me the most faithful daughter and sister that ever Princes had.'

She soon had a chance to put her love to the test. Monsieur's death created a crisis in the French succession, since there seemed no likelihood that Henry III, with his Court of *mignons*, would have children. He had married Louise de Vaudmont, a cousin of the Duke of Guise, in the first year of his reign, but to the Queen Mother's disappointment there was no issue. As the Salic Law prevailed in France, the Crown could not descend through the female line, and the heir to the French throne after Catherine's youngest son was Henry of Navarre, the Huguenot leader, who was a direct descendant of St Louis. Henry III announced that he would recognise him as Dauphin if he would become a Catholic, but Henry of Navarre knew no one would take such a sudden conversion seriously, so he told the King his conscience would not allow it. Henry III turned to his dear sister of England who was so proud of her skills as a mediator, to see if she could help avert the crisis by persuading Henry of Navarre to change his mind. Elizabeth's image had already been tarnished in Protestant eyes by the treacherous behaviour of the French in the Netherlands, and not surprisingly, despite her deep sympathy for Henry III, her conscience did not permit her to intervene in the delicate matter of Henry of Navarre's faith.

A month after Alençon's death a young Burgundian, Balthasar Gerard, assassinated William of Orange. He was the only member of the Dutch nobility with the stature to bind the seventeen provinces with their differing traditions and beliefs into any lasting alliance. Elizabeth was still wearing mourning for Monsieur and the Prince of Orange in December 1584, when the German traveller Lupold von Wedel toured England. He described her dining in state at Greenwich in a gown of 'black velvet embroidered with silver and pearls. Over her robe she had a silver shawl, that was full of meshes and diaphanous like a piece of gossamer tissue.' The young man from Pomerania was fascinated by the ceremony with which the great Queen was served from forty dishes, all of silver-gilt. She sat alone under a cloth of gold canopy of estate, while her page, also in black velvet, carved for her. Another page dressed in green poured her wine, and remained kneeling beside her until she had finished drinking. At a table nearby five countesses took their seats, but, while the Queen was eating, the gentlemen stood. Charles Howard, the Lord High Admiral, was in attendance, also 'my lord of Leicester, the Master of the Horse, who', wrote von Wedel, 'is said to have had a love affair with the Queen for a long time. Now he has a wife. Then there was the Lord High Treasurer and the Keeper of the Privy Purse, my lord Hertford, who they say of all Englishmen has the most right to the throne. He it is who got one of the Queen's ladies with child, and married another, much against the Queen's will.' There was also Sir Christopher Hatton, whom von Wedel thought had been her lover after Leicester. 'All of them', he said, 'had white staffs in their hands and were handsome old gentlemen.'

Such a one as one day would give God the vomit

Parliament met in November 1584, three months after the assassination of William of Orange, and amidst the uproar that followed the sensational disclosures of the Throckmorton Plot. Francis Throckmorton, a Catholic nephew of Sir Nicholas, had been caught secretly corresponding with Mary Stuart, who still remained in the custody of the Earl of Shrewsbury. Lord Shrewsbury had his own share of domestic problems, having become involved in an appalling property battle with his wife, the redoubtable Bess of Hardwick. Elizabeth offered to mediate in their squabble, and the couple's financial affairs were sorted out with meticulous attention to detail, inventories of their household goods being made down to the countess's last pair of sheets.

During this interlude Mary had written regularly to the French and Spanish ambassadors. Walsingham, who had developed an excellent secret service, read most of the letters, which were in cipher, or invisible ink, or hidden in doublet-linings and shoe-heels. He set spies on Francis Throckmorton, who was arrested in November 1583. Amongst his papers two lists were found, one naming Catholic noblemen who could be relied on to rise in favour of Mary, and one of English ports where troops could be landed if the Pope's Enterprise against England, which had been discussed for so long, should ever set out. Throckmorton was racked until he confessed the names of his accomplices. Mendoza was summoned by the Council and asked to leave England. He told them he was 'not fond of staying in another person's house as an unwelcome guest', and he threatened that Philip would avenge with war insolence such as theirs to a nation as mighty as Spain.

The discovery of Throckmorton's lists created a great stir. Walsingham wrote to Sir Edward Stafford on 10 January: 'The Spanish ambassador was yesterday by her Majesty's order commanded to depart the realm within fifteen days.' He was 'discovered to have practised the disquieting of the realm and to have had secret intelligence with the Queen of Scots'.

In Antwerp the writer of the Fugger newsletter had heard as early as 7 January 'of the plot against the Queen. Many nobles are said to have been arrested, but two of the ringleaders seem to have escaped. There is talk here of the King of Spain fitting out a great fleet against the Netherlands, because he hoped the plot against the Queen's life would succeed.'

A month before Parliament assembled a Bond of Association was formed to protect Elizabeth. Thousands of gentlemen from all over England added their signatures and seals, swearing that, if the Queen was harmed, they would kill outright anyone who plotted against her. The Bond did not mention Mary by name, although it was originally devised to prevent her, or her son James, from claiming the English throne. The Commons wanted to enforce the Bond in an Act for the Queen's Safety. Their enthusiasm threatened to be an embarrassment to Elizabeth, who was engaged in a last delicate negotiation to get her cousin back to Scotland, there to rule jointly with her son. She intervened to delay both the bill for her safety and one to introduce stiffer penalties against Jesuits and seminary priests. These were put aside until after the Christmas recess, so that the Council could discuss them more thoroughly.

During the breathing space James VI rejected the idea of sharing his throne with his mother, and a further plot to make Mary Queen of England was discovered, involving Dr Parry, a member of the House of Commons who, with his associate Neville, had calmly contemplated assassinating Elizabeth as she walked in St James's Park. When Parliament reassembled in February, there was no holding the Commons. They thought an ordinary traitor's death too good for Parry and begged the Queen to let them invent a more horrible form of torture for him, which they would legalise by statute, but Elizabeth gave orders for Parry to be punished according to the existing forms of law. She was immensely heartened by the great demonstrations of love and loyalty in the country and the Commons, which was represented by the Association. Their seals alone filled several trunks, which were brought to her at Hampton Court. On 22 March she wrote to Mary to tell her of the fury in the Commons, stressing that once again she had intervened to save Mary's life.

'We suppose you cannot be ignorant how since the time of Parry's wicked intent has been disclosed and known to our loving and devoted subjects, they are grown so jealous of our safety – the rather for that the said Parry confessed before certain of our council appointed to examine him that his attempt tended purposely to the restoring of the Catholic religion by advancing you to this crown – that in open Parliament motion has been made with a general applause of the whole house to revive the former judicial proceedings against you propounded thirteen years past in Parliament, which as you know being assented to by both the Nobility and Commons, was only stayed at the time by us as it was also at this present on the same motion and not without the great misliking and discontentment of our best and devoted subjects.'

Her own safety was not Elizabeth's chief concern. At the end of the session she thanked Parliament for 'the safekeeping of my life for which your care appears so manifest', but it was a passing reference, a prologue to a homily on the matter which perturbed her far more, the uniformity of the Anglican Church. On Grindal's death, in September 1583, she had appointed John Whitgift as her third Archbishop of Canterbury. He shared her desire to enforce the Thirty-nine Articles, which were to them, as to future generations, the foundation of the Church of England, and to curb the Puritans and any other deviant sects. Several councillors, including Lord Burghley, disapproved of Whitgift's methods of enforcing the official doctrine, but Elizabeth believed firmly that the articles drawn up in 1562, embracing ancient Christian doctrine but steering a moderate course between Roman superstition and high Protestant newfangledness, were sound.

At the end of February she addressed Whitgift and other senior clergy in an audience at Somerset Place. She thanked them graciously for their share of the subsidy, sympathising with those of them who had been under fire from the House of Commons.

'We understand', she said, 'that some of the Nether House have used divers speeches against you, tending greatly to your dishonour, which we will not suffer.' If they did not administer their dioceses properly it rebounded on her. She too had been criticised, for it appeared to others that the Church of England had no clear doctrines of its own. A letter had come from overseas, written, she said, by someone 'who bore her no good will'. She had seen and read it and it predicted that the Papists would prevail in England, because the Protestants themselves misliked her. 'I have heard that some of them of late have said that I was of no religion – neither hot nor cold, but such a one as one day would give God the vomit. I pray you look unto such men.'

Then she turned to the unpleasant topic of those who tolerated Puritans in their dioceses, expressing particular disapproval of John Aylmer, Bishop of London, who was not present, but who had allowed things to go so far that in the City 'every merchant must have his schoolmaster and nightly conventicles, expounding scriptures and catechising their servants and maids'. She had heard that in some cases the maids had 'not sticked to control learned preachers and say that such a man taught otherwise in our house'.

'You suffer many ministers to preach what they list,' she complained, 'and to minister the sacraments according to their fancies, some one way, some another to the breach of unity. Yea, and some of them are so curious in searching matters above their capacity as they preach they wot not what – that there is no Hell, but a torment of conscience. Nay, I have heard there be six preachers in one diocese the which do preach six sundry ways. I wish such men to be brought to conformity and unity.'

After Whitgift had apologised, and Burghley had intervened with the shocking story of the Bishop of Lichfield and Coventry, who had made seventy unlearned men ministers in one day, Elizabeth asked how many livings there were in the realm. When the Archbishop explained that he could not find enough educated clergy to fill England's thirteen thousand parishes, Elizabeth made her famous exclamation:

'Jesus, thirteen thousand! It is not to be looked for.'

The Church whose overruler God hath made me

Religion was still uppermost in Elizabeth's mind when she spoke to Parliament at the end of the session. She had sent a message by the Speaker that the Commons were not to 'meddle with matters of the Church' and she supported Whitgift staunchly by vetoing all bills concerning ecclesiastical affairs. She had had time to organise her thoughts since the meeting at Somerset Place and, referring only briefly to the most dramatic business of the session, the bill for her safety, she launched into a homily on her responsibilities as Supreme Governor of the Church, pointing out her own unique responsibilities for the post.

ᘓ One matter touches me so near as I may not overskip [she told them]; religion is the ground on which all other matters ought to take root, and being corrupted may mar all the tree; and that there be some fault finders with the order of the clergy, which so may make a slander to myself and the Church whose overruler God hath made me, whose negligence cannot be excused if any schisms or errors heretical were suffered.

Thus much I must say that some faults and negligence may grow and be, as in all other great charges it happeneth; and what vocation without? All which if you, my Lords of the clergy, do not amend, I mean to depose you. Look ye therefore well to your charges.

I am supposed to have many studies [she reminded them] but most philosophical. I must yield this to be true, that I suppose few that be no professors have read more. And I need not tell you that I am so simple that I understand not, nor so forgetful that I remember not. And yet amidst so many volumes I hope God's book hath not been my seldomest lectures; in which we find that which by reason, for my part, we ought to believe – that seeing so great wickedness and griefs in the world in which we live but as wayfaring pilgrims, we must suppose that God would never have made us but for a better place and of more comfort than we find here. I know no creature that breatheth whose life standeth hourly in more peril for it than mine own; who entered not into my state without sight of manifold dangers of life and crown, as one that had the mightiest and the greatest to wrestle with. Then it followeth that I regarded it so much as I left myself behind my care. And so you see that you wrong me too much if any such there be as doubt my coldness in that behalf. For if I were not persuaded that mine were the true way of God's will, God forbid I should live to prescribe it to you. Take you heed lest *Ecclesiastes* say not too true; they that fear the hoary frost the snow shall fall upon them.

I see many overbold with God Almighty making too many subtle scannings of His blessed will, as lawyers do with human testaments. The presumption is so great, as I may not suffer it. Yet mind I not hereby to animate Romanists (which what adversaries they be to mine estate is sufficiently well known) nor tolerate newfangledness. I mean to guide them both by God's holy true rule. In both parts be perils. And of the latter I must pronounce them dangerous to a kingly rule: to have every man according to his own censure, to make a doom of a validity and privity of his Prince's government with a common veil and cover of God's word, whose followers must not be judged, but by private men's exposition. God defend you from such a ruler that so evil will guide you. Now I conclude that your love and care neither is nor shall be bestowed upon a careless Prince, but such as for your good will passeth as little for this world as who careth least. With thanks for your free subsidy, a manifest show of the abundance of your good wills, the which I assure you, but to be employed to your weal, I could be better pleased to return than receive.

To change this our former course

The death of Alençon and the assassination of William of Orange left Elizabeth no choice but to intervene in the Netherlands. Parma captured Ghent and began a long siege of Antwerp. under the leadership of the Sieur de Sainte Aldegonde the town resisted through the autumn and winter of 1584, while Parma blockaded the Scheldt to cut off supplies, and the Dutch argued about who should become their leader. The choice lay between Henry III and Elizabeth. Henry was by now under considerable pressure from the Duke of Guise and Mendoza, whom Philip had sent as Spanish ambassador to France, to make a united stand against the heretics. The States turned to Elizabeth, who refused sovereignty but agreed to send an army. A formal treaty was signed at Nonsuch on 10 August 1585.

There can seldom have been a more reluctant aggressor. Elizabeth issued a twenty page pamphlet, *A Declaration of the Causes moving the Queen of England to give aid to the Defence of the People afflicted and oppressed in the Low Countries*: it was printed in English, French and Dutch and distributed widely in England and on the Continent. Ascribed usually to Burghley and Walsingham, this deliberate piece of propaganda has an imposing frontispiece of the royal arms fully achieved with '*Dieu et Mon Droit*' emblazoned across the page to emphasise its official nature. The wording suggests Elizabeth almost certainly helped to compile it.

The Declaration describes the time-honoured friendship between England and Burgundy and the 'mutual and natural concourse and commerce' that had gone uninterrupted 'for many ages until recently the King of Spain hath appointed foreigners and strangers of strange blood, men more exercised in war than in peaceable government'. These new rulers had 'violently broken the ancient laws and liberties of all the countries and in a tyrannous sort have banished, killed and destroyed without order of law within the space of a few months many of the most ancient and principal persons of the natural nobility that were most worthy of government'.

CB   We have [announced the pamphlet] by many friendly messages and Ambassadors by many letters and writings to the said King of Spain our brother and ally declared our compassion of this so evil and cruel usage of his natural and loyal people.

And furthermore as a good loving sister to him and a natural good neighbour to his low countries and people, we have often and often again most friendly warned him that if he did not otherwise by his wisdom and princely clemency restrain the tyranny of his governors and cruelty of his men of war, we feared that the people of his countries would seek foreign protection.

The pamphlet assured its readers that Elizabeth had treated Philip's ambassadors well, except for 'Girald de Spes, a very turbulent spirited person', and Bernardino Mendoza, who had 'devised how an invasion might be made into our realm, setting down in writing the manner how the same should be done with what number of men and ships'.

CB   Hereupon we hope no reasonable person can blame us if we have disposed ourselves to change this our former course and more carefully to look to the safety of our self and our people.

The last five pages refute the notion that she was in any way ungrateful to Philip or plotted to take his life.

CB   He is one of whom we have ever had an honourable conceit in respect of those singular and rare parts we always have noted in him which hath won unto him a great reputation as any man of this day living carrieth of his degree and quality and so have we always delivered out by speech unto the world. Given at Richmond 1 October 1585.

The Declaration was no call to arms by a warrior Queen. She did not want open war and she dithered and delayed over the business of sending out men and munitions for so long that Antwerp finally surrendered to Parma on 17 August, the day after Sir John Norris set sail with an army for its relief. Elizabeth plied him with anxious messages to take defensive, not offensive, action, begging him to take special care of 'the lives of the young gentlemen of best birth', so that the flower of nobility should not be wasted.

Jesus! what availeth wit?

Elizabeth's commanders saw the campaign in an entirely different perspective from the Queen. They were hampered at every turn by her cautious femininity. Norris's advance guard was backed up in December by the arrival of the main force led by the Earl of Leicester. Despite his great distinction in the tilt yard, and his considerable experience in managing large cavalcades of ladies and gentlemen, farthingales and baggage, horses and provender, Dudley had not seen active military service for thirty years. Nor was he fully conversant with the changes that had taken place in warfare since he had fought in Philip and Mary's armies at St Quentin – yet he was to be matched against Parma, the most efficient soldier in all Europe.

Elizabeth created appalling delays even before he set out. On 1 September he wrote to Walsingham from Kenilworth stressing that he was fully prepared to accept the command if only Elizabeth would make up her mind. He enclosed one of her letters, so that Walsingham could see what he was up against, lamenting that the Queen 'ever took occasion to withdraw any good from him on account of his marriage'. On the 21st he wrote again to the Secretary: 'the Queen was very desirous to stay his journey to Holland. She used pitiful words to him. She fears she shall not live, and would not have him from her.' He begged Walsingham to send word to his wife that he could not be in London before Thursday. On the 24th Elizabeth finally gave Leicester permission to go, but her instructions made it perfectly clear that he was not to accept any title which made it appear that she (or he) was seeking sovereignty. Like Norris he was to stick to defensive, not offensive, tactics. She procrastinated further, giving and countermanding orders, while he was trying to requisition men and armour. He finally landed at Flushing on 10 December, after changing an order of his own which caused half the fleet to put in at Brill. The Dutch welcomed him immediately as their saviour and protector.

Banquets and fireworks heralded the earl's arrival at Flushing. There were torchlight processions, lavish entertainments and triumphal arches in the streets, inscribed with congratulatory verses to Elizabeth and Leicester. Whatever his sovereign's command, the Dutch made it clear that he was not expected to keep a low profile. At Delft the citizens erected a backdrop to the feasting, a castle of crystal and pearl, sheltered by the figure of a protective maiden. By January he was urging the Council in England to let him accept the title 'Governor-General' in the Queen's name, explaining that to refuse would hurt morale and offend the Dutch. On 25 January 1586 he was formally invested at The Hague. Elizabeth's rage knew no bounds. She wrote to him on 10 February in her own hand and the anger still leaps from the page.

CB How contemptuously we conceive ourself to have been used by you, you shall by this bearer understand, whom we have expressly sent unto you to charge you withal. We could never have imagined (had we not seen it fall out in experience) that a man raised up by ourself and extraordinarily favoured by us above any other subject in this land would have in so contemptible a sort broken our commandment, in a cause that so greatly toucheth us in honour, whereof although you have showed yourself to make but little accompt in so most undutiful a sort, you may not think that we have so little care of the reparation thereof as we mind to pass so great a wrong in silence unredressed: and therefore our express pleasure and commandment is that all delays and excuses laid apart, you do presently upon the duty of your allegiance obey and fulfil whatsoever the bearer hereof shall direct you to do in our name whereof fail you not, as you will answer the contrary at your uttermost peril.

Her temper was not improved by a rumour that Lady Leicester intended to join her husband 'with such a train of ladies and gentlemen and such rich litters, as her Majesty hath none such'. On 6 March Ambrose Dudley wrote to his brother, 'her malice is great and unquenchable'. The Council tried to calm her, fearing her violent rage might offend the Dutch to the point of breaking the alliance. Sir Thomas Heneage tried to mediate by diplomatically softening the message he had been given for Leicester. Elizabeth learned of this and wrote to Heneage on 27 April. 'What phlegmatical reasons soever, had persuaded him were lost upon her.

CB Jesus! what availeth wit when it fails the owner at greatest need? Do that you are bidden and leave your considerations for your own affairs. For in some things you had clear commandment, which you did not, and in other none, and did. We Princes be wary enough of our bargains. Think you I will be bound by your speech to make no peace for mine own matters without their consent.

Once again she made it clear that she had had no wish to be drawn into the Dutch war, but only to act as a mediator. 'It is enough that I injure not their country nor themselves in making peace for them without their consent. I am assured of your dutiful thought but I am utterly at squares with this childish dealing.'

The Queen was so angry that she delayed the funds needed for paying the army. Eventually the Council succeeded in soothing her and a way was found to make the new title acceptable. Leicester was *her* Lieutenant-General, 'Governor' applied only when he was on Dutch soil. At the St George's Day celebrations in Utrecht an empty throne was placed at the head of the banqueting table to signify her authority, while Leicester sat on a stool at the other end of the table. The arrangement seemed to satisfy her. Elizabeth's violent reactions did not only stem from a dislike of sharing her own power; desperate fear that Philip and Parma would construe her actions as aggressive also prompted her outbursts and increased her caution. She had in fact forgiven Leicester by the summer of 1586. When he was away from Lettice, chivalrously dedicating his life to his royal mistress in the wars, the old trust and tenderness were restored. In July she wrote as though no rift had ever been between them, signing herself with her old intimate nickname for him, the symbol for two 'Eyes'.

ᗣ Rob,

I am afraid you will suppose by my wandering writings that a midsummer moon hath taken large possession of my brains this month, but you must needs take things as they come in my head, though order be left behind me. When I remember your request to have a discreet and honest man that may carry my mind and see how all goes there, I have chosen this bearer, whom you know and have made good trial of. I have fraught him full of my conceits and those country matters and imparted what way I mind to take and what is fit for you to use. I am sure you can credit him and so I will be short with these few notes. First that Count Maurice and Count Hollocke find themselves trusted of you, esteemed of me and to be carefully regarded if ever peace should happen, and of that assure them on my word that yet never deceived any. And for Norris and other captains that voluntarily without commandment have many years ventured their lives and won our nation honour and themselves fame let them not be discouraged by any means, neither by new come men nor by old trained soldiers elsewhere. If there be fault in using of soldiers or making of profit by them, let them hear of it without open shame and doubt not but I will chasten them therefor. It frets me not a little that the poor soldiers that hourly venture life should want their due, that well deserve rather reward. And look in whom the fault may duly be proved, let them smart therefore. And if the Treasurer be found untrue or negligent according to desert he shall be used; though you know my old wont, that love not to discharge from office without desert; God forbid. I pray you let this bearer know what may be learned herein; and for this treasure I have joined Sir Thomas Shirley to see all this money discharged in due sort where it needeth and behoveth. Now will I end that do imagine I talk still with you, and therefore loathly say farewell, $\overline{OO}$, though ever I pray God bless you from all harm and save you from all foes with my million and legion of thanks for all your pains and cares. As you know, ever the same,

E.R.

We Princes, I tell you, are set on stages

The Babington Plot sealed Mary Stuart's fate. In January 1585 she had been moved to Tutbury Castle in Staffordshire, and placed in the custody of Sir Amyas Paulet, who had been Elizabeth's ambassador in Paris. He proved a sterner gaoler than Lord

Shrewsbury, depriving Mary of her secret post for almost a year. It was restored, with Walsingham's connivance, at Christmas 1585, when the Queen of Scots was moved to Chartley, the manor where Lettice had entertained Elizabeth before her marriage to Leicester. It now belonged to her son, the nineteen-year-old Earl of Essex.

Walsingham had persuaded Gilbert Gifford, a young man in minor orders training for the Catholic priesthood and working as a courier for Mary, to act as a double agent. Her letters were carried to and fro in waterproof packets hidden in a beer keg. The brewer was at first ignorant of what was going on, but Paulet and Walsingham drew him into their network. Mary's letters from abroad arrived in the French ambassador's packet and were given to Gifford, who showed them to Walsingham before delivering them to Chartley. If they were in cipher, Walsingham's cryptographer, Thomas Phelippes, took copies, the originals being restored to Gifford and, with Paulet's knowledge, hidden in the beer barrel. The outgoing post worked the same way in reverse, and the brewer received double payment, from both Mary and Walsingham, although this did not prevent him from trying to raise the price of his beer.

A group of Catholics were planning to assassinate Elizabeth as part of the Enterprise. One of their number, Anthony Babington, a young Derbyshire gentleman, had been a page in Shrewsbury's household as a boy. When he came of age and into his own fortune, which was considerable, Babington frequented the French ambassador's circle. He wrote to Mary telling her that six gentlemen were to be involved in murdering Elizabeth, while others would ride to Chartley to rescue her. Walsingham intercepted the letter and added a forged postscript to Mary's reply, asking Babington to reveal the names of the conspirators. He delayed his answer, thus depriving Walsingham of the final and conclusive evidence he needed, but Mary was lured into a hunting expedition, during which her private papers were searched at Chartley. The conspirators were arrested, to the great joy of the citizens of London, who rang bells and lit bonfires to celebrate their sovereign's deliverance. Elizabeth wrote to Paulet without mincing her words.

'Let your wicked murderess know how with hearty sorrow her vile deserts compel these orders, and bid her from me, ask God forgiveness for her treacherous dealings towards the saviour of her life many a year, to the intolerable peril of my own, and yet not content with so many forgivenesses must fault again so horribly far passing woman's thought.'

The Council wanted Mary to be sent to the Tower, but she was taken to Fotheringhay Castle in Northamptonshire, where she was tried and found guilty. The charge was that she had connived at the murder of Elizabeth, but Mary wrote to the Duke of Guise that she was to die in the cause of religion. Elizabeth is supposed to have written a peremptory note before the trial, when Mary was protesting that she was a twice-anointed Queen, not subject to the ordinary laws of England:

'You have in various ways and manners attempted to take my life and to bring my kingdom to destruction by bloodshed. It is my will that you answer the nobles and peers of the kingdom, as if I were myself present.'

The original of this letter has never been found.

Parliament had been prorogued until November 1586, but the Council had it dissolved and called a new one, which could sit a month earlier to deal with the urgent situation. Elizabeth remained at Richmond, trying to dissociate herself from the proceedings as long as possible. under the Act for the Queen's Safety, to which she had given her assent eighteen months earlier, it was inevitable that she must now put Mary Stuart to death. Hatton and Sir Walter Mildmay detailed Mary's treacheries to an attentive House. Hatton called her 'the hope of all idolatery'; Mildmay described the purpose of the Babington Plot: 'to advance this Scottish lady to the present possession of this crown, and thereby to overthrow the Church of God, not only here but in all other countries, where the Gospel is professed, and so to restore Popery'.

On 12 November a deputation from the Lords and Commons went to the Queen at Richmond with the petition she dreaded. She spoke at length. First she thanked God for her own miraculous preservation. It had been 'rare and singular'. She could not 'sufficiently set forth His wonderful works and graces which to me have been so many, so diversely folded and embroidered one upon another, as in no sort am I able to express them'. She had reigned twenty-eight years, perceiving 'no diminution of good wills' in the hearts of her subjects. 'And now', she said, 'I find my life hath been full dangerously sought and death contrived by such as no desert procured it.'

Mary was her near kin; she wished she could have saved her; she wished they were 'but as two milkmaids with pails upon our arms'; but they were not private persons – they were Princes 'set on stages, in the sight and view of all the world'. If the plot had succeeded she would have been 'loth to die so bloody a death', she said, but God would undoubtedly have given her the grace to be prepared for such an event. As Lords and Commons wept over the picture she evoked, she turned to the matter in hand. She would have preferred to have proceeded 'by the ancient laws of this land', not by 'the last statute', which had not been made particularly to entrap Mary, but rather as an admonition.

'You lawyers', she said, turning to a favourite grudge, 'are so nice and precise in sifting and scanning every word and letter that many times you stand more upon form than matter, upon syllables than the sense of the law. For in this strictness and exact following of common form, she must have been inducted in Staffordshire, been arraigned at the bar, holden up her hand and then been tried by a jury; a proper course forsooth, to deal in that manner with one of her estate. I thought it better therefore for avoiding of these and more absurdities to commit the cause to the inquisition of a good number of the greatest and most noble personages of this Realm, of the judges and others of good account, whose sentence I must approve.

'But I must tell you one thing more: that in this late act of Parliament you have laid an hard hand on me, that I must give direction for her death, which cannot be but most grievous, an irksome burden to me. And lest you might mistake mine absence from this Parliament, yet hath it not been the doubt of any such danger or occasion that kept me from thence, but only the great grief to hear this cause spoken of, especially that such one of state and kin should need so open a declaration, and that this nation should be so spotted with blots of disloyalty.'

She thanked them for their loyalty, showed so spontaneously the previous year when the Association had been formed for safeguard of her person. She punned on the word bond, saying her own should be the stronger, but she refused to take immediate action. She said she would pray about the matter, beseeching God to illuminate her understanding, for she knew delay was dangerous, and she promised 'inviolably' to do whatever was right.

My surety cannot be established without a Princess's head

Elizabeth's remark that she and Mary were 'set on stages in the sight and view of all the world' was to prove prophetic. Mary Stuart's death could not have been more dramatic, or memorable. On Monday 14 November Hatton delivered a further message from the Queen to the Commons. She would forbear taking Mary's blood if any other means could be devised for the safety of her Majesty's own person and the realm. They were not met to make laws this session, but to discuss the great matter, and to advise their sovereign.

On 24 November, coincidentally the day on which Leicester returned from the Netherlands, the delegation of Lords and Commons went again to Richmond. Once more Elizabeth seems to have spoken extempore, later amending the lengthy draft of her remarks with her own hand, so that the text was fit to be published as an official defence of her actions.

CB Since now it is resolved [she said] that my surety cannot be established without a Princess's head, I have just cause to complain that I who have in my time pardoned so many rebels, winked at so many treasons, and either not produced them, or altogether slipped over them with silence, should now be forced to this proceeding against such a person. I have beside during my reign seen and heard many opprobrious books and pamphlets against me, my Realm and my State, accusing me to be a tyrant. I thank them for their alms. I believe therein their meaning was to tell me news: and news it is to me indeed. I would it were as strange to hear of their impiety. What will they now say that for the safety of her life a maiden Queen could be content to spill the blood even of her own kinswoman? I may therefore full well complain that any man should think me given to cruelty: whereof I am so guiltless and innocent as I should slander God, if I should say he gave me so vile a mind. Yea I protest I am so far from it that for mine own life I would not touch her. Neither hath my care been so much bent how to prolong mine, as how to preserve both; which I am right sorry is made so hard, yea so impossible.

I am not so void of judgement as not to see mine own peril; nor yet so ignorant as not to know it were in nature a foolish course to cherish a sword to cut mine own throat; nor so careless as not to weigh that my life daily is in hazard.

But since so many have both written and spoken against me, I pray you give me leave to say somewhat for myself, and before you return to your countries let you know for what a one you have passed so careful thoughts. And as I think myself infinitely beholding unto you all that seek to preserve my life by all the means you may so I protest that there liveth no Prince – nor ever shall be – more mindful to requite so good deserts.

She spoke eloquently, convincing her audience that their petition had won her fullest approval, but she arrived at no decision and asked them 'to accept my thankfulness, to excuse my doubtfulness and to take in good part my answer answerless'.

Leicester was now able to add his persuasions to those of Burghley and Walsingham. Mary had been declared guilty on 25 October. The death sentence was officially proclaimed on 4 December, after a great deal of drafting and re-drafting of the wording. In London the citizens rang the church bells and made bonfires, but still Elizabeth flinched from signing the death warrant. Burghley had made one out at the end of December, and it was given to William Davison, the under-secretary, for safekeeping. Ambassadors arrived from Henry III and James VI to plead for Mary's life. The King of Scotland's equivocal attitude towards his mother's execution was influenced by the fact that she had bequeathed her claim to the English throne to Philip II.

In January Walsingham scented another plot against Elizabeth. The French ambassador, de Mauvissière, was placed under house arrest since he confessed that he had known of Babington's plans, but not mentioned them to the English government. On 1 February Elizabeth signed the warrant, giving it to Davison with a bitter joke that he should show it to Walsingham, who was ill. 'The news thereof', she said, 'will go near to kill him'; and she bade Davison to get the warrant sealed. He went straight to Burghley, who called a Council, remembering her vacillations over the Duke of Norfolk's execution. They acted immediately, sending the necessary instructions to Northamptonshire.

Mary Stuart died courageously. She was executed on 8 February in the great hall at Fotheringhay. A real stage had been erected, a scaffold draped all in black. Mary mounted it with immense dignity in a gown of black velvet with a white coif over her auburn hair. When she was helped out of the gown she was seen to be dressed in a satin bodice and a velvet petticoat all in crimson, the colour of Christian martyrdom. The Dean of Peterborough besought her to change her religion as a sign of repentance, but she replied, 'Master Dean, trouble me not, I am resolved in the Roman Catholic Faith.' She laid her head on the block, repeating: '*In manus tuas, Domine, confide spiritum meum.*'

When the executioner lifted her severed head, not only did the auburn wig slip revealing the grey hair beneath, but the lips continued to move as though in prayer. The dean had the presence of mind to shout, 'so perish all the Queen's enemies', and the Earl of Kent echoed him, but Lord Shrewsbury wept and Mary's dog, which had hidden beneath her skirts, crept out and lay pathetically beside his mistress's corpse. Walsingham ordered the body to be placed in a leaden coffin to deter religious fanatics from seeking relics.

Elizabeth had betrayed her own ideals, and the psychological crisis was acute. She gave way to hysterical weeping and ordered Davison to be sent to the Tower. He was sentenced in the Star Chamber, being ordered to pay a fine of £10,000 and to remain in prison during the Queen's pleasure. The fine was eventually remitted and Davison received a pension for the rest of his life, but he was not released from the Tower until 1588. Elizabeth raged and wept alternately, saying Davison never should have let the warrant out of his keeping. To James VI she wrote:

'I would you knew the extreme dolour that overwhelms my mind for that miserable accident which (far contrary to my meaning) hath befallen.'

She sent a messenger to tell him what Davison had done.

'If I had meant it,' she wrote, 'I would never lay it on other's shoulders; no more will I damnify myself that thought it not.'

A book and a bull

Leicester had returned from the Netherlands to the sad task of burying his beloved nephew, Philip Sidney, who had been wounded at the siege of Zutphen. Sidney's wife, Walsingham's daughter Frances, came out to nurse him, but the wound became infected with gangrene and Sidney died. Dudley returned to the Low Countries in June 1587 with three thousand fresh troops and a fleet of warships under the command of Charles Howard, the Lord High Admiral. They were to go to the relief of Sluys, for Parma had been ordered by Philip to concentrate on taking the coastal towns in preparation for the attack on England. Leicester's plan was to send a fireship to burn the floating bridge which the duke had erected at the mouth of the Scheldt. The earl proposed to attack from the water, but Parma was ready for him. He swung back part of the bridge so that the hellburner passed through into the shallow water, harmlessly exhausting itself.* Parma then rebuilt the bridge and the Dutch navigators refused to enter the narrow channel. While they were arguing the tide turned and Leicester's plan could not be put into action. Sluys surrendered on 26 July.

Elizabeth did not wish to waste any more men or money. She wrote to Leicester: 'We have thought good considering the broken state of things to yield to the treaty. We think you should acquaint the States General with this our disposition.' She did not upbraid Leicester, but she felt keenly 'the great touch of honour we have received by the loss of Sluys through the malice or other foul error of the States.'

The Dutch blamed the English, believing Elizabeth had intended to treat with Philip all along. Leicester was finding it impossible to bring the States to the conference table. On 10 November Elizabeth recalled him.

Philip, meanwhile, continued to arm his great fleet. In April 1587 Drake, who was more successful with the hellburners than Leicester, had made his daring raid on Cadiz Harbour, sending the fireships to destroy Philip's fleet in the episode which became known as 'the singeing of the King of Spain's beard'. In retrospect it is difficult to see how Elizabeth believed she could negotiate for peace after this touch to Philip's honour, although she continued to treat with Parma, complaining that Philip's councillors were preventing her messengers from reaching the King himself. As late as 8 July 1588 she was to assure Parma that 'if any reasonable conditions of peace should be offered' she would accept them.

Philip had written to the duke in September 1587, telling him to prepare to invade England. He was to land at Margate and the Marquis of Santa Cruz would join him with the King's warships. Parma believed the plan would work, and he set about preparing flat-bottomed boats for transporting his troops to England even before Leicester's withdrawal. He hired sixteen ships in Hamburg, seized thirteen French and seventeen Flemish vessels and chartered 170 barges.

Elizabeth continued to pin her hopes on the peace negotiations. England was ill-prepared for war. Although Sir John Hawkyns had made improvements to the navy, the country had no standing army. Troops had to be called by musters, and although each shire was supposed to give a week's military training annually to bands of picked men, the system had been neglected. On 21 December 1587 Elizabeth made Howard Lieutenant-General and Commander of the Navy. Leicester divided his time between Wanstead and Kenilworth; he had no great wish to be at Court after the Sluys fiasco, and he had resigned his office as Master of the Horse to his stepson, the Earl of Essex. In January Dudley wrote to Elizabeth begging her to behold 'his wretched and depressed estate'. She was more concerned in trying to bring the Dutch war to a formal conclusion. It was February before Lord Burghley called the Council to calculate the cost of raising troops to repel an invading army.

---

* The hellburners were packed with gunpowder and long-fuse cannon; they were not manned, and exploded in a fusillade of destructive debris. They were used against Parma at Antwerp, later by Drake at Cadiz, and under the direction of the Italian expert Federico Giambelli against the Armada itself in Calais Roads.

In April 1588 Elizabeth sent Dr Valentine Dale, formerly her ambassador in Paris, to treat with Parma. Talks were proposed at Ostend and Ghent, but eventually they opened at Bourbourg, a tiny village outside Dunkirk. On 30 May, the first day the commissioners met to discuss peace, the Armada of 130 ships sailed from Lisbon under the command of the Duke of Medina Sidonia. By prolonging the Bourbourg negotiations the English retained a vantage point from which they could spy on Parma's preparations. Thousands of copies of a bull in which the Pope reiterated Elizabeth's excommunication and authorised Philip's Enterprise had been printed at Antwerp to be scattered among Elizabeth's Catholic subjects when the Spanish armies landed. Cardinal Allen had also published a pamphlet, *An Admonition to the Nobility and People of England*. It referred to Henry VIII as Elizabeth's 'supposed father' and called Anne Boleyn 'an infamous courtesan'.

Elizabeth was extremely distressed by the book and the bull. She insisted Dr Dale should tackle Parma personally on the subject. Dale wrote back to Walsingham complaining of the 'tickleness' of his commission, but he managed to have an audience with the duke at Bruges and wrote to Elizabeth on 8 July, describing in detail how he had conveyed her message. She was prepared to give up Flushing and Brill, which were still held by the English, but first she desired Parma to 'deal plainly', and tell her if he knew of:

ℰ a book printed at Antwerp and set forth by a fugitive of England, which calleth himself a Cardinal, touching the execution of the sentence of the Pope against the Queen my sovereign and mistress. There is also a bull set forth by this Pope Sixtus V, whereby the Pope doth pronounce a sentence to declare my said sovereign and mistress illegitimate and an usurper with other matter too odious for any prince or gentleman to name or hear.

The duke said he had not read Allen's book and knew nothing of the Pope's bull. He was only sorry for the '*mal entendu*' between Philip and Elizabeth. As a soldier he must do the commandment of his master.

It was known by June that the Armada had set sail. Howard and Drake had been anchored off Plymouth since May. On 23 June the Lord Admiral wrote to Elizabeth from aboard the *Ark Royal*:

'For the love of Jesus Christ, Madam, awake thoroughly and see the villanous treasons round about you, against your Majesty and your realm, and draw your forces round about you like a mighty Prince to defend you. Truly Madam if you do so there is no cause to fear. If you do not there will be danger.' On 17 July, only two days before the sighting of Medina Sidonia's ships off the Lizard, Elizabeth finally broke off the peace negotiations. She could believe that Parma had not read Allen's book, it 'being in English', but she could not believe, she wrote scornfully, 'that he has not heard of it'. Dr Dale was to say that:

'The King and the Duke will be much deceived if they hope that fear will cause her to accept any conditions not sufficient and honourable. With the protection of Almighty God and those means which he has given her, she awaits with confidence the outcome of such an assault, being comforted by the testimony of a good conscience for she has never coveted other princes' dominions.'

In the midst and heat of the battle

The ships were sighted on 19 July. It took three days for the news to reach London. Lord Burghley, who had been heard to wish openly that they would come before the money ran out, drew up a memorandum on 23 July for prayers to be said in all the churches. On the 22nd the Earl of Leicester, who had been in charge of the army in the south of England since April in his capacity as a Privy Councillor and Lord-Lieutenant of Hertfordshire, bustled up to Leicester House, checking the defences along the Thames. He fired off a reminder to Walsingham that he had no authority to muster men in Kent or Suffolk if the enemy should land in the wrong place, and was hastily made Lieutenant-General. Lord Hunsdon was in command of the troops around London.

All the better regiments wanted to guard the Queen, and by mid-July Leicester still had only 4,000 men in the main camp at Tilbury. Throughout the summer he had busied himself with men and munitions. On paper the Council thought they could assemble 50,000 foot soldiers and 10,000 horse. Leicester believed Parma would try to sail down the Thames, and he arranged a bridge of boats beside Tilbury fort to act as a blockade. His experience in the Netherlands had made him keenly aware of the importance of victualling. On 26 July he wrote to Walsingham of the great want of victuals. He had 'as gallant and willing men as ever were seen' but a detachment had arrived after a twenty-mile march with 'not a barrel of beer nor a loaf of bread' among them. He ordered a thousand men who were to be sent from London to stay where they were if they did not have provisions with them. 'Great dilatory wants are found upon all sudden hurly burlies,' he wrote.

The knowledge that Parma was a liar and no gentleman helped to galvanise Elizabeth. Having striven so long to maintain peace, she threw herself energetically into the field of war. She had been declaring for some weeks that if necessary she would ride to the confines of her realm at the head of an army. The Council was anxious that she should do no such thing. On 27 July, a little after he had heard of the taking of Don Pedro de Valdes' ship, Leicester wrote reassuringly:

CB My most dear and gracious Lady,

A most just God that beholdeth the innocency of your heart, and the cause you are assailed for is His and His church's, and He never failed any that faithfully do put their chief trust in His goodness. He hath to comfort you withal given you great and mighty means to defend yourself, which means I doubt not but your Majesty will timely and princely use.

Her army, he said, was gathered about her, ready for action at a few hours' notice; she should 'give the charge thereof to some special nobleman' and place her officers 'that every man may know what he shall do'.

CB Now for your person being the most dainty and sacred thing we have in this world to care for, a man must tremble when he thinks of it; specially finding your Majesty to have the princely courage to transport yourself to the utmost confines of your realm to meet your enemies and to defend your subjects. I cannot, most dear Queen, consent to that, for upon your well doing consists all the safety of your whole kingdom and therefore preserve that above all.

It was his idea that she should visit Tilbury to raise the troops' morale, and with the skill and experience he had derived from the years of managing her progresses he told her to go to her house at Havering, which was fourteen miles from the camp. She should spend 'two or three days to see both the camp and the forts.'

CB I trust you will be pleased with your poor lieutenant's cabin and within a mile there is a gentleman's house, where your Majesty may also be. You shall comfort not only these thousands, but many more shall hear of it. And thus far, but no farther can I consent to adventure your person.

She arrived on 8 August: it was the last great progress he would arrange for her. She travelled by river, a causeway having been built for her to ride from the landing place to the camp. Everything was perfectly stage-managed. Leicester had heard of the success of the main engagement, but it had crossed his mind that Burghley might try to dismantle the army prematurely. He wrote anxiously to Walsingham to point out that nobody yet knew what Parma would do. For Elizabeth's overnight stay at Tilbury he had requisitioned Mr Rich's little manor, 'a proper sweet cleanly house' about a mile from the camp. He knew the effect her appearance would have on the men's morale. 'Good sweet Queen,' he wrote on 5 August, 'alter not your purpose.'

Thomas Deloney wrote an eye-witness account, *The Queen's Visiting of the Camp at Tilsburie*; it was rushed up to London and entered in the Stationer's Register on 10 August before permission had even been given for the imprint.* When Elizabeth

---

* This brief summary of Elizabeth's speech (a single broadsheet of a ballad to be sung to the tune of 'Wilson's Wild') is the first printed reference. It circulated widely, a fact which greatly annoyed James Aske, the author of *Elizabetha Triumphans*, which was not published until November. Aske complained in his preface that the popularity of Deloney's ballad had ousted the importance of his own work. There is no evidence that Aske was

disembarked she passed briefly through the camp and, according to Deloney, the army fell on their knees. She bade them stand up and wept to behold them. After this show of emotion she dined with her general under canvas. The following day they found a breast-plate for her to wear, for there were those in the Council who thought it a rash plan for her to ride about the open camp site. They strapped the plate armour over her bodice and it shone magnificently between the lace of her ruff and the rich fabric of her gown. She rode 'on prancing steed attired like an angel bright', preceded by the Serjeant-Trumpeter, Garter King of Arms and the Serjeants-at-Arms. Then came Leicester and the Lord Marshal with Essex and Sir John Norris bringing up the rear. The cavalry horses stamped and there was either a march-past or clamorous applause, for Deloney reports, 'the earth and air did sound like thunder'. Her shoulders straight and her body stiff from riding more than a mile in a piece of plate armour, Elizabeth must have held herself proudly that day. Perhaps her mind slipped back to the times when she had seen Henry VIII inspecting a guard or attired for the tilt. It was not surprising that she felt herself 'in the midst and heat of the battle'.

There is no need to doubt the authenticity of the words she spoke. Soldiers at the back of the ranks could not hear the Queen clearly and that evening Leicester called Dr Leonel Sharp, one of the military chaplains, and told him to re-deliver Elizabeth's uplifting oration 'to all the army together to keep a Public Fast'. Sharp recalled that this was 'the next day after her departure'. He kept his copy of the speech, and some thirty years later he gave one to the Duke of Buckingham at the time of the Palatinate match. 'This I thought would delight your Grace and no man hath it but myself and such as I have given it to.' This suggests Sharp treasured the draft given him by Leicester, although it was not printed until 1654. Sharp was a distinguished elder statesman by the time he made his gift to Buckingham. He had been chaplain to Leicester, to Essex and to the discerning Prince Henry. 'I remember in '88 waiting upon the Earl of Leicester at Tilbury Camp,' he told Buckingham, describing how the Queen 'rode through all the Squadrons of her army as Armed Pallas'. 'She made an excellent Oration,' he said, 'her words were these.'

CB My loving people, we have been persuaded by some that are careful of our safety to take heed how we commit our self to armed multitudes for fear of treachery, but I assure you, I do not desire to live to distrust my faithful and loving people. Let Tyrants fear, I have always so behaved myself that under God I have placed my chiefest strength and safeguard in the loyal hearts and good will of my subjects. And therefore I am come amongst you as you see at this time not for

---

an eye-witness, as Felix Barker recently suggested he was. In mentioning the Dorset regiment that offered £1,000 to guard the Queen's person, Aske stated that he had the story from a reliable person who was in the camp, implying he was not. Deloney's summary captures the spirit of the text preserved by Sharp (see p. 285) and is closer to it than Aske's account. Significantly, Aske published his version on 23 November, the eve of the Thanksgiving Service at St Paul's.

my recreation and disport, but being resolved in the midst and heat of the battle to live or die amongst you all. To lay down for God and for my kingdom and for my people my honour and my blood even in the dust. I know I have the body of a weak and feeble woman but I have the heart and stomach of a King, and of a King of England too, and think foul scorn that Parma or Spain or any Prince of Europe should dare invade the borders of my Realm to which rather than any dishonour shall grow by me, I myself will take up arms, I myself will be your General, Judge, and Rewarder of every one of your virtues in the field. I know already for your forwardness you have deserved rewards and crowns and we do assure you in the word of a Prince, they shall be duly paid you.

In the meantime my Lieutenant-General shall be in my stead, than whom never Prince commanded a more Noble or worthy subject, not doubting but by your obedience to my General, by your Concord in the Camp and your valour in the field we shall shortly have a famous victory over those enemies of God, of my Kingdom and of my People.

CHAPTER XII

His last letter

On 9 August news reached the camp that Parma was ready to set out. Elizabeth thought it would be dishonourable to desert her troops in the field and was all for staying at Tilbury. Leicester demurred, gently sending her back to London, where Lord Hunsdon's army was assembled to defend her. Medina Sidonia had anchored in Calais Roads on 28 July, but Parma did not know he was there. The duke could not sail nearer to the Dutch coast because of the sandbanks and shallow waters in which the Spanish ships, with their deep keels, would have run aground. Justin of Nassau, William of Orange's son, was also patrolling the coastline with 130 highly manoeuvrable fly boats.

By the evening of 29 July the English had sent in their fireships, so that by the time Elizabeth delivered her famous words at Tilbury the decisive battle of Gravelines was over, the two Spanish dukes had missed their rendezvous, and the remnants of the mighty Armada were already being driven northwards by the winds. Leicester did not yet realise this, and messengers posted in all directions, often with conflicting reports. On 9 August Drake announced that the Spanish forces intended to land at Dungeness. Sir Thomas Scott wrote to ask whether he should march 700 musketeers there to repel them. Drake's despatch referring to the battle of Gravelines, 'the Duke of Parma is as a bear robbed of his whelps', was written from the *Revenge* on 10 August. Heneage, meanwhile, heard from the *Ark Royal* that the Admiral had put in to the North Foreland, having left off pursuit of the Spaniards for want of victuals. 'The Lord Admiral', he wrote to Walsingham, 'has been obliged to eat beans.'

On 16 August Lord Henry Seymour, whose squadron was still guarding the Narrow Seas, had news that Parma had reinforced the flat-bottomed boats to bring over 40,000 men, but it was thought they would wait until the following spring. The army was to be disbanded as quickly as possible, mainly because there was no money to pay them. 'To spend in time convenient is wisdom,' ran Burghley's memorandum, 'to continue charges without needful cause bringeth repentance.' By 25 August the Council were already asking Leicester if the captains had taken money for the release of the trained bands. An outbreak of dysentery ravaged the navy. Howard, Hawkyns and Drake paid for wine and arrowroot from their own pockets for the sick crews rather than waste time in waiting for money to arrive from London. The Admiral had heard that 'the beer brewed at Sandwich was sour; the men think this was the greatest cause of infection'. The epidemic killed thousands. Howard

The Armada Portrait,
showing Elizabeth wearing
the pearls given to her by
Leicester (p. 212)

wrote to Burghley of the pitiful sight at Margate where the men were dying in the streets.

When the victory was assured, Elizabeth was ready to make Leicester Lieutenant-General of England and Ireland. He had not fired a shot, but he rode triumphantly into London to a hero's welcome, while the Earl of Essex thrilled the citizens with a military review, which Elizabeth and Leicester watched from the palace windows. Mendoza's London agent reported that Leicester dined nightly with the Queen, but the idyll was not to last; Robert was exhausted and ill. By the end of the month he had extricated himself from the festivities to join Lettice at Wanstead. He then set out for Buxton to take the spa waters. He had with him his wife and some special medicine bestowed by the ever-practical Queen. He spent the night at Rycote, where he and Elizabeth had often been guests of Lord and Lady Norris. He scribbled a note to thank her for the medicine and to ask 'how my gracious lady doth', signing it 'from your old lodging at Rycote ready to take my journey'. On 4 September he died. Elizabeth shut herself in her chamber until Burghley ordered the door to be broken down. Fifteen years later, when Elizabeth herself died, they found the note from Rycote in a cabinet she kept by her bed. Across the scrap of folded parchment she had written 'His last letter'.

Robert's will had been drawn up the previous year at Middleburg, a week after the surrender of Sluys. It was written in his own hand in the absence of lawyers, for the Dutch campaign had left him 'very little leisure since my arrival to get any time for my private business'. He wrote sincerely and reflectively, a soldier in the field, wondering how best to bestow his remains amidst the conflicts that life, and love, and the desire to have legitimate issue had brought upon him. He began with 'a true Testimony of Faith':

'In this faith I now live and in this faith I trust to change this life with continual prayer to the throne of grace to grant me during this pilgrimage of mine a true humble and penitent heart for the recognition of all mine offences and the willing amendment of the same, and to fly instantly to the sure anchorhold my Lord and Saviour, Jesus Christ.'

He appointed Lettice as his executrix, but it clearly crossed his mind that he might die in battle, and that Elizabeth might want to give him a State funeral, so he left open the question of where he should be buried:

'I have always wished, as my dear wife doth know and some of my friends, that it might be at Warwick, where sundry of my ancestors do lie, either so or else where the Queen's Majesty shall command, for as it was when it had life a most faithful, true, loving servant unto her, so living and so dead let the body be at her gracious determination, if it shall so please her.'

He left to Elizabeth, 'my most dear and gracious Sovereign whose creature under God I have been, the jewel with three great emeralds with a fair large table diamond in the middle without a foil and set about with many diamonds without foil and a rope of fair white pearl to the number of six hundred'. She wore the pearls in the

Armada portrait by George Gower, and in many subsequent pictures. They have been mentioned by most of her biographers, but perhaps not always in context. The clause describing them in Robert's will explains that it 'was once purposed' to give her the jewel at Wanstead, where he obviously hoped that Lettice might act as hostess if only the two women could be reconciled. He left Kenilworth to Ambrose during his lifetime and thereafter to Robert Dudley, his base-born son by Lady Sheffield. He had already settled Lettice's jointure, perhaps anticipating the rapacity with which Elizabeth might set upon his widow for the repayment of his debts, but he really did not want the two women to scrap over his body, and Elizabeth had the grace to let it lie at Warwick beside the 'Noble Imp', who had died in 1584.

Instruments to daunt our foes

The Queen roused herself from her grief for the official Thanksgiving Service which was held on 24 November at St Paul's. She travelled in a chariot drawn by two white horses, its canopy a gilded crown. It was the opinion of all true Englishmen that God had purposely sent the winds to scatter Philip's fleet, and the theme of Elizabeth as a figure served by the elements themselves continued in patriotic literature through the rest of her reign. She gave Sir Thomas Heneage an enamelled pendant showing Noah's Ark resting safely on an azure sea. Several golden medallions were struck bearing Elizabeth's head on the obverse, with pictures of the Spanish ships struck by lightning on the reverse. '*Non ipsa pericula tangunt*' reads the legend on the most famous, inscribed across a picture of England upon which a symbolic bay tree flourishes, untouched by wind or storm. '*Sevas tranquilla per undas*', proclaimed another, though Maurice of Nassau perhaps had the best of the commemorative Latin with '*Flavit et dissipati sunt*' encircling the crippled Spanish fleet.

At St Paul's Elizabeth prayed accordingly:

CƐ Most omnipotent Creator, Redeemer and Conserver: When it seemed a most fit time to thy worthy Providence to bestow the workmanship of this world's globe with thy rare judgement, thou didst divide into four singular parts, the form of all this Mold which after time hath termed Elements; all they serving to continue in this orderly Government of all the Masses, which all when of thy most singular bounty and never yerst seen care, thou hast this year made serve for instruments to daunt our foes, and to confound their malice. I with most humbly bowed heart and bended knees do tender my humblest acknowledgements and lowest thanks. And not least for that the weakest Sex hath been so fortified by the strongest help, that neither my people need find lack by my weakness nor foreigners triumph at my ruin. Such hath been thy unwonted grace in my days, as though Satan hath never made Holy day in practising for my life and state, yet thy mighty hand hath overspread both with the shade of thy wings, so that neither hath been overthrown nor received shame, but abide with blessing to thy most glory and their greatest ignominy. For which Lord of thy mere goodness grant us grace to be hourly thankful and ever mindful. And if it may please thee to grant my request give us thy countenance and favour in my days of like goodness that my years never see change of such grace to me and especially to this Kingdom, which Lord grant (for thy Son's sake) may flourish many ages after my end.

AMEN

The first reports to reach Philip had given false news of a great Spanish victory, but by the end of August the King had learned that his fleet had been blown completely off course. No one expected that the battered remnants of the great Armada would sail round Scotland and then the west of Ireland, to be wrecked mercilessly on the rocky coastline of Donegal. Throughout September Philip waited anxiously for news until Medina Sidonia, his flagship letting in water, led eight ruined galleons into Santander. He was followed by Diego Flores de Valdes with twenty-two battle-scarred ships and Don Miguel de Oquendo who reached Biscay with five more. The Duke dictated the first circumstantial account to the King. Stories of Philip's stoic acceptance of the disaster are mostly apocryphal. A letter has recently come to light in which he poured out his anguish to his chaplain Mateo Vasquez.

'Very soon we shall find ourselves in such a state that we shall wish we had never been born. If God does not send us a miracle (which is what I hope from Him) I hope to die and go to Him before all this happens – which is what I pray for, so as not to see so much ill fortune and disgrace.'

On New Year's Day 1589 Hatton gave Elizabeth a necklace of golden scallop shells, set with rubies, diamonds and pearls. She was the Queen of the Seas, and the most respected sovereign in all Europe.

Departing in such sort without our privity

The Treasury was exhausted, the danger not over. In one version of the Armada portrait Elizabeth stands with her finger delicately pointing to Spanish America on a globe placed at her right hand. Behind her, also on the right, is the Crown of England, backed by an inset of the English fleet in full sail. On the left side of the Queen the ships of the wrecked Armada lurch through the stormy seas.

Privateering became big business in the 1590s; syndicates were formed in the city, sometimes with the Queen as an investor. As early as September 1588 Drake and

Sir John Norris approached her with a plan to launch an attack on Lisbon, which was to be followed up by a plundering expedition in the Azores. A large-scale military and naval offensive on the Portuguese capital, with the object of placing Dom Antonio on the throne, would, it was argued, force Philip to seek peace on terms favourable to Elizabeth. The ambitious project was launched as a joint-stock enterprise. The Queen was to furnish £20,000, six ships, two pinnaces, a siege train, arms and armour and three months' victuals. £10,000 was raised in the City and Drake contributed a further £5,000. The Dutch agreed to join the enterprise, for Parma's attention had been diverted by the troubles in France, where the Catholic League was foundering after the murder of the Duke of Guise. Parliament met in February. Sir Christopher Hatton, Lord Chancellor since 1587, said in his opening remarks that they had been granted 'a most notable victory', but the enemy was still to be feared:

'We have lopped off some of his boughs, but they will sooner grow again than we think of.'

By the end of the session both Lords and Commons were advising the Queen to declare open war on Spain. Both Houses, the Speaker declared, offered their 'bodies, their lives, lands and goods', if Elizabeth wished to attack. The idea was expensive, and the Queen preferred Drake's plan of hit-and-run.

He set sail in March 1589, managing to divert sixty Dutch fly-boats, which were headed for La Rochelle where they intended to load salt. He had eighty-five ships and 3,000 sailors under his command, and Norris had collected 11,000 soldiers. The Dutchmen joined them, anticipating a richer cargo than salt. The young Earl of Essex, eager for glory, up to his neck in debt, and resentful at being left behind among the women when many of his contemporaries had gone to join Drake's lucrative voyage, also rode off to Plymouth, embarking on Sir Roger Williams's ship, the *Swiftsure*. It put to sea ahead of the rest of the fleet. Essex had succeeded his stepfather as Master of the Horse at the end of 1587. Leicester had trained him for the post, and when the young man ran away to sea he had already been an officer of the Court for two years, responsible for the movements of the royal household. It was natural that after his stepfather's death he should become the favourite. He could not take Dudley's place, but he often kept the Queen company, playing cards with her far into the night. As a boy he had been educated in Lord Burghley's household, where he was brought up with Burghley's son Robert Cecil, but it was at his stepfather's side that Essex learned to be a soldier and a courtier. He had fought in Leicester's campaigns at Zutphen and at Sluys. His father, Walter Devereux, a soldier of distinction, had served Elizabeth faithfully in Ireland. She did not expect the young man to desert his post at Court and sent his grandfather, Sir Francis Knollys, down to Plymouth to fetch him back with a peremptory note telling him what she thought of him for leaving without her permission.

Robert Devereux, Earl of Essex, by Marcus Gheeraerts (Trustees of the Bedford Estates, Woburn Abbey)

CƷ Essex,

Your sudden and undutiful departure from our presence and your place of attendance you may easily conceive how offensive it is, and ought to be, unto us. Our great favours, bestowed on you without deserts, hath drawn you thus to neglect and forget your duty; for other constructions we cannot make of those your strange actions. Not meaning therefore to tolerate this your disordered part, we give directions to some of our Privy Council to let you know our express pleasure for your immediate repair hither; which you have not performed, as your duty doth bind you, increasing greatly thereby your former offence and undutiful behaviour, in departing in such sort without our privity, having so special office of attendance and charge near our person. We do therefore charge and command you forthwith, upon receipt of these our letters, all excuses and delays set apart, to make your present and immediate repair unto us to understand our further pleasure. Whereof see you fail not, as you will be loth to incur our indignation, and will answer for the contrary at your uttermost peril.

When she learned that the *Swiftsure* had already sailed, Elizabeth wrote to Norris and Drake calling for Sir Roger Williams's head.

'Although we doubt not but of yourselves you have so thoroughly weighed the heinousness of the offence lately committed by Sir Roger Williams, that you have both discharged him from the place and charge which was appointed him in that army and committed the same to some other meet person, yet you should also know from ourself by these our special letters our just wrath and indignation against him and lay before you his intolerable contempt against ourself, and the authority you have from us in that he forsook the army and conveyed away also one of our principal ships from the rest of the fleet.'

'His offence', she wrote angrily 'is in so high degree that the same deserveth by all laws to be punished by death, which if you have not already done then we will and command you that you sequester him from all charge and service. And if Essex be now come into the company of the fleet, we straitly charge you that all dilatory excuse set apart, you do forthwith cause him to be sent back hither in a safe manner; which if you do not you shall look to answer for the same to your smart, for these be no childish actions nor matters wherein you are to deal cunning of devises, to seek evasions as the causes of lawyers is; neither will we be so satisfied at your hands. Therefore consider well of your doings herein.'

I never feared and what fear was my heart never knew

In the will written at Middleburg after his failure to recapture Sluys, Leicester made a short prayer that God would let Elizabeth live to be 'the oldest Prince, that ever He gave over England', also the godliest, the most virtuous and 'the worthiest in his sight'. She outlived her councillors. Sir Walter Mildmay died in 1589, Ambrose Dudley and Sir Francis Walsingham in 1590. Burghley and Knollys remained, the one revered, the other doddering. Hatton died in 1591, the year when Burghley, seventy and tortured by gout, begged to retire. Elizabeth teased him for wanting to become a hermit; she had a mock charter drawn up for presentation to him during a visit to Theobalds, solemnly enjoining him in best legal English to the enjoyment of his own house.

Robert Cecil had been trained to succeed his father in office in the same way that Essex had been brought up to follow Leicester as Master of the Horse. Although Cecil became a councillor, he was not given the Secretary's post until 1596. At Court the 'New Men' formed rival factions, Essex heading the war party. The Portugal voyage of 1589 had not been a success, despite Sir John Norris's gallant attack on Corunna. The English stormed the town, but they could not garrison it. They failed to destroy the Spanish fleet, which had been the main object of the expedition. Thousands of soldiers and sailors died of dysentery, six ships were lost and the Queen got no return for her £20,000 investment. Essex was allowed, however, to go to France in 1591 in command of a substantial army to aid Henry IV at the siege of Rouen.

In Europe the cast of 'Princes set upon a stage' was also changing. Catherine de' Medici died in January 1589. In a bid to protect himself against the outrages of the Paris mob, fomented by extremists in the Catholic League, Henry III had the Duke of Guise murdered. He had been forced to flee his own capital during the summer of 1588, and in April 1589 he joined Henry of Navarre in an attack on Paris. The King was assassinated, leaving Navarre the uncrowned King of France. The Protestant Prince refused three times to change his religion, which won him Elizabeth's respect. He turned to her for financial aid, and when she sent Essex to Normandy in 1591, she wrote to Henry asking him to keep an eye on the earl, fearing 'the rashness of his youth' made him sometimes 'too precipitate'. She praised the King's valour, begging Henry to remember that Essex would need 'the bridle rather than the spur', adding sternly that Henry was to look after her soldiers, treating them 'not as those who serve as mercenaries, but freely from good affection, also that you will not carry them into too great danger'.

When Essex arrived in France the King was at Compiègne. Leaving the main body of his army at Dieppe, the earl rode with a small escort of gentlemen across enemy territory. He entered Compiègne dressed in orange velvet with gold lace, preceded by six pages in the same colours and by a procession of trumpeters. Henry and his battle-scarred troops succumbed to the young man's charm, spending several days in feats of arms and field sports. The King and his nobles challenged the earl and his gentlemen at the high jump, and the story goes that 'Essex did overleap them all'. After this show of prowess, he had to call on his infantry to get him safely back to base. Henry, meanwhile, decided to postpone the siege of Rouen to attend the marriage of the Catholic Duchess of Bouillon and the Huguenot general, the Viscount of Turenne. This he deemed a political necessity, which would win him the allegiance of many of his Catholic subjects.

Elizabeth was furious that her troops had been paid to stand by while the King of France went to a wedding. Essex led an assault on a fort near Rouen, during which his younger brother, Walter Devereux, was killed. Elizabeth reprimanded Essex for his rash conduct; she hated waste of life. Essex sulked and fumed, finding it intolerable that she should reproach him in a time of personal grief. Elizabeth heard that Parma was marching to Rouen at the head of a Spanish army to relieve the besieged Catholics. Henry prepared to attack Parma in a pitched battle, but the duke built another bridge of boats, and swiftly marched his army back across the Seine towards Brussels. Elizabeth by now considered herself something of an expert on military tactics. She was following the progress of different armies on maps of Europe, and appeared to think that the whole campaign could be directed from her Presence Chamber. She complained of Henry's 'preposterous actions', accused him of mismanagement, criticised him for dividing his army and gathered in daily reports of the King of Spain's activities in Brittany. In the end she recalled Essex, leaving a small force in France under Sir Roger Williams.

When Parliament met in 1593 another Armada was expected. Elizabeth spoke confidently, referring to her father, and echoing the words and sentiments of Leicester's letter written to her from Gravesend in 1588.

'Many wiser princes than myself you have had, but one only excepted, whom in the duty of a child I must regard, and to whom I must acknowledge myself far shallow[er], I may truly say none whose love and care can be greater, or whose desire can be more to fathom deeper for prevention of danger to come, or resisting of dangers if attempted towards you shall ever be found to exceed myself.

'You have heard in the beginning of this Parliament, some doubt of danger, more than I would have you to fear. For mine own part I protest I never feared and what fear was my heart never knew. For I knew that my cause was ever just and it standeth upon a sure foundation – that I should not fail, God assisting the quarrel of the righteous, and such as are but to defend.'

She knew, she said, that Philip could not prevail, when she had 'so mighty a protector' on her side. She asked the members when they returned to their counties not 'to strike fear into the minds' of her people. She had heard that at the time of the Armada some 'dwelling in a maritime shire fled for fear farther into the middle of the land'. She had paid a recent visit to the coastal towns, where she made a point of inspecting ships as her father had done, and now she spoke personally to those members of the 1593 Parliament who were Lords-Lieutenant in their own counties:

'You that in the shires have the leading of the most choice and serviceable men under your bands,' she said, 'let me charge you that you see them sufficiently exercised and trained, and that all decays of armour be presently repaired and made sufficient.' She had evidently not forgotten that at the time of the Armada, when Leicester had sent from Tilbury for plate armour, some had arrived from the store in the Tower in such a condition that the men refused to wear it.

Incredibly, the new Armada was prevented from sailing by storms, confirming Elizabeth's calm certainty that God was on her side. Parma had died the previous year, and the only event which perturbed Elizabeth was Henry IV's sudden conversion to Catholicism in July 1593. Unable by virtue of his former religion to gain control of his own capital, he quipped that 'Paris is well worth a Mass', and earned Elizabeth's unqualified disapproval. Her soul groaned at the news, she wrote, but she wrote in French and the violent agitation with which she began her letter does not translate effectively.

'*Ah! quels douleurs, oh! quels regrets, oh! quels gémissements*,' she exclaimed, reminding us again of what an actress she was, throwing herself completely into any role, and when she used a foreign language, mimicking exactly the inflections and gestures appropriate to the sentiments she wished to convey.

CB My God! is it possible [she asked Henry] that worldly considerations can so erase the fear of God which threatens us? Can we in reason expect any good result from an act so impious? He who has supported and preserved you through the years, can you imagine that he will forsake you in time of greatest need? Ah! It is dangerous to do evil, even for a good end. I hope that you will return to your senses. In the meantime I shall not cease to put you foremost in my prayers, that the hands of Esau do not snatch away the blessing of Jacob. And as for promising me all amity and faithfulness, I have merited it dearly; I have not tried to change my allegiance to my father. For I prefer the natural to the adopted parent, as God well knows. May He guide you back to the right way. Your most assured sister, if it is after the old manner, for with the new, I have nothing to do.

E.R.

Despite his defection, Elizabeth remained in firm alliance with Henry IV.

Neither in vain do we put our trust in God

Still in her mood of calm assurance Elizabeth settled down in the autumn of 1593 to translate Boethius' *De Consolatione Philosophiae* into English. She took great pride in the speed with which she accomplished this, and bothered Mr Bowyer, the Keeper of the Records in the Library at Windsor Castle, to work out how long it had taken her. With exceptions for Sundays and time off for riding in the park, he made it seventeen days.* Previous translators had included King Alfred, Chaucer and Caxton. Elizabeth worked partly in verse and partly in prose. She started to write out the translation in her own hand, but quickly tired, and dictated the rest to a secretary, Thomas Windebank, the Clerk of the Signet. Derided by some critics as her least impressive 'Englishing', it has not been generally realised that she was experimenting with the 'antique style' favoured at the time for translating classical authors. Elizabeth's spelling is a law unto itself. It is not uncommon to find three different renderings of the same word in one manuscript, but in the draft of Boethius, she has occasionally crossed out Windebank's version of a word, deliberately replacing it with a more archaic form.

Although it is a short work, *The Consolation of Philosophy* suited Elizabeth's frame of mind that autumn, dealing as it does with questions of great magnitude, suitable to be understood by Princes. She began the work one month after her sixtieth birthday, and was clearly fascinated by the fifth and last book in which the philosopher examines the concepts of luck and chance, free will, divine prescience, providence and eternity. Passages of Boethius are echoed in her last two parliamentary speeches, and, in berating Essex, she occasionally parodies the philosopher's method of reasoning.

When she came to a passage that interested her, Elizabeth forgot about the antique style and went straight for the sense:

'Wherefore if thou wouldest weigh his foreknowledge by which he all understandeth, thou wouldest judge that he hath not a foreknowledge of things to come alone, but rightlier a science of never worn continuance. Wherefore we must not call it foresight but providence which being set over all things, yea in the meanest, views them all as out of the very top and spring of all.'

The argument for divine providence runs counter to the argument in favour of divine prescience. It is clear why the topic absorbed Elizabeth, for if there was prescience, or predestination, this would invalidate human prayer.

'There lasteth also a viewer of us all the foreknowing God whose ever present

---

* Three computations were made; all concur that Elizabeth began work on 10 October 1593 and worked for a period of about twenty-five or twenty-seven days, but they differ in the deductions made for Sundays, holidays and riding in the park. One computation assures Elizabeth that she completed the whole work in twelve hours! Miss Pemberton has proved that this would have been impossible.

eternity of sight agreeth with the following property of our actions and so dispenseth to good reward, to ill their deserts. Neither in vain do we put our trust in God, neither of small price our prayers, which being truly made can never fall in vain. Avoid vice therefore, prize virtue, your minds lift up to true hopes and settle your humble prayers in highest place.'

By her own constant prayers she felt she had kept her people safe, and the failure of the Armada of 1593 even to set sail against the winds and storms confirmed her most cherished theory of State.

You have made me famous, dreadful and renowned

The bad weather which kept the Spaniards in their ports in 1593 continued into the following year. It ruined the English harvests, heralding a period of food shortage and severe inflation. 1596 was a critical year for England and the Council brought in emergency measures to deal with the needs of the poor. The Sheriffs and Justices of the Peace were required to enforce compulsory sale of grain at reasonable prices. Fast days were declared on Wednesdays and Fridays when, instead of the customary fish being eaten, the rich were asked to go supperless, giving the price of their meal to the poor in each parish. At the end of the year the Queen lifted the import duties on wheat and rye, believing the merchants would buy in foreign grain in the port towns. Nevertheless, in some counties there were bread riots.

Amidst this background of domestic turbulence Elizabeth allowed Essex to prepare his spectacular assault on Cadiz. The previous summer four Spanish ships had sailed over from the coast of Brittany, burned Penzance, and invaded the tiny village of Mousehole. They sailed away but created sufficient alarm from the Council to order the strengthening of the coastal defences. Drake and Hawkyns had again gone privateering in the Spanish Main, and in the spring of 1596 Elizabeth still hoped they would return with plunder to fill her treasury. It was not until May that Sir Thomas Baskerville returned to tell the tale of Nombre de Dios and of the death of her two best commanders. By March she was ready to listen to Essex's persuasions that the time had at last come for her to take offensive rather than defensive action. Essex's scheme was to take Cadiz and garrison it, establishing a foothold for the English in Spain itself. A mighty revenge for Mousehole! He did not at first discuss the whole operation with the Queen, avowing rather his intention to intercept the returning Spanish treasure fleet, a plan which he knew she would approve.

While preparations were still in their initial stages, a Spanish fleet from the Netherlands attacked Calais. The Queen immediately gave orders for Essex to go with 6,000 men to help Henry IV in 'succouring the Citadel of Calais now besieged'. The following day, 14 April, the Spanish cannon fire could be heard across the

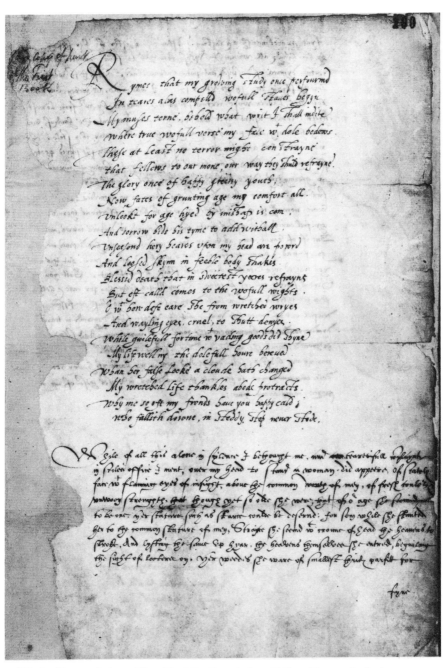

Elizabeth's translation of Boethius' *De Consolatione Philosophiae*, made during Autumn 1593

Channel in London. Elizabeth was inspecting ships. At the sound of the battle she wrote to Essex from aboard the *Due Repulse*. It is very clear from the wording of her letter that she had never forgotten Câteau Cambrésis, and she would have bargained with Henry IV to get Calais back if there had been any way of wresting it from him.

'As distant as I am from your abode,' she wrote to Essex, 'yet my ears serve me too well to hear that terrible battery that methinks sounds for relief at my hands; wherefore rather than for lack of timely aid it should be wholly lost, go you on in God's Blessed Name, as far as that place where you may soonest relieve it, with as much caution as so great a trust requires. But I charge you, without the mere loss of it, do in no wise peril so fair an army for another Prince's town. God cover you under his safest wings, and let all peril go without your compass. Believe Cecil in the rest. From the *Due Repulse*, where this day I have been.'

On 15 April Calais surrendered, and Essex and Howard resumed preparations to raid Cadiz. Henry IV proposed a league between England and France that was to be 'offensive as well as defensive', and Elizabeth composed a prayer for the success of her army and navy. Essex and Howard set out on 3 June, anchoring outside Cadiz harbour on the 20th. Under their joint command they had 150 English ships. Even the Spaniards said it was 'the most beautiful fleet that ever was seen'. They had orders to attack the town first, but Walter Raleigh persuaded the admiral to change plans, letting the English ships enter the harbour to attack the four galleons which guarded the narrow entrance. Essex threw his hat into the sea for joy when he heard the new order, while Raleigh called out from the *Warspite* '*Intrabimus*'. The English ships fired on the galleons and after a battle of several hours the commanders of the *San Felipe* and the *San Tomaso* set fire to their ships rather than face defeat.

'The Spanish navy being thus defeated,' ran the official despatch, 'the generals prepared the same day to land their men and attempt the town.' The local forces included 800 horsemen, but the English beat them back. The town gates were shut, and some of the retreating cavalry tried to leap over a low wall into a suburb. 'The Earl of Essex, perceiving an entrance that way, ran up to the top of the wall and made his men leap after them, and would have been ready to leap after, had not the Marshal by that time beaten open the ports and with this sudden fury the town was taken without the loss of a man of name, save Sir John Wingfield, who was slain in the market place.'

Before the English soldiers sacked the town, Essex allowed the women and children to take as much as they could carry and to go off to a place of safety. This legendary piece of gallantry won him a reputation as the most Christian soldier in all Europe; in contrast, during the sacking of the town, the Duke of Medina Sidonia sent orders for the ships from the Indies, which were berthed nearer to the river, to be fired. They were reputed to be worth eight million crowns. The English fleet then set sail for home, missing the remainder of the Indies fleet by forty-eight hours. Reports of the victory reached Elizabeth before the news that Medina Sidonia had burned the treasure ships. Her first reaction was to draft her congratulations to both her commanders.

'If my pen had as many tongues as the flock of owners had feathers, they shall scarce express the Lauds that my soul yieldeth to the Highest for this great Victory which his graceful hand hath given us. You have made me famous, dreadful and renowned not more for your Victory than for your Courage, nor more for either than for such plentiful life, nor of mercy which may well match the better of the two.'

As the details of the expedition reached Elizabeth, and the financial implications became clear, her letters grew less gracious.

The law of nature and of nations

Elizabeth praised and blamed alternately. Abroad, her reputation had never been higher. In Venice people were clamouring for her picture; she was called 'The Great Queen of England', 'The Queen of the Seas'. At home she had no money to pay the army and navy. Cadiz had been a prestigious but unprofitable victory, and the Lord Admiral was demanding back pay for the fleet, even though the soldiers and sailors had pilfered much of what was due to the Crown. Philip had fared rather worse. The burning of the treasure ships caused him to go bankrupt yet again. It is said he seized a candelabrum and vowed he would pawn it rather than not be revenged. The Admiral of Castile, Don Martin de Padilla, was ordered to prepare another Armada forthwith.

Elizabeth gave Essex command of a small fleet which set out to attack the Spanish ships in port. Afterwards they were to set sail for the Azores in the hope of capturing the Spanish treasure fleet. Storms delayed their departure and by the end of July 1597 Essex had to put back to Plymouth, where he waited for the weather to change.

The Court was at Greenwich when an ambassador from the King of Poland arrived. He was the son of the Duke of Finland, who had wooed Elizabeth almost forty years earlier as the proxy of Erik of Sweden. Robert Cecil, now firmly established in the Secretary's post which Elizabeth had granted him while Essex was at Cadiz, wrote to the earl aboard ship, describing the ambassador as 'a gentleman of excellent fashion, wit, discourse, language and person'. Elizabeth was struck by his appearance and evident intelligence. She decided to receive him publicly in the Presence Chamber. He wore a long robe of black velvet covered with jewels, and came to kiss Elizabeth's hand as she stood under her canopy of estate. Then he backed away to begin his speech. As the Latin phrases resounded through the Presence Chamber, astonishment covered the faces of the assembled courtiers. The quarrel between the Queen of England and the King of Spain was affecting the King of

Poland's merchants, disrupting his trade routes and violating the law of nature and of nations. Elizabeth had been expecting a complimentary address. She paused for a few seconds then, turning on the young man, she began her reply in flawless extempore Latin:

> ଔ *O quam decepta fui* [rasped the indignant voice] *expectavi legationem mihi vero querelam adduxisti.* How I have been deceived! I was expecting a diplomatic mission, but you have brought me a quarrel! By virtue of your testimonials I have received you as an ambassador, but I have found you instead a challenger. Never in my life have I heard such audacity. I marvel, indeed I marvel at so great and such unprecedented impertinence in public. Nor can I believe that had your King been here he would have spoken in such words. But if he had, indeed, happened, which I can scarcely credit, to entrust some such matter to your hands, even though the King is young and a King not by birth but by election – and newly elected at that – he would show himself as having a very imperfect understanding of the manner in which such matters are handled between Princes, a manner observed towards us by his betters and which he will perhaps observe in future. As for yourself, you give me the impression of having studied many books, but not yet of having graduated to the books of Princes, rather remaining ignorant of the dealings between Kings. As to the law of nature and of nations of which you make so much mention, know that the law of nature and of nations is thus: when war is declared between Kings, either may cut the other's lines of supply, no matter where they run from and neither may they make it a precondition of their losses that these be made good. This, I say, is the law of nature and of nations. And as for your alliance with the House of Austria by which you set so much store, let it not escape your memory that there was one of that house, who attempted to wrest the kingdom of Poland from your King. For the other matters which are too numerous to be dealt with here and now, you shall wait until you hear what is considered by certain of my counsellors appointed to consider them. Meanwhile farewell and hold your peace.

'It was one of the best answers in extempore Latin that ever I heard,' wrote Cecil to the absent Essex. Tradition has it that Elizabeth, conscious of her success, turned her back on the unfortunate young diplomat, remarking loudly to her courtiers, 'My lords, I have been forced this day to scour up my rusty old Latin.'

You have learned upon our expenses

Shortly after Leicester's death Lettice had married Sir Christopher Blount, Master of the Horse in her own household. He was fifteen years younger than the countess, and he served under his stepson at Cadiz. Amidst the continuous juggling for office that was part of Court life, the Earl of Essex had never ceased to sue for his mother. In 1597 he finally succeeded in getting Elizabeth to receive Lettice at Court. The reconciliation was brief and took place in the Privy Chamber; Essex wanted a repeat performance before a larger audience, but Elizabeth said she did not wish 'to be importuned in these unpleasing matters'. Whenever Essex sulked or disobeyed her, she was inclined to say he had inherited his difficult nature from his mother.

Since the Island's Voyage the Council had become more sharply divided into two parties, Essex still calling for war, the fragile, ailing Lord Burghley urging peace, if only it could be honourably procured. An ugly scene took place in July 1598, when a few of the Queen's most trusted advisers were discussing the Irish problem. Under their new, immensely competent leader Hugh O'Neill, Earl of Tyrone, the Irish had won a resounding victory at the Yellow Ford on the River Blackwater. Over a thousand English soldiers were said to have been killed. Elizabeth wanted Tyrone suppressed; she suggested that Essex's uncle, Sir William Knollys, should go to Ireland as Lord Deputy. Essex preferred Sir George Carew, but the Queen would not listen to him. In a fit of uncontrollable rage, the earl turned his back on her. Elizabeth flew at him, boxing his ears, and telling him to be hanged. His hand went to his sword; Howard, who had been made Earl of Nottingham for his exploits at Cadiz, stepped forward to restrain him. Essex swore violently, saying he would not have borne such an insult, even at the hands of Henry VIII, and he left the Court. His friends wrote after him; Lord Keeper Egerton suggested that the best means of reconciliation would be for him to apologise humbly, but in a famous reply Essex wrote:

'I owe her Majesty the duty of an earl and of Lord Marshal of England. I have been content to do her Majesty the service of a clerk, but I can never serve her as a villein or slave. Cannot Princes err?' he asked. 'Cannot subjects receive wrong? Is an earthly power or authority infinite?'

At the end of the month Lord Burghley fell ill. Elizabeth sat at his bedside feeding him broth. He died on 4 August: Essex appeared at his funeral as one of the chief mourners. A month later Philip II died, but his son Philip III continued the feud with Elizabeth. She had decided to appoint Lord Mountjoy as Lord Deputy of Ireland, but after much importuning for the post, Essex persuaded her that he could prevail over the Irish himself.

Elizabeth raised the largest and best-equipped army that she had ever mustered. Essex's fame attracted large numbers of young gentlemen eager to prove themselves in battle. He left London on 27 March 1599 on an unprecedented wave of popularity, riding through the City followed by cheering crowds. He took with him an army of 16,000 foot-soldiers and over a thousand horse. The cost of the whole campaign was later reckoned at £250,963 10s 10d. On arrival in Dublin Essex delayed marching against Tyrone in his northern stronghold, deciding he would first subdue the province of Munster. He captured Cahir Castle, hanging all captives for, unlike the Cadiz expedition, this was a campaign against rebels. By midsummer he had still not set out for Ulster to crush Tyrone, which was the main object of the expedition.

Sir John Harington, who was with Essex in Ireland, left a wonderful description of Elizabeth's dealings with her councillors in general. She would write down what they had said, and then draw it out some months later, when they had changed their ground, defeating them with their own former opinions. She had listened many times to Essex's scornful views on the military tactics mistakenly employed by previous Lords Deputy. On 19 July she wrote in reply to a despatch he had sent her not long after the storming of Cahir.

'It seemeth by the words of your letter that you have spent divers days in taking account of all things that have passed,' she observed grandly, 'yet have you in this despatch given us small light either when or in what order you intend particularly to proceed to the northern action, wherein if you compare the time that is run on, and the excessive charges that is spent, with the effects of anything wrought by this voyage, you can little please yourself hitherto with anything that hath been effected.

'For what can be more true (if things be rightly examined) than that your two months' journey hath brought in never a capital rebel, against whom it had been worthy to have adventured one thousand men. For of their two comings in that were brought unto you by Ormonde (namely Montgarrett and Cahir) whereupon ensued the taking of Cahir Castle, full well do we know that you would long since have scorned to have allowed it for any great matter in others to have taken an Irish hold from a rabble of rogues, with such force as you had, and with the help of the cannon, which was always able in Ireland to make his passage where it pleased. And therefore, more than that, you have learned upon our expenses, by knowledge of the country, that those things are true, which we have heretofore told you, if you would have believed us, how far different things would prove than from your expectation.' She reminded him that 'the eyes of foreign Princes' were upon her actions and that while she was spending money on war it was incumbent upon her to 'comfort and cherish' the hearts of her people 'who groan under the burden of continual levies and impositions, which are occasioned by these late actions.'

Prestige mattered a good deal to Elizabeth; it displeased her, she wrote, that it was being said 'that the Queen of England's fortune (who hath held down the greatest enemy she had) to make a base bush kern to be accounted so famous a rebel, as to be a person against whom so many thousands of foot and horse besides the force of all the nobility of that kingdom must be thought too little to be employed.'

A further cause of her displeasure was that Essex had made his friend, the Earl of

Southampton, Master of the Horse. The earl was in particular disgrace for having first seduced, and then married one of the Queen's maids-of-honour.

Stung by her words Essex called a Council of War in Dublin, and wrote back to Elizabeth that it would be unwise to attack Tyrone that year. She answered on 14 September with a series of trenchant replies to his excuses:

Let him leave off his 'impertinent arguments', she said. 'Our Lord-Lieutenant we do tell you plainly, and you that are of our Council, that we wonder at your indiscretion. If you say that our army be in a list nineteen thousand, that you have them not, we answer then to you, our Treasurer, that we are evil served, and that there needs not so frequent demands of full pay. If you say that the muster-master is to blame, we must muse then why he is not punished. We say to you our General that all defects by musters have been affirmed to us to deserve to be imputed to the General.'

The letter took some time to reach him, for he had set out on 28 August to march towards the borders of Ulster. On 7 September Essex and Tyrone met for a parley near Carrickmacross. They agreed on an immediate truce, and Essex announced that Tyrone would receive the Queen's pardon if he submitted to her authority. A Captain Lawson was sent to tell Elizabeth, who immediately told the exhausted courier to go back to Ireland.

'We never doubted', she wrote sarcastically, 'but that Tyrone, whensoever he saw any force approach either himself or any of his principal partisans would instantly offer a parley, specially with our supreme general of that Kingdom, having done it with those of subaltern authority, always seeking these cessations with like words, like protestations and upon such contingents as we gather these will prove.

'It appeareth by your journal that you and the traitor spoke half an hour together without anybody's hearing, wherein though we that trust you with our kingdom are far from mistrusting you with a traitor, yet both for comeliness example and your own discharge, we marvel you would carry it no better.'

For this Elizabeth had sent out over 16,000 troops, spending over a quarter of a million pounds, a sum undreamed-of. 'If we had meant that Ireland, after all the calamities in which they have wrapped it, should still have been abandoned,' she wrote, 'then it was very superfluous to have sent over a personage such as yourself.'

That man is above me

Before Lawson reached Dublin with the stinging rebuke, Essex himself had set out for England, to explain his actions in person. He arrived at Nonsuch on 28 September, having ridden through the night. Elizabeth was still dressing, and the famous story goes that he burst into her bedchamber in his mud-spattered clothing to behold her as no man ever had, without the red wig and with 'her grey hairs about her ears'.

On 2 October she dismissed him from all his offices, placing him under the surveillance of Lord Keeper Egerton at York House. She wanted him to stand trial in the Star Chamber, but the Council dissuaded her on account of the earl's popularity. He fell ill; Elizabeth sent broth and a consortium of doctors. By March 1600 he was allowed to go back to Essex House. He had freedom to go anywhere except the Court. When John Harington took a message from him to Elizabeth, she burst out in rage:

'By God's son, I am no Queen, that man is above me.'

She bade Harington get out of her sight. 'If all the Irish rebels had been at my heels, I should not have had better speed,' Harington remembered, 'for I did now flee from one whom I both loved and feared too.'

Essex's magnetism was such that his supporters openly criticised the Queen's behaviour towards the former favourite. Robert Cecil and Francis Bacon had managed to persuade her against the Star Chamber trial. Walter Raleigh wrote to Cecil:

'I am not wise enough to give you advice but if you take it for good counsel against this tyrant you will repent it when it shall be too late. His malice is fixed and will not evaporate by any of your mild courses.'

Since it was now rumoured in London that Essex had been condemned unheard, Elizabeth ordered him to be tried before a special commission. He was not charged with disloyalty, but nor was he vindicated. Deprived of his income as Master of the Horse, his main livelihood came from his lease on the custom of sweet wines. It expired in August and Elizabeth did not renew it. He had already been in correspondence with Lord Mountjoy, the new Lord Deputy in Ireland, and with Southampton, planning a *coup d'état* by which James VI should be declared heir to the throne. He was encouraged to regain his position at Court by his sister, Lady Penelope Rich, who for many years had carried on an open liaison with Mountjoy. Essex formed a plan to storm the Court and raise the Londoners.

On Saturday 7 February 1601 some of his followers paid Shakespeare's company to put on a special performace of *Richard II* at the Globe Theatre. That evening the Council summoned Essex, but he refused to go before them. The following morning his uncle, Sir William Knollys, Lord Keeper Egerton, the Earl of Worcester and the Lord Chief Justice went to Essex House to fetch him. A tumultuous assembly thronged the Strand, setting upon the Court officials and shouting for the Great Seal of England to be cast into the river. Essex took the four councillors as hostages, and set out with an armed band of some two hundred men to raise the City, shouting 'for the Queen, for the Queen, a plot is laid for my life'. He rode up Ludgate Hill and along Cheapside, closely followed by a herald who proclaimed him a traitor, for Robert Cecil had already anticipated his moves and had warned the mayor and aldermen. There was a little skirmishing, but when he got back to Essex House, the earl found his prisoners had been released. By the evening his old comrade-in-arms, the Lord Admiral, had arrived on the scene. He was threatening to send for a keg of gunpowder to blow Essex House to pieces if the earl did not give himself up. He surrendered after burning his papers.

The trial was in the Star Chamber. Essex asked for a private execution, which took place on Tower Green on 25 February 1601. Wearing a red waistcoat, he recited the Creed and the Lord's Prayer, and he prayed for the Queen to have a long life. All who watched were in tears. A memorandum arrived from the Council just before his execution, for it was feared he might try to rouse popular feeling with a curtain speech. Southampton was arrested and reprieved; Sir Christopher Blount, another of the conspirators, was executed. Lettice survived until she was ninety-four.

I have reigned with your loves

Elizabeth made two curtain speeches, both magnificent. In the autumn of 1601 Philip III sent a Spanish army to aid Tyrone, which landed at Kinsale in late September. Lord Mountjoy was proving a loyal and able Deputy, but progress in Ireland was slow and expensive. Parliament was called so that a subsidy might be levied for extraordinary expenses. The Lord Keeper's opening speech on 27 October explained briefly the need for the subsidy; no difficulties were anticipated as it was for the defence of the realm.

The Queen hoped Parliament would be dissolved well before Christmas. Essex's lease on the sweet wines had been part of a complex system by which the Queen farmed out the privilege of fixing the prices of certain commodities, or trading in them with other countries. Many people were indignant about these monopolies, which led to excessively high prices. Elizabeth was fully aware of the abuse, but it was a useful way of providing income for her courtiers without incurring extra expenses herself. On 18 November a Mr Hyde called for an act 'containing but twelve lines. It is an exposition of the Common Law touching these kinds of patents, commonly called monopolies.' The House of Commons became unruly. Elizabeth sent a message promising to stop the malpractices by a royal proclamation. Overwhelmed with joy, the Members sent their thanks, but the Queen observed drily that they should wait until she had performed her promise. The proclamation was drawn up within three days, and Elizabeth announced she would receive a deputation in the Presence Chamber at Whitehall. When they were deciding who should go, some members started a cry of 'All, all'. This was reported to Elizabeth, who pointed out that there was very little space.

On the afternoon of 30 November, 140 Members of the Commons, 141 with the Speaker, crowded into the Presence Chamber and fell on their knees as their sovereign entered the room. She was sixty-eight and in excellent health, but perhaps some guessed that this would be her last Parliament. She had come to deliver what should have been a rasping harangue on finance, but she turned it into 'golden words', which were to be reprinted time and time again up to the eighteenth century, whenever England was in danger, as the Golden Speech of Queen Elizabeth.

Several versions survive, including a printed pamphlet which it is thought Elizabeth may have checked and corrected, but its text is inferior to the moving account by the diarist, Hayward Townshend, who was among those kneeling before her that November afternoon in the Presence Chamber.

Cℨ Mr Speaker,

We have heard your declaration and perceive your care of our estate. I do assure you there is no prince that loves his subjects better, or whose love can countervail our love. There is no jewel, be it of never so rich a price, which I set before this jewel: I mean your love. For I do esteem it more than any treasure or riches; for that we know how to prize, but love and thanks I count invaluable. And, though God hath raised me high, yet this I count the glory of my Crown, that I have reigned with your loves. This makes me that I do not so much rejoice that God hath made me to be a Queen, as to be a Queen over so thankful a people. Therefore I have cause to wish nothing more than to content the subject and that is a duty which I owe. Neither do I desire to live longer days than I may see your prosperity and that is my only desire. And as I am that person that still yet, under God, hath delivered you and so I trust by the almighty power of God that I shall be his instrument to preserve you from every peril, dishonour, shame, tyranny and oppression, partly by means of your intended helps which we take very acceptably because it manifesteth the largeness of your good loves and loyalties unto your sovereign.

Of myself I must say this: I never was any greedy scraping grasper, nor a strait fast-holding Prince, nor yet a waster. My heart was never set on any worldly goods. What you bestow on me, I will not hoard it up, but receive it to bestow on you again. Therefore render unto them I beseech you Mr Speaker, such thanks as you imagine my heart yieldeth, but my tongue cannot express. Mr Speaker, I would wish you and the rest to stand up for I shall yet trouble you with longer speech.

The Commons had been kneeling, but at this point the diarist interpolates, 'So we all stood up and she went on in her speech, saying':

Cℨ Mr Speaker, you give me thanks but I doubt me I have greater cause to give you thanks, than you me, and I charge you to thank them of the Lower House from me. For had I not received a knowledge from you, I might have fallen into the lapse of an error, only for lack of true information.

232

Since I was Queen, yet did I never put my pen to any grant, but that upon pretext and semblance made unto me, it was both good and beneficial to the subject in general though a private profit to some of my ancient servants, who had deserved well at my hands. But the contrary being found by experience, I am exceedingly beholden to such subjects as would move the same at first. And I am not so simple to suppose but that there be some of the Lower House whom these grievances never touched. I think they spake out of zeal to their countries and not out of spleen or malevolent affection as being parties grieved. That my grants should be grievous to my people and oppressions to be privileged under colour of our patents, our kingly dignity shall not suffer it. Yea, when I heard it, I could give no rest unto my thoughts until I had reformed it. Shall they, think you, escape unpunished that have oppressed you, and have been respectless of their duty and regardless of our honour? No, I assure you, Mr Speaker, were it not more for conscience' sake than for any glory or increase of love that I desire, these errors, troubles, vexations and oppressions, done by these varlets and lewd persons not worthy of the name of subjects should not escape without condign punishment. But I perceive they dealt with me like physicians who, ministering a drug, make it more acceptable by giving it a good aromatical savour, or when they give pills do gild them all over.

I have ever used to set the Last Judgement Day before mine eyes and so to rule as I shall be judged to answer before a higher judge, and now if my kingly bounties have been abused and my grants turned to the hurt of my people contrary to my will and meaning, and if any in authority under me have neglected or perverted what I have committed to them, I hope God will not lay their culps and offences in my charge. I know the title of a King is a glorious title, but assure yourself that the shining glory of princely authority hath not so dazzled the eyes of our understanding, but that we well know and remember that we also are to yield an account of our actions before the great judge. To be a king and wear a crown is a thing more glorious to them that see it than it is pleasant to them that bear it. For myself I was never so much enticed with the glorious name of a King or royal authority of a Queen as delighted that God hath made me his instrument to maintain his truth and glory and to defend this kingdom as I said from peril, dishonour, tyranny and oppression. There will never Queen sit in my seat with more zeal to my country, care to my subjects and that will sooner with willingness venture her life for your good and safety than myself. For it is my desire to live nor reign no longer than my life and reign shall be for your good. And though you have had, and may have, many princes more mighty and wise sitting in this seat, yet you never had nor shall have, any that will be more careful and loving.

A Prince set upon a stage, there seems no doubt that she delivered her lines magnificently that November afternoon, placing particular emphasis, according to Townshend, on the last words.

'For I, oh Lord, what am I, whom practices and perils past should not fear? Or what can I do? That I should speak for any glory, God forbid.' And turning to the Speaker and her councillors she said, 'And I pray you, Mr Comptroller, Mr Secretary and you of my Council, that before these gentlemen go into their countries, you bring them all to kiss my hand.'

Constant to the grounds of honour

When Philip II died on 13 September 1598, Queen Elizabeth had little to say on the matter. Francesco Soranzo, writing to the Doge of Venice, described him as 'one of the richest Princes the world has ever seen. Yet', he added, 'he has left the revenues of the Kingdom and of the Crown burdened with about a million of debts. Profoundly religious, he loved peace and quiet. He displayed great calmness and professed himself unmoved in good or bad fortune alike. He had vast schemes in his head – witness his simultaneous attack on England and France.'

His heir Philip III had no quarrel with Elizabeth save a hereditary one, and at the close of the 1601 Parliament the Queen chose to make some remarks on the subject. Many of the new members were young men who had grown up in the decade when England was at war with Spain; the thirty years of peace had been before their time. The Parliament granted the subsidies, for if the Spanish army in Ireland prevailed, a further attack on England was to be expected. In fact, Mountjoy won a resounding victory at the end of the year, ending Tyrone's dream of an independent Ireland, but the news had not reached London in the last week of Elizabeth's last Parliament. On 10 December she sent them a message to speed up their business, as she wished to close Parliament before Christmas. They had finished by the 18th, but the Queen postponed the closing ceremony until the next day. Although no draft survives in her own hand, she must have thought out carefully what she had to say, and it has been surmised that she made notes which she later lent to Lord Henry Howard, in whose hand the only copy of her speech is written.

'Before your going down at the end of the Parliament,' she began crisply, 'I thought it good to deliver unto you certain notes for your observation, that serve aptly for the present time.'

She proposed to give them a short review of her reign and policies, 'both concerning civil and foreign causes', that they might 'more easily discern in what kind of sympathy' her care to benefit them had corresponded with their 'inclination to obey'.

If any present on that December afternoon had thought of Elizabeth as a majestic but frail old woman, they were in for a surprise. Contemporary accounts concur that her cheeks were a little hollowed, her neck wrinkled and several of her teeth had fallen out or were blackened with decay, but her mind seemed sharper than ever as she proceeded to outline the history of her long quarrel with Spain.

'First civilly yourselves can witness that I never entered into the examination of any cause without advertisement, carrying ever a single eye to justice and truth. For though I were content to hear matters argued and debated pro and contra as all princes must that will understand what is right, yet I look ever as it were upon a plain table[t] wherein is written neither partiality nor prejudice.'

She thanked them for their gift of the subsidy; it was for the defence of the realm and 'like rivers coming from the ocean' it would 'return to the ocean again'.

'I have diminished my own revenue that I might add to your security, like a taper of true virgin wax, to waste myself and spend my life that I might give light and comfort to those that live under me.'

She spoke of the Spanish Armada: 'those that did not only threaten to come, but came at last in very deed, with their whole fleet'. And she spoke of the many attempts on her own life, which it had pleased God to spare, making her 'an instrument of his holy will in delivering the state from danger and myself from dishonour'. Then she treated them to a long discourse on her foreign policy.

'I take God to witness that I never gave just cause of war to any prince, which the subjects of other states can testify nor had any greater ambition than to maintain my own state in security and peace. For to let you know, what is not perhaps understood by any other, than were or are conversant in state matters and keep true records of dealings past – even that potent Prince, the King of Spain (whose soul I trust be now in Heaven) that hath so many ways assailed both my realm and me had many provocations of kindness by my just proceedings.

'It is neither my manner nor my nature to speak ill of those that are dead but that in this case it is not possible without some touch to the author to tax the injury. For when the colour of dissension began first to kindle between his subjects of the Netherlands and him – I mean not Holland and Zeeland only, but of Brabant and the other provinces which are now in the Archduke's possession – about the bringing in of the Inquisition, a burden untolerable, increase of impositions, planting foreigners in the chiefest offices and places of government, then I gave them counsel to contain their passions and rather by humble petition than by violence or arms to seek ease of their aggrievances: nay which is more I disbursed great sums of money out of my own purse to stay them from revolt till a softer hand might reduce these to harmony.' She told them what she had said in *The Declaration* of 1585, dwelling on the ancient amity between England and Burgundy, and describing how fifteen years ago she had warned the King of Spain that if he did not respect the ancient liberties of the people of the Low Countries they would invite some foreign prince to be their leader. She told them of Alva's arrival in the Netherlands and of Philip's interference in her own land. 'In recompense of this kind care and faithful dealing, he first begins to stir rebellion within the body of my realm, encouraging the Earls of Northumberland and Westmorland to take arms against myself.' But, she told them proudly, by the victory she had over her own rebels, she had made even Philip II 'see how hard a matter it was to prevail against a Prince, confident in the protection of God and constant to the grounds of honour'.

'Now that the father is at rest the son, whom I did never in my life offend, assails me in another parallel, seeking to take away one of the two crowns.'* Such a quarrel, she said, 'unworthily begun and unjustly prosecuted without provocation by the least offence', could never prosper. Philip III must acknowledge it in his own conscience and, she concluded with assurance, 'God will punish it'.

By New Year 1602 Mountjoy wrote of his victory over Tyrone, also telling Elizabeth of the Spanish surrender.

When thou dost feel creeping Time at thy gate

Elizabeth remained in good health until the autumn of 1602. In August, a little before her sixty-ninth birthday, she could still ride ten miles in one day, and then go hunting afterwards. She ate sparsely, walked a good deal and she continued to take an avid interest in Irish affairs. In December 1600, before his great onslaught against Tyrone, Mountjoy had complained to her that he did the work of a scullion, and she had written him a letter of encouragement in which she teasingly nicknamed him 'Mistress Kitchenmaid'. As he continued to subdue the province, and strengthen the English settlements in the centre of Ireland, she still directed affairs, sending him clear instructions on the treatment of the rebels, and warning him that Tyrone, 'the arch traitor', might 'let slip of purpose' Irishmen who would pretend to submit to the English, for the purpose of spying on or betraying them.

On 15 July 1602, she added a postscript in her own hand to a letter to Mountjoy, thanking him for his mopping-up operation:

ଔ We con you many lauds for having so nearly approached the villainous rebel and see no reason why so great forces should not end his days, whose wickedness hath cut off so many, and should judge myself mad, if we should not change your authority for his life, and so we do by this. Since neither Spaniard, nor other accident, is like to alter this mind, as she that should blush to receive such indignity after so royal prosecution. We have forgotten to praise your humility,

---

* Of England and of Ireland.

that after having been a Queen's kitchenmaid, you have not disdained to be a traitor's scullion. God bless you with perseverance.

Your Sovereign, E.R.

In February 1603 the Doge and Senate of Venice sent Giovanni Scaramelli to England; he was the first official Venetian ambassador since Elizabeth's accession, and she received him graciously at Richmond in a gown of silver and white taffeta, embroidered with gold; it was low necked and 'showed her throat encircled with pearls and rubies down to her breast'. She no longer dressed in the height of fashion and Scaramelli observed that 'her skirts were much fuller and began lower down than is the fashion in France. Her hair was of a light colour never made by nature, and she wore great pearls like pears round the forehead. She had a vast quantity of gems and pearls upon her person; even under her stomacher she was covered with golden jewelled girdles and single gems, carbuncles, balas-rubies and diamonds. Round her wrists in place of bracelets she wore double rows of pearls of more than medium size.' On her head was an Imperial Crown. Scaramelli was so awed to come face to face with the great lady, who was a legend in her own time, that he bent very low and tried to kiss the hem of her garment. She raised him up and gave him her right hand to kiss, saying:

'Welcome to England, Mr Secretary. It was high time that the Republic sent to visit a Queen, who has always honoured it on every possible occasion.'

When the ambassador had finished his address, which touched on the same unpleasant matters of which the King of Poland had complained, namely that English corsairs were making the quarrel between Elizabeth and Spain an excuse to attack foreign shipping indiscriminately, Elizabeth's reply was razor sharp. She pointed out with disarming sweetness that it had never been possible for her to deal directly with matters concerning such attacks, as there had been no Venetian ambassador resident in England.

> ℭ I cannot help feeling that the Republic of Venice during the forty-four years of my reign has never made herself heard by me except to ask for something, nor for the rest, prosperous or adverse as my affairs have been, never has she given a sign of holding me or my Kingdom in that esteem which other princes and other potentates have not refused. Nor am I aware that my sex has brought me this demerit, for my sex [she said confidently] cannot diminish my prestige, nor offend them who treat me as other Princes are treated to whom the Signory of Venice sends its ambassadors.

She promised to appoint commissioners to look into the matter: 'I will do all that in me lies to give satisfaction to the serene Republic,' she answered Scaramelli. Then she changed the subject, saying gently, 'I do not know if I have spoken Italian well; I think so, for I learned it as a child and believe I have not forgotten it.'

At the end of the month the Admiral's wife, the Countess of Nottingham, died. She was the granddaughter of Elizabeth's aunt, Mary Boleyn, and one of her closest remaining friends. The Queen ordered a State funeral, but sank into a mood of great depression. Lady Nottingham's brother, Robert Carey, came to Richmond early in March and found Elizabeth in one of her withdrawing chambers, seated among her cushions. It became obvious that she was failing. At first she refused to give in, admonishing Robert Cecil: 'Little man, little man, the word *must* is not to be used to Princes,' when he told her she really should go to bed.

Her godson John Harington had tried to raise her spirits by telling her a joke, but she replied: 'When thou dost feel creeping Time at thy gate, these fooleries will please thee less.'

Carey tried to persuade her from her melancholy humour. He heard her fetch 'forty or fifty great sighs' and was grieved, 'for in all my lifetime before', he wrote, 'I never knew her fetch a sigh, but when the Queen of Scots was beheaded.'

On 21 March they sent for the Lord Admiral, who was away from Court in mourning for his wife. He finally persuaded Elizabeth to go to bed. They had to saw the Coronation Ring from her finger, for it had grown into her flesh. She had still not formally named her successor. By Wednesday the 23rd, an inflammation in her throat was preventing her from speaking although, according to the Venetian ambassador, she rallied a little, asking for rose-water and some currants that were on a table at her bedside. Cecil begged her to give a sign that James VI was her choice. Lifting both her hands she made her fingers into the shape of a crown. Then she raised her hands to her head.

Elizabeth died at Richmond on 24 March 1603. It was a Thursday, the same day of the week on which Henry VIII had died. Archbishop Whitgift had arrived at six the previous evening and remained on his knees praying until it grew late and everyone departed except for her chaplain, Dr Parry, and some of her women. Between 2 and 3 o'clock in the morning, 'mildly like a lamb, easily like a ripe apple from the tree', Elizabeth slipped away. Dr Parry 'sent his prayers before her soul', wrote one of the attendants, 'and I doubt not but she is among the royal saints in heaven.'

Allegorical portrait of Elizabeth with Time and Death

APPENDIX

The following is the text of Elizabeth's Latin translation of the title-page of Queen Katherine's *Prayers and Meditations* and of her dedication to her father (see p. 6).

CB Precationes seu meditationes quibus mens comovetur ad omnes perturbationes huius vite patienter ferendas ad vanam prosperitatem huius mundi contemnendam et ad eterna foelicitatem asidue expetendam. Ex quibusdam pys scriptoribus per Nobilis et Pietiss. D. Catherinam Anglie, Francie, Hibernicq. reginam collecte et per D. Elizabetam ex anglico converse.

Illustrissimo ac Potentissimo regi Henrico octavo Anglie, Francie Hibernicque regi fidei defensori et secundum christum ecclesie anglicane et hibernice supremo capiti Elizabeta Maiest.S humillima filia omne foelicitatem precatur et benedictionem suam suplex petit. Quemadmodum immortalis animus immortali corpore prestat ita sapiens quisque iudicat animi res gestas pluris estimandas et maiori laude dignas esse ulla corporis actione. Cum itaque maiestas tua tante excellentie sit ut nulli aut pauci tecum sint comparandi in regis et amplis ornamentis et ego obstricta sum tibi lege regni ut domino lege nature ut domino et patri meo lege divina ut amplissimo domino et singulari ac benignissimo patri et omnibus legibus et officiis variis ac pluribus modis obstricta sim maiestati tui libenter querebam (id quod officium meum fuit) quo parto amplitudini tue prestantissim{um} munus offerem quod tum facultas tum industria mea invenire possent. In quo solum vereor ne tenera et inchoata studia et puerilis ingenii maturitas minuant illius rei laudem et commendationem quam perfecta ingenia in argumento divinissimo pertractarunt. Nam nihil acceptius esse debet regi quem philosophi deum in terris esse sentiunt quum illud opus animi quod nos in coelum tollit et in terra coelestes atque in carne divinos facit: et quum perpetuis ac infinitis miseriis implicati simus tunc etiam beatos nos et foelices reddit. Quod quum tam pium sit et pio studio atque magna industria Regine illustrissime fuerit anglice collectum et propterea ab omnibus magis expetendum et a maiestate tua in maiori precio habendum sit accommodatissimum mihi visum est ut hoc quod argumento suo rege collectione vero regina dignissimum est a me filia tua in alias linguas converteretur que non modo virtutum tuarum imitatrix sed illarum etiam heres esse debeam in quo quicquid meum non est amplissima laude dignum est quemadmodum totus liber est tum argumento pius tum ingeniose collectus et aptissimo ordine dispositus. Quicquid vero meum est si in eo aliquis error insit tamenpropter ignorationem etatem breve tempus studii et voluntatem venia meretur et si mediocre sit, etiam si nullam laudem mereatur, tamen si bene accipiatur me vehementer excitabit ut quantum annis cresco tantum etiam scientia et dei timore crescam itaque fiet ut illum religiosius colam et maiestatem tuam officiosius observem. Quamobrem non dubito quin paterna tua bonitas et regia prudentia hunc internum animi mei laborem non minoris estimabit quam aliud ullum ornamentum et sentiet divinum hoc opus quod est pluris estimandum quia a serenissima regina coniuge tua colligebatur, paulo in maiori precio habendum esse quia abs filia tua convertebatur. Ille rex regum in cuius manu corda regum sunt ita gubernet animum tuum et vitam tueatur unt in vera pietate ac religione diu sub maiestatis tue imperio vivamus

Harfordiae 30 die decembris.

LIST OF ILLUSTRATIONS

List of Illustrations

SOURCE NOTES

LIST OF ABBREVIATIONS

Bedingfield Papers	*Miscellaneous Tracts of the Norfolk Archaeological Society* IV (Norwich 1885)
BL	British Library
Cal. Pat. Rolls	*Calendar of Patent Rolls*
CSP Dom. Ed. VI	*Calendar of State Papers, Domestic: Edward VI*
CSP Dom. Eliz.	*Calendar of State Papers, Domestic: Elizabeth*
CSP Dom. Mary	*Calendar of State Papers, Domestic: Mary*
CSP Foreign	*Calendar of State Papers, Foreign* (London 1863–1959)
CSP Ireland	*Calendar of State Papers, Ireland* (London 1860–1912)
CSP Scotland	*Calendar of State Papers relating to Scotland* (Edinburgh & Glasgow 1889–1979)
CSP Spain	*Calendar of State Papers, Spanish* (London 1862–1954)
CSP Span. Eliz.	*Calendar of State Papers, Spanish, Elizabeth* (London 1892–9)
CSP Ven.	*Calendar of State Papers, Venetian* (London 1864–98)
Feria's Despatch	M.J. Rodriguez-Selgado and S. Adams, 'The Count of Feria's Despatch to Philip II of 14 November 1558', *Camden Miscellany XXVIII* (Camden Fourth Series 29) (London 1984)
Foxe, *Acts and Monuments*	J. Foxe, *The Acts and Monuments of John Foxe* ed. J. Pratt (London 1877, rptd New York 1965)
Fraser, *Mary Queen of Scots*	Lady Antonia Fraser, *Mary Queen of Scots* (London 1972)
HMC	*Historical Manuscripts Commission*
Miscellaneous State Papers	*Miscellaneous State Papers 1501–1726* ed. Earl of Hardwicke (London 1778)
LP Hen. VIII	*Letters and Papers, Foreign and Domestic, of the reign of Henry VIII* (London 1862–1932)
Neale, *Elizabeth I and her Parliaments*	Sir J. Neale, *Elizabeth I and her Parliaments* (London 1953)
Nichols, *Progresses*	J.A. Nichols, *The Progresses of Queen Elizabeth* (London 1823)
Nugae Antiquae	*Nugae Antiquae* ed. H. Harrington (London 1767–75)
Passage of our Sovereign Lady	*The Passage of our most dread Sovereign Lady Queen Elizabeth through the City of London, 1558* Printed by R. Tothill (London 1558)
PRO SP	Public Record Office, State Papers
Proceedings in Parliament	T.E. Hartley, *Proceedings in Parliament* (Leicester 1981)
Tudor Royal Proclamations	Hughes and Larkin, *Tudor Royal Proclamations* (Yale 1964–9)

Source Notes

INTRODUCTION

page 1, *line* 32 P.A. Forbes, *A full view of the public transactions in the reign of Queen Elizabeth I* (London 1740)

G.B. Harrison, *The Letters of Queen Elizabeth* (London 1935)

Leicester Bradner, *The Poems of Queen Elizabeth I* (Rhode Island 1964)

p 1, *l* 35 *Proceedings in the Parliaments of Elizabeth I*

p 5, *l* 5 BL MS facs. 218, 'Queen Elizabeth's Book of Devotions': first English prayer.

p 5, *l* 17 *L P Hen. VIII* 10, no. 908 (377). See also nos. 1107, Lord Rochford's child; 909, Mr Norris's bastard; 1043 and 1044, the child of a villein or poor person.

p 5, *l* 24 *L P Hen. VIII* 11, no. 312

p 5, *l* 32 *L P Hen. VIII* 10, no. 913, '18 Jan. Boat hire from Greenwich to London and back to take measure of caps for my lady Princess's purple satin cap to mend it.'

p 5, *l* 40 BL MS Cotton Otho C.X f.234; printed *L P Hen. VIII* 11, no. 312

p 6, *l* 25 BL MS Cotton Otho C.X f.284

p 7, *l* 10 *L P Hen. VIII* 10, no. 860

p 7, *l* 16 *Succession to the Crown Act, 29 Hen. 8* c. 1 sections 3, 10 and 21

p 7, *n** *L P Hen. VIII* 11, no. 860

p 9, *l* 6 *L P Hen. VIII* 12.i, no. 815

p 9, *l* 20 *Succession to the Crown Act, 35 Hen. 8* c.1 sections 3 and 4

p 10, *l* 5 *L P Hen. VIII* 11, no. 147

p 10, *l* 12 *Hamilton Papers* 1, no. 35 (p.40) letter from Henry to Margaret of Scotland, 27 December 1536

p 10, *n** *L P Hen. VIII* 11, no. 48

p 11, *l* 13 E. Hall, *Chronicle* (London 1548) 864–6

p 11, *l* 18 *L P Hen. VIII* 20.ii, no. 1030

CHAPTER I

p 13, *l* 9 *L P Hen. VIII* 18.i, nos. 740,873

p 13, *l* 13 Ibid. no. 918

p 13, *l* 20 *L P Hen. VIII* 19.i, no. 780

p 13, *l* 25 Ibid. no. 799

p 14, *l* 12 *L P Hen. VIII* 19.i, nos. 979, 1019; ii, nos. 39, 58, 136. Letters from Katherine Parr to Henry VIII at siege of Boulogne.

p 14, *n** *L P Hen. VIII* 19.ii, no. 688 (pp.406–7)

p 15, *l* 6 F.A. Mumby, *The Girlhood of Queen Elizabeth* (London 1909) 22: 'For some obscure reason Elizabeth seems to have fallen out of her father's favour again very soon after Catherine Parr had obtained his consent to her return to Court.' Mumby seems to base his assumption on the word '*exilio*' in the Italian letter.

Cf. Elizabeth Jenkins, *Elizabeth the Great* (London 1958) 17 'she offended the King. Nothing is known of the offence, only of its consequences. She was banished from his household, and it was a year before her humble entreaties and the Queen's good offices brought her back to the family circle.' There is no foundation for these assertions; Henry's letters to Katherine from Boulogne always included blessings to all his children.

p 15, *n*† *L P Hen. VIII* 18.ii, no. 39

p 15, *l* 33 BL MS Cotton, Otho C.X f.235. The MS was damaged in the Cotton fire, but was printed in Thomas Hearne's *Sylloge Epistolarum* (Oxford 1716). I have varied from the translation made by Mrs Green in *Letters of Royal and Illustrious Ladies*, and used by G.B. Harrison in *The Letters of Queen Elizabeth* (London 1935) principally by retranslating '*volutrice*' and '*clementia*'. The capitals are Elizabeth's own; at ten her handwriting was round and clear.

p 16, *l* 3 H.M. Colvin, *A History of the King's Works* (London 1979) III, 255 also *L P Hen. VIII* 14.ii, nos. 696, 697

p 16, *l* 9 *L P Hen. VIII* 19.ii, no. 726

p 16, *l* 14 Oxford Bodleian Library, MS Cherry 36

p 16, *l* 26 Anne Lake Prescott, 'The Pearl of the Valois Elizabeth I', in Margaret Patterson Hannay (ed.), *Silent but for the Word* (Ohio 1987) 71

p 18, *l* 33 Oxford, Bodleian Library, MS Cherry 36 f.1, 2

p 19, *l* 7 Susan E James, 'The Devotional Writings of Queen Catherine Parr', *Transactions of the Cumberland and Westmoreland Antiquarian and Archaeological Society* (1982) 135–9

p 19, *n** *L P Hen. VIII* 20.ii, nos. 639, 764, 856, 890, 1038

p 21, *l* 35 BL MS Royal 7 D. X. I am indebted to Dr Elizabeth Leedham Green, Assistant Keeper of the University Archives, Cambridge, for this dignified translation. The Latin text is in the Appendix, see p. 319.

p 22, *l* 10 J. Scarisbrick, *Henry VIII* (London 1968) 454 et seq.

p 22, *l* 20 Originally Erasmus' doctrines of 1520, later printed as *The Bishop's Book*, but after the Supreme Head found time to revise it, it was known as *The King's Book*. Before the end of 1544 it went into fifteen editions, *STC* 5168–5178. See also *Tudor Royal Proclamations I*, 373

p 22, *n** D. Starkey, *The Reign of Henry VIII* (London 1985) 145

p 24, *l* 7 BL MS Harleian 5087, no 28, f.IIV

p 24, *l* 16 Janet Arnold, 'The Picture of Elizabeth I when Princess', *Burlington Magazine*, May 1981

p 25, *l* 26 BL MS Cotton Vespasian F.III f.46

p 26, *n** CSP *Span.* 1547–49, 123

p 26, *l* 17 BL MS Cotton Nero C.X f.13

p 27, *l* 23 *Paraphrases of the New Testament*, unpaginated. From Udall's Epistle to Katherine Parr.

p 27, *l* 42 Oxford, Bodleian Library, MS Cherry 36. *A Godly Meditacyon* f.26v has 'maketh me a newe godly and bewtyfull creature.

p 28, *l* 17 *STC* 848, 849 and 850 were printed from Marburg, a fake imprint for Wesel.

p 28, *n** *A godly meditacyon* f.7

p 29, *l* 5 *A godly Meditacyon* f.41

p 29, *l* 15 Ibid. f.8v

p 29, *l* 21 *STC* 17320; the first edition has the Wesel imprint. There were four English editions *STC* 17320.5–17322.5.

p 29, *l* 27 Ibid. f.41

p 30, *l* 30 Ibid. f.37v, f.38r. In 'The Pearl of the Valois' cited above, Anne Lake Prescott assumes Elizabeth worked from the edition of *Le Miroir* printed at Geneva in 1539. I think she used the 1531 edition printed at Alençon by Maître Simon du Bois. On the title page there is a prominent design of heart-shaped leaves. In the Bodleian MS Elizabeth uses an identical motif as a 'line filler', and occasionally as a random calligraphic embellishment. f.3 'an instrument of yron or of other metayle waxeth soone [motif] rusty onles it be continually occupied'. f.5 'To the reader [motif] if thou dost rede thys whole worke'.

Source Notes

CHAPTER II

p 31, l 12 Haynes, *Burghley Papers* (London 1740) 62

p 31, l 26 *Acts of the Privy Council* II, 104

p 31, l 32 Sir John Neale, *Queen Elizabeth I* (London 1952) 26

p 32, l 19 *Burghley Papers* 99: confession of Katherine Ashley

p 32, l 27 PRO SP 10/6 nos. 19, 20, 21, 22

p 32, l 39 J. Ridley, *Elizabeth I* (London 1987) 39

p 32, n* Alison Plowden, *The Young Elizabeth* (London 1971)

p 34, l 2 E. Jenkins, *Elizabeth the Great* (London 1958)

p 34, l 30 PRO SP 10/2 no. 25

p 35, l 1 Thomas Hearne, *Sylloge Epistolarum* (Oxford 1716) 151–2

p 35, l 21 BL MS Otho C.X f.236v

p 35, n* *CSP Dom. ED. VI* VIII, no. 35

p 35, n† PRO SP/5 no. 5

p 35, n‡ PRO SP10/6 no. 14

p 36, l 30 *Archaeologia* 72, 249

p 36, n* PRO SP10/5 no. 4

p 36, n† *Burghley Papers* 77–8

p 37, l 13 Oxford, Bodleian Library, MS Add. c. 92 f.12, printed in Hearne's *Sylloge Epistolarum*

p 37, l 19 *Burghley Papers* 102–103: confession of the Lady Elizabeth's Grace.

p 37, l 26 PRO SP 10/6 no. 10

p 37, l 29 *Acts of the Privy Council* 1547–1550 II, 247–256

p 37, n‡ *Statutes at Large* 28 Hen. 8 c.18

p 38, l 4 J. Nichols, *Literary Remains of King Edward VI* (London 1857) 57

p 38, l 8 W.K. Jordan, *Edward VI: The Young King* (London 1968) 45

p 38, l 12 PRO SP 10/6 no.7; deposition of the Marquis of Dorset

p 38, l 22 J. Nichols, *Literary Remains of King Edward VI*, cxix

p 40, l 7 Hatfield House, MS 1/64

p 40, l 25 Oxford, Bodleian Library, MS Ashmole 1729. Printed G.B. Harrison, *Letters of Queen Elizabeth I* (London 1935) 11–12

p 40, l 32 *Historical Manuscripts Commission, Hatfield* 285

p 42, l 5 BL MS Lansdowne 1236/33

p 42, l 10 *Burghley Papers* 75–76

p 43, l 16 BL MS Lansdowne 1236/35

p 43, l 41 J. Latimer, *Sermons* (Cambridge 1844) 228–229

p 45, l 10 *The Whole Works of Roger Ascham*, ed. J.A. Giles (London 1865) 191

p 45, l 30, n† BL MS Nero C.X f.16v

p 46, l 3 *CSP Dom. Ed. VI* IX, 33: a letter of 9 October to both Princesses sets out the malpractices of the Lord Protector.

p 46, l 15 *CSP Span.* IX, 489

p 46, l 30 *Ibid.* X, 206

p 46, *l* 38 Ibid. X, 209–12

p 47, *l* 1 *Original Letters Relative to the English Reformation* (London 1846) I, 76

p 47, *l* 13 *CSP Span.* X, 215

p 47, *l* 25 Ibid. x, 214

p 47, *l* 41 Ibid. X, 207

p 48, *l* 14 BL MS Royal 16 E I. f.Ir/v

p 48, *l* 37 J. Aylmer, *An Harborrowe for Faithful and Trewe Subiectes* (Strasbourg 1559) unpaginated

p 49, *l* 6 B. Ochino, *Prediche* (Basel, 1543) Sermon XII

p 49, *n** *STC* 18764–18769, the *STC* lists six printings of Ochino's *Sermons* in English. The earliest is translated by R. Argentyne, printed Ipswich by A. Schloker 1548. Anne Cooke's later translation of fourteen sermons is not dated. It is dedicated to her 'beloved Mother, the Lady F,' and printed by John Day and William Seres, *STC* assumes 1551.

p 50, *l* 7 Oxford, Bodleian Library, MS Bodley 6

CHAPTER III

p 51, *l* 15 BL MS Cotton Nero C.X f.51v and Nichols, *Literary Remains of Edward VI* 381–3 n.3

p 51, *l* 20 BL MS Cotton Nero C.X. f.52v

p 52, *l* 2 *CSP Span.* 1550–1552 X, 493

p 52, *l* 7 BL MS Cotton Nero C f.58v

p 52, *l* 15 BL MS Cotton Nero C f.75v

p 52, *l* 28 W.K. Jordan, *Edward VI The Threshold of Power*, 517

p 52, *n†* H.M. Colvin, *History of the King's Works* (London 1982) VI, 252–3; *Cal. Pat Rolls* 1549–51, 238 and 415

p 53, *l* 5 BL MS Harleian 6986 f.23

p 53, *l* 14 Jordan, *Edward VI The Threshold of Power*, 512–20; for a fuller description of the events leading up to the Devise and for the background of Northumberland's dynastic plans.

p 53, *l* 20 *CSP Span.* XI, 38

p 53, *l* 22 Ibid. 46

p 53, *l* 23 Ibid. 50

p 53, *l* 27 Ibid. 54

p 54, *l* 4 Ibid. 82

p 54, *l* 22 W. Camden, *Annales Elizabetha*, ed. Thomas Hearne (Oxford 1718) I, 14–15: '*Illa modeste respondit, cum Maria sorore natu majore prius transigendum qua superstite, se nibil juris sibi posse arrogare*'

p 54, *n** Jordan, *Edward VI* II, 516–517

p 55, *l* 4 *CSP Span.* XI, 80

p 55, *l* 19 *Proceedings in Parliament* I, 146–148

p 55, *l* 30 *CSP Span.* XI, 115

p 55, *l* 37 *The Diary of Henry Machyn*, ed. J.G. Nichols, Camden Society (London 1848) 37

p 56, *l* 18 *CSP Span.* XI, 251

p 56, *l* 31 *Tudor Royal Proclamations* II, 5–8

p 57, *l* 12 F. Madden, *Privy Purse Expenses of the Princess Mary* (London 1831): 'item: ii payr of Bedes of corall, the one red the other white trymed wt gold the white given by the quene's highness at Seint James xxi Sept 1553 to the Lady Elizabeth's grace'.

Source Notes

p 57, *l* 20 *CSP Span.* XI, 252/3

p 57, *l* 29 Ibid. 263

p 57, *l* 41 Ibid. 274

p 58, *l* 22 BL MS Lansdowne 94, f.21

p 58, *l* 29 *CSP Span.* XI 230

p 59, *l* 7 Ibid. 466

p 59, *l* 13 Ibid. 418

p 59, *l* 30 Ibid. 440–441

p 60, *l* 29 *CSP Span.* XII, 50

p 61, *l* 21 Foxe, *Acts and monuments* VI, 414–15

p 61, *l* 36 *CSP Span.* XII, 52

p 62, *l* 10 *CSP Dom. Mary* II, no. 20: letter from Gardiner to Petre

p 62, *l* 17 *CSP Span.* XII, 120

p 62, *l* 40 Ibid. 167. It has been assumed Winchester was the other peer, because of Elizabeth's letter to him, q.v.

p 62, *n** Ibid. 151/4

p 63, *l* 11 *CSP Span.* XII, 166–167

p 65, *l* 24 PRO SP 11/4, 2

CHAPTER IV

p 66, *l* 8 *CSP Span.* XII, no. 309

p 66, *n** *CSP Span.* XIII, nos. 1 & 2

p 67, *l* 2 *CSP Span.* XIII, no. 11 (p.11)

p 67, *n** Geoffrey Parker, *Philip II* (London 1978) 82

p 68, *l* 10 *CSP Dom. Mary* II, no. 20 (Gardiner's letter to Petre) & *CSP Dom. Mary* II, nos. 39, 40

p 68, *l* 18 Elizabeth's prayer at the time of her coronation: *the passage of our Sovereign Lady*

p 68, *l* 37 Foxe, *Acts and monuments* VIII, 611

p 69, *l* 19 *Bedingfield Papers* 157/8

p 69, *l* 32 Foxe, *Acts and monuments* VIII, 616

p 69, *l* 37 *CSP Span.* XII, nos. 285, 286

p 70, *l* 4 *Bedingfield Papers* IV, 182/3. Mary's letter was written from Farnham where the court was awaiting Philip's arrival.

p 70, *l* 21 Ibid. 192/3

p 70, *l* 31 Ibid. 203

p 71, *l* 1 Ibid. 205

p 71, *l* 5 Ibid. 210–12

p 72, *l* 10 Ibid. 215–16

p 72, *l* 21 Oxford, Bodleian Library, MS e Musaeo 242

p 72, *l* 28 T. Warton, *Life of Sir Thomas Pope* (London 1772) 73/74, Nichols, *Progresses* I, 10, F.A. Mumby, *The Girlhood of Queen Elizabeth* (London 1909) 185–6. All quotes Warton's original mistakes, 'goodliesome herbs' for 'goodly green' and the letters EC supposedly for Elizabeth Captiva.

p 72, *l* 32 *STC* 2878 ff.

p 74, *l* 1 *CSP Span.* XI, 216

p 74, *l* 16 *CSP Span.* XIII, 60: Ruy Gomez's letter

p 74, *l* 22 Ibid. 101/2

p 74, *n** *CSP Span.* XI, 227

p 74, *l* 33 Foxe, *Acts and monuments* VI, 568–71

p 75, *n** Ibid. VI, 582

p 76, *l* 11 *CSP Span.* XIII, 251

p 77, *l* 9 BL MS Harleian 39, f.14

p 77, *l* 20 *CSP Ven.* VI.i, 505, 510, 514

p 77, *l* 25 Ibid. 514

p 77, *l* 36 Warton, *Life of Pope* 65

p 79, *l* 12 MS Lansdowne 1236, f.37

p 79, *l* 15 *CSP Ven.* VI.ii, 836

p 79, *l* 27 *CSP Span.* XII, no. 287, 'He will not seek on account of the marriage by direct or indirect means to draw England into the war now in progress between the Emperor, his father and Henry, King of France, but to preserve peaceful relations between England and France.'

p 79, *l* 30 *The Diary of Henry Machyn* 120

p 80, *l* 6 Lord David Cecil, *Guide to Hatfield House* (London 1973) 2

p 80, *l* 12 *CSP Ven.* VI.ii, 1105

p 80, *l* 29 Ibid. VI.iii, 1059

p 81, *l* 3 Ibid. 1059

p 81, *l* 8 Ibid. 1216

p 82, *l* 7 BL MS Cotton Vitellius C.XVI, f.333. Damaged in Cotton fire. MS Harleian 444, f.28, a copy, has been used where original was charred.

CHAPTER V

p 83, *l* 10 R. Holinshed, *Chronicles of England, Scotland and Ireland* (London 1807/8) IV, 137

p 83, *l* 21 *CSP Span.* XIII, 138, Renard to the Emperor

p 84, *l* 14 *CSP Dom. Mary* XII, no. 3

p 84, *l* 17 Ibid. no. 6

p 84, *l* 19 Ibid. no. 29

p 84, *l* 24 Ibid. no. 20

p 84, *l* 29 Ibid. no. 38

p 85, *l* 4 *CSP Span.* XIII, 378

p 85, *l* 17 *Feria's Despatch*, 316

p 85, *l* 23 *CSP Ven.* VI, 1455

p 85, *l* 26 BL MS Harleian 6949

p 85, *l* 35 *CSP Span.* XIII, 378/9

p 85, *l* 42 *CSP Span.* XIII, 400

p 86, *l* 7 H. Clifford, *The Life of Jane Dormer, Duchess of Feria*, ed. J. Stevenson (London 1887) 80

p 86, *l* 20 *CSP Ven.* VI, 12, 85

Source Notes

p 86, *l* 24 Sir J. Neale, 'The Accession of Queen Elizabeth I', *History Today* 3 (1953) 293–300. Neale maintains (296) that Elizabeth was 'organised and ready to fight for her throne if need be.'

p 87, *l* 7 BL MS Cotton Vespasian F III f.27

p 87, *l* 14 *CSP Span.* XIII, 440 and *Feria's Despatch*

p 87, *l* 34 *CSP Span.* XIII, 440

p 88, *l* 21 *Feria's Despatch*, 330

p 89, *l* 3 Ibid. 331

p 89, *l* 22 Ibid. 332

p 89, *l* 33 Ibid. 333

p 90, *l* 27 Ibid. 335

p 91, *l* 12 *Nugae Antiquae* I, 113–16

p 91, *l* 40 Ibid. 114–16

p 92, *l* 31 *Tudor Royal Proclamations* II, 99

p 92, *l* 37 Ibid. 103

p 93, *l* 28 *Passage of our Sovereign Lady*

p 94, *l* 2 *Passage of our Sovereign Lady*

p 94 *n** *CSP Ven.* VI, 1668.

p 94, *n†* *CSP Ven.* VIII, 15

p 95, *l* 4 A. L. Rowse, 'The Coronation of Queen Elizabeth I' *History Today* 3, (1953) 303

p 95, *l* 26 *CSP Ven.* VII, 16/17

p 95, *l* 28 BL MS Egerton 33320

p 96, *l* 5 Rowse, *History Today* 3 (1953) 310: 'But immediately upon the consecration of the elements beginning, it seems undoubted that the Queen withdrew to her traverse.'

p 96, *l* 20 *CSP Ven.* VII, 17. In a previous letter (ibid., 3) Schifanoya also tells us the name of the Chaplain, Dr Carey DD.

CHAPTER VI

p 97, *l* 8 *CSP Ven.* 22, *CSP Span. Eliz.* I, 25

p 97, *l* 11 *The Passage of our Sovereign Lady*

p 97, *l* 32 *CSP Ven.* VII, 23

p 98, *l* 17 Neale, *Elizabeth I and her Parliaments* I, 38–9

p 99, *l* 2 *Proceedings in Parliament* I, 31–9

p 99, *l* 9 Ibid. 4

p 99, *l* 12 Ibid. 44. Text from BL MS Lansdowne 94. Hartley (I, 33–9) cites 12 other versions.

p 100, *l* 35 Ibid. 44–5

p 101, *l* 2 *CSP Ven.* VII, 11

p 101, *l* 12 Ibid. 27

p 101, *n** H. Robinson, *Zurich Letters* (Parker Society 1845) 62–3, *CSP Span. Eliz.* I, 39. Feria: *CSP Span. Eliz.* I, 18

p 102, *l* 8 *Proceedings in Parliament* 12–17

p 102, *l* 17 *Tudor Royal Proclamations* II, 109–11

p 102, *l* 20 *CSP Span. Eliz.* I, 38

p 102, *l* 25 Ibid. 49

p 102, *l* 29 *CSP Ven.* VII, 64–5

p 103, *l* 8 *Proceedings in Parliament* 27–32

p 103, *l* 12 *CSP Ven.* VII, 80–1

p 103, *l* 21 PRO SP 12/IV 39

p 103, *l* 32 PRO SP 12/V 18

p 103, *l* 36 PRO SP 12/V 25 f.ir.

p 103, *l* 41 PRO SP 12/56 and 57

p 105, *l* 6 J. Strype, *Annals of the Reformation* (Oxford 1824) I, 218. Strype also prints the bishops' letter, 216–217. He alleges his source was the papers of Sir Henry Sidney. The Privy Council Register for the period May 1559 to May 1562 is missing.

p 105, *l* 32 *CSP Ven.* VII, 24

p 106, *l* 28 *CSP Span. Eliz.* I, 40

p 107, *l* 19 *CSP Span. Eliz.* I, 53

p 107, *l* 27 V. von Klarwill, *Queen Elizabeth I and some foreigners* (London 1928) 76

p 108, *l* 2 *CSP Span. Eliz.* I, 119

p 108, *l* 15 Ibid. p. 18. An undated memorandum in the PRO which must have been compiled before 29 December 1558 suggests Arundel's post as Lord Steward at the coronation may even have been a temporary appointment. (SP 12/1 f.110v) 'Sir Richard Sackville kt to take the charge of the whole Coronation. Item the High Steward of England for the day of ye coronation to be named by the Queen's Majesty.'

p 108, *l* 23 *CSP Span. Eliz.* I, 8, 67, 73–4. Pickering laughed when de Quadra tried to question him and said he knew 'Elizabeth meant to die a maid.'

p 112, *l* 14 *CSP Foreign Eliz.* I. 1558–9 401. PRO SP II/70 f.5: her first draft dated 22 February 1560. Ibid. ff. 76 and 77. The postscript is taken from f.77.

p 113, *l* 21 *CSP Span. Eliz.* I, 58

p 113, *l* 37 Ibid. 63

p 113, *l* 41 *CSP Ven.* VII, 81

p 114, *l* 17 *CSP Span. Eliz.* I, 95

p 114, *l* 22 Klarwill, *Queen Elizabeth I and some Foreigners*, 152

p 114, *l* 24 *CSP Span. Eliz.* I, 107

p 114, *l* 39 Ibid. 175–6

CHAPTER VII

p 115, *l* 27 I.A. Aird, 'The death of Amy Robsart', *English Historical Review*, LXXI 75–6

p 115, *n** Derek Wilson, *Sweet Robin* (London 1981) 120

p 116, *l* 1 Ibid. 72

p 116, *l* 10 Ibid. 71

p 116, *l* 16 *Miscellaneous State Papers* I, 164

p 116, *l* 23 *HMC Hatfield* no. 796

p 116, *l* 34 *CSP Foreign Eliz.* 1560–61 no. 625

p 116, *l* 37 Ibid. no. 621

p 116, *l* 37 *CSP Span. Eliz.* IV. 182

Source Notes

p 117, *l* 2 Ibid. no. 623

p 117, *l* 8 Ibid. no 627

p 117, *l* 13 *Miscellaneous State Papers* 165

p 117, *l* 38 *Miscellaneous State Papers* 168

p 118, *l* 5 *CSP Span. Eliz.* I, 178

p 118, *l* 23 Ibid. 208

p 119, *l* 9 *CSP Dom. Eliz.* XIX, 31

p 119, *l* 16 *Miscellaneous State Papers* 177

p 120, *l* 10 Hatfield House, MS 1.261

p 120, *l* 33 *CSP Foreign 1558–9*, no. 1297

p 122, *l* 6 *CSP Scotland* I, no. 1002. Cf. Knox's letter to Cecil of June 1559, *CSP Scotland* I, no. 475: 'I never offended her Grace and she ought not to repute me an enemy', also ibid. no. 496 Knox's letter to Elizabeth herself. Despite his wish to be well thought of, *The First Blast* only went into one edition in England.

p 122, *l* 10 *CSP Scotland* I, no. 1005

p 122, *l* 24 Ibid. 1006

p 122, *l* 38 Ibid. 1010

p 123, *l* 27 Ibid. 1006

p 123, *l* 34 Ibid. 1008

p 124, *l* 10 Ibid. 1017

p 124, *l* 22 Ibid. 1046

p 124, *l* 26 Ibid. 1083

p 125, *l* 26 P. Forbes, ed., *A Full View of the Public Transactions in the Reign of Queen Elizabeth I* (London 1740) 53–5 (Latin and English) also *CSP Foreign 1562*, no. 682.

p 125, *l* 29 *CSP Scotland* I, no. 1174

p 126, *l* 16 *Archaeologia* XIII (1800) 201–3

p 126, *l* 32 *CSP Span. Eliz.* I, 263

p 127, *l* 5 *Proceedings in Parliament* 87–9

p 128, *l* 5 Ibid. 114. Text used here is BL MS Lansdowne 94 f.30

CHAPTER VIII

p 129, *l* 7 Nichols, *Progresses* 160

p 130, *l* 7 Ibid. 176–9

p 130, *l* 19 Ibid. 155

p 130, *l* 29 Baldassarre Castiglione, *The Courtier*, translated by Sir Thomas Hoby (London 1561) unfoliated. Hoby was later Elizabeth's ambassador in Paris. The 1561 edition has a forward by Sir John Cheke. Elizabeth would probably have read it in the original Italian, since it contains flattering references to her father's education.

p 131, *l* 1 Neale, in *Elizabeth I and her Parliaments* I, 101ff, suggested the opposition came from the Commons themselves; Elton, in exploding the myth of Neale's 'Puritan choir', traces the early outlines of a Dudley faction. Sir Geoffrey Elton, *The Parliament of England 1559–1581* (Cambridge 1986) 358–74

p 131, *l* 32 *CSP Span. Eliz.* I, 404–5

p 132, *l* 7 Ibid. 520

p 132, *l* 13 PRO SP 52/10 f.68

p 133, *l* 38 *CSP Span. Eliz.* I, 312–13

p 134, *l* 14 Sir James Melville, *Memoires* (London 1683) 49

p 134, *l* 24 *CSP Scotland* II, 80

p 134, *l* 27 Ibid. I, 233

p 134, *l* 41 Melville, *Memoires* 56

p 134, *l* 42 *CSP Scotland* II, 126

p 134, *n** PRO SP 12/34 f.178–9

p 135, *l* 3 *CSP Span. Eliz.* I, 441

p 135, *l* 32 Fraser, *Mary Queen of Scots* 253

p 136, *l* 7 *CSP Scotland* II, 361

p 136, *l* 17 Melville, *Memoires* 70

p 136, *l* 42 Fraser, *Mary Queen of Scots* 302

p 137, *l* 7 The original MS has '*feu et mon tue*'. Rendered '*vieux mari et mon* [cousin] *tue*' this translates logically, with '*vieux*' in the sense '*ancien*'.

p 137, *l* 17 *CSP Scotland* II, 477

p 137, *l* 26 *CSP Span. Eliz.* I, 620

p 137, *l* 31 T. Thomson, ed., *Diurnal of Occurents* (Edinburgh 1833) 108

p 139, *l* 5 *CSP Scotland* II, 336–7: draft by Cecil in French, Translated in *Calendar*. A fuller version is printed in G.B. Harrison, *The Letters of Queen Elizabeth* (London 1935) 50–1

p 139, *l* 19 *Burghley Papers* 444

p 139, *n** *CSP Span. Eliz.* I, 472

p 140, *l* 5 *CSP Dom. Eliz.* XXXIX, 41

p 140, *l* 9 PRO SP 12/39 f.105. Leicester's writing is not clear: the last word of this extract could be 'honour' or 'conclude'.

p 140, *l* 24 *CSP Span. Eliz.* I, 164

p 143, *l* 6 Ibid. 146–9

p 143, *l* 29 BL MS Lansdowne 1236, f.42

p 143, *n** *Tudor Proclamations* II, 150, 160, 169

CHAPTER IX

p 145, *l* 5 Fraser, *Mary Queen of Scots* 280

p 145, *l* 8 *CSP Scot.* II, 366–7

p 146, *l* 19 BL Cotton MS Caligula C.I f. 517

p 147, *l* 1, *n** Neale, *Queen Elizabeth I* 159 and 173–4; Fraser, *Mary Queen of Scots* 391–408. H. Villius ('The Casket Letters', *Historical Journal* 28 (1985) 517–34) compares the two texts of 'The Glasgow Letter' and ingeniously arrives at a supposition of the original text. This article proves conclusively that although the letters shown to the tribunal were forged, the original Glasgow Letter implicated Mary.

p 147, *l* 27 BL MS Cotton Caligula C.I f.367

p 149, *l* 9 Fraser, *Mary Queen of Scots* 420

p 149, *l* 14 BL MS Cotton Caligula C.I f.466 et seq.; BL Additional MS 30156, printed Digges, *The Compleat Ambassador* (London 1665), 9

p 149, *n** *CSP Span, Eliz.* I, 654

Source Notes

p 150, *l* 32 Fraser, *Mary Queen of Scots* 386 and 415

p 152, *l* 12 *CSP Span. Eliz.* II, 370

p 152, *l* 30 Oxford, Bodleian Library, MS Ashmole 1729/7 f.13a

p 154, *n** Nichols, *Progresses* I, 304. Neale, *Elizabeth I and her Parliaments* I 287

p 155, *l* 12 BL Additional MS 30156 f.326. *CSP Foreign 1572–4* 158

p 155, *l* 28 BL Additional MS 30156 f.329. *CSP Foreign 1572–4* 159–60

p 155, *l* 35 Nichols, *Progresses* I, 527

p 155, *l* 39 Conyers Read, *Lord Burghley and Queen Elizabeth* (London 1960) 86

p 157, *l* 2 BL Additional MS 30156, f.380

p 157, *l* 21 Ibid. f.437

p 157, *l* 36 Ibid. f.440

p 158, *l* 13 Nichols, *Progresses* I, 527

p 158, *l* 26 MS in the Ellesmere collection, USA. Conyers Read, 'A letter from Robert Earl of Leicester to a Lady', *Huntingdon Library Quarterly* (April 1963) 25

p 159, *l* 15 *CSP Dom. Eliz. 1547–1580* 442 (86, no. 35 and 88, no. 1)

p 159, *l* 21 *CSP Span. Eliz.* II, 511

p 159, *l* 26 *CSP Dom. Eliz. 1547–1580* 531 (109, no. 37)

p 159, *l* 32 Nichols, *Progresses* I, 444

p 160, *l* 13 George Gascoigne, *The Princely Pleasures of Kenilworth* (London 1576, reprinted 1821) 1

p 160, *l* 30 Nichols, *Progresses* I, 444

p 161, *l* 1 Gascoigne, *The Princely Pleasures of Kenilworth* 21

p 161, *l* 5 Ibid. 29

CHAPTER X

p 162, *l* 7 *Nugae Antiquae* II, 149

p 162, *l* 10 Ibid. 149–154

p 162, *l* 16 Ibid. I, 62–3

p 163, *l* 18 *Proceedings in Parliament* 421

p 163, *l* 29 Elton, *The Parliament of England* 351–4

p 164, *l* 4 *Proceedings in Parliament* 495

p 164, *l* 5 Neale, *Elizabeth I and her Parliaments* I, 363

p 164, *l* 16 *Proceedings in Parliament* 495 and Elton, *The Parliament of England* 13

p 164, *l* 23 Neale, *Elizabeth I and her Parliaments* I, 364

p 168, *l* 10 *Proceedings in Parliament* 471–3; Fitzwilliam of Milton MS Political 177

p 169, *l* 25 George Gascoigne, *The Spoyle of Antwerp* (London 1576) unpaginated

p 169, *l* 42 *CSP Span. Eliz.* II, 353

p 170, *l* 29 *CSP Span. Eliz.* II, 550. Latin translated in *Calendar.*

p 171, *l* 7 Ibid. 559

p 171, *l* 23 C. Read, *Lord Burghley and Queen Elizabeth* (London 1960) 152

p 172, *l* 2 *CSP Span. Eliz.* II, 627

p 172, *l* 5 Ibid. 664

p 172, *l* 24 Hatfield House, Cecil Papers 148/23r

p 172, *l* 32 *HMC Hatfield* 241. In an earlier memorandum in the hand of Sir Edward Stafford this line of argument is used in Answer to Objection 8.

p 173, *l* 1 Hatfield House, Cecil Papers 148/23v, 25r&v

p 173, *l* 4 Ibid. 148/24

p 173, *l* 17 *CSP Foreign 1578–9* 504–6

p 173, *l* 24 *CSP Span. Eliz.* II, 675

p 174, *l* 41 *Tudor Royal Proclamations* II, 445–9

p 175, *l* 3 *Nugae Antiquae* II, 188–9

p 175, *l* 18 BL ML Facs 194

p 175, *l* 31 *HMC Hatfield* II, 273

p 176, *l* 2 Hatfield House, Cecil Papers 149/24

p 176, *l* 24 W. Camden, *The History of Elizabeth Queen of England* (London 1625) II, 232–3

p 177, *l* 6 *CSP Span. Eliz.* III, 2

p 177, *l* 10 Wilson, *Sweet Robin* 228–231

p 177, *l* 20 Longleat House, Dudley Papers III, f.190

p 177, *l* 24, *n** Nichols, *Progresses* II, 223 and 337 note 1; Thomas Churchyard, *A Discourse of the Queen's Majesty's Entertainment in Suffolk and Norfolk* (London 1578) unpaginated

p 178, *l* 3 *CSP Span. Eliz.* III, 477

p 178, *l* 28 Ibid. 14–5

p 180, *l* 5 Hatfield House, Cecil Papers 135/21

p 181, *l* 16 BL Additional MS 15, 981 f.19 r&v

p 182, *l* 8 *CSP Span. Eliz.* III, 226–7

p 182, *l* 12 Ibid. 227

p 183, *l* 15 Ibid. 188

p 183, *l* 32 BL MS Facs 218

CHAPTER XI

p 187, *l* 33 *HMC Hatfield* III, 10

p 189, *l* 12 BL MS Cotton Galba E, VI, f.244

p 189, *l* 36 Klarwill, *Queen Elizabeth and some Foreigners* 353–6

p 190, *l* 8 Ibid. 322

p 190, *l* 30 *CSP Span. Eliz.* III, 513–15

p 190, *l* 35 *CSP Foreign 1583–4* 301

p 191, *l* 4 *Fugger Newsletters* (London 1926) 80

p 191, *l* 39 *CSP Scotland* VII, 597

p 192, *l* 42 *CSP Dom. Eliz. 1581–1590* 229 (176, no. 68)

p 194, *l* 12 BL Harleian MS 540 f.115 et seq.

p 195, *l* 27 *A Declaration of the Causes moving the Queen of England to give aid to the Defence of the People afflicted and oppressed in the Low Countries* (London 1585). In the General Catalogue of the British Library this pamphlet is ascribed to Burghley and Washingham. Certain turns of phrase lead me to believe that the Queen helped to compile it.

Source Notes

p 195, *l* 34 *CSP Foreign 1586* 126

p 196, *l* 15 *CSP Dom. Eliz. 1581–1590* 265 (182, no. 1)

p 196, *l* 18 Ibid. 267 (182, no. 24)

p 197, *l* 11 BL MS Cotton Galba C. VIII f.27

p 197, *l* 15 J. Bruce, *Correspondence of Robert Dudley, Earl of Leicester, during his Government of the Low Countries 1585–6* (Camden Society 1844) 151

p 197, *l* 24 BL MS Cotton Galba C. IX, f.204

p 198, *l* 31 *CSP Foreign Holland & Flanders* 21.ii, 94

p 199, *l* 34 BL MS Lansdowne 1236, F.44

p 200, *l* 2 A. Strickland, *Lives of the Queens in England* IV (London 1854) 511

p 201, *l* 14 Neale, *Elizabeth I and her Parliaments* II, 107–108

p 201, *l* 11 Both Elizabeth's speeches to the Lords and Commons Deputation are four pages long; the following texts are therefore greatly abridged. Text and précis from Exeter College, Oxford MS 127, ff.51–3. Also Neale, *Elizabeth I and her Parliaments* II, 116–21

p 201, *l* 23 Ibid. 126 and 130–1; Neale discusses why he believes she spoke extempore.

p 202, *l* 18 Text and précis from BL MS Lansdowne 94, ff.86–8. See also Neale, *Elizabeth I and her Parliaments* 126–9

p 203, *l* 25 BL MS Cotton Caligula C.X, f.201

p 204, *l* 8 *CSP Foreign 1587* 227

p 204, *l* 26 S. Adams, 'The Spanish Armada; the Lurch into War' and G. Parker, 'The Spanish Armada; why the Armada Failed', *History today* 38 (1988), quote the records of the Armada de los Estados de Flandes.

p 204, *l* 36 *CSP Dom. Eliz. 1581–1590* 457 (208, no. 10)

p 205, *l* 11 Cardinal W. Allen, *An Admonition to the Nobility and People of England and Ireland concerning the present warres made for the execution of his Holines Sentence by the high and mightie King Catholike of Spain* (Antwerp 1588)

p 205, *l* 28 *CSP Foreign* July-December 1588, 33

p 206, *l* 4 Ibid. 52

p 206, *l* 26 *CSP Dom. Eliz. 1581–1590* 514 (no.46)

p 207, *l* 20 Ibid. 525 (no.34)

p 207, *n** Felix Barker, 'If Parma had landed', *History Today* 38 (1988) 29

p 208, *l* 21 *Cabala* (London 1654) 260

p 208, *l* 24 Ibid. 257–60

CHAPTER XII

p 210, *l* 16 *CSP Dom. Eliz. 1581–1590* 526–7 (nos. 47, 48, 49, 52)

p 210, *l* 17 Ibid. 527 (no. 52)

p 210, *l* 19 Ibid. 529 (no.65)

p 210, *l* 22 Ibid. 527 (no. 53)

p 210, *l* 28 Ibid. 530 (215, no. 3)

p 212, *l* 18 *CSP Span. Eliz.* IV, 431

p 213, *l* 1 Wilson, *Sweet robin* 336 (Appendix II: The Will of Robert Dudley)

p 213, *l* 23 C. Eisner, *British Commemorative Medals* (London 1987) 32–3

p 214, *l* 10 Sorocold, *Supplication of Saints* (London 1612) 267–273 ('Queene Elizabeth's Prayer of Thanksgiving for the overthrow of the Spanish Navy sent to invade England Anno 1588')

p 214, *l* 25 C. Martin and G. Parker, *The Spanish Armada* (London 1988) 258

p 215, *l* 15 Lambeth Palace, MS 178, f.81

p 217, *l* 16 W. Devereux, *Lives and Letters of the Devereux Earls of Essex* (London 1853) I, 204–5

p 217, *l* 34 BL MS Cotton Galba D I, f.283

p 218, *l* 4 Wilson, *Sweet Robin* 336

p 218, *l* 10 MS sold at Sotheby's (16 December 1980, lot 299) to a private collector. Printed Strype, *Annals of the Reformation* IV, no. 54 (p. 108)

p 218, *l* 35 Harrison, *The Letters of Queen Elizabeth* 209

p 219, *l* 23 J. Stevenson, ed., *Unton Correspondence* (London 1847) 43 (letter to Sir Henry Unton, Elizabeth's resident ambassador in France, 22 August 1591)

p 220, *l* 6 J. Stow, *Annales of England* (London 1605) 1273

p 220, *l* 33 *HMC Hatfield* IV, 343

p 221, *n** C. Pemberton, ed., *Queen Elizabeth's Englishing of Boethius* (Early English Text Society, London 1899) Introduction, xi. The original MS in the Public Records Office (SP 12/289) runs to 89 closely written folios. The calculations on f.7, 9, 10 appear to me to be two rough drafts of the same sum, which is written fair on f.7. Whoever wrote the calculation on f.7 also began to copy out the whole translation neatly, but only two pages f.100, 101 survive.

p 221, *l* 30 Pemberton, *Queen Elizabeth's Englishing of Boethius* 118, PRO SP 12/289 f.82

p 222, *l* 5 Ibid. 120, PRO SP 12/289 f.83v

p 222, *l* 35 *CSP Dom. Eliz. 1595–1597* 203 nos. 25, 26

p 224, *l* 12 Ibid. 205 no. 32

p 224, *l* 34 *CSP Dom. Eliz. 1595–1597* 272 no. 114

p 225, *l* 8 BL MS Cotton Otho E. IX

p 226, *l* 30 BL MS Additional 29, 275

p 226, *l* 32 *CSP Dom. Eliz. 1595–1597* 473–4

p 227, *l* 30 J. Neale, *Queen Elizabeth* (London 1934) 349

p 228, *l* 12 *Nugae Antiquae* II, 218

p 228, *l* 41 *CSP Ireland* VIII, 98–101

p 229, *l* 13 Ibid. 150–3

p 229, *l* 32 W. Devereux, *Lives and Letters of the Devereux Earls of Essex* (London 1853) 73–4

p 230, *l* 13 *Nugae Antiquae* II, 216

p 232, *l* 9 There are several versions of this famous speech. The pamphlet, a copy of which survives at Harvard, is definitely the most leaden. '*Her Maiesties most Princelie answere, delivered by her selfe at the court at Whitehall, on the last day of November 1601*. The same being taken verbatim in writing by A.B. as neere as he could possibly set it down' (*STC* 7578). Neale believed Elizabeth authorised this version. In the Stowe MS there is a more 'golden' account: 'The Journall or abstracts of soe mush as passed in the Lower House at the Parliament holden 27 Oct. 19 Dec. 1601'. this account is by the diarist Hayward Townshend who was himself present when Elizabeth spoke, as he interpolates 'so we all stood up and she went on'.

p 234, *l* 8 BL MS Stowe ff.169–72

p 234, *l* 15 *CSP Ven.* IX, 342–3

p 234, *l* 29 Neale, *Elizabeth I and her Parliaments* II, 428

p 236, *l* 8 BL MS Cotton Titus C. vi ff. 410–411

p 236, *l* 11 F. Moryson, *An Itinerary Containing His Twelve Years Travel* (London 1617) III, 187

Source Notes

p 237, l 3 Ibid., III, 187

p 237, l 39 *CSP Ven.* IX, 531–4

p 238, l 8 Robert Carey, *Memoirs* (London 1759) 138

p 238, l 13 Ibid. 140

INDEX

Index

Index